De Nova Villa:

OR,

THE HOUSE OF NEVILL

IN SUNSHINE AND SHADE,

BY

HENRY J. SWALLOW,

FELLOW OF THE ROYAL SOCIETY OF LITERATURE; THE SOCIETY OF ANTIQUARIES OF SCOTLAND, &c., &c.

"To visit the most remarkable scenes of history, to record the impressions thence derived in their immediate vividness, to restore as it were each place and its inhabitants to freshness, and to present them freed from the dust of ages to the general reader—*this is the proper labour of the antiquary.*"—*Howitt.*

"It is HISTORIE that hath given us life in our understanding since the WORD itself had life, having made us acquainted with our dead Ancestors ; and out of the depth and darkness of the earth delivered us their Memorie and Fame.—*Sir Walter Raleigh.*

NEWCASTLE-ON-TYNE:
ANDREW REID, PRINTING COURT BUILDINGS, AKENSIDE HILL.
LONDON :.
GRIFFITH, FARRAN, & CO., ST. PAUL'S CHURCHYARD.
1885.
[ENTERED AT STATIONERS' HALL.]

BY KIND PERMISSION,

Tɒis ⱬook

IS DEDICATED TO THE REPRESENTATIVE HEADS OF THE

HOUSE OF NEVILL,

THE MOST HONOURABLE WILLIAM NEVILL,

MARQUIS OF ABERGAVENNY;

AND

THE RIGHT HON. CHARLES CORNWALLIS NEVILLE,

BARON BRAYBROOKE.

PREFACE.

THIS book is an attempt to produce a record of the Nevill family, which may be of some interest both to the antiquary and the general reader. If, in making this attempt, I have courted the fate of the proverbial person who seeks to occupy two stools, I can only say that the acrobatic performances of this person are somewhat amusing; and I, at least, have succeeded in amusing myself.

Fifty-five years ago Daniel Rowland wrote his *Historical and Genealogical Account of the Noble Family of Nevill.* Only sixty copies of this very costly work were printed; and several of these have been destroyed. But the writer had his reward.

"It has beguiled and alleviated many hours of weariness. It has occupied my mind, diverting it from the memory of pleasures, which can return no more."

I have built on Rowland, esteeming him to be a tolerably sure foundation; and I have spent three years in independent research. Several manuscripts which appear in this book have never been printed before.

My sincerest thanks are due to the Marquis of Abergavenny, and to several members of the Carlton Club, for the kindly interest they have taken in the

book—to Lord Boyne for the use of Brancepeth
Castle Library; to the Dean and Chapter of Durham,
and the Rev. Canon Greenwell, for the use of the
Chapter Library; to John Stansfield, Esq., F.S.A., for
the use of his library; to Mr. Froude, for permission
to make extracts from his invaluable History; to the
Bishop Suffragan of Nottingham; to Rev. the Hon.
Latimer Neville; to the Hon. Ralph Pelham Nevill,
of Birling; to Rev. Bury Capel, Vicar of Abergavenny;
to Rev. Douglas G. Blakiston, Vicar of East Grinstead;
to Rev. Joseph Wix, Vicar of Littlebury; to Rev. S.
H. Reynolds, Vicar of East Ham; to Rev. F. Ruxton,
Vicar of Well; to Rev. J. F. Hodgson, Vicar of
Witton-le-Wear; to Rev. J. J. Burton, Vicar of Eridge;
to Rev. T. Stevens, Vicar of Saffron Walden; to Rev.
R. Wentworth Fawkes, Rector of Frant; to W. H. D.
Longstaffe, Esq., F.S.A., of Gateshead; to Mr. C. M.
Carlton, of Durham; to Walter de Grey Birch, Esq.,
F.R.S.L.; and to several officers of the British Museum
and the Public Record Office, who have given me
assistance.

I am indebted to Captain Robinson, of Hardwicke
Hall, for the sketch of Barnard Castle. The block of
Nevill's Cross is copied (with some necessary altera-
tions) from a design kindly lent me by Mr. Murray, of
Albermarle Street. The portrait of the ill-fated Earl
of Westmoreland is from a very fine steel engraving,
copied from the original picture in the possession of
Lord Abergavenny. The picture was moved from
Birling to Kidbrooke, and from thence to Eridge
Castle. The portrait of the Countess is copied from

Sir Cuthbert Sharp's *Memorials*, and was originally taken from her father's tomb at Framlingham. The Kingmaker's portrait is a reproduction from Rowland's work. The Warwick engravings are from the original steel plates, in the possession of Messrs. Cooke and Sons, Warwick. The permanent photograph of Brancepeth is an adaptation from a larger one, kindly presented to me by Messrs. Frith and Co., of Reigate.

To prevent the book from becoming too costly, I have been obliged to forego my intention to present the reader with engravings of the principal Nevill monuments, and also to suppress a great quantity of matter, chiefly copies of wills and other documents, in Latin and Norman-French. For the same reason I have only ventured upon a passing notice of the minor branches of the Nevill family.

With regard to the name Nevill, it will be noticed that the Abergavenny branch reject the final "e," whilst the Braybrooke branch retain it; and, for the sake of further distinction, the Grove, Hornby, Chevet, Holbeck, Skelbrooke, and Wellingore divisions omit one "l." In the old manuscripts, from *De Nova Villa* we get Neuville, Nevylle, Nevyll, Nevyl, Nevill, and Nevil, whilst the Latimers are frequently styled Nevell; but the prevailing form is Nevyll or Nevill. I have adopted the latter spelling, and have thereby made an incalculable saving of the letter "e."

H. J. S.

Brancepeth, Durham,
May, 1885.

CONTENTS.

INTRODUCTION.

THE SAXON.

"Rex est qui metuit nihil;
Hoc regnum sibi quisque dat."
—SENECA. *Thyestes, a. II.*

A MANUSCRIPT in the British Museum *(Harl. Collect.)* carries the Nevill pedigree through Woden and Hengist to Adam the father of us all. In *Salomon and Saturn* we are also told that Adam himself was created of eight pounds by weight; a pound of earth, whence his flesh; a pound of fire, whence his hot and red blood; (for they knew nothing about corpuscles in those good old days), a pound of wind, whence his breath; a pound of cloud, whence his unsteadiness of mood; a pound of grace, whence his stature and growth; a pound of blossoms, whence the variety of his eyes; a pound of dew, whence his sweat; and a pound of salt, whence his tears.

Genealogists tell us it is useless to go back to early Saxon times, for the lines of historical fact are shrouded by a dense mythical mist, and in the dim light of superstition it is difficult to distinguish gods from men.

"Geat begat Godwulf, who begat Finn, who begat Frithowulf, who begat Fritholaf, who begat Woden, who begat Wecta, who begat Witta, who begat Wictgils, who begat Hengist," and so on.

An old historian *(Daniel)* declares that "the beginning of people and states are as uncertain as the heads of great rivers, and cannot add to our virtue, and peradventure little to our reputation to know them."

"*Peradventure little to our reputation.*" What a truly terrible warning! Nevertheless, dear old Daniel, I intend to go straight back now to the wondrous days when Woden and Thor reigned in Angleland.

The history of the Nevill family is almost collateral with the history of our country. The one cannot be understood without the other. Indeed, a great portion of English history was *made* by the Nevills. But in order fully to understand the sources of that extraordinary vigour of character which made the name of Nevill terrible on many a well fought field in Europe, we must search among the shadowy forms of heroes haunting battle fields long since obliterated; we must wake again the sleeping warrior gods, and the savage sanguinary priests; we must put out of sight our own civilisation, and see instead immense hordes of cruel creatures rushing to battle; we must listen to wild weird songs, set to music still wilder and more weird than the words, pourtraying war as the very gate of heaven, and the means of escape from hell; we must banish from our society every false swearer, cold-blooded coward, and sneaking assassin; we must consign all such to the serpents of Nastrond; and the man who alone must be exalted, and in whose presence all other men must be abased, is he, who, strong in his ever present manhood, rejoices to find himself alone in the thick of battle, who fears no fall, who scorns a helper.

> "I trust my sword, I trust my steed,
> But most I trust myself at need." *

In the last great encounter when Allfather goes forth to meet His foes the Hero will find a vantage place, and the joy of hoping for that tremendous battle will create his heaven.

The Teutonic tribes revered their gods, and these gods in war and pleasure alike were terribly earnest.

> "Endless was
> The love of Geat,
> So that the pain of love
> Took all the sleep from him."
> —(*Trans. Cod. Exon. p.* 378.)

> * " Först troer jeg mit gode svärd,
> Og saa min Gode hest,
> Dernäst troer jeg mine dannesvenne,
> Jeg troer mig self allerbedst."
> —*Danish Battle Song.*

The Teuton monarch was no puppet of the people. He was their heaven-born king. In his veins throbbed the fierce blood of all the warlike gods. Beowulf relates how Sceaf, the great ancestor of the Saxon heroes, floated as a lovely sleeping boy to the shores of Scamphta in a tiny mystic skiff. Great treasure came with him, but not a living soul. The islanders loved and reared him as their own. He founded a royal race, and dying, floated away as he came. *

The pagan pantheon to which he returned possessed few gods of a peaceful disposition. *Tiw* (the Saxon Mars), after whom the third day of the week is still called, was the supreme giver of victory, and the bravest god of all. But the Saxons most loved the warrior Woden.

"And by the roadsides
Made him offerings,
And upon high hills."

Localities named after him are still very common on rising ground.†
The roaming Teutons loved him as the Greeks loved Odysseus.

"The many sided man,
Who wandered very much."

—Odyss. Bk. I.‡

* Whatever genealogy we follow, we find ourselves fairly afloat at last. The Ark mentioned in the Saxon Chronicle as the birthplace of Sceaf, is apparently synonymous with the German skiff indicated by Jornandes *(De Rebus Gothicis)*. Even the people of Teochiapan told Humboldt that their great ancestor assisted in building a high tower, and was grandson to an old man who was saved on a raft.

† Woden and Thor (Wednesday and Thursday) naturally go together. Thor, the Thunderer, was known in Germany as *Hamar*, from the heavy mace he carried. This has become almost synonymous with devil. In Surrey, the Devil's Jumps, and the Devil's Punchbowl, and Hammerponds are close to *Thursley*, which place is also in close proximity to *Tewsley*, Thunderhill, Dragon Hill, and Wanborough, formerly Wodnesbeorh. The first meeting of the Picts and the Saxons (under Hengist and Horsa) is represented as taking place near Stamford. Horsey Hill and Horsegate are supposed to preserve the tradition. It is said that Horsa had a sister called Swane. Swanborough and Horsted lie together in Sussex, Swanwick and Horsley in Derbyshire, Swanthorpe and Horsdon in Hampshire, Swanage and Hengistbury Head in Dorsetshire, and there are three Swantons in Norfolk, a few miles to the west of a group of parishes bearing the name of Horsa.—*Vide Haigh's Anglo-Saxon Conquest.* Zahn calls the similarity of names "a rock on which uncritical heads are much in the habit of splitting;" but the names given above are certainly significant. Baldersby (Yorks.), and Balderston (Lancs.), keep fresh the memory of the god of beauty (Baldr). I am told that the inhabitants of these places are very good looking. This is quite as it ought to be.

‡ "Ἄνδρα —— πολύτροπον, ὃς μάλα πολλὰ
πλάγχθη."

c

They worshipped him as the devastating god who had ravaged
Europe—the god who for the sake of his own sons wore a kindly
human form, and wandered here on earth.

Fricge, Woden's wife, gave her name to the sixth day. She
was the Northern Venus, and appears to have been a female form
of the god Frea, the only Saxon deity who mislaid his sword in his
desire for the beautiful.

Baldr, the god of light, grace, and beauty, perished in the midst
of so many contending deities, yet there was a promise of his
restoration if all created things could weep for his loss. All nature
wept save one old crone, who refused her tears, for Baldr had never
made her beautiful, and she hated him. Then Nanna, the lovely
spouse of the god of grace, refused to outlive her lord, and all the
gods and goddesses stood mournfully around the funeral pile of
Baldr and Nanna. And they swore that Baldr should rise again
after the twilight of the gods.

As time went on this faith was strengthened and elevated until
it embraced the entire renewal of Allfather's kingdom.

> Then sees she rise
> A second time
> The world from ocean
> Wondrous green.
>
> Then unsown
> The swath shall flourish
> All bale mend and
> Back come Baldr.
>
> There sees she stand
> Than sunlight fairer
> Gimli's hall
> With gold all covered.
>
> There the just shall
> Joy for ever,
> And in pleasure
> Pass the ages.
>
> —*Vaula Spa. Kemble's Trans.*

The warlike worship of Woden was not without its charms.
Who does not admire the honest manliness of Beowulf's hero king?

> "Lives there no folk-king of kings about me,
>   Not any one of them
> Dare in the war strife welcome my onset;
> Time's change and chances I have abided,
>   Held my own fairly,
> Sought not to snare men.
> Oath never sware I falsely against right;
> So for all this may I glad be at heart now
>   Sick though I sit here,
>   Wounded with death wounds."
>
> —*Beowulf, v. v.* 5458—5474.

The warrior who could desert his chieftain in the hour of need was reckoned an outcast, and all his *mægburh* (family connections) lost their civil rights.

> " Death is better
> For every warrior
> Than a life of shame."—*Beowulf* 1, 5765.

But the death that succeeded a life of shame was indeed dreadful.

> . "A dwelling deadly cold
> With winter covered in
> And snake dwellings
> Thirst and hunger
> Mighty terror
> Joylessness."
> —*Salomon and Saturn, Kemble's Trans.*

Hell was no place of fire and brimstone, for the Teuton loved fire too well to regard it as an object of terror. But at the thought of Nástrond, with its cold shame and frosty serpents, he literally shuddered, and many a legend tells of violent death embraced through the horror inspired by that fearful future.

The HERO inherited the glories of *Wælheal*. Looking upwards, from the field of some midnight battle, with his last glance, he saw, traced along the star-lighted sky, his pathway to eternal honour. In Allfather's home he would quaff the life-giving wine. Gazing there upon the flashing eyes of the Shieldmaidens, and animated by their songs of carnage, he would be inspired to go forth in mysterious ærial warfare, and, returning with re-kindled desire and ever increasing strength, his entranced soul would listen for the signal of the last great battle.

The graphic pen of Tacitus shows how true the Teuton was to his warlike religion.

"Traitors and deserters they hang on trees; *cowards, the unwarlike, and infamous of body they bury alive in mud and marsh* with a hurdle cast over them. The difference of the penalty has this intention as it were, that crimes should be made public, but infamous vices hidden while being punished. They transact no business either of a public or private nature without their weapons. If the king's opinion please them they dash their lances together. The most honourable form of assent is by clashing of arms."—*Germ. xiii.*

Teutonic tradition and religion reeked with the smoke and blood of battle. If art and poetry existed, they existed only for the sake of the soldier. Literature had never laid her light hand upon the mailed warrior. The Teutons did not learn writing from Greek or Roman. It was part of the tradition which descended to them from the time when the human race was still one family. But it was considered a mysterious accomplishment; indeed it was little better than a *black art.**

* The *rún*, or inscribed tablet, was supposed to *whisper* secrets that could only be heard and understood by the initiated. A riddle in the Exeter book has reference to a tablet constructed out of timber taken from a ruined pier. It forms a beautiful explanation of the way in which the art of writing was regarded by our forefathers.

Ic wæs be sande	I was by the sand
sæ-wealle neáh	nigh the sea wall,
æt mere-farothe.	at the ocean-shore.
Mínum gewunade	I dwelt in my
frum-stathole fæst.	first station fast.
Feá ænig wæs	Scarce any was there
monna cynnes,	of mankind,
thæt mínne thær	that there
on ánæde,	in the loneliness,
eard beheóld.	my dwelling beheld.
Ac mec, uhtna gehwám,	For me each early morn
yth sio brúne	the brown wave
lagu-fæthme beleolc.	locked in its watery bosom.
Lyt ic wénde	Little I weened
thæt ic, ær oththe síth,	that I, early or late,
æfre sceolde,	should ever,
ófer meodu,	over mead,
múthleas sprecan,	mouthless speak,
wordum wrixlan.	converse with words.
Thæt is wundres dæl,	That is a deal of wonder
on sefan gearolíc,	curious in the mind,
thám the swylc ne conn,	to those who such a thing
	understand not,
hú mec seaxes ord,	how me the knife's point,
and seó swíthre hond,	and the right hand,
eorles ingethonc,	man's sagacity,
and ord somod,	and the point together,
thingum gethydan,	purposely associate,
thæt ic with the sceolde,	that I with thee should
for unc ánum twám	for us two alone,
ærend-spræce	a speech-errand
abeódan bealdlíce;	boldly announce;
swá hit beorna má	so that it more men
uncre word-cwidas	our word sayings
widder ne mænden.	further imagined not.

. Even of late Saxon times Dugdale speaks disdainfully :—

"Neither did they much minde learning, till little before the Conquest by Duke William. Before the coming of the Normans, the clergy were scarce able to stammer out the words of the Sacrament. So that it is not such a Merveil that we have no more light of storie to guide us in those elder times, as 'tis a wonder there is anything at all left to us by reason that learned men were exceeding scarce."

Doubtless fierce fighting was the one thing in which the Saxons most believed. They poured ale into the skulls of their fallen foes, and drank to Woden, their warrior king, priest, and god. Even their sport was warlike, for many a fierce beast lurked in the forests.

Such were the people who came (A.D. circum. 450) to Britain. Under the care of the Antonines, Britain had grown beautiful, though being a slave she was necessarily weak. When Rome drew off her legions in her own defence, the Britons, wearied by incessant harryings from Pict and pirate, welcomed the proffered shield of the Saxon sword.

Slowly but surely the Saxon sword did its work until Britain was no longer Britain, but Angleland. It took two centuries of bitter warfare to do this. Then the Briton was driven into Cambria for all time. But the old hero still lives in the writings of Geoffrey of Monmouth, the father of English fiction.

As the ages passed, many beautiful traits of character developed themselves under the shelter of the Saxon shield. Truth and kinship were strong among the English people. Every bold-faced Saxon meant the words he said, and comrades were bound together by a life-long fellowship in arms. "Every outrage was held to have been done by all who were linked in blood to the doer of it, every crime to have been done against all who were linked in blood to the sufferer from it." In the brief periods of peace no Saxon hand was idle. Busy households clustered round the sacred tree in every village. The women were workers—spinsters, spinning the wool which their own hands had shorn from the full fleeces of the flock. After all, the brave Saxon must have valued the serenity of home when he called woman the weaver of peace. She was his Fulgia— his good guiding star of destiny.

Very beautiful indeed became the Saxon character when moulded by the graces of the Christian faith.*

* The master mind of Gregory the Great, soldier, statesman, musician, priest, and Pope, recognised the fitness of the Saxon mind for the reception of Christian dogma;

Heroism was sanctified in the lives of Oswald, Eadwine, and Ælfred. The one English king whom we call "Great" was purely Saxon.

Brave and sturdy to the last was the Saxon soldier. His ruin was only wrought by his own "strong spirit of localisation, and consequent want of imperial unity." The country lacked cohesion. Shire would not help shire. Therefore Edmond Ironside fell before the Dane, and the strong sons of Godwin were literally hacked to pieces by the Norman. The lover of Saxon history as he reads how Harold bled for England on the field of Senlac must ever ask: Why was the hero left alone at the last great scene of all? Where was Eadwine, where was Morkar, where was Waltheof? As he sorrows to see these noble Saxon chieftains struggling alone and vainly against the concentrated cunning and strategy of the Conqueror, he feels the force of the old saying, "Unity is strength."

Yet Father Time has dealt gently with the Saxon. The fair faces still left to us to love are Saxon, the quaint old words that stir our hearts and strengthen our hands are Saxon. Eight hundred years have passed since the monks of Waltham sang their requiem over the body of their beloved Harold, yet "where is now the Norman, where is *not* the Saxon?" We might extend the question by asking, where is *not* the Nevill?

In literature he is represented by the Master of Magdalene College, Cambridge; in social and courtly life he is represented by the noble families of Abergavenny and Braybrooke; in the walks of mercy and benevolence he is represented by the Baroness Burdett-Coutts, the lineal descendant of John Nevill, last Lord Latimer; and as a HERO he has been represented even in these latter days by HENRY ALDWORTH NEVILLE, who, after sharing in the glorious

and so the old myth of the death of Baldr gave way to the more beautiful story of the sacrifice of Christ; and the Twilight of the Gods, and the Glories of Allfather's Kingdom were absorbed in the more abundant Revelation of St. John the Divine.

One hundred and forty-seven years after the traditional landing of Hengist at Ebbsfleet, a little company of Benedictines landed at the same place, having in their hands only a silver cross, and on their lips a solemn litany that Gregory himself had taught them in their beloved convent on the Cælian Hill.

It was fitting that to the noble Saxons noble evangelists should be sent. To the south came Augustine, a man of gigantic stature, and shrewd sense. To the north came Paulinus, with the spirit of John the Baptist; and holy Aidan; and Cuthbert, who, when the snow closed up the coast, and the wild storm barred his passage across the sea, quieted his little crew with a steady smile, and an assurance that "the way to heaven still lay open."

victory of Alma, was killed in action during that ever memorable battle of Inkerman, when the British soldiers, having exhausted their cartridges, defended themselves with stones and the butt ends of their muskets, until succour arrived.

The blood of the old Saxon soldier, who could fight but could not run, ran also in the veins of GREY NEVILLE,* who perished at Balaclava.

> "Stormed at with shot and shell,
> Nobly he rode and well,
> Into the jaws of death,
> Into the mouth of hell."

---

* Lieut. Col. Edward Neville, Scots' Fusilier Guards, served in the Crimean campaign, and obtained medal with three clasps, Turkish medal, and 5th class Medjidie, and Legion of Honour. He is the son of the late Very Rev. The Hon. George Neville-Grenville, Dean of Windsor, second son of 2nd Baron Braybrooke. His brother, *Glastonbury Neville*, captain in the Royal Engineers, was killed at Baroda in India, January 31st, 1858. Horace John Nevill, grandson of the late Rev. The Hon. George Henry Nevill, second son of the 1st Earl of Abergavenny, served and received a medal in the Zulu War, 1879. The Earl of Lewes is Lieut. W. Kent Yeo. Cavalry; and his brother, Lord Henry Nevill, is captain in the same troop. Lord George Nevill was Lieut. West Kent Militia. Lord William is Lieut. 3rd Batt. Queen's Own. The Nevills may therefore still be considered as a military family.

BAMBOROUGH CASTLE.

THE HOUSE OF NEVILL.

CHAPTER I.

SAXON AND NORMAN.

> " Those dauntless chiefs,
> Who clad in armour bright, and lofty crests,
> Dealt death with many a ghastly wound."

UPON a certain day in the year 1028, a lovely girl named Harlotta, the daughter of a tanner, was washing clothes in a brook near the strong castle of Falaise. Upon the cliff above sat Robert the Devil, in whose veins flowed the fierce blood of the famed Rollo. Rumour told how this same Robert had poisoned his brother. Be that as it might, he was then Duke of Normandy in consequence of his brother's death, and his evil eye rested upon the fair Harlotta as she stood in the sunshine.

Afterwards, William Talvas de Belesme saw, in a cradle, a babe born of the tanner's daughter, and he cursed the little boy with all the energy of a high-minded Norman baron. Whether Robert the

Devil cared anything for the curse, I cannot say; but as he neared the end of life, seized by remorse, he went on pilgrimage. He sowed his pathway to the Holy Land with gold, and his steeds were lightly shod with silver shoes, which readily dropped upon the road and testified to the wealth of the Norman Duke. Thus Robert the Devil became Robert the Magnificent before he died.

His bastard boy, left to the care of Alan of Brittany, developed a remarkably rigid disposition. He would not peaceably give up the possession of anything, and his toys were broken in the efforts made by his guardians to wrench them from his baby fists. As the child grew towards manhood his strength of will seemed superhuman. He fed and thrived on opposition. When he approached Alencon, the citizens roused by the taunts of Talvas de Belesme spread skins upon the walls, and cried out, "Hides for the tanner." Their gibes entered into the heart of Harlotta's son ; and the hands, and feet, and eyes of thirty jesters were thrown over the city wall by the order of this remarkable man.

All Normandy soon lay at his feet. His foes rotted in the deepest dungeons. "No knight under heaven was his peer. No man could bend his bow. Earls that did aught against his bidding he cast into bonds, bishops he stripped of their bishopricks, abbots of their abbacies. He spared not his own brother. Stark man he was, and great awe men had of him." In 1060, he was chief among the Princes of France. In 1066, he was King of England. His might was his right. Europe was silenced by his irresistible energy, and the Pope sent him a consecrated banner with the *very* hair of S. Peter. Being born to conquer, he was fitly called The Conqueror.

Richard de Nova Villa was cousin to the Conqueror on his mother's side. The name and parentage of his wife remain in obscurity; but it is known that he left four sons, Gilbert, Robert, Richard, and Ralph. From Gilbert descended the houses of Westmoreland, Warwick, Latimer, and Abergavenny.

"Gilbertus Normanus," commonly called the *Admiral*, is placed at the head of the Nevill pedigree by all the early genealogists. Leland styles him the Conqueror's Admiral, on the authority of a "roulle of the genealogie of the Erles of Westmoreland." Henry Drummond—into whose work Stapleton's researches into the Norman ancestry of the Nevills were incorporated—considered Leland's information as a mere family tradition, introduced towards the close of the 15th century. Whether the device of the ship on the seal of Henry de Nevill (date circ. 1200) supports the tradition, or whether the tradition arose from the seal, is a matter on which opinions differ. Foulk d'Anou, the uncle of Gilbert, certainly furnished forty ships for the invasion of England. There is no other evidence to support Leland's assertion that Gilbert himself was Admiral.

"From a passage in Odericus Vitalis it is clear that the Norman family of Nevill issued from a Teutonic stock, some members of which offered their services to Richard; second Duke of Normandy, and are known to have held high office, contracted important alliances, and possessed large fiefs in England *previous* to the Conquest. Baldric Teutonicus was Lord of Bacqueville en Caux, and *Archearius* under Duke William. He married a niece of Gilbert Compte de Brionne, grandson of Duke Richard I., and Regent of Normandy in 1040."

"The fourth son of Baldric was called Richard de Nova Villa,* or De Neuville, from his fief of Neuville sur Tocque, in the department of the Orne, the arrondissement of Argenton, and the Canton of Gacé. Hawisia, sister of Richard de Nova Villa, married Robert Fitz Erneis, who fought and fell at Hastings."—*Vide Planché's Norman Ancestry of the Nevills, a paper read at Durham in* 1865, *and published in the British Archæological Journal, Vol. XXII, p.* 279.

We have now to show how Saxon and Norman became united in the Nevill family.

"In the year of grace 548, began the kingdom of Northberland, for the chiefs of the Angles, having after great and long-continued toil subdued the country, chose Ida, a noble *youth* (*juvenis nobilissimus*) as their king. He had by his queen six sons, and six by concubines. All these came into Britain in sixty ships, and landed at Flammisburgh."—Flamburgh. (*Roger de Wendover.*)

* The name of Richard de Nevill is given by M. Leopold de Lisle in his catalogue of the companions of the Conqueror, and by Vicomte de Magny in his book, entitled *Le Nobiliaire de Normandie.* The name of Ralph occurs in the *Clamores in Westreding, co. Lincoln.* Ralph Nevill held Thorpe of Turold, Abbot of Peterborough, but the name is omitted by Sir Henry Ellis in his *Introduction and Indexes to Domesday.* De Nova Villa *is* found in the Roll of Battle Abbey, and in other lists of doubtful authority, but Odericus Vitalis makes no mention of the presence of any Nevill at the battle of Hastings, nor does Wace in his *Roman de Rou;* but that some of the brothers, sons, or nephews, of the elder Richard de Nova Villa, if not Richard himself, were present at that battle is very probable.

This noble youth built Bamburgh, and called it Bebbanburch, in honour of Bebba, his queen.—(*Sic Saxon Chronicle; disputed by Nennius and others.*)

The chiefs who held court at Bamburgh were at different periods known under the title of king, duke, or earl.

In the year 993, Earl Eadulf, being old and feeble, was blockaded in his regal fortress by the Danes. Bamburgh was taken by storm, and much booty with it. Taking advantage of this circumstance, the Scots, under Malcolm, laid siege to Durham. Eadulf, it would appear, perished in the Bamburgh blockade; but Uchtred, his son, collected the strength of Northumbria, and forced Dane and Scot out of the country.

With Uchtred the history of the Saxon branch of the great Nevill family properly begins.

Uchtred married three times.

The first was not for love. It was in this way. The soul of good Aldune, Durham's first bishop, was greatly exercised about the living body of his daughter, as well as the dead body of St. Cuthbert, for both bodies were really very tiresome. But Ecgfrida, being a girl, and not a saint at any time, gave most trouble. Uchtred, the martial Earl of Northumbria, was therefore respectfully invited to have, and to hold her, if indeed he could. As some compensation for the lack of the virgin's love, Aldune gave him the lands of Bermetun, Skirningheim, Eltun, and some other possessions, which had recently been bequeathed to the Church by Styr, the son of Ulf, well known in Deira for his wealth.

It was not long, however, before the stout Earl was glad enough to give up Bermetun and Skirningheim, if so be he might give up Ecgfrida too. Fortunately, Kilvert, the son of Liulf, a Yorkshire thane, agreed to take her for better for worse. But she was more than a match for the Yorkshire thane as well as the Northumbrian earl. She was therefore returned to Durham, as were also her lands. The bishop said, "Daughter be at peace;" and Ecgfrida took the veil.

Now, Styr, the son of Ulf, had an inveterate foe, called Turebrand. He had also a daughter, called Sigen. Earl Uchtred looking round for another wife, well endowed with money, and with a better temper than the first, beheld the daughter of Styr. "Faint heart never won fair lady;" but in this case the conditions of marriage were stern enough to daunt the bravest heart, for Styr said, "Rid me of my enemy, and you shall have Sigen." Uchtred had failed in contending with a woman, but he thought nothing of overcoming a man. Therefore Turebrand bit the dust. Many a dreadful tragedy, darkening the page of Northumbrian history, may be traced back to the deed which caused the daughter of Styr to reign in the halls of Bamburgh. What was the exact fate of this lady, I am not able to say; but in process of time Uchtred was out courting again. The third time is always lucky. The stalwart Earl had been as a tower of strength against the Scots to Ethelred the Unready; and the king, who had married well himself, was kind enough to wish that Uchtred might do the same. As a special mark of gratitude, therefore, his daughter, Elfgiva, or Algiva, own sister to Edmond Ironside,* was bestowed on Uchtred.

The Earl never deserted his King, and steadfastly refused allegiance to Cnut the Dane, whilst Ethelred lived. Afterwards, as the *Saxon Chronicle* pathetically relates, he "submitted from need," and was treacherously slain in the royal presence, by Turebrand, the Hold, a son probably of his old opponent, A.D. 1016.—*(Symeon.)*

Assassination and anarchy wrought dire confusion in Northumbria until long after the coming of the Conqueror; but into this history happily we need not enter.

The accompanying table will readily show how the Nevills were descended from Uchtred, and how strongly they established themselves in the north, by becoming Barons of Raby, Brancepeth, and Sheriff Hutton.

By all early writers the Nevills are denominated De Nova Villa. Ingenious philologists have traced the origin of the provincial word *nevel*, to pummel with the fist, to the pugnacious character of the early lords of Raby and Brancepeth, but very likely one provincial word, *nevel*, is derived from another provincial word, *neave*, the fist.

---

* "This Eadmund was not born of Emma, but of some other person whom fame has left in obscurity."—*(Vide Malmesbury.)*

According to Florence of Worcester, the name of Ethelred's first wife was Elfgiva. Roger of Wendover says that she was "the daughter of a certain duke," and he gives the date of the marriage, A.D. 981. The date of Ethelred's second marriage to Emma, the descendant of Rollo, is variously given.

CHAPTER II.

SETTLEMENT OF THE NEVILLS IN LINCOLNSHIRE.

"There level ploughlands—and aye a heavy crop
They mow in season, for rich the soil beneath."[*]
Odyssey, Book IX., 135. *Bigge-Wither's Trans.*

"All his gold and his goods hath he given
To holy church for the love of heaven ;
And hath founded a chantry with stipend and dole,
That priest and that bedesmen may pray for his soul."
—*Scott.*

WHEREVER the Norman went he identified himself with the erection and endowment of ecclesiastical buildings on a magnificent scale.

"You might see churches rise in every village, and monasteries in the town and cities, built after a style unknown before. You might behold the country flourishing with renovated rites ; so that each wealthy man accounted that day lost to him which he had neglected to signalise by some magnificent action."—*Malmesbury.*

The earliest settlement of the Nevills appears to have been at Horncastle, and they soon became associated with ecclesiastical establishments in the county of Lincoln. They were the founders of *Tupholme*, a priory of the Order of Præmonstratensians, who observed the rule of St. Austen. Unfortunately the records concerning their various benefactions are rather conflicting.[†]

The heart of many a weary wayfarer across the fens of Lincolnshire has blessed the kindly hospitality provided by the foundation

---

[*] Ἐν δ᾽ ἄροσις λείη· μαλα κεν βαθὺ λήιον αἰεὶ
Εἰς ὥρας ἀμῷεν, ἐπεὶ μάλα πῖαρ ὑπ᾽ οὔδας.

[†] Robertus de Nova Villa tenet in Broclesby dimidium feudum militis, de domino rege in capite, de conquestu. Abbas de Thoupholm tenet illud in elemosinam de dicto Roberto, tam in dominico, quam in servitio à primâ fundatione domus.

Abbas de Thoupholme tenet. VI. bovatas terræ in Harburc in elemosinam de dono Roberti de Nova Villa a prima fundatione domus.

of Nevill; but the heavy heel of Henry VIII. rested upon the religious houses, and the lights of Tupholme suddenly went out.

> " Time was when they were sacred
> As the place of Jacob's rest,
> And their altars all as spotless
> As the virgin mother's breast."

But that day has passed. The bells of Tupholme are heard no longer across the waste. The following short entry occurs in *Comput Johnis ffreman Armigii Receptoris*, dated 31st and 32nd Henry VIII.:—

XX

TUPHOLME: in plumbo iiij^{li} in campanis . . . xxxij^{li}. xijd*i*. vjd. in tot' cxiij^{li}. xijd*i*. vjd.

In a letter from Robert Goche, Receiver of the County to the Commissioners for Lead and Bells, dated 14th May, 1556, occurs the passage:—"I have spoken to my L. Willoughby for the belle remayninge in his handes at Tupholme beinge verie smalle ys contente to pae for the same at your worshipfull discretions." *Land Revenue Records—Church Goods, Linc. P.R. Off. Quoted in North's Church Bells of Lincolnshire.*

De diversis terris, Canonicis de Tupholme (in comitatu Lincolniæ) spectantibus. Ex Rot. Hundr. in arce Lond. anno. 3 Ed. 1. Linc.

" *Tupholm*, an abbey of Præmonstratensian Canons, dedicated to the blessed Virgin, *founded by Alan de Nevill, and Gilbert his brother*, temp. Henry II., wherein about the time of the Dissolution were nine religious, who had the yearly income of £100 14s. 10d. (Dugdale) £119 2s. 8d. (Speed). The site was granted 30 Henry VIII. to Sir Thomas Henneage."—*Notitia Monastica.*

Tupholme abbat or Præmonstraten uno a Bardeney milliari. Ranulphus de Nevill. D. de Raby 1's fundator.
(Lelandi Collect. Vol. 1, p. 92).

" *Tupholme*, founded by Robert de Nova Villa. The said Robert held several lands of the King in capite from the Conquest, which he gave to the Abbot of Tupholme at the first foundation of this House. Gilbert de Nevill, and Alan his brother, Henry de Nevill, and Henry 1st, King of England, were benefactors to this Priory in several lands and churches; all of which were confirmed to God, St. Mary, and the Abbot and Canons of the Order of Præmonstratensians. Nov. 22, Anno. Regni 20."—*Magna Britannia, Vol. 2.*

"Geoffrey de Nevill, otherwise called Geoffrey Fitz Robert, gave six ox gangs of land in Harburck, Lincolnshire, to the Canons of Tupholme, and the church of Randley, with certain lands in Burreth in Lincolnshire, and one ox gang in Thinesto and Shill Milne with the Marsh."—*Rowland.*

Surtees says that the grandfather of this Geoffrey was the *founder* of Tupholme, but he does not state his authority for this remark.

An impression in green wax of the common seal of Tupholme, of the date of 1276, is among the Harleian Charters in the British Museum marked 45 A. 14. It represents the Blessed Virgin with the Divine Infant in her lap. Legend—SIGILLUM ABBATIS ET CONVENTUS. S. MARY DE TOPEHOLM. It has also a counter seal.

One ruined wall alone remains of Tupholme Priory. The upper part appears to have formed a side of the refectory, and contains lancet windows, and a small gallery, in which the person sat who read to the brethren during their meals.

Whilst we are talking of Lincolnshire, I may observe that the name of Ranulphus de Nevill occurs among the signatures to the letter addressed by the British barons to Pope Boniface VIII. This document, which was drawn up at Lincoln, holds a conspicuous place in the history of English liberties. In the year 1297, Edward I. found himself very much in want of money. This state of things was by no means new to him, but it was none the less unpleasant. The barons granted him a twelfth, the burgesses an eighth. But the people who possessed the most wealth were least inclined to part with it. "The possessions of the clergy," says Dr. Henry, "daily increasing, were now swelled to an enormous bulk, and threatened to swallow up the whole lands of the kingdom." During the reign of Henry III. nine cathedrals were either entirely erected or greatly enlarged, and one hundred and fifty abbeys, priories, and other religious houses were founded. But a large proportion of this wealth found its way to Rome. In a few years, in the transactions connected with the crown of Sicily, the Pope was computed to have drawn from England a sum equal to more than nine millions of our present money. When Edward asked Winchelsey for means to carry on his wars, the Primate replied that "obedience was chiefly due to our *spiritual* lord, and *his holiness loved peace.*"

The clergy refused to pay their fifth, and were outlawed. Winchelsey hurled excommunication against all those who disobeyed the Pope, but the barons upheld the right of the King, and the clerics eventually gave way.

But "about the beginning of the year 1300," says Walsingham (himself a Benedictine monk of S. Alban's), "*the Scotch, knowing all things to be saleable at Rome,* sent over rich presents to the Pope, praying him to stop the King of England." And the bold Boniface actually sent his mandate to Edward commanding him to abstain from all proceedings against the realm of Scotland, "*which realm,*" said he, "*did and doth still belong in full right to the Church of Rome.*"

Then King Edward issued writs for a meeting of Parliament at Lincoln, on January 23rd, 1301.

"At the park afterwards his Parliament set he,—
The good King Edward, at Lincoln his citie:
At St. Katherine's house the earl marshal lay;
In the Broadgate lay the Bruse, erle was he that day;
The king lay at Nettleham; it is the bishop's towne,
And other lords there came, in the countrie up and downe."

—Langtoft.

Representatives were summoned from one hundred and thirty-seven cities and boroughs. "Letters were also sent to the universities, and the principal religious houses, desiring them to send some of their most learned men with copies of any records, which might be in their possession, bearing upon the questions agitated in the papal mandate." To this appeal the nation responded right loyally. "The spectacle at Lincoln was lively and singular." From all parts of the kingdom puissant nobles, with their "goodlie companies," entered the city gates to support the king in his right. An enormous amount of provision was consumed. London allowed her four representatives twenty shillings, equal to £15 of present money, for their daily entertainment, and the member for Lincoln, Samuel Stanham, merchant grocer, made a good thing of it, his bill against the King alone for fish and sweetmeats, being £151 0s. 5d.

"The Parliament at Lincoln," says the author of *The Greatest of the Plantagenets*, "deserves a high place among the notable events of English history. In it we find the parliamentary system firmly established, in all its dimensions, features, and characters. To its principal act—the reply to Pope Boniface—we find appended the names and seals of no fewer than one hundred and four earls and barons."

And this is what they told the Pope.

"By a custom which has always been inviolably observed—a privilege arising from the pre-eminence of the regal dignity—the Kings of England have never pleaded, or been bound to plead, respecting their rights in the forementioned kingdom, or any other, their temporal rights before any judge, ecclesiastical or secular. Wherefore, after discussion and deliberation respecting the contents of your letters, it was our common and unanimous resolve, and by the grace of God shall for ever remain such, that with respect to the rights of his kingdom of Scotland, or other his temporal rights, our aforesaid lord the King shall not plead before you, nor submit in any manner to your judgment; nor suffer his foresaid right to be brought into question by any inquiry; nor send agents or procurators for that purpose into your presence. For *such proceedings would be to the manifest*

B

disherison of the rights of the Crown of England, and the royal dignity, the evident subversion of the state of the kingdom, and the prejudice of the liberties, customs, and laws which we have inherited from our fathers—to the observance and defence of which we are bound by our oaths, and which we will maintain to the best of our power; and by the help of God will defend with all our might. Neither do we, nor will we, permit—as we neither can nor ought—our aforesaid lord the King to do, or attempt to do, even if he wished it, the things before mentioned; things so unwarranted by custom or obligation, so prejudical and otherwise so unheard of."—Rymer's Fædera, Vol. II., p. 927.

These same barons had consecrated their wealth to the building up of our glorious cathedral and collegiate churches. They were true Churchmen, yet true Englishmen. They wrote a plain page of history which ought never to be forgotten.

The vices of Ralph de Nevill have often been pointed out. It should be remembered also that his name is written among the charters of our national liberties.

Ralph served in Gascony in the reign of Edward I., and joined in a disastrous campaign in Scotland in 1310. He is described as but slightly engaged in secular business, and devoted to the society of the monks of Merton and Coverham; but his character as a religious man is seriously injured by the records in Bishop Kellawe's Register. "Citacio Dom. Ranulphi de Nevill publicata tam in ecclesia de Stayndrop in manerio suo de Raby, xvii. Oct. a 3 Pontific, pro incestu et adulteriis cum Antasia filia sua, uxore Dom. Walteri de Fauconberg." Another notice says, "Richardus de Kellaw Ranulphum de Nova Villa pro incestu cum filia propria ad pænitentiam publicam coegit." Ralph Nevill defended the *privileges of the King against the Pope*, and the *privileges of the people against* the oppressive encroachments of *the Bishop* (Anthony Bek), who compelled the tenants of St. Cuthbert to serve in Scotland, whereas they were not bound to go beyond the Tyne or Tees, either for king or bishop. The men of Durham, known as *Holywerefolc*, or the tenants of St. Cuthbert, were simply sworn to defend the rights and relics of the saint. Ralph held Raby and eight adjoining townships by a yearly tax of £5, and a stag to be offered on St. Cuthbert's Day to the Prior of Durham; but disputes arose regarding this tenure. His mother, Mary of Middleham, apparently held him in no great estimation, for she settled Middleham and Coverdale upon her grandson Robert. At Well Church there is an ancient monument which Whitaker (History of Richmondshire) supposes to be that of Margery, daughter of John Thweng, and second wife of Ralph de Nevill.

**Hic jacet Merge Ria Domina
Nebile uxor secum
Da R. Dni Nebile cui Deus pro
Picietur. Amen.
Merci. Ei. T. De L'Alme.**

Lord Ralph was buried at Coverham Abbey.

His eldest son, Robert de Nevill, died 1318 V.P., without issue. For description of his monument in Brancepeth Church, see chapter on Nevill Monuments.

"As Richard Marmaduc, Seneschal to the Bishop of Durham, did ride to hold the County Court, he was slain upon the old bridge of Durham (Elvet), by his kinsman, Robert Nevill. In the following year the same Robert Nevill, in his pride and wantonness, got together a gang of excommunicated thieves and vagabonds, intending to take a prey in the marches of Scotland, but at Bewyk Park he was killed by James, Earl of Douglas; and Ralph Nevill, his brother, was led away prisoner, and kept in custody by Patrick, Earl of Dunbar. After a time he was ransomed."—*Harl. MSS.*

From his great love of finery, Robert de Nevill was known as "*The Peacock.*"

JOHN DE NEVILL, the fourth son of Lord Ralph, was slain at Halidon Hill, July 19th, 1333. The hill stands outside the town of Berwick. "The commanding border position, and massive fortress of Berwick made it, like Ramah of Benjamin in ancient times, a constant object of acquisition in war, and a frequent scene of international struggles. Sir Alexander Seton held the garrison for Scotland, and refused to surrender even when Edward III. hanged his own son, Thomas Seton, a comely and noble looking youth, before the very gate of the town. On the 19th of July, Sir Archibald Douglass came to the relief of the beleaguered fortress. Contrary to the dying injunctions of Bruce, who instructed his captains never to hazard a battle if they could by any means protract the war, Douglas led his troops across the soft marsh which separated them from the English position. An irresistible storm of arrows swept through their ranks as they wallowed in the morass. The vanguard broke, and fell upon the rear in wild disorder, but the bravest still struggled on to the fore, and, pressing up the hill, attacked the English with great fury. But they were soon left breathless by the very fierceness of their struggle, whilst Edward's troops were both fresh and lusty. Scottish bravery was beaten to death against the strength of Halidon Hill. The English men-at-arms bore down upon the rout, the Welsh and Irish irregulars rushed in upon the flanks with their long knives, and such bloody carnage ensued that men thought the day of Scotland was over at last. John de Nevill was reckoned among the few Englishmen whose lives were sacrificed in the defence of Halidon Hill. Berwick was given up 'tower and town' to Edward, and 'remained thenceforward an integral part of the English dominion, the only territorial trophy of Edward's Scottish victories which was never lost.'"—*Warburton's Edward III., and Tytler's Hist. Scot., Vol. II.*

"The Englishe made arrowes flee as thick as motes on the sonnebeme (sun-beam), and so thei smote the Skottes, that thei fell to grounde by many thousands. And anone the Skottes begane to flee fro the Englishmenne to save their pere lyves; butt when the knaves and the Scottishe pages, that weren behinde the Skottes to kepe their horses, seyen the discomfiture, thei prikened ther maisters horses awey to kepe themselfe from perille, and so thei towke no hede of theyre maisters. And then the Englishmenne towken many of the Skottes' horses, and prikeden after the Skottes, and slewe them downrighte. And ther men might see the nowbell Kinge Edwarde of Englande, and his folke, houghe mannefully thei chaseden the Skottes."—*Harl. MSS.* 4690, *fol.* 79.

CHAPTER III.

LORD RALPH NEVILL OF NEVILL'S CROSS.

"While danger on our frontier stalks around,
We need not fear our soldiers will repose
Upon the lap of indolence and ease."

RALPH DE NEVILL, Lord of Raby, Brancepeth, Sheriff Hutton, Middleham, Warkworth, and Clavering, married Alice, daughter of Sir Hugh de Audley, and sister to Hugh, Earl of Gloster. She afterwards married Ralph, Baron of Graystock, and died in 1374.

In the 7th year of Edward III., Lord Nevill was Commissioner to settle articles between Edward of England and Edward Baliol; and, with Henry Percy, was Warden of the East and Middle Marches. He was also Governor of Bamburgh Castle during the succeeding year.

In the 12th year of Edward III., he lent the King all the money arising from the sale of wool on the manor of Flaxfleet, Yorks.

In 15th of Edward III., he was on the Commission to treat with David Brus, titular of Scotland, for a final peace.

In 17th year of Edward III., he was on Commission to treat with Philip de Valois.

In 26th year of Edward III., he was on Commission at Newcastle to treat for the release of David Brus.

In 29th year of Edward III., he was Governor of Berwick.

From 29th to 35th year of Edward III., he was Warden of the Marches.

In 33rd year of Edward III., he attended the King into France, and placed himself in ambush with Lord Mowbray and other knights three leagues from Paris, where after a sharp skirmish the French were defeated.—*Froissart.*

After a life of incessant action and great achievements, he died August 5th, 1367, and was buried in the Cathedral at Durham, being the first secular person thus honoured.

" He obtained this favour from the Prior and Convent, for a vestment of red velvet richly embroidered with gold, silk, great pearls, and images of saints, standing in tabernacles given by him to S. Cuthbert. His body was drawn in a chariot and seven horses, unto the bounds of the churchyard, and then carried by the shoulders of knights into the middle of the church, where the Abbot of S. Mary's, in York (by reason of the Bishop's absence, and the impotence of the Prior), performed the office for the dead, and celebrated mass, at which were offered eight horses, viz., four of the war, with four men armed, and all their harness and habiliments; and four others for peace; as also three cloths of gold, of blue colour interwoven with flowers; four of which horses were redeemed by John Nevill, his son and heir for 100 marks (£1,100.) · Besides all this Alice, his widow, sent to the sacrist £120 in silver to repair the Cathedral, and gave for celebrating his anniversary one vestment, two tunicles, one cope, three albs, three stoles, four manipples of black satin, and another vestment for the celebration of the Sacrament, embroidered with the arms of Nevill and Audley."—*Rowland.*

He revived the dispute, begun by his father, with the Prior of Durham, about the offering of a stag to the Priory on S. Cuthbert's Day. This offering had been a recognised feature in the tenure of

Raby since the days of Cnut, but these bold barons could brook no custom that lessened their importance. They required, therefore, that the prior should feast them, and all their company, on S. Cuthbert's Day; that the whole retinue should lie all night at the Priory, and breakfast next morning; that only the Raby retainers should wait at table, the menials of the prior not being allowed that honour; and that thus, and thus only, should the stag be offered. The Lord Nevill having gratified his whim, and gained his point, brought but few with him; and these more for the honour of the prior than a burthen, and shortly after dinner took his leave; but left one of his servants to lodge all night and breakfast there, pretending that, as a son and tenant of the Church, he would not be burthensome to it, by bringing a great train; "for," said he, "*what does a breakfast signify to me? Nothing.*"

Sometimes these disputes grew a little lively. On one occasion the Nevill retainers began to beat the monks, but the undaunted clerics, who always loved a scrimmage, seized the huge wax tapers that adorned the altar, and belaboured the Raby servants with such zest that they cried out for mercy.

The name of Ralph Nevill is inseparably connected with the battle of Nevill's Cross. Of the magnificent cross, which once stood on the Brancepeth road, there remains now only a portion of the octagonal shaft, into which an obliterated milestone has been fixed.

Until quite recently, any earnest archæologist, who wished to examine this little relic of antiquity, did so at his peril, for the cross—if cross it can be called—stood on the summit of a slippery mound, at the base of which was an accumulation of filth. During the present year the remnant of this once beautiful monument has been very properly protected, and re-established. The work has not given universal satisfaction; but I never yet heard of any "restoration" that did.

"It is to be regretted," writes a Durham gentleman, "that, when the old toll-bar was removed, the stones were not examined, for I distinctly remember many years ago seeing sculptured stones built into the walls of the cow-byre. In boyhood's day we used to walk nine times round the cross; and then, closing the eyes and placing an ear upon the remnant of the monument, we listened intently, fancying that we could hear the clash of arms and din of battle. This used to be a very favourite pastime."

"The cross," says Surtees, "is generally considered to have been erected as a memorial of the battle, yet the expressions used by the earliest historians would almost lead one to suppose that a cross of some sort did actually stand here before this memorable day."

Fordun says, "The English formed their army on the moor, *juxta crucem quæ Nevil Cross dicitur.*"

Minot, a contemporary bard, entitles his eighth song or ballad—

> "How Sir David had of his own grete loss
> With Sir Edward at the Nevel Cross."

And, again—

> "At the Nevel Cross nedes had them knele,
> For Cuthbert of Doren
> Haved thai no dout:
> Tharefore at the Nevel Cros
> Law gan thai lout."

"I have seen," says Raine (*Saint Cuthbert*, p. 106), "documents in the Treasury, of a date long antecedent to the battle in question, which prove that there was *then and there* a Neville's Cross, but whether of wood or stone I know not."

Surtees suggests that, "if it existed anterior to the battle, it was doubtless restored and richly adorned in honour thereof, and remained a stately monument of prowess and high command, on which every Nevil, as he passed from Brancepeth to Durham, might cast a glance of hereditary pride. It fell, in 1589, a victim to wanton mischief or to fanatic feeling, soon after the fall of the noble house with whose name its history is connected. The traditional account of the cross first printed by Davies, in his *Rites and Monuments*, 1674, is taken from an old roll, compiled probably by a monk of Durham after the Dissolution."

"On the west side of the city of Durham, where two roads pass each other, a most famous and elegant cross of stone-work was erected to the honour of God for the victory there obtained, known by the name of Nevil's Cross, and built at the sole cost of Lord Ralph Nevil, which cross had seven steps about it every way squared to the socket wherein the stalk of the cross stood, which socket was fastened to a large square stone, the sole or bottom stone being of a great thickness, viz., a yard and a half every way; this stone was the eighth step. The stalk of the cross was in length three yards and a half up to the boss, having eight sides all of one piece; from the socket it was fixed to the boss above, into which boss the stalk was deeply soldered with lead. In the midst of the stalk, in every second square, was the Nevil's cross, a saltire in an escutcheon, being Lord Nevil's arms, finely cut; and at every corner of the socket was a picture of the four evangelists, finely set forth and carved. The boss at the top of the stalk was an octangular stone finely cut and bordered, and most curiously wrought, and in every square of the nether side thereof was Nevil's cross in one square, and the bull's head in the next; so in the same reciprocal order about the boss. On the top of the boss was a stalk of stone (being a cross a little higher than the rest) whereon was cut on both sides of the stalk of the said cross the picture of our Saviour Christ crucified; the picture of the Blessed Virgin on one side, and of St. John the Evangelist on the other, both standing on the top of the boss. All which pictures were most artificially wrought together, and finely carved out of one entire stone, some parts thereof through carved work, both on the east and west sides of the cross, with a cover of stone likewise over their heads, being all most finely and curiously wrought together out of the said hollow stone, which cover of stone was covered over."

"And, furthermore, in the said Red Hills, on the north side of Nevil's Cross, a little distance from a piece of ground called the Flasse, above a close lying hard by North Chilton Pool, and on the north side of the hedge where the Maid's Bower had wont to be, and where the prior and monks standing made their prayers to God with the Holy Relique of St. Cuthbert during the said battle, there was erected by the said prior monks a fair cross of wood, in remembrance of that Holy Relique by them carried to the battle, which being finely wrought, very large, and two yards in height, stood there and continued. The priors and monks ever after, in memory of the said Holy Relique after the said victory achieved, did in their recreation as they went and came to and from Beau Repair to Monastry and Abbey, make their humble and solemn prayers to God and Holy St. Cuthbert at the foot of the said cross in perpetual praise and memory of the said victory and recovery of the said battle, till it was suddenly defaced and thrown down by some lewd and ill-disposed persons, who despised antiquity and worthiness of monuments after the suppression of abbeys."

In the Baron's Hall at Brancepeth Castle, there is a sword described in the Armour Catalogue as "the original sword of Ralph Nevill, with which he fought at Nevill's Cross." It bears his name, and the date, 1345.

THE BATTLE OF NEVILL'S CROSS.

CHAPTER IV.

THE BATTLE OF NEVILL'S CROSS, TUESDAY, OCTOBER, 17TH, 1346.

"Now tell us all about the war,
And what they fought each other for."
* * * *
"Why 'twas a very wicked thing!"
Said little Wilhelmine.
"Nay, nay, my little girl," quoth he,
"It was a famous victory."
* * * *
"But what good came of it at last?"
Quoth little Peterkin.
"Why that I cannot tell," said he,
"But 'twas a famous victory."

Battle of Blenheim.—Southey.

Yes, Wilhelmine, it was a very wicked thing. They were "children of one family," but they could not "agree." King David married the sister of King Edward, but the Scot harried Edward, and

Edward harried the Scot. Like the "comely squires" of Spenser's *Fairie Queen*, they were in "conflict brothers, yet most unbrotherly." The sister of Philip de Valois was mother to King Edward's wife, but that did not in the least prevent Edward from making war against Philip de Valois. "He was unto him a grievous adversarie." Poet and historian, *i.e.*, Ovid and Tacitus, are agreed. "*Tanta est discordia fratrum. Acerrima proximorum odia.*" Relationship and religion always give quarrels a keen edge. Professedly pious men, especially when they happen to be near of kin,

> "Will stop each other's breath,
> And eat each other up, as spiders do."

And if these things are so now, why need we wonder that the Bruce should bring into battle the Black Rood* of Holy Rood, or why need we wonder that certain monks, seeing, from their station on the bell tower of Durham Cathedral, the glorious victory of the holy corporax cloth, should break forth into loud singing of *Te Deum Laudamus*, which the English soldiers hearing "more sharply followed their enemies, and more strongly trode them under foot"? *(Knyghton.)* But without further comment let us now try to get a "righte plaine and proper understanding" of this same battle of Nevill's Cross.

King Edward had gone into France to recover the "heritage of his mother." The adoption of such a generous hearted policy did not arise out of any affection for his mother, because he had previously shut her up quite safely as a State prisoner in Castle Rising; nor did it arise out of any affection for the people of France, because they had given him clearly to understand that they did not desire him as their king; and, by the Salic law, France could not be "the heritage of his mother." But Edward cared nothing for the Salic law, nor did the English barons care much for it. Shut up in their solitary frowning strongholds, without any penny papers or

---

* In the *Cronikils of Scotland*, and in the "*Rites and Monuments*" of Durham, it said that the "Black Rood" was taken from King David at *Nevill's Cross*, but Symeon says that it was *bequeathed to the Priory by St. Margaret*. It was a crucifix with figures of the Virgin and St. John, on each side of our Lord, the three "being richly wrought in silver, and smoaked black all over." The figures were over 3 feet in height, and were surmounted with three crowns of pure gold. The "*holy croce*" was believed to have dropped miraculously into the hands of David from the antlers of a hart during the chase in the neighbourhood of Edinburgh. "The hart fled away with gret violence, and evanist in the same place quhare now springs the Rude Well. The King returnit to his castel; and in the nicht following was admonist by ane vision in his sleip to big ane abbay of channonis regular in the place quhare he gat the croce. And from France and Flanderis he brocht richt crafty masonis to big this abbay; syne dedicat it in the honour of this holy croce."

working men's clubs to divert their minds with details of the differences between right and wrong, how could they brook the dreary monotony of domestic life? They were tired of the stag and the joust. War—real war with a great nation like France— nothing but war with France could chase away the dullness of their beclouded spirits.

They had their wish. Disaster could not check them. Year followed year. Many a weary hour did Queen Isabel pass in Castle Rising, and many a smiling homestead of Brittany lay in ashes, but again and again Edward hurled his legions upon France to recover the "heritage of his mother." Edward Woodstock, late of the Queen's College in the University of Oxford, had won his spurs at Creci, and certain noble gentlemen of Calais were now being reduced to that state of starvation which was to send them "bare-footed and bareheaded, with halters round their necks," into the presence of the King of England.

Philip de Valois, from the Sandgatte Hill, saw the sad state of Calais, and found himself powerless to render assistance. It was high time for Philip to look round for an ally, and he found one in Edward's "*dearest brother.*"

Ambassadors were sent to King David, requiring him "that with an armie he should enter England, and doo what damage he might unto the Englishmen, to trie if by that meanes, King Edward would be constrained to leave his siege, and return home for the defence of his own countrie." *(Hollinshed.)* The am-bassadors assured King David that there "did not remain in England any unless husbandmen and shepherds, and imbecile and decrepit chaplains." *(Knyghton.)* The *Te Deum* that these imbecile chaplains afterwards chanted must have sounded sadly in the ears of the deluded Scot.

King Edward, anticipating the action of Philip, had already sent John de Mowbray, William de Ros, and Thomas de Lucy, on a mission, to persuade the Scots to preserve a pacific attitude towards England. But the King of France had been kind to David in exile. Moreover David was "stout and right jolly, and desirous to see fighting."* *(Wyntown.)* Every Scot was anxious to wipe out with fresh blood the disgrace of Halidon Hill, and no Scot—

* In the entrance hall of Brancepeth Castle, a suit of armour, richly inlaid with gold, is pointed out as the one in which David fought at Nevill's Cross. If the King did indeed get into this suit the historian must have drawn very largely upon his imagination when he described him as *stout.* In the *Chronicle of Lanercost,* it is

least of all the son of Robert Bruce—could afford to throw away this golden opportunity for the re-assertion of national independence. Thus whilst Edward was engaged in starving to death the citizens of Calais,

> " The Scot on his unfurnished kingdom,
> Came pouring like the tide into a breach."

After the battle of Halidon Hill, July 19th, 1333, it was said that "the Scotch wars were over at last," for there was not a man left in Scotland, who had skill or material to muster an army; nevertheless before the end of September, 1346, an enormous martial force gathered at Perth; troops being drawn from the islands, as well as the mainland. But the Highland chiefs brought their deadly feuds with them. The Earl of Ross assassinated Ranald of the Isles, in the monastery of Elcho; and, dreading the royal vengeance, led his men back to their mountains, a circumstance which in those days of superstition was considered by the rest of the army a bad omen of success. The soldiers of the Isles, deprived of their leader, dispersed in confusion, and many of the inferior Highland lords, anxious for the preservation of their lands, privately deserted, and returned home. David, however, pressed forward from Perth; and, reaching the border, sat down before the Castle of Liddel, then commanded by Walter Selby, a fierce, freebooting chief, ready to lend himself to the party that could purchase his sword at the highest rate. He had espoused the quarrel of the Baliol, from whom he received a grant of lands in Roxburghshire. David demolished the castle, put the garrison to the sword, and ordered Selby to instant execution. Sir Wm. Douglas, the veteran Knight of Liddesdale, then advised a retreat, but his counsel was rejected by the youthful ardour of the King, and the jealousy of the nobles. *(Tytler's Hist. of Scot.,* Vol. II., *p.* 68.)

By the light of a full moon, the Scottish army passed through Cumberland. Lanercost Abbey was sacked, and a long line of burning villages marked the route of the wild soldiery.

Passing by Naworth, they came to Hexham, and there plundered both abbey and town. Corbridge and Haydon Castle capitulated. Crossing the Tyne at Ryton, David was menaced by S. Cuthbert, who disturbed his evening slumbers, and threatened him with

said that on the morning of the battle the Bruce had no breakfast, for the servants allowed the pot to boil over, and the meal was destroyed. If this kind of thing happened often, and the King found himself able to overlook it, he must at least have been "*right jolly*," although not stout.

direst vengeance if he continued in his evil course. But the King was a "goodlie youth of twentie-three, not given unto superstition." He therefore despised the admonition of the Saint.* After crossing the Derwent, and halting at Ebchester, his soldiers finally encamped beside a wood at Beauepaire (Bearpark), two miles from Durham, where they pillaged, and feasted to the full. The position was ill-chosen, showing that though David had the valour, he had not the discretion of his father.

A broken country, intersected by hedges and ditches, hindered the divisions of the army from supporting each other, whilst the undulating character of the landscape gave the enemy an opportunity of approaching unobserved. (*Tytler.*) The Knight of Liddesdale, leading a strong squadron of heavy armed cavalry, the vanguard of the Scottish army, advanced for forage as far as Sunderland Bridge, and suddenly found himself in the presence of a strong force of English cavalry coming down from Merrington. In the encounter that ensued he lost 300 men. (*Chron. de Lanercost.*) This happened on the morning of the 16th of October. Douglas retired with his shattered squadron to Beaurepaire, but his news did not alarm the King, who slumbered peacefully at the Manor, without even taking the trouble to station any sentinels. (*Surtees*, Vol. I., 50.)

Henry de Percy, Ralph de Nevill, and William de la Zouch, Archbishop of York, had been appointed by the Regency commanders of the English army (*Rot. Scotiæ*, *Vol. I.*, 673), which numbered about 18,000 men, according to Surtees; but the total fighting force of both armies is very variously given. King David is represented as commanding any number of men, from 36,000 (*Knyghton*) to 62,000 (*Walsingham*). The English headquarters were at Auckland Park.

By nine o'clock, on the morning of the 17th, the whole English force had passed Nevill's Cross. A huge crucifix was carried in front of the line, and around it waved innumerable banners and pennons, gorgeously embroidered. As the army came upon the Red Hills, there was heard "a great sound of singing." The chaplains were chanting the "*Miserere.*"

---

* David's contempt for sacred territory excited the greatest resentment and horror. Amidst all the cruel destruction of those early days the property of the Church was religiously spared. Some English soldiers fired the French Abbey of Beauvais, but Edward immediately hanged twenty of them as a salutary warning to the army.

In many a border battle the Percy had "led the way." It was therefore perfectly natural that the Earl of Northumberland should command the van at Nevill's Cross. Gilbert de Umfreville, Henry le Scrope, and Thomas Musgrave were also in the forefront. Ralph Lord Nevill, with his son, Sir John Nevill, the Lord Hastings, and the Archbishop of York, with the "*Halywerefolc*" (tenants of St. Cuthbert), led the central division. Sir Thomas Rokeby, Lord Mowbray, and John de Leyburn, with the men of Yorkshire and the Lancashire Archers, formed the left wing. William Ross of Hamlake, commanded a company of reserve. From the letter of thanks, dated from the Tower, Oct. 20th, and addressed by the Regent to the commanders at Nevill's Cross, it would appear that William Dyencourt, Robert de Ogle, Thomas de Gray, Thomas de Lucy, and Robert Bertram were also present. But no name is better known in connection with this battle than that of John de Coupeland.*

The undaunted Bruce pressed forward over "a grievous countrie" to meet his fate. There is some contradiction among authorities about the disposal of the Scottish host, but it would appear that the King commanded the centre, the Earl of Moray the van or right wing, and the High Steward, with the Earl of Dunbar, the left. To the "*Miserere*" of the "imbecile chaplains," Bruce responded with the wild strains of Scottish pipes and clarions.

When the English archers had advanced almost within bowshot, Sir John de Graham reminded the King of Halidon Hill, and earnestly besought him to command the cavalry to charge these terrible archers in the flank. It was the same manoeuvre which had been successful at Bannockburn, but from ignorance or youthful obstinacy, David was deaf to this advice. "Give me," cried the veteran Graham, in an agony of impatience, as the fatal phalanx of the archers advanced nearer and nearer, "give me but a hundred horse, and I will engage to disperse them all." Yet even this was unaccountably denied him ; and the brave baron, seconded by none except his own few followers, threw himself upon the

---

* After the battle, Coupeland was created a knight banneret, and Governor of Roxburgh Castle. In 1361, he was Warden of the East Marches. By his will, proved in 1365, it appears that he possessed lands in Lincolnshire, Yorkshire, Lancashire, and Westmoreland. He probably fell by the hands of his own countrymen. The county of Northumberland obtained pardon for his death by a payment of 1,000 marks in 1366. For a detailed account of this knight, together with an admirable description of the battle of Nevill's Cross, see a very valuable paper published in *Archæologia Æliana*, 1857, 8vo. series, *Vol. I.* Unhappily, like most good things, this volume is rather scarce.

bowmen; but it was too late; time had been given them to fix
their arrows, and the deadly shower had sped. Graham's horse
was shot under him, and he himself with difficulty escaped back to
the army.—*(Wyntown and Fordun quoted in Tytler)*.

Entangled among hedges and ditches, and greatly galled by the
steel shower, which fell incessantly upon them, the Earl of Moray's
men were specially marked out for slaughter. The English cavalry
charged through the broken line until the Scottish van was altogether routed, and Moray himself slain. "The English then
attacked the main centre of the Scots, where David commanded in
person; and as this also was drawn up in the same broken and
enclosed ground, the various leaders and their vassals were separated,
and fought at a serious disadvantage." Their flank, too, was
exposed to the discharge of a great body of English bowmen, and
as the distance diminished, the arrows flying with a truer aim and
more fatal strength, told fearfully against the Scots.—*(Tytler, Vol.
II., p. 72)*.

It then became painfully evident to King David that Philip de
Valois had spoken falsely. All the best men of England were *not*
in France. The Chronicle of Lanercost draws a graphic picture of
the barons who fought "for England and for Edward at the Nevill
Cross."

"Percy, a short man, of much forethought, putting forward his
own body to meet the enemy, encouraged all to do the same.
Nevill was strong, cautious, brave, much to be feared. He fought
so that traces of his blows stuck to the enemy. Sir Henry de
Scrope took his station in front, cutting down the foe. John
Mowbray was full of grace and goodness; his worthy fame was
widely spred." Upon the High Steward and the Earl of March
there fell the disgrace of deserters. Authorities differ as to the
time when they fled the field, but it seems pretty certain that they
"became discreet" at an early stage of the battle. "*The residue
of the Scots, continuing faithfully with the King, stood about him
like a round tower, keeping him in the middle, who so continued till
there were scarce forty of them left alive, of which not one of them
could escape.*" *(Annales Stowe.)* The fighting became tremendous. "The like was never seen before." The fury of Flodden
was but a repetition of the fury of Nevill's Cross. The High
Steward and the Earl of March turned their backs upon their brave
young King—

But as they left the dark'ning heath,
More desperate grew the strife of death.
The English shafts in volleys hailed,
In headlong charge their horse assailed,
Front, flank, and rear, the squadrons sweep,
To break the Scottish circle deep,
    That fought around their King.
But yet, though thick the shafts as snow,
Though charging knights like whirlwinds go,
Though bill-men ply the ghastly blow;
    Unbroken was the ring;

The stubborn spearmen still made good
Their dark impenetrable wood,
Each stepping where his comrade stood,
    The instant that he fell.
No thought was there of dastard flight,
Link'd in the seried phalanx tight,
Groom fought like noble, squire like knight,
    As fearlessly and well."
            —*Marmion, Canto VI.*, 34.

David had been anxious to see fighting. Little did he expect
to see such a ghastly heap of slain. In that heap lay Moray, the
last in the male line of his heroic race. There, too, lay Charles,
he High Chancellor; and Peebles, the Lord Chamberlain; and
Keith, "Scotia's Marshall and Dunnottar's Lord;" and David de
la Haye, the Constable, with the Earl of Strathern, and above
thirty other of Scotland's best barons. The Knight of Liddesdale,
the Earls of Fife, Menteith, Sutherland, and Wigton, and fifty
other noblemen were prisoners; but with obstinate and hereditary
valour, the Bruce fought on to the bitter end. Disarmed, overpowered, grievously wounded, and covered with blood, he still
struggled in the strong embrace of John de Coupeland, and with
his gauntlet dashed out the front teeth of the Northumbrian squire.
It was the last blow of the last Bruce for liberty. Two arrows had
pierced his body. The extraction of one of these caused him the
sharpest agony. Then the fallen monarch was lifted on horseback,
and hurried through the country to the castle of Sir John Ogle, a
distance of twenty-four miles.

Mounted on a tall black courser, and accompanied by the mayor,
aldermen, and craftsmen of the city, and a guard of several thousand

men-at-arms, he was soon afterwards paraded through the streets of London, and lodged in the Tower. *

"After the victory, the prior and monks of Durham, accompanied by Ralph Lord Nevill, and John Nevill his son, Lord Percy, and other nobles, returned to the Abbey Church, joining in prayer and thanksgiving to God and Holy Saint Cuthbert for the conquest obtained that day."—*Sir John Lawson's MSS.*

The name of Bruce, though it must ever be associated with deep sin and sorrow, still remains as the inspiration of the noble songs of Caledonia. Yet Robert de Brus, the hero of Scotland's liberty, was in reality no Scot at all, being descended from one of those enterprising gentlemen who came over with the Conqueror to put an end to Saxon freedom. (*Wallace Documents, Maitland Club,* 1841.) "The Norman house of Brus formed a part of the Yorkshire baronage, but it had acquired, through intermarriages, the Earldom of Carrick, and the Lordship of Annandale." (*Green's Hist. Eng. People,* Vol. I., p. 369.) Brus bought the throne of Scotland at a fearful cost. He murdered Comyn. He sacrificed his family. He had a splendid band of brave brothers. He saw three die on the scaffold. The fourth perished miserably. His wife and children were captives, exposed to the peril of those fearful days when the wild passions of evil men found vent upon the helpless and the innocent. If the mental anguish and physical privation that he endured could be told, no work of fiction could equal such a story in extremity of horror. He reigned with an intrepid yet lonely heart, and died of leprosy in 1331, leaving an only son. That son spent his young life as an exile in France, and after Nevill's Cross he was a prisoner for eleven years in the Tower. The cancer of confinement ate away the patriotism of his heart, for "in the Chapter House of Westminister there yet remain two

* Knyghton says the King was taken at Merrington, and sent to Bamburgh. This is altogether absurd. Merrington is seven miles south of Nevill's Cross; to have reached it, the King must have fought his way through the English army. The tradition that he fled and was captured under a bridge, spanning the river Browney, is also opposed by authentic historians. We have already quoted Stowe's description of the last stand made by the Scots around the King. The pursuit of fugitives "as farre as Prudhow and Corbridge" is also noticed by him. These fugitives probably formed the rear guard of the division retreating under command of the High Steward and the Earl of March.

Many other reports relative to the battle are untenable. There is no reliable evidence that Queen Philippa, or Baliol, or the Archbishop of Canterbury, or the Bishops of Lincoln and Carlisle were present. Hatfield, Bishop of Durham, was at Calais. The Latin letter of Prior Fossor describing to him the battle is printed in *Raine's Northern Registers,* p. 338.

instruments, in which David recognises the King of England as his Lord Paramount, and consents to take the oaths of homage." (*Tytler*, Vol. II., p. 80.)

He returned home to be the slave of passion. Margaret Logy, a woman of inferior birth, but surpassing beauty, was exalted to a throne which had been filled by the sister of Edward III. For some dark reason she was divorced, and died; and David was robbed of his people's affection by his own selfish, sordid passions. Unhonoured and unloved, the soul of the last of the short line of Bruce passed to its Maker on the 23rd February, 1370.

From the days of Bruce to the days of Elizabeth, at least a quarter of a million souls were hurried to their long home by the Border battles. The loss of property and of material prosperity during the same period cannot easily be estimated. The Scots, during these wars, were looked upon as excommunicated barbarians. All connection with them was avoided and forbidden. The merchant who trafficked with them—the priest who said a mass in their presence—all were involved in the same ecclesiastical sentence, which bound the members of the offending nationality. No Scot was allowed to become a citizen of York and Newcastle. In the civic registers of the former city there are many certificates to show the English origin of men who were kept back from rising in their trades by being falsely charged with having been born across the Borders. (*Raine's Northern Registers, Preface.*)

I fall back again on Southey's poem. The old man spoke to little Peterkin of the glory of Blenheim; but "what good came of it at last" he could not tell. Neither can I tell what good came of the battle of Nevill's Cross; but as I stood one day by the relic of the Cross, thinking of all the feuds between two great nations, now happily united as one people, I felt heartily thankful that the *Halywerefolc* could gather upon the Red Hills no more; and that from the site of the Maiden's Bower there could be heard no sound of battle, but only the silvery Minster bells telling of "peace on earth, good will toward men." I saw, it is true, one "Flying Scotchman," for the East Coast Railway passes across the battlefield like a bond of union between the two kingdoms.

The events which immediately followed the battle may be briefly told.

Roxburgh Castle, the key of the kingdom on the Borders, surrendered to Henry Percy and Ralph Nevill, and the English over-ran the districts of Tweeddale, the Merse, Ettrick, Annandale, and Galloway. Availing themselves of the panic and confusion which ensued upon the captivity of the King, they pushed forward into Lothian, and boasted that the marches of the kingdom were from Coldbrandspath to Soutra, and from thence to Carlops and Crosocryne. Soon after, Lionel, Duke of Ulster, the son of Edward III., became engaged in a mysterious transaction relative to the affairs of Scotland, upon which, unfortunately, no contemporary documents throw any satisfactory light. By an agreement, entered into between this English Prince and the Lords Henry Percy and Ralph Nevill, these barons undertook to assist Balliol with a certain force of men-at-arms. Only the title of this treaty remains. *

Our old chronicler, Holinshed is not always considered a reliable authority, but this account of the battle of Nevill's Cross would be incomplete if he were not allowed to have his say. I therefore append his version of the affair:—" The next day the King of Scotts, with forty thousand men, 'one and another, came and lodged within three English miles of the town of New Castelle, in the land of the Lord Nevill. And the King sent to them within the towne that if they would issue out into the fielde he would fight with them gladly; and they had answere that they would come out and fight with him in the field. Then the Lords and Prelates of England sayde unto the Queen—We are content to adventure our lives with the right and heritage of the King of England our maister. And then they all issued out of the towne, and were in number twelve hundred men of arms, three thousand archers, and seven thousand of others, with the Welchmen. Then the Scottes came and lodged against them nere together; and every man was set in order of battaile. There was ordayn'd four battayles, one to aid to another. The first was in the governance of the Bishop of Durham and the Lord Percye. The second, the Archbishop of York and Lord Nevyll. The third, the Bishop of Lincoln and the Lord Mowbray. The fourth, Lord Edward Ballioll, captain of Barwick, and the Archbishop of Canterbury, and the Lord Roos. And the Queen went from battayle to battayle, praing them to do their devoire for the defence of the honor of their lord

---

* "Indentura tractatus inter Leonellum filium Edwardi tertii primogenitum, Comitem de Ulster, ex una parte, et Monsieur Henry Percy et Rauf. Nevill, ex altera parte, per quam ipsi Henricus et Radulphus conveniunt se servituros in Scotia pro auxilio prestando Edwardo de. Baliol Regi Scotia cum 360 soldariis." 12, Ed. III, *Ayloffe's Ancient Charters, quoted in Tytler*, Vol. II., p. 75.

and maister the King of England, and in the name of God every man to be of good heart and courage, promising them that she would remember them as well and better as though the King her lorde were there personally; and so the Queen departed from them, recommending them to God. The battayle was cruel and dangerous. They began at nine o'clock in the morning, and fought until it was noon. The Scottes had with them great axes, hard and sharp, and gave with them many sore and cruel strokes."

CHAPTER V.

ISSUE OF RALPH, LORD NEVILL, OF NEVILL'S CROSS.

"We shall increase in numbers, and in strength;
Our hearts for England glow with warmer love;
Our ruined forts will rise, our valleys smile
With joyful harvests, and our armies rush
Cheerful to battle, as the lark that sings
Sweet roundelays to hail the blushing morn."

(An adaptation from Rev. J. Hodgson's Poem on Nevill's Cross.)

"All hurtling through the darken'd air the arrowy sleet fell fierce and fast,
And drooping low, in very shame, the Oriflamme to earth was cast.
Bohemia lost his ostrich-plume—Lorraine his spotless shield of pride—
While through the vale rang out the shout, 'St. George for England!' far and wide.
Alencon, humbled, bit the dust—sped Philip headlong from the fight—
And all the bloody plain was dark with dying serf and bleeding knight;
And thus Prince Edward won his spurs; his was the honour of the fray;
Oh! I wot that English hearts will e'er remember Crecy's wondrous day!"
—*W. H. D. L.*

Ralph, Lord Nevill=Alice, daughter of Sir Hugh de Audley.

1. *John de Nevill* FOUGHT AT NEVILL'S CROSS Oct. 17, 1346.	2. *Robert*, FOUGHT AT CRECI, Aug. 26, 1346. Afterwards knighted. Mentioned in Froissart and Hollinshed as having served under the banner of the Black Prince. He married the widow of Sir Thomas Grey.	3. *Sir R. Nevill*, of Condell, was the founder of the family of the NEVILLS OF THORNTON BRIDGE. Sir Thomas Nevill, Knight, High Sheriff of Leicestershire in 1539, 1552, 1561, married Clara, a daughter of Ralph Nevill of Thornton Bridge, and the latter family merged into that of the Nevills of Holt.	4. *Alexander,* Archbishop of York. (*See below.*)	5. *Thomas,* died Bishop-elect of Ely.
6. *William*, created Knight in retinue of the Earl of Salisbury. Relieved the Castle of Brest when besieged by French. Afterwards made Admiral. In 1378 again employed in French war. He then became Knight of the King's (Rich. II.) Chamber, and was also appointed Commissioner to treat for peace in Scotland. He was specially distinguished as a leader of the Lollards.	**7.** *Margaret*, married 1st, William Lord Roos of Hamlake, ancestor to Duke of Rutland; 2nd, Henry Percy, 1st Earl of Northumberland, who fought at Nevill's Cross.	**8.** *Catherine*, married Lord Dacre of Gillsland.	**9.** *Alianor,* married Geoffrey, Lord Scroope.	**10.** *Eufamia,* married 1st, Reginald de Lucy. 2nd, Robert Clifford, Lord of Westmoreland, who died without issue in 1357; 3rd, Sir Walter Hellerton.

How difficult it is to follow fully any service in Durham Cathedral! Every stone, eloquent with history, leads you away into endless trains of thought. The pinnacles of the Nevill screen, bathed in soft light, rise before you like ghosts of long gone years; and soon you find yourself away with John de Nevill among the Red Hills, or with his brother Robert in the thick of the battle of Creci.* Young Edward is down; Richard de Beaumont, bearer of the banner of Wales, has flung the red dragon of Merlin over the fallen hero. The boy has not yet seen fifteen summers. He . must not be allowed to die. The sturdy Welshmen, and the still sturdier Northumbrians fight on, through the autumn twilight. Night comes at last, and victory!

The blazing watchfires shine upon the gory battlefield; they light up the old weird windmill that stands upon the hill, and before the eyes of every soldier, they "gild with a glorious glow" the embrace of the warrior father with his warrior son. There is a "hush of happiness," whilst the monarch says, "Fair son, God give you good perseverance; right royally have you behaved this day."

The altar screen at Durham was John de Nevill's gift of thanksgiving for the preservation of his father, his brother, and himself, in "sundrie grievous and righte deadlie battels." It is still very beautiful after all its sufferings at the hands of the spiteful Scot. A description of it will be found in the chapter on the Nevill Monuments.

John de Nevill succeeded his father as Lord of Raby. As already noticed, he commanded at Nevill's Cross. He also distinguished himself in the French wars, and was created a Knight of the Garter, with Lord Fitzwalter. In the 44th Edward III. (1371), he was Admiral of the King's Fleet, and served in France with one hundred men-at-arms, one hundred archers, and two hundred

---

* "There was a large park near a wood, on the rear of the army which King Edward enclosed, and in it placed all his baggage, waggons, and horses, for the men-at-arms and archers were to fight on foot. He afterwards ordered that the army should be divided into three battalions. In the first, he placed the young Prince of Wales, and with him the Earls of Warwick and Oxford, Sir Godfrey de Harcourt, the Lord Reginald Cobham, Lord Thomas Holland, Lord Stafford, Lord Manley, the Lord Delaware, Sir John Chandos, Lord Bartholomew Burghersh, *Lord Robert Neville*, Lord Thomas Clifford, the Lord Bouchier, the Lord Latimer, and many other knights and squires whom I cannot name. There might be in the first division about 800 men-at-arms, 2,000 archers, and 1,000 Welshmen, all of whom advanced in regular order to their ground, each lord under his own banner and in the centre of his men."—*Froissart.*

mariners. In 1369, he was a Commissioner for the custody of the East Marches towards Northumberland. In 1374, he served in Brittany with three hundred men-at-arms, three hundred archers, and fourteen knights. In 1378 (1st Richard II.), he was constituted Governor of Bamborough Castle for life. He besieged and took Berwick-on-Tweed from the Scots in the following year. About the same period he became Seneschall of Bordeaux. Being Lieutenant of Aquitaine, "he reduced that province to peace, and in those parts eighty-three walled towns, castles, and forts were surrendered to him." He also fought against the Turks. He acted as Commissioner to treat for the ransom of David of Scotland, and received 24,000 marks as part of the said ransom. After the decease of Sir Robert de Mowbray, Bolton in Allerdale reverted to him. In 1381, he received a license to castellate his house of Sheriff Hutton. The license for Raby was given two years earlier. In 1385, he attended Richard II. to Scotland, with a train of 500 men. He married first, Maud, daughter of Henry, Lord Percy, by whom he had six children, of whom we shall speak presently. He married secondly, Elizabeth, daughter and heir of Sir William de Latimer, and had livery of her lands delivered to him. By her he had two children. She afterwards married Sir Robert de Willoughby, and died in 1396. Her son, John, became Baron Latimer. See table given below.

Lord John Nevill* died at Newcastle, October 17th, 1389, the anniversary of the battle of Nevill's Cross, and was buried in Durham Cathedral.

His brother, *Alexander de Nevill*, was born at Raby. He was consecrated Archbishop of York in 1374, and was made Lord High Chancellor of England. He beautified and strengthened the Castle of Cawood. Being much in favour with Richard II., the enemies

---

* "In the morning a certayne nombre of gentylmen that were in the town (Newcastle) yssued out to the nombre of C C speres (200 spearmen) to make a skry in the Scottysshe host; they dashed right on the Earl of Moret's tentes, who bare on his armour syluer three creylles goules; ther they took hym in his bed, and slewe many, or thoost was moued, and wan great pillage. Than they returned into the towne boldely with great joye and delyuered therle Moret as prisoner to the captayne of the castell, the Lord John Nevill."—*Bernard.*

"When the Scots had marched from before Newcastle, the Governor, Lord John Nevill, having mounted a fleet courser, passed by them, for he was well acquainted with all the by-roads and passes of the country, and made such haste that in five days he came to Chertsey where the King of England was."—*Froissart.*

If Lord Nevill knew all the by-roads, it was more than Sir John Froissart did; for before the battle of Otterbourne he makes Earl Douglas' train "cross the Tyne, three leagues above Newcastle, near Brancepeth, where they entered the rich country of Durham."

of the King designed to imprison the Archbishop in Rochester Castle, but he fled for protection to Pope Urban at Rome, who, partly out of pity (that he might have something for his support), and more out of policy, that York might be at his own disposal after the removal of this Archbishop, translated him to St. Andrew's, in Scotland. But Scotland was poor, and the Scots, looking at that time with jealousy upon all Englishmen, were especially opposed to a Nevill, since that family had been so active against them in war. "Half a loaf is better than no bread, but this new translation was rather a stone than a loaf, not filling his belly, but breaking his teeth if feeding thereon. This made him preferre the pastorall charge of a parish in Louvaine before his arch-no-bishop-ricke, where he died in the 5th year of exile (1394), and was buried in the church of the Carmelites. So may God reste his soul." —*Fuller.*

A full account of the "Proceedings in Parliament against Alexander Nevill, Archbishop of York, Robert Vere, Duke of Ireland, Michael de la Pole, Earl of Suffolk, Robert Tresilian, Lord Chief Justice of England, and Nicholas Brambre, some time Mayor of London, and others for High Treason," February 3, 1388, (11th Richard II.), will be found in *State Trials*, Vol. I.

"It was asserted that by wicked contrivance they would not permit the great men of the Kingdom, nor good Counsellors to come near the King, thereby encroaching to themselves the Royal Power. Divers people had been hindered of the benefit of the Common Law of England, and put to great delays, losses and costs, and the aforesaid traitors took great bribes in many cases in the name of the King for maintenance of Quarrels and Suits, and once took bribes of both Sides or Parties, etc.

"The persons accused being summoned for the third time, *and not appearing*, the Lords proceeded to Judgment, and did adjudge the said Archbishop, Duke, and Earl, to be convicted of Treason, and to be drawn and hanged as such, that their Heirs should be disinherited for ever, their lands forfeited to the King, and the Temporalities of the Archbishop of York should be taken into the King's hands, etc."

"On this day the Lord Mayor, Sir Nicholas Brambre, *did appear*, and being charged, answered, 'Whosoever hath branded me with this ignominious Mark with him I am ready to fight in the Lists to maintain my Innocency whenever the King shall appoint.'

E

And this spake he with such a Fury that his eye sparkled with Rage, and he breathed as if an Etna lay hid in his breast, chusing rather to die, gloriously in the Field, than disgracefully on a Gibbet. The Appellants so hearing, with resolute Countenance answered they would readily accept of the Combat, and the whole company flung down their Gages before the King that they seemed like Snow on a Winter's day. Yet the Lords resolved that Battle did not lie in that case, wherefore the most damnable traitor was drawn on a hurdle to Tyburn, and being suddenly turned off from the ladder, and the Executioner likewise cutting his throat, he died." Tresilian the Lord Chief Justice being found in a ditch, and being "stript of certain images painted like unto the Signs of the Heavens, and the Heads of many Devils painted together with their Names, which so long as he wore he could not die, he was forced up the ladder with staves and so perished."

This trial is given with great minuteness. It affords a very sad and graphic picture of the course of "justice" in the reign of Richard II.

Issue of John, Lord Nevill, by his first wife, Maud, daughter of Henry, Lord Percy, and aunt to Henry, first Earl of Northumberland.

1. *Ralph*, Lord of Raby, and first Earl of Westmoreland. (*See next chapter.*)	2. *Thomas*, summoned to Parliament 1383, as BARON FURNIVAL, *jure uxoris primæ.* (*See below.*)	3. *Alice*, married William, Lord Deincourt.	4. *Matilda*, married William, Lord Scroop.	5. *Idina*.	6. *Eleanor*, married Ralph, Lord Lumley, who was attainted, 1. Henry IV. 1399.

Issue of Lord John Nevill, by his second wife, Elizabeth, daughter of Lord Latimer of Danby.

1. *John*, summoned to Parliament as BARON LATIMER in right of his mother, 1404 to 1430, when he died, S.P. He married Maud, daughter of Lord Clifford and widow of Richard, Earl of Cambridge.	2. *Elizabeth*, married Sir Thos. Willoughby, son of Robert, Lord Willoughby de Eresby.

Thomas de Nevill married Joane, daughter and heir of William, Lord Furnival, 1384, and had livery of her lands. He was the same year summoned to Parliament as Baron Furnival. He was Warden of all Anandale, and Constable of Loughmaban, in the West Marches of Scotland, 4th Hen. IV. ; also Governor of Berwick, Alnwick, and Warkworth, and High Treasurer of England. He married secondly Ankaret, widow of Sir Richard Talbot, and daughter of John, Lord Strange of Blackmere. Lord Furnival's daughter, Maud, was married to the famous Sir John Talbot, who in her right was summoned to Parliament as Lord

Furnival, and who was afterwards created Earl of Shrewsbury. The manor of Farnham was held by the Furnivals by the tenure of finding a glove for the King's right hand on the coronation day, and supporting the left arm so long as he held the royal sceptre. The Talbots surrendered the manor of Farnham to Henry the Eighth, in exchange for that of Worksop, and the service was continued by the Dukes of Norfolk, in consequence of their connection with the Furnival family. Furnival's Inn was originally a house of Lord Furnival's. It formed part of the Talbot property, until Francis, Earl of Shrewsbury, in consideration of £120, sold it to Edward Gryffin, Esq., Solicitor-General to the King (1st Edward VI.) for the use of the society of Lincoln's Inn. (*Vide Origines Juridiciales.*) The first mention of the family of Furnival is the record of Girard de Furnival's association with Richard I. in Palestine. Thomas de Nevill died seized of the manors of Farnham, Bucks; Sutton Maddock, Corsham, Wrockardine, Salop; Eccleswell, Wormlow, and Penyard with the Lordship of Goodrich Castle, and the hundred of Irchenfield in Herefordshire; Aiveton in Staffordshire; Treton and Hoton Bainell, with the castle and manor of Sheffield in Yorkshire, and the manor of Wirksop in Nottinghamshire. By his will dated March 12th, 1406, he bequeaths his body to be buried without pomp in the Priory of Worksop. To the King he gave his best gold cup with its cover; to the fabrick of the steeple at Worksop, £40; to his sister, the Lady Alice Deincourt, £200; to John Talbot and his wife Maud his best bed with its furniture. He willed that his devises of certain lands in Worksop should cause his obit to be solemnly kept every year in the Priory Church with *placebo* and *dirige*, and mass of requiem by note. *Vide Dugdale and Rowland.*

"He lyeth at Wirksop above the quire, in a fair tomb." *Vide Chapter on Nevill Monuments.*

By his second wife, Ankaret, he had a daughter Joane, who married Sir Hugh Cooksey.

CHAPTER VI.

RALPH DE NEVILL, FIRST EARL OF WESTMORELAND.

BARDOLPH. "On, on, on, on, on! to the breach, to the breach!"
PISTOL. "Knocks go and come; God's vassals drop and die;
   And sword and shield,
    In bloody field,
   Doth win immortal fame.
BOY. "Would I were in an ale-house in London!
   I would give all my fame for a pot of ale, and safety."

  * * * * * * *

WESTMORELAND.   "O that we now had here
   But one ten thousand of those men in England
   That do no work to-day!"
KING HENRY.   "What's he that wishes so?
   My cousin Westmoreland? No, my fair cousin:
   If we are mark'd to die, we are enow
   To do our country loss; and if to live,
   The fewer men the greater share of honour.
     O, do not wish one more!
   Rather proclaim it, Westmoreland, through my host,
   That he which hath no stomach to this fight,
   Let him depart; his passport shall be made,
   And crowns for convoy put into his purse:
   We would not die in that man's company
   That fears his fellowship to die with us.
   This day is call'd the feast of Crispian:
   He that outlives this day, and comes safe home,
   Will stand a tip-toe when this day is named,
   And rouse him at the name of Crispian.

  * * * * * * *

This story shall the good man teach his son :
And Crispin Crispian shall ne'er go by,
From this day to the ending of the world,
But we in it shall be remembered ;
We few, we happy few, we band of brothers :
For he to-day that sheds his blood with me
Shall be my brother ; be he ne'er so vile,
This day shall gentle his condition :
And gentlemen in England now a-bed
Shall think themselves accursed they were not here,
And hold their manhoods cheap whiles any speaks
That fought with us upon Saint Crispin's Day."

—*Henry V., Act III.*

RALPH NEVILL was united in the Commission with his father and the Earl of Northumberland, for receiving the ransom of King David of Scotland, 1384. In 1386, he was made Governor of the Castle and City of Carlisle, and a Warden for the West Marches. He was also Warden of all the King's forests beyond Trent for life. About the same time he obtained a Charter for a weekly market, and yearly fair, in his lordship of Middleham. In 1391, he was on the Commission to treat with France and Scotland for a truce. In 1397, he was appointed Constable of the Tower of London. From Sir John Montagu he obtained the Castle of Warke-upon-Tweed, in exchange for other lands. On the 29th of September, 1397, he was created a Knight of the Garter, and *Earl of Westmoreland.* Being a member of the Privy Council to King Richard II., he obtained from him the honour of Penreth, as also all the royalties which belonged to the Crown, and had been unjustly withheld by the heirs of Richard de Vipont. From John of Gaunt, Duke of Lancaster, he had a grant of Fiendeleze in Richmondshire.

Having received many favours from Richard II., it may seem strange that Ralph Nevill should ever desert that monarch ; nevertheless it is a fact that when Henry, Duke of Lancaster, landed in 1399, the Earls of Westmoreland and Northumberland, the Lords Percy, Roos, Willoughby, and others resorted to him ; and, taking an oath from him that he would not do King Richard any bodily harm, they did homage to him, and marched to London. The Earl of Westmoreland was one of the Lords who attested, in the Tower, the resignation of the imprudent and unhappy Richard. Beyond this, he took no part in the proceedings against that monarch.—(*Hall's Chronicles.*)

Ralph Nevill was created by Henry IV., on his assuming the Crown, Earl Marshal of England. In his patent it was granted "that he, by reason of his office, might have, bear, and carry, as well in the King's presence as absence, a golden staff, ringed about both ends with black, and with the King's seal of arms engraven in the upper end, and the seal of arms of the said Earl of Westmoreland, in the lower end of the staff, notwithstanding that all Earls in time past who held the same office of Earl Marshall of England, were accustomed to bear and carry a staff of wood." The vast lordship or honour of Richmond was likewise given to Ralph Nevill for his life.—*Rowland.*

And now we enter upon the fifteenth century. Homildon Hill was fought in 1402. Great numbers of Scotch nobles—Earl Douglas among them—were taken prisoners by Percy, Earl of Northumberland, and his renowned son, Harry Hotspur. Although he owed his throne in great part to the valour of the Percys, and although he was deeply in debt to them, Henry IV. commanded that their prisoners should not be ransomed. His commands were disregarded. Douglas was set at liberty.

The death of Richard II. left the young Mortimer, Earl of March, the next claimant in blood to the Crown. With his two sisters, he was therefore very promptly put in prison by Henry IV., and his uncle, Sir Edmund Mortimer, was taken captive by Owen Glyndwr (great grandson of Llewellyn), who had been a faithful adherent of the late King, and was now in open revolt. But Henry was only too pleased to hear of the captivity of any Mortimer, and he refused to ransom him. This was the last straw of ingratitude which broke the back of Percy's loyalty, for Mortimer was his brother-in-law.

Meanwhile Mortimer was caught in a double chain of captivity, for he fell in love with his gaoler's daughter, and straightway was made into a very great rebel. In fact Glyndwr, Mortimer, Douglas, and the Percys, became confederates in a huge conspiracy to place the Earl of March upon the throne. Henry Percy marched towards Wales, but instead of meeting with Glyndwr, he met with the King. Then the gallant Hotspur

> "Threw many a northward look to see his father
> Bring up his powers, but he did look in vain."

It had been agreed that a second army should advance under command of the Earl of Northumberland to support the rebels;

but while the Percys revolted, the Nevills adhered faithfully to Henry; and Ralph Nevill drove the old Earl of Northumberland, · his former associate in arms and policy, back to Prudhoe Castle.

Everybody knows how Hotspur died, as only such a hero could die, on the fatal field of Shrewsbury, July 23rd, 1403.

Northumberland retired almost heart-broken to Warkworth; but in the merry month of May, 1405, he was out again among the rebels.

Scroop, Archbishop of York, and Lord Mowbray assembled a body of 15,000 men on Shipton Moor, expecting to be joined by Northumberland. Ralph Nevill met the insurgents, and finding them numerous, he had recourse to stratagem, or treachery, as some say. Like the witches of Macbeth,

> "He paltered with them in a double sense,
> And kept the word of promise to their ear,
> And broke it to their hope."

"He sent to ask what were their grievances, that if reasonable they might be redressed. He then invited the Archbishop and other leaders to a conference, in which they stated their demands. To all these he agreed, and solemnly pledged himself to procure the King's ratification. When he had thus completely lulled them into security, he persuaded them to send messengers to their troops, to tell them that peace was made; and that they might return to their homes,* promising on his own part to do the same. But whilst the Archbishop, unsuspicious of any fraud, sent orders to his

---

* HASTINGS. My lord, our army is dispersed already:
　　　　　Like youthful steers unyoked, they take their courses
　　　　　East, west, north, south; or, like a school broke up,
　　　　　Each hurries towards his home and sporting place.

WESTMORELAND.
　　　　　Good tidings, my Lord Hastings: for the which
　　　　　I do arrest thee, traitor, of high treason:
　　　　　And you Lord Archbishop, and you Lord Mowbray,
　　　　　Of capital treason I attach you both.

　　　　　*　　　*　　　*　　　*　　　*

WESTMORELAND.
　　　　　There is not now a rebel's sword unsheath'd,
　　　　　But Peace puts forth her olive everywhere.
　　　　　The manner how this action hath been borne
　　　　　Here at more leisure may your highness read,
　　　　　With every course in his particular.

KING.　　O Westmoreland, thou art a summer bird,
　　　　　Which ever in the haunch of winter sings
　　　　　The lifting up of day!　　　　—*Henry IV.*

men to disband, the wily Nevill gave his own message to a person whom he had previously ordered not to deliver it; and, as soon as he had preceived that the insurgent camp was broken up, and the men dispersing, he caused a body of his own soldiers to come suddenly to the place of conference, and carry off the archbishop, and all those who accompanied him, prisoners to Pontefract, where they were all beheaded." This is the first instance in English history of a prelate suffering capital punishment. Northumberland escaped to Scotland, but was slain among the insurgents on Bramham Moor in 1408.

Ralph Nevill served Henry faithfully, too faithfully indeed, since to serve him he broke faith with others. Perhaps his marriage with the King's half-sister secured his loyalty.

When Henry V. ascended the throne he found that the "temporal lands, devoutly given, had been disordinately spent by religious and other spiritual persons."

A bill was introduced in the Parliament, at Leicester, 2nd Henry V.; and it was ordained, "that this matter should then be well studied, pondered, and brought to a good conclusion," so that "the King might have in his coffers £20,000, the values of religious houses which overpass."

"Now this same bill was much noted and feared amongst the religious sort, whom in effect it mightily touched and unhinged, insomuch that the fat Abbots did sweat after a profuse sort, the proud Priors frowned, the poor Friars cursed, the silly Nuns wept, and altogether were nothing pleased nor content."—*Hall.*

Indeed it was a terrible bill. "The very existence of Holy Church was threatened like as by a foul and filthy plague." The clergy felt so sure of this that they determined "to replenish the King's brain with some pleasant study," and what could be more pleasant than a war with France? "Why should their sovereign lord look greedily upon their poor patrimony when the whole realme of France with all its prerogatives and preheminencies belonged to him as heir to his great-grandfather?" Archbishop Chicheley, "a man much regarding God's law, but more loving his own lucre, after low obeysance, made an oration" to the effect "that the glory of kings consisteth not only in high blood and haute progeny, not in haboundant riches and superfluous substance, nor in plesant pasttime and joious solace; but the very tipe of the magnificence of a Prince resteth in populous rich regions, wealthy subjects, and beautiful citys and towns, all of which wealthy subjects, rich regions, and beautiful citys were to be found in this same kingdom and realme of France."

Henry rather thought that the question lay between his great-great-grandmother and the Salic law, but the good Chicheley made short work of this same Salic law.

> " There is no bar
> To make against your highness' claim to France
> But this, which they produce from Pharamond
> 'In terram Salicam mulieres ne succedant;'
> No woman shall succeed in Salique land:
> Which Salique land the French unjustly gloze
> To be the realm of France, and Pharamond
> The founder of this law and female bar,
> Yet their own authors faithfully affirm
> That the land Salique is in *Germany*.
>
> * * * *
>
> The sin upon my head, dread sovereign!
> For in the book of Numbers is it writ,
> When the man dies let the inheritance
> Descend unto the daughter. Gracious lord
> Stand for your own; unwind your bloody flag,
> Look back into your mighty ancestors:
> Go, my dread lord, to your great-grandsire's tomb,
> From whom you claim; invoke his warlike spirit,
> And your great-uncle's, Edward the Black Prince,
> Who on the French ground play'd a tragedy
> Making defeat on the full power of France,
> Whiles his most mighty father on a hill
> Stood smiling to behold his lion's whelp
> Forage in blood of French nobility.
> O noble English, that could entertain
> With half their forces the full pride of France
> And let another half stand laughing by,
> All out of work and cold for action!"

But we must leave Shakspeare, much as we love him, for the more sober chronicle. When the Archbishop had finished, "Ralf, Earl of Westmoreland, a man of no less gravity than experience, and of no more experience than stomach, which was then High Warden of the Marches towards Scotland, and therefore thinking that if the King should pass over into France with his whole puissance, that his power should be too weak to withstand the strength of Scotland, rose up, and making obeysance, said, 'Surely, sir, as my Lord

Canterbury hath clerkly declared, the conquest of France is very
honourable, and when it is gotten and obtained, very profitable
and pleasant: but saving your Grace's reformation, I say and
affirm, that to conquer Scotland is more necessary, more apparent
easy, and more profitable to this realme, than is the gain of France.
For though I am not so well learned as my Lord Archbishop is,
nor have proceeded to degree in the University, yet I have read,
and heard great clerks say, that strength, knit and combined
together, is of more force and efficacy than when it is severed and
dispersed. As for an example, sprinkle a vessel of water, and it
moisteth not, but cast it out wholly together, and it both washeth
and nourisheth. This notable saying, before this time hath
encouraged Emperors, animated Kings, and allured Princes, to
conquer realmes to them adjoining, to vanquish nations to their
dominions adjacent, and to subdue people either necessary for
their purpose, or being to them daily enemies and continual
adversaries.

"'Do you not remember how the whole Isle of Britain was one
entire monarchy in the time of your noble ancestor, King Brute,
first king and ruler of your famous Empire and glorious region?
which dividing his realme to his three sons, gave to Lothrine, his
eldest son, that part of Britain, which your Highness now enjoyeth,
and to Albanact, his second son, he gave the country of Albany,
now called Scotland, and to Camber, his third son, he gave the
country of Cambria, now called Wales; reserving always to him,
and his heirs, homage, liege, and fealty loyal for the same countries.
By this division, the glory of the monarchy of Britain was clearly
defaced; by this separation, the strength of the British kings was
sorely diminished ; by this dispersion, intestine war began, and
civil rebellion sprang first within this region.

"'Wherefore my Counsel is first to invade Scotland, and by
God's grace, to conquer and join that region to your Empire, and
to restore the renowned monarchy of Britain to her old estate and
pre-eminence, and so beautified with realmes, and furnished with
people to enter into France for the recovering of your righteous
title, and true inheritance, in observing the old ancient proverb
used by our forefathers, which saith,

'Who so wyll France wynne,
Must with Scotland fyrst beginne.'

"There was much more to the same effect. Then the Duke of Exeter spoke; and then all men cried, '*War, War! France, France!*' "wherefore the dissolving of religious houses was clearly forgotten and buried, and nothing thought of, but only the recovering of France; and so the Parliament was dissolved."

Shakspeare follows Hollinshed in representing the Earl of Westmoreland as the person who wished for more men from England at Agincourt. Monstrelet says that "one, Walter Hungerford, a gallant knight, expressed a wish that some of the men-at-arms and archers, then fat and idle in England, were with them to do battle, and the King exclaimed, 'No, by my life I would not have one more! If we win the battle, as I trust we may, the fewer we are, the greater shall be our honour, and if we lose, we are too many already.'" Shakspeare's historical accuracy has here been called in question. Walter Hungerford wished for more men; therefore it was not Westmoreland who wished for more men; therefore Hollinshed and Shakspeare are wrong. The less we have of this kind of criticism the better. That two people in the same circumstances should wish for the same thing is most natural. That their wishes, after being expressed to the same person, should meet with the same answer is also natural. "Many there were who wished for absent comrades, many there were who looked bitterly up to heaven, and implored the Divine mercy, and the protection of the Blessed Virgin, and of England's patron, Saint George, to save them from the imminent perils by which they were surrounded."—*Old Clerical Chronicler, quoted in Sir Harris Nicholas' Chronicle of Agincourt.*

But modern criticism proceeds to further assertions. "*The Earl of Westmoreland, being in England and not at Agincourt, could not wish for more men from England.*" I do not know who first found this out, but evidently such an idea never occurred to the far searching mind of Durham's great historian.

"In the Roll of Agincourt, the Earl Marshall (Westmoreland), had in his train, five knights, thirty-three lancers, and eighty archers. Some of the names are immediately familiar to a northern ear—Thomas Rokeby, Knight; Sir John Hoton, Edmund Rodham, Roger Ratcliffe, John Swynborne, Thomas Rokesby, William Hagthorpe, John Wardale, John Wytton, &c."—*Surtees' History of Durham*, Vol. IV.

Several names on the Agincourt roll occur also in the registers of Brancepeth until late in the seventeenth century. The rector of Staindrop, with whom I communicated on this point, has noticed a like occurrence in the Staindrop registers. I imagine, then, that these names represent the descendants of Brancepeth and Raby men, who fought in Westmoreland's train at Agincourt.

The Agincourt roll appears to be only a fragmentary transcript; and it would be exceedingly difficult, at this date, to say who was, and who was not, at Agincourt; but I see no reason for doubting the presence there of the Earl of Westmoreland. The inference for his absence was probably drawn from the fact that he had been appointed warden to defend the Scottish marches.* Rowland denies the presence of the Earl at Agincourt, but he provides a crumb of comfort to the admirers of the Nevill family, by stating that Lord John de Beauchamp, Lord de Despencer Burgavenny, and the Earl of Worcester, ancestors of the Abergavenny branch of the house of Nevill, fought on that field.

The Earl of Westmoreland married, first, Margaret daughter of Hugh, Earl of Stafford, for which marriage a special dispensation from Pope Urban the Fifth was obtained, she being within the third and fourth degrees of consanguinity. She died on the 9th of June, 1370, and was buried in Brancepeth Church. The opponents of intermarriages will not fail to notice that the issue of the Earl's first marriage was far less distinguished than that of the second, which sprang from the Royal Joan Beaufort (widow of Lord Robert Ferrers of Oversley), daughter of John of Gaunt, Duke of Lancaster, and fourth son of Edward III. Joan was half-sister to Henry IV., and to Lady Philippa Plantagenet, wife of John, King of Portugal. She was also cousin-german to Richard II., and aunt to Henry V. By his first wife Ralph Nevill had nine children, by his second fourteen. Joan Beaufort died Nov. 13th, 1440, and was buried in the choir of Lincoln Cathedral. (See chapter on Nevill Monuments, where also will be found particulars of the tombs and chantries erected to perpetuate the memory of the first Earl of Westmoreland.) By her first husband (Baron Ferrers) Joan Beaufort had two daughters—Elizabeth, who married John, Baron of Greystock; and Mary, who married Ralph Nevill of Oversley, second son of the Earl of Westmoreland by his first countess.

* The Earl Marshal (Westmoreland) was at Southampton on the 2nd of August, 1415, as a Commissioner to try the Earl of Cambridge and others for high treason. Cambridge was executed on the 5th, and the expedition sailed to France on the 11th.

Earl Ralph was first cousin to Hotspur, and grandfather to King Edward IV. and Richard III. He died Oct. 21st, 1426, and was buried at Staindrop.

Henry IV. granted him by charter free chase in all his demesne lands at Kettlewell; and Henry V. in third year of his reign, granted him free chase in all his lands of Burton in Bishopsdale, Walden, West Witton, and Penhill.

He was Lord of Raby, Branspeth, Sheriff Hutton, Middleham, and Coverham, and he died seized of upwards of four score manors, viz., the manor and half hundred of Clavering, in Essex; the manors of Isenhampstead, Latimer Crowley, and Boughton, in Bucks; Dylewike, Wotton, Kerkington, Rouhale, Bromham, Sutton, and Stratton juxta Biggleswade, and Potton juxta Sutton, in Bedford; Wilby, and Carleton juxta Rockingham, in Northampton; of the manor of Tarbroke, called Woodhall, in Norfolk; Helpringham and Shekington, in Lincolnshire; Bolton Gameslesby, and Unthan, in Cumberland; Bywel, Styford, and the Castle of Bamborough, in Northumberland; Danby, with the hamlets of Crowecliff, Glassdale, and Letom; the manors of Thornton, in Pickering Lithe, Scarnston, Sinelington, Tiverington, Leverton, Sheriff Hoton, Quenby; two parts of the manor of Walton; the manors of Riseburgh, Stokesley, Flemington, Sutton in Galtres; Well, with the advowson of the hospital, Snape, Crakehall, Middleham, Carleton, Coverdale, and Thoraldby, in York; twenty knights' fees in Sharnebroke, Pavenham, Hinewike, Thorncote, Carlton, Turvey, Stachesden, Wooton, Bromham, Bidenham, Houghton Conquest, Horcliff, Chalgrave, Evershot, Potsgrave, Chikeland, Stotford, Stondon, Helew, South Yevel, Stanford, Wardon, Kerdinton, Conpoll, Wiliton, Harewedon, Wrastlingworth, Taddelow, Wiboldston, Bereford, Rouhale, Ravensden, Goldington, Rish Belnhurst, Caisho, Aspel, and Astwike; as also divers lands in Briddale, and Scotton, in York.

ADDENDA.—THE BATTLE OF AGINCOURT, FRIDAY, OCTOBER 25TH, 1415.

"What news, what news, my trusty page?
What news, what news dost thou bring to me?"
"I brings such news from the King of France,
That you and he can never agree.
He says you are young and of tender age,
Not fit to come up to his degree;
He has sent you home some tennis-balls
That with them you may learn for to play."
Oh! then bespoke our noble King,
A solemn vow then vowed he;
"I'll promise him such English balls
As in French land he ne'er did see—
Go! call up Cheshire and Lancashire,
And Derby hills that are so free;
But neither married man, nor widow's son,
Nor widow's curse shall go with me!"
—*Song of Agincourt.*

(The special mention of Cheshire, Lancashire, and Derby in this song may be accounted for by the fact that Henry was Duke of Lancaster, and Earl of Chester and Derby.)

"Agincourt is a commune or parish consisting of a most uninteresting collection of farmers' residences and cottages, once, however, distinguished by a Castle, of which nothing now remains but the foundation. The scene of the contest lies between this commune and the adjoining one of Tramecour, in a wood belonging to which latter the King concealed those archers whose prowess and vigour contributed so eminently to the glorious result."—*Paper read before the Royal Society of Literature.* 1827.

"By God's help we will see a little more of this bonny land of France—of this France which is all our own. We are resolved to undergo every peril rather than suffer the French to taunt us with fearing them. We will go, an' it please God without harm or danger; but should they hinder our journey, why, then, we will fight them, and the victory and the glory will be ours. In our marches through the country nothing shall be compelled from the villages, nothing taken but paid for; none of the French upraided or abused in disdainful language; for when lenity and cruelty play for a kingdom the gentlest gamester is the soonest winner."

So spoke Henry, when, on the 8th of October, he quitted Harfleur, resolved to march through Normandy to his own town of Calais. His little army diminished by dysentery, numbered then about 6,000 souls.

He could ill afford to lose even one, yet when a soldier was detected in sacrilege, having hidden in his sleeve a copper-gilt pix, the man was promptly hanged.

Whatever else the army lacked it possessed discipline. Reaching Abberville on the 13th, Henry found all the bridges of the Somme broken, and the enemy posted on the opposite bank. But nothing daunted the heart of Henry of Monmouth. "On the morning of the 19th, after wearily toiling through sand and mud, discovering an unguarded ford between Betencourt and Perouenne, he boldly carried his army across the river, and with shouts of joy they occupied the opposite bank. Crossing the swift rolling Ternois at Blangy on the 24th, he discerned the *innumerable hosts* (estimated from fifty to a hundred thousand) of the French retiring upon Agincourt as he approached, and covering the marshy plain with their glittering pennons."—*Adam's Memorable Battles.*

Henry passed the night in a small hut in the village of Maisoncelle. The rain fell heavily. The soldiers were weary and half famished. They betook themselves to prayer. Henry was up by break of day. Having attended mass, he mounted a small grey horse, and drew up his army in line of battle.

On his head was a polished helmet, encircled by a crown of gold, sparkling with gems; but the light in his face gladdened the hearts of all men. On his coat he wore the arms of France and England.

"I swear," said he, "England shall pay no ransom for me, nor shall France triumph over me in life. This day shall either be famous for my death, or in it I will win honour."

The French covered the country like a mighty forest. The sun shone on a thousand banners of embroidered arms.

Sir Thomas Erpingham, a knight fearless and magnificent, with snow-white hair, advanced and threw up into the air his truncheon. This signal was answered by such a shout as Frenchmen had never heard before. The archers planted their stakes into the ground, and standing behind them, rained their arrows against the enemy. The French cavalry were gored to death by the iron pikes. Horse and rider rolled helplessly together on the filthy field. "Many an English soldier was bare-headed and half naked; but his heart was warm with loyal courage. With short knife, with sword and dagger, with lead loaded mallet, he dealt death around. The Constable of France fell; the Duke of Brabant, spurring fresh upon the field, was slain."—*De Barante, quoted in Adams.*

As calm as if sitting at the council, the English King from the midst of the battle, even where it was fiercest around him, issued his commands, and marked with words of commendation, the conduct of the foremost in the fight.—*G. R. James' Agincourt.*

Eighteen knights, all sworn to take him or kill him, set upon him as he was defending the stricken Clarence. The guard closed round. The eighteen were slain. The Duke D'Alençon, "the prime hope, and Flower of France," followed by sixty knights, pressed forward. His axe cleft the King's Crown, and dashed to earth the Duke of York. In another moment he was himself a corpse. Men's breath came in quick hoarse gasps, so sharp was the strife. "The English stood on heaps of dead bodies which exceeded a man's height, and felled their adversaries below with swords and axes."—*MS. Sloane.*

As the battle waged, hundreds of Picardy peasants, believing the English vanquished, came to plunder the camp. Henry, mistaking these for armed reinforcements, under the Duke of Burgundy, gave order for the slaughter of the prisoners, and multitudes were massacred in cold blood. In this battle France lost the chief of all her chivalry. England lost the Duke of York, the Earl of Suffolk, Sir Richard Keighley, Thomas Fitz-Henry, John de Peniton, and the famous David Gamme (*i.e.*, David of the squint eye), who, being questioned as to the number of the enemy, replied: "There are enow to be killed, enow to be taken prisoners, and enow to run away."

When Henry returned to Dover, "the crowd plunged into the waves to meet him, and the conqueror was carried in their arms from his vessel to the beach. The road to London exhibited one triumphal procession. Pageants were erected in the streets; sweet wines ran into the conduits; bands of children, tastefully arrayed, sang his praise; and the whole population seemed intoxicated with joy."— *Lingard.*

Indeed, Henry grew quite tired of hearing about Agincourt. By a formal edict, he ordained that for the future no songs should be recited by harpers or others, in honour of the recent victory, since it tended only to vanity. It is somewhat singular that in the Pepysian collection at Magdalen College, Cambridge, there is preserved a song composed in 1415, to celebrate the battle, and "it is the only English song of so early a date of which the original music has been preserved."—*Burney's History of Music, quoted in Tyler's Henry V.*

I append the concluding verse:—

> "Now gracious God he save owre Kynge,
> His peple, and all his well wyllinge;
> Gef him gode lyfe, and gode endynge,
>   That we with merth may safely synge.
> Deo gratias, Anglia! redde pro Victoria!"

I understand the music is not pretty.

CHAPTER VII.

HOUSE OF WESTMORELAND CONTINUED.

> "Of changing sentinels the distant hum,
>   The mirth of feasts, the clang of burnish'd arms,
>   The braying trumpet, and the hoarser drum,
>   Unite in concert with increased alarms."—*Byron.*

RALPH DE NEVILL succeeded his grandfather as Earl of Westmoreland in 1426. After the death of his mother, he had £40 allowed by the King for his maintenance, being then in his minority. In the 4th Henry VI., this was augmented to £50 16s, 8d., payable out of the fee farm of Newcastle-on-Tyne. The Earl married first, *Elizabeth*, daughter of Henry, Lord Percy (Hotspur), and widow of John, Lord Clifford, by whom he had issue, John, son and heir, who died *vita patris*, *S.P.* (This John was a zealous Lancastrian, and was slain at the first battle of St. Alban's, 1455. His widow, Anne, daughter of John Holland, Duke of Exeter, remarried Sir John Nevill, uncle of her first husband. *Vide Rowland.* He also died in the Lancastrian cause, being slain at Towton in 1461.) Second, *Margaret*, daughter of Reginald, Lord Cobham, of Starborough; the only issue being a daughter, Margaret, who died in infancy. This second Countess was buried at Doncaster.

In 1433, the Earl was in command in France, under the Regent, the Duke of Bedford. Hollinshed describes him as "a man as politique in peace, as hardy in warre, and yet no more hardy in warre than merciful when he had the victory." He lived to a good old age, dying in 2nd Richard III., 1484. During his life feuds between the branch of the Nevill family, descended from the first Earl by his first wife, and the other branch, descended from the second wife, appear to have been both fast and furious, as will be seen by the following document :—

BY THE KYNG. HENRY 6TH.

Worshipful fader in God, Right trusty and welbeloved, We have now late herd and well understande unto oure grete displeasaunce of c'tain mysgouv'nances and debates late moeved and sturred betwix oure cousin therele of Westm'lande Sir John Neville and Sir Thomas Neville oon the oon p'tie, and oure cousines the Countesse of Westm'lande therele of Salesbury and the lord Latymer on the othr' partie. Of the which' diverse e'ithr' ageinst othr' by manere of warre and insurreco'on have late assembled grete rowtes and compaignies upon the felde and doon firth' more othr' grete and horrible offenses aswele in slaught' and distrucc'on of oure peuple, as oth'wise the which' thing is gretly ayeins oure estat and the wele of paix of this oure Roy'me, and also expressely ayens our lawes, whereof also the subversion of pollitike gouv'nance and oth' grete inconvenientes and mischiefs be like to followe, which' God forbede and defende in oure dayes, on lasse thanne by oure auctorite hit be the rather appaised and redressed. Wherfore we wol and charge yow, tht ye doo oure writtes severaly to be made and directed unto the said Erles, lord Latymer and knightes, yeving theym and everich' of theym straitly in co'mandement upon ligeance to appere before us in thaire personnes the morowe upon saint Hillary day next co'myng wheresoever we shal be within this oure Roy'me, to answere in ye said maters as lawe and reson wol require. And firth'more tht ye yeve theym straitly in co'mandement by the same to absteyne and surcesse from hensforth, from al such' misgouv'nances as is abovensaid, and to kepe and doo oure paix to be kept booth' by theym and theyr servantes and adherentes upon the p'il tht wol falle th'upon. Yeven, under oure signet at our Castle of Kenelworth' the xxviij day of Decembr'

To the worshipful fader in God, Oure right' trusty and welbeloved the bisshop' of Bath' oure Chauncell'r of Englande.

Excerpta Historica.

Holinshed relates that when the dissensions between the Duke of Gloucester and the Bishop of Winchester were adjusted in the 4th Henry VI., the Kyng caused a solemn feaste to be held on Whitson Sondaie, at which feaste the Duke of Bedford adorned the Kyng with the high ordre of Knighthode, which on the same daie dubbed with the sweard these Knights, Richard, Duke of York, John, Duke of Norfolk, the Earl of Westmerland, Henry Lord Percy, and thirty-one others.

John, son of the second Earl made a will as follows :—

"In Dei Nomine. Amen. The first day of December ye yere of our Lord 1449. I, John Nevill, Knt., sonne and heire to Rauf, Erle of Westmerland, being in good hele and good minde, remembering ye uncertente of this warlde, and as it is due to every creature to dispose and ordeyne for ye helth of his saule, as well when he is in good hele as when he is visited by the sonne of God, this I ordeyne and make my testament. First, I bequeath my soule to God Fadre Almyghty, therewith to doe his blessed will, and for my body to be buried in the church of Hautenprice within the quere, in the midds of the chancell, and that I lye honestly, as in according to mine estates by the advise and discrec'on of them that I shall make myn executors; also I bequeath to the same place where my body shall rest for my cors p'sant, a coursour cald Lywd Nevill;* also I will that myn executors ordayne an honest and a kunning priest to sing for my soul a twelmonth, and that he have for his sallary X marc; also I bequeath to the same place, for to make of vestments, a gown of cloth of gold blew, a doublet of ye same, a gown of black velvet, and all my doubletts of velvet; also I bequeath to the same place a standinge cup of silvr and gilt, called ye Kataryne, and thereof to make a chalys. Also I bequeath to my wife Anne all the rem'aunt of my menable and unmenable, and sche to be myne executor of myn testament, and with the said goods to pay my debts well and trewly, as my servants' wages yat they be behynde, as all myn own creditors, yat I be in no p'ill y'refore; also I bequeath my wife Anne to helpe also towards the paiment of my seid detts, C Marcs due to me by my lord, her father, of her marriage, if sche can recure it, and if sche cannot, yat that be no impediment to the paiment of my said debts; als I bequeth my said wife all the money that is due to me by my said lord her fadir; also I bequeth all my ffurrs to my wife Anne; als I will that my said wife have holly all the liflode yat schew be inducedinne even like as I have it. Also I will yat the servants yat I have freed by my l'res patentes, that they have it still like as their patentes make menc'on; and I will that my said wife make Thomas Prowfrott que' of X marc yearly terme of his life tyme; also for my servants yat be not freed, I will that they be rewarded by discretion of my said wife. These I ordayne to be myn executors; first, my wife Anne principall, and then John Crakenthorp, Thomas Prowfrott, Sir Nicholas Marchell, my chapleyne, and they fulfil my will. Proved 30th March, 1451.

Ralph Nevill, who became third Earl of Westmoreland, was the son of Sir John Nevill, who fell at Towton fighting for Henry VI. This Ralph was twenty-eight years of age in the second year of Richard III., when he succeeded to the title (1485). He married Matilda, daughter of Sir Roger Booth of Barton. She was buried at Brancepeth. Ralph died at Hornby Castle, Richmondshire, in the year 1523. It is reported as an amiable trait in his character that his death was owing to his great grief at his son's decease. He was buried in Hornby Parish Church. He lived during the commencement of the iron sway of the Tudors. By the Wars of the Roses the Baronage of England had been so destroyed that it was totally unable to cope with the Crown. In the first Parliament of Edward IV. (1461) the nobility consisted of one duke, four earls, one viscount, and twenty-nine barons; all the nobles of the Lancastrian party having been killed in battle, fallen on the scaffold, or fled from the victor. *Rowland.*

---

* *Lywd Nevill,* also written Lidiard and Lyart, means *Grey* Nevill. Chargers were named after families and friends.
        "Saddle grey Surrey for the field to-morrow."
Blakiston of Malton mentions in his will *Bay* Salvin.—*Vide Surtees' History of Durham. Whitaker's History of the Cliffords.*

Ralph Nevill was a great leader in the English army commanded by Thomas, Earl of Surrey, 9th Henry VII. (1494), when James of Scotland invaded England.

"In persoun with his army did the King causit siege the castell of Norame (Norham), quhair he lay long tyme; bot seeing he couth not win the same, albeit he had done great domage and skaith thereto, he returnit within his realme."

James had espoused the cause of Perkin Warbeck, and married him to Catherine Gordon, a near relative of his own, and the daughter of the Earl of Huntly.

Her beauty, amiability, and high qualities made her a fitting match for any Prince. James, with the "Duke of York" (Perkin) ravaged the border; but seeing "that no Inglishmen did resort to the saide Richard, and considering that the said Richardes promesseis of the assistance of his friendes followed not in deid according to his wordis, causit the King to chaunge the guid opinione quhilk he had of him; and the soldiers laden with spoil, and perceiving that no succours come out of England to the newly invented Duke, contrary to that which he had made them believe would come to pass, they determined to retire with assured gain rather than tarry the uncertain victory of that counterfeit Duke."—*Vide Holinshed and Lesley's History of Scotland.*

The Earl of Surrey's army numbered 20,000, and among its leaders were Lords Dacre, Nevill, Strange, Latimer, Lumley, Scrope, Clifford, Ogle, Coniers, and Darcy. They pressed northwards, taking several strongholds on the way, James meanwhile retiring into Scotland. Henry sent the Bishop of Durham to persuade James to withdraw his support from the "foolish feignet boy." Sundry *pleasant* things for the war were sent from Flanders to aid Scotland in the invasion. Perkins's own army is described as 1,400 strong, "of all manner of nations." *Bothwell.*

Ralph Nevill, grandson of the third Earl, had livery of his grandfather's lands in 22nd Henry VIII., and became *Fourth Earl of Westmoreland.* He married Catherine, daughter of Edward Stafford, Duke of Buckingham. She died in 1553, and was buried in St. Leonard's, Shoreditch.

This Earl was one of those who subscribed the letter to Pope Clement the Seventh, intimating to his Holiness that unless he complied with the wishes of King Henry as to his divorce with Catherine of Arragon they would shake off the supremacy of Rome.

This remarkable document may be found in Rymer, Vol. VI., p. 160. It is also printed in Froude, Vol. I. In 1531, Queen Catherine was removed to the More, a house in Hertfordshire, which had been originally built by George Nevill, Archbishop of York, and had also been the favourite and most beautiful haunt of the luxurious Wolsey.

Earl Ralph before his death was made a Knight of the Garter. He died in 3rd Edward VI., 1549.

In the Cottonian manuscripts there is a letter from Ralph Nevill, 4th Earl of Westmoreland, to Lord Cromwell, about the living of Brancepeth. The year is not mentioned, but it must have been before 1540, when Cromwell, the favourite of Henry VIII., fell from power. A request from the Minister of Henry VIII. was no doubt very much like a Royal command.

"May it please your Lord'p to be advertized, that I have received your loving letter, wherein you write to me, in the favour of Doctor Bellasis, your chaplain, concerning the parsonage of Brancepeth, to be as good to him as I would be to yourself. My Lord, of surety (the King, my master, excepted, and my Lord Prince) there is no man living that I would do so much for as I woll do for you, desiring your Lordship to take no displeasure with me, in every thing. Now the trowth concerning the same parsonage, which is this: That upon grete labour made unto me by old Sir William Bulmer, Knt., and Sir Thomas Bentley, being then my chaplayn, I granted the next advoydance of the same benefice, after the death of Doctor Lupton, incombent thereof, unto the said Sir William Bulmer and the said Thos. Bentley, and then it chanced afterwards that upon importunate suyte of the Lord Burgavenny, and not having in remembrance the former grant, negligently, I made one other grant of the next advoydance of the same parsonage for one Doctor Walbye, after whych grant made, one Doctor Natives being in some charitie with the said Sir Thomas Bentley, hath obtained of him the said former grant, by reason whereof he is now presented thereunto. And of surety, my Lord, I have here declared unto your Lordship the verye treuth thereof, and how it has passed my hands to have givene, your Lor. sholde have had it as heartilye as hart can thynke to have doone therewith with plesure. Besecheing yor Lor. to thynke none other in me, and be not displesed with me, I pray nowe, that the answer cometh no sooner unto you; as may fortune yor Lord, thinketh it might have doone, for of a surety the failour thereof is not in me, for it was the 18th last past afore yor letter came unto me, wych were delyvred by the hands of the Chancellor of Dyshouses unto me—At Brancepeth, 20th day of March.

"Yor Lor,
"RAUFE WESTMORLAND."

"To my very good Lord, my Lord Privy Seal,
good Lord'p these be d——d."

We have already noticed that Sir John Nevill, father of the third Earl, was slain at Towton. Sir Humphrey Nevill, a cousin of the third Earl, lay hidden for five years in a cave on the banks of the Derwent. After the battle of Hexham he was taken prisoner, and beheaded at York, by order of Edward IV.

———

HENRY, FIFTH EARL OF WESTMORELAND, was Warden of the West Marches, while Lord Wharton held the general wardenry. The records that remain concerning him relate almost exclusively to his wardenry, and his marriages. He married, first, Anne, daughter of Thomas Manners, Earl of Rutland; secondly, Jane, daughter of Sir Richard Cholmly (by Catherine, daughter of Sir Robert Constable), and widow of Sir Henry Gascoigne. His third marriage is not mentioned by Rowland, nor have I noticed a record of it in any Nevill pedigree. The reason of this we shall soon see.

A full account of the ceremonies observed on the occasion of his first marriage is contained in one of the manuscripts in the British Museum.—*Additional Cat. MSS.*, 6,113.

"The marriage of the Earl of Oxford's Westmoreland's and Rutland's children, solemnized, celebrated, and made the 2nd day of July, in the year of our Lord God 1536, and in the 28th year of the reign of our dread Sovereign, Lord King Henry the Eighth, King of England and of France, Defensor of the Faith of Christ, Lord of Ireland, and in earth the supreme head under Christ immediately of the Church Catholick of England. On Monday, the 2nd day of July, were solemnized and made, the day and year above rehearsed, the marriage of the three noble Earls' children, their sons and their heirs, under one solemnization, at Haliwell, at the Earl of Rutland's place, with great royalty and honor, as ever chanced unto any Earl's children, the day of the spousage or wedding; and thus were these weddings ordered. First, Lord John Viscount Bulbeck, son and heir to Sir John Vere, Earl of Oxenford, married the Lady Dorothe Nevill, eldest daughter of Sir Raulf Nevill, Earl of Westmorland; and Lord Henry Nevill, son and heir to Sir Raulf Nevill, Earl aforesaid, married the Lady Anne, eldest daughter of Sir Thomas Manners, Earl of Rutland; and Lord Henry Rose, son and heir to the said Earl of Rutland, married the Lady Margaret, daughter to the said Earl of Westmorland, in the Church at Halywell: all three at one mass, as hereinafter shall be declared.

"The preparations towards the Church, and the order of setting forth, and the description of the spousal apparel. First in the morning, at the . . . hour of the day, were made ready all the spousals aforesaid, to go to the church, for the receiving the Holy Sacrament of Matrymony. The Bridegrooms and their Spouses ornately garnished of and after one manner, in no kind of apparel disagreeing, the kind whereof was this:—The three young Lords were . . . with doublett and coate of radiant gold, and gownes of pure white damask, with brede garde of white velvit laced with silver. The three Ladies in kyrtles of yellow damask, and gowns of white damask, and upon their heads circles of gold set with pearls, and stones rich, and of great value and precious, besides their chains of fine gold and pearl sarcenet artificially wrought: their necks were envyroned and garnished to the goodly, decent, and seemingly setting forth of their several beauty, to the delight of the beholders, and the great magnificence, praise, and honors of the progenitors' and parents' nobility. The Church also was hanged with cloth aras, rich and sumptuous. The pavement strawed, and covered with goodly carpets, and stools also, and upon the form where they should kneel a carpet of great riches, and thereupon four cushions of clean gold, most ornately wrought, and of four no less precious were had for them to kneel upon. Unto the which Church these goodly Ladies were brought, by the young Gentlemen Batcherlors of their lineage, with a great nobility of Knights, Esquires, and Gentlemen, aliis multis, which did precede; and after them did follow the Barons, Earls, and Dukes as hereafter followeth. First, Thomas Audley, Lord Chancellor of England; Thomas Howard, Duke of Norfolk, and Lord Treasurer and Marshall of England; Charles Brandon, Duke of Suffolk; Marquis Gray Dorset; Marquis Henry of Exeter; John, Earl of Oxford; Ralf, Earl of Westmorland; Earl of Surrey, son of Duke of Norfolk; Bouchier, Earl of Essex; Stanly, Earl of Derby; Clifford, Earl of Cumberland; Manners, Earl of Rutland; Ratcliffe, Earl of Sussex; Hastings, Earl of Huntingdon."

Henry Nevill, married the third time for love only, and therefore plunged himself into very hot water, as so many well-meaning and highly respectable do, whenever they have sufficient audacity to follow the dictates of affection, and despise all other dictates.

I traced the course of Henry Nevill's true love through a considerable number of fusty old manuscripts. I therefore present it to the reader as an original thing. Sixteenth century people thought it a little too original. Good Queen Bess thought it horribly original. So thought the Archbishop of York, and so thought the first Protestant Bishop of Durham, and so doubtless will think many other good people in this present day of Grace; for Henry Nevill's true love was love for *his deceased wife's sister* —love for Margaret, own sister to his second wife Jane!

He had "*good reasons*," so he tells us; I append some of them:—

1. It is the duty of every man to marry.—(I. *Cor.* vii. 2.)

2. It is the duty of every man to marry the woman he loveth best.

3. That a man should marry the sister of his late wife, is a thing not contrary to Scripture, or experience, ór common sense.

4. That many a worse thing hath oft been covered over by the mantle of religion, the dispensation of the Pope, and the will of the King.

The Earl's "opynyon" was "gathered out of the Leviticall Lawes, and though there were that quoted the Old Testament against him, such did so to the hindrance of their own cause, for they remembered not the patriarch Jacob, who took unto himself two *live sisters*."

It "seemed better" to him openly to marry than to do those things "which were recommended for the sake of convenience," and yet "*had in them no symptoms of manliness, or vigour of courage.*"

Doubtless the Earl expected that Elizabeth would remember her own father's exploits in the matrimonial field, and would therefore look leniently at the lesser liberties of her barons; but he was altogether mistaken. The Virgin Queen had nò such intention.

I have selected the following letters from among the existing documents, relating to the Earl's marriage. They have never been published before :—

HENRY, EARL OF WESTMERLAND, TO CECIL.

State Papers Domestic, Elizabeth.—Vol. XII. No. 54.

After my most hartie recommendacons unto you wth like thanks for your frendly and gentle lettres, sent me by my s'vant George Stafford, whereby appeareth the contynuance of the zeale and good hert ye have alwaye borne me. And for the faithful frendship wch I found in you once, (wch I neither can or will ever forgit) I must acknowledge myself bound unto you so long as I live. Assuring you ther is neither venyson (for the wch ye give me more thaunks then it is worth), nor no other thing that I have, but yt is at yo . . commandement to use as yor owne. Yt seameth somewhat strang unto me that you being a man of wisdome and know . . . shuld wryt unto me ye have bene moch pplexed sence . . . com'yng into these pts for that ye have herd my lait mariage spoken and judged much to yer discomfort against my estimacons. And that how so wer yt hath bene considered by me ye finde none that can allowe of it. What haith bene reported unto you I know not, but *I believe I have done nothyng but God's law doth allowe yt.* Though ye say ye can find none that so doth. But I am sory to here you say that howe so ever some devines may in argument seke to defend yt, ther ys no law in any comen wealth that doth approve yt, *for I know no devine can defend yt, but by Godes worde whereupon, as I take yt, all lawes in every christian comen wealth ought to be grounded. And can not the one disapprove that the other alloweth.* This I knowe so long as the canonicall lawes of the Busshopp of Rome were in force in this realme I might not, without licence, (*w'ch for moneye might at all tymes have bene obteyned*), have done yt; but they being taken away, and the libertie of the gospel restored, I think I have offended no lawe in that I have done w'ch me thinks ye being learned could have answered moch better than I, if ye had herd any thing to the contrary. And whereas ye seme to thinke great danger might by this mariage followe to my posteritie, if yt shuld depend theruppon, I doubt no such thing onless the Busshop of Rome shuld recover his former usurped jurisdiction within this realme, w'ch I trust shall never be. And if he shuld (as God defend) *I fere not but ther covitousness will so remayne with theyme it might for money be dispenced withall, seing yt is not against God's law, though it agre not with ther constitucons.* I will follow yoe good counsell in bestowing my sone, and place him either in as good or better house than myne own, where he may be likely to have yssue, w'ch care for his well bestowing haith so remayned alway in my heade. I have wryton thus playnly unto you, as to my most assured frend to th'end (the end) ye shuld not only knowe my hole mynde in the premisses, but also, as my trust is, answer for me in this caise when ye shall here yt in talk, even as ye knowe God's worde doth allow, and bere yt. I render unto you most hertie thaunks for yor newes. And so I comyt you to Almightye God, who send you most prosperous successe in all the Quen'es Ma'ty's affaires. From my Mannor at Kirbymoressad (Kirbymoorside) the xxi. day of June 1560.

> Your assured loving friend, to my power even as ye have bound me,
> —H. WESTMLAD.

Addressed.—To the right honorable and my very loving frend, Sr. Willm Cecill, Knight, Secretary to the Quenes Ma'tye.

Endorsed.—xxj. of June 1560. Erle of Westmorland to my Mr.

THE QUEEN TO ARCHBISHOP YOUNG.
State Papers, Domestic, Elizabeth, Vol. XIX., No. 25.

To ye Archb. of York.

> R. Reverend father, &c.

We have hard good report made of your dilligence used in Visitatio' of your diocese, but yet we find it strang that in yor diocese or provy'ce the Erle of West-m'land is permitted to kepe the sistar of his former wiffe in manner as his wiffe being as we thynk contrary to the law of God, and if ma' such examples so sufferred must nedes offend God and do great hurt in slandery'g of our realme, we therefore will that you take order in your provy'ce that nether this nor such like disorder be suffered uncorrected; and this we correct ye rather for the weale of the said erle, being our coosynd, and a principall me'bre of our realme, to whom we wish well for many respects, as we dout not but he knoweth our favorable mean'ng towards hym, and his howse. Our pleasure is in this matter ye shall procede by ye authorite which ye have as Archbishop without notifying to hym of theis our lettres, written to your Grace under our signett.

Endorsed.—17 August, 1561. M. of the Q. Ma'ties lettre to ye Archb. of York pro coi't Westm'land.

Draft in Burghley's hand.

THE EARL OF WESTMORLAND TO CECIL.
State Papers, Domestic, Elizabeth, Vol. XIX., No. 53.

After my most hartie commendacons wth lyke thankes for all your gentlenes and most faithfull and assured frendshipp, w'ch I have alway found and by yor late lettres doo perceyve it to contynu towards me. Whereby I doo not only acknowleg my self bounde unto you so long as I lyve, but allso am thereby imboldened in all

H

my troubles and adversities to open my mynde and the very secrets of my hart to you, as my faithfull frende. And although my fortun hath heretofor ben such that I have ben subject to many troubles, and at tymes susteyned sundry Injuries, part whereof at length by yor good helpe have overpassed. Yet chaunced there never a thinge unto me, wherewith I was so sor pplexed, and grewe so werey of my lyfe, as wth this matter of my mariage, for the w'ch I am by my L. Archebusshop of Yorke's grace called into the spirituall courte. And although yt semeth to me my L. to be so wyse and hon'able that he will do me no wrong nor offre me any injustice; yet he hath gyven me very shorte days of annswering, in which tyme I cannot possible bring doune my councell. *I am troubled (as it is thought as well to many well learned men as to me) wrongfully, seinge I have done therein nothing either against Godes Lawes or the Lawes of this Realme.* But for that there runneth a Rumor all over the cowntry, and meteth me well nigh in every place where I goo, that the Quene's Ma'tie shold take it in evell part, and be my heavye Ladye and Mrs, wch is my gretest grefe, and doth most trouble me; for I am assured I never offended hir Ma'tie by woord, dede, or thought, as God, yf he were here, could Witnesse. So that yf yor lettres for the intertaynment of the French Lordes had not come to me, I was determyned to have gone upp unto hir grace. I protest before God, who knoweth the secrets of all men's harts, I have alway borne, doo, and will beare as true and faithfull harte unto hir Ma'tie according to my bounden dewty as any subject she hath, howsoever hir grace have ben, by any that are not my frends otherwise incensed. And the straingers once passed by, and some money gathered for my chargs (w'ch was never worse to gett in this cuntrie) I mynd, God willing, to come up, and make my purgacon off these matters attempted against me.

And in the meane tyme for easing of my troubled and unquyet mynd, I hartely pray you to let me (by this bearer my servaunt and kinsman, George Stafford, whome ye may trust as myself), have yor gudd advice and councell, that I may prepare my doings accordingly. And lyke as heretofore ye have ben friendly unto me, so I hope you will styll contynue as my speciall trust is in you. For a man never tryeth his frendes but in adversytye, wherein I have ever found you faithfull, which of me shall never be forgotten. The greatest ease and comfort that any man can have in adversytye is a faithfull frend to whome he dare fully open his mynd and hole harte, and such an one yor frendshipp hath bound me to conceyve you to be, and now in myne extremytye make an accoumpte still to fynd it so. In this case I knowe I have nether offended God's Lawes or the Lawes of the Realme. Therefore I am the more bold upon the trust I have in you to desyre you to be a suter for me unto the Quenes Matie, that hir grace (in consideracon of my true and faithfull service done unto her father, brother, and sister, and my true harte to serve her highness with such good will that yf evry here off my hede were a man I wold spend them in her quarrel, and yf my lands and goods were tenne tymes more than they are, I wold spend them in her service) will have consideracon on me, and for my true harte and faithfull service not to see me defaced in my cuntrie. Whereby I shall never be able to serve hir when they have once conceyved hir evill opynyon in me, which is dayly expected by all men to my discreditt and dishonour for ever.

Yet I trust by yor mediation and sute hir Mtie will vouchsafe to graunt me hir graces lettres unto my L. Archbushopp of Yorke to desist any further to proced with me untill I have made my repayre unto her Mtie, at whose hands myne onlie trust is to find succor since *I have not offended God's Lawes,* as you shall perceyve by myne opynyon gathered out of the Leveticall Lawes, which yf you will conferre with learned men that have the feare of God before theyre eyes they cannot deny. Nowe my trust is that her Grace will consider the service that my howse hath done unto hir P.decessors, and is hable to doo, and will be alwayes ready for to doo unto hir Mtie. Thus I bid you most hartely farewell from Brauncepith, the 20th of Septembre, 1561.

Your lovinge and assured frende,

H. WESTMRLD.

Addressed.—To the right honorable and my very loving frende Sir Willm Cicill, Knight, Secretary to the Quenes Mtie.

Endorsed.—20 Septembre, 1561. Erle of Westmland to my Mr touchinge hys wyfe.

BISHOP PILKINGTON TO CECIL.

State Papers, Domestic, Elizabeth, Vol. XX., 5.

Jesu Helpe!

Gratia et pax. Paulu' cu' bestiis pugnait Ephesi. 1 Cor. xv. So fight I here. The more I trie the more grefes I finde. God be mercifull to us. Here is a double jurisdictio', and whither is more troublesome I well know not, oneli I live sub spe contra spe as Abraham did. In my judgement, this I see, that here nedes rather authorite and power to be give tha take awai. The takig awai off the bisshop's living, wherebi his power is the lesse, and so lesse is he regardet. Therl of Westmer lies not here, the L. Euri is off no grete power. I am afraid to think what mai folow. The worshipful of the shire is few and of small power, the people rude and heddi, and bold. I can not finde 10 hable justices of peaces off wisdom and authorite off nather religion. The weake state of this cuntrie therfor bi this yor wisdom mai better consider. Iff Mr. Nevel and others refusing the othe off their allegeace (oath of allegiance) mai be on the Council in authorite still, and have their doings for gudd, it will encorage other to the like. Gudd service must nedes faile thogh mi will were never so gudd.

I have had p'vate conferes with therle of Westm. for his mariage. He has declared his ansors and consellors. I have said something to the contrari, butt had raither other mene shuld be judges opeli, lest he shuld think me a evil neighbor, and where yet we agre wel p.adventure afterwards he might change. Thus for this time I bidde you fare well, and daili in mi prairers comend yor estate to God's holi tuition, that ye may p.serve the realme to God's glorie. Iff I mai doo yor pleasure ye mai worthily comand. 13 Octobr.

Yors assured in the Lord,

J. DUNELM.

(The signature is given in Greek characters in the original.)

ARCHBISHOP YOUNG TO CECIL.

State Papers, Domestic, Elizabeth, Vol. XX., 22.

After my right hartie comendacons. It may be please you to be advertised.

As concerning the Earle of Westmerland's matter, this bearer, my Chancellor, can make reporte thereof, whoe hath alsoe with hym the copie of all my p.ceedings hetherto therein. *He is marvelouslye affected* to this hys *pretensed wyffe. I think*

*that manye lawfull husbandes in England be not nearlie in such grate love with theyr
lawfull wyffes.* He hath ben with me hymself and hath made manye earnest
requestes for his quietnesse and continuance with a greate numbre of teares. My
answeres and pswasions in that behalfe hath not ben very pleasaunte unto hym,
nevertheless he staundeth falslie in hope that Judgemente must passe on hys syde,
being encouraged by Mr Whitehed and suche other singler divines, and not altogether destitute of the helpe of lawers, for the Deane of the Arches hath allready
ben here, being retayned of hym and doth intende to come agayne against the next
sittinge, which shal be the 18th of January next at Yorke, at which tyme I think we
shall shortely grow to an ende.

And thus I cease, comytting you to the tuicon of the Almightie God, who ever
p.serve you and governe you in all yor affayres and doings. From my mannor at
Cawood, this xth of Novembre, 1561.

Yor loving frende assuredly,

THO. EBOR.

Addressed.—To the right honorable Sir Willm. Cicill, Knight, Chefe Secretaire
to the Quenes Matie.

Endorsed.—10 Nov. 1561.   ArchB. of York to my Mr.

The lady, concerning whom all this commotion was made,
eventually died, and was buried at S. Dunstan's in the West,
April 2nd, 1570.

The Earl himself died in the autumn of 1563, and was buried
in Staindrop Church. *Vide Nevill Monuments.*

ADDENDA.

LETTER OF HENRY, 5TH EARL OF WESTMORELAND, TO THE EARL OF SHREWSBURY.

After my most heretie commendac'ons unto yo' good Lordship, these may advertise the same that I do send this bearer, my s'unt, George Stafford, unto yo' L., to declare unto you in what caise I was yesterday very sore handled with a fyt of an ague, so that the burnyng thereof held me extremely twelve howers; but, thanked be to God, I ame better to-day, and doo purpose, God willing, if I may sett on horseback, to goo forwards to-morrow, and wilbe with my Lord of Northumbreland as shortly as I may; desyring to knowe yor L. pleasure if I may taik my holle power here in Yorkshier wth me. And, my Lord, if yt so be the Dowager of Scotland, wth the power thereof, be comed to the borders, my poor advise is, yor L. shuld likewise come forward wth yor holle power streight way never regarding the lake of money, in respect of the p'sent daunger of the frounters, and to bring with yo'r L. all the worshipfull and wealthiest of the countrie, so that every man of worshippe may have the conduction and guyding of his owne frends and ten'nts, to the intent that if any murmar or grudge shuld arise amongest the soldiers for lak of money before the same may be p'vided, every man of worshippe may help to relieve his own company; and, as I think, the herts of the people is suche that they will sooner be p'swaded by their own natural lords and masters, and more willinglie s'rve under theym for love than with strangers for money. Thus, wishing yo'r L. most p'sperous successe in all the King's and Quene's affaires, and as well to doo as I would myselff, I comytt the same to Almightie God. From my Manor at Kirbymoreshead, the xviii. of August, 1557.

Yor good L. most assured loving friend,

H. WESTM'LA'D.

Post Script.—My Lord, I pray your L. give creditt to this bearer. After the signing of this l're word is comed unto me that my brother Xtopher is already gone towards my Lord of Northumbreland. To the Right Honorable and my very good Lorde th' Erle of Shrewsburye, Lord P'sident of the King's and Quene's Ma'ts counsell established in the Northe Parts, and ther Highnes Lieuten'nt Generall from Trent Northward.

LETTER OF WESTMORELAND TO EARL OF SHREWSBURY.

After my moste heretie comendac'ons unto yor good Lordship, these shall be t advertise the same that I came to Alnwike yesternight, in whiche travell I susteyned some paynes, because I wold no fault shuld be imputed unto me as long as I am hable to labor. The waters was so great as I never saw then greater; so that although we were driven to leve the hyeway and seke byeways, yet did o'r horses swyme in many places, where if your L. had been, ye shuld have seen suche dowking of men and horses as yf yt had bene for hete of Mydsomer. I was also glad to leave my carraiges at Morpeth, which could not passe for watter. I met here three l'res, two to yor L. and one to myself; wherein my L. Warden wrytteth unto me that he haith given commandment to his harbengers to place me and my men at Belforthe, where I purpose to be this day accordyng to his appoyntment, and ther to remayn untill I here further from his Lordshipe. I opened one of yo'r L. l'res, whereby I understand the Bushopriche men doth covet to come home, and that they passe nott cccc men of theym. As I remember yo'r L. told me there was a hundreth horsemen of the Bushopriche, but I believe yt will fawlle out ther is no horssmen here but myne, except yt be Robert Tempest. I have sene the Bushopriche s'rve at such a tyme with a thousand men, but it will be so no more, so long as the gentlemen and riche farmers are suffred to tary at home, and a sort of poor creators and men hired for moneye sent furth w'tch haith nothing to help themselves with all. I ame sorry to see suche an untowardness to s'rve in the Bushopriche men as ys now, but I know not in whom the fault ys. Thus I comyt yo'r good L. to Almighty God. From Alnewik the xiiith day of October, 1557.

Your good L. assured friend,

H. WESTM'LA'D.

To the Right Honorable and my very good Lord th' Erle of Shrewsbury, Lord P'sident of the King and Quene's M'ts counsell establised in the North, and ther Highnesse's Lieuten'nt Generall from Trent Northwards.

ABSTRACTS FROM NEVILL RECORDS IN STATE PAPER OFFICE.

Sept. 17, 1552.—Richmond.—*Henry, Earl of Westmoreland, to Cecil.*—Sends up John Burge, whom he has examined as to slanders against Northumberland.—*Dom., Ed. VI.*, Vol. XV., 7.

Henry, Earl of Westmoreland, to the Bishop of Durham.—I enclose copies of two letters, one signed, the other unsigned, taken from a man who declares that Scarborough Castle has been taken by the traitor Stafford. Give me your advice whether, as appointed, to come to Newcastle, or go and set upon these rebels with such power as I can make. I will spend my life in the King and Queen's service.—Kirby-moor-side, 24 April, 1557.—*Dom. Addenda, Mary*, Vol. VIII., 4.

June 6, 1557.—Raby.—*Henry, Earl of Westmoreland, to the Queen.*—Solicits the office of Steward of Richmondshire and keeper of the forest of Galtres, vacant by the death of John Lord Conyers.—*Dom., Mary*, Vol. XI., 5.

Aug. 8, 1557.—Richmond.—*The Queen to the Earl of Westmoreland.*—We find from your letters that you have put in readiness such men as you are able, and for defence of the Borders, have sent thither such as you have in the Bishopric of Durham, and in Northumberland, under conduct of your brother, for which forwardness we thank you.—*Dom. Add. Mary*, Vol. VIII., 33.

Jan. (?), 1558.—*The Queen to the Mayor and Aldermen of Newcastle.*—Having appointed the Earl of Westmoreland Lieutenant-General in those parts, we think it necessary to have a mass of treasure ready in some sure place in those parts. We have therefore sent Edw. Hughes with £10,000, to be kept in your custody for our use, and not disbursed, but upon special warrant.—*Dom. Add. Mary*, Vol. VIII., 76.

April, 1558.—*The Queen to Lord Eure.*—You are to permit the Earl of Westmoreland, Lieutenant-General, and the Earl of Northumberland, Lord Warden of the

East and Middle Marches, Sir Jas. Crofts, Sir Rich. Lee, and John Brend, to take down the inside of the Castle at Berwick to a convenient height, which is thought necessary by those in charge, to prevent it from hurting the defences of the town.—*Dom. Add. Mary*, Vol. VIII., 89.

May 1, 1558.—*The Council to the Earls of Westmoreland and Northumberland.*—We have much complaint for lack of justice ministered to manifest offenders in Tynedale and other places upon the Borders, and are informed that not only are poor men's cattle stolen, but men taken out of their houses and carried prisoners into Scotland, and that by their own neighbours, without punishment, so that the honest inhabitants of the Borders say that they are worse handled by the Tynedale men than by the Scots themselves. This we think strange, considering your charge to see thereto, viz., you my Lord of Northumberland, by force of your wardenry of the East and Middle Marches, and you my Lord of Westmoreland, by force of your lieutenancy of that country. In case this outrage be not reformed, and that country brought to better order, Her Majesty must think a great negligence of duty in you, which we would be loath she should do. Therefore lend yourselves wholly to advance her service, and administer justice, weighing what danger may ensue by your disagreeing, as well to your own persons as to the whole country.—*Dom. Add. Mary*, Vol. VIII., 91.

May 14, 1558.—Brancepeth.—*Earl of Westmoreland to the Queen.*—I have received your letters of thanks addressed to me, and the Earl of Northumberland, the Lord Eure, and Sir Henry Percy, for service done in the North, and, though my service deserves it not, it encourages my fervent zeal in your service. I shall never be merry till I have done as much as any of my ancestors. The people of Edinburgh and Leith are in great fear, and a few have conveyed away their goods into places of safety, looking daily for invasion by the French.—*Dom. Add. Mary*, Vol. VIII., 95.

June 16, 1558.—*The Queen to Sir James Crofts.*—We are advertised out of Flanders by Sir William Pickering, that 3,000 Almains are ready to be transported out of Flanders, and will be at Newcastle by the 26th June. You are to consult with the Earl of Westmoreland, our lieutenant, how they may be best employed on their arrival.—*Dom. Add. Mary*, Vol. VIII., 102.

June 25, 1558.—*The Queen to the Earl of Westmoreland.*—According to the desire of those in charge of the works at Berwick, for some person of authority to see and report on them, we send the Bishop of Ely and Sir William Cordell, Master of the Rolls, to see the town and Borders, and redress grievances. We desire you to confer with them touching the said fortifications, the estate of the Borders, the placing of the Almains, the employment of our garrisons, &c., that our great charges in maintaining them may be countervailed, and the country kept quieter.—*Dom. Add. Mary*, Vol. VIII., 107.

Feb. 14, 1558.—Newcastle-on-Tyne.—*Earl of Westmoreland to the Queen.*—The King's (Philip) ambassador to Scotland has dined with me; he is a discreet gentleman, and has learned much of the disposition of the Scots. He says they seem desirous of peace, but they probably dissimulate. The chief mark whereat they shoot is Berwick; but for that they would gladly have peace. They know we shall be too strong for them without aid from France, and they think the King will keep the French King too much occupied this summer to spare them aid. Sir Wm. Ingleby says I am only to have £5 a day entertainment, less than any lieutenant had before; for other lieutenants have had it, besides wages for 100 men, and so I was promised, and I trust I may have it. I shall spend it all, and my lands, and not spare my life in your service.—*Dom. Add. Mary*, Vol. VIII., 81.

March 9, 1558.—*The Queen to the Earl of Westmoreland.*—Having seen your letters to Council about the state of Bamborough, we have written to Sir John Foster, captain, either to reside at the Castle entrusted to him, or deliver up the charge and profits, that we may commit it to some other. You must deliver our letters to Foster, and see that he accomplishes our pleasure, and all others whom you think should be resident at their charges; in case of refusal, give us the names of a few others meet to take charge of Bamborough Castle, whom we may appoint thereto.

The Queen to Sir John Foster.—The charge of Bamborough Castle has been committed to you, but we are informed that it is not kept in such order of defence as its importance requires, and as you are bound to keep it, and that you, being required by our lieutenant to reside at the Castle, denied to do so, which we take ill, as such places should be in defence. Unless therefore you are willing to reside on the place, we must commit it to the keeping of some other, who will better see to it.—9 March, 1558.—*Dom. Add. Mary*, Vol. VIII., 83.

Dec. 17, 1558.—London.—*Henry, Earl of Westmoreland, to Cecil.*—Requests him to further the suit of George Nevill, Archdeacon of Carlisle, to be appointed Queen's chaplain.—*Dom. Elizabeth*, Vol. I., 36.

1561.—Account of arrears due to the Queen by Henry, Earl of Westmoreland, in the office of Anthony Reve, Auditor of the Exchequer. Lat.—*Dom. Elizabeth*, Vol. XX., 61.

March 26, 1562.—London.—*Westmoreland to Sir Thos. Chaloner.*—Desires to purchase or rent his house in London during his absence.—*Dom. Elizabeth*, Vol. XXII., 23.

WILL OF THE FIFTH EARL.

Aug. 18, 1563.—I Henrye Erle of Westmerlande, one of the moste noble order of the Gartyr, knyght, do accordinge to the libertie of one Act of Parliamente, maide and ordayned at Westmynster, in the thyrtye yeare of the raygne of our late soveraigne lorde, of famous memorye, Kynge Henrye th' Eight, ordayne and make thys my last will and testamente. I bequeathe and commende my soule unto Allmyghtie God, and my bodie to be buried in the Parysh Churche of Stayndropp, under the tombe that last was maide, nighe unto my late wyfe Ladye Jane, yf I die in Englande, and my funeralls to be honorablye celebrated and done accordinge to the discretion of myne executors. I will devyse two parts of all my manors, &c., unto Syr Richerde Cholmeley, knight, and Robert Bowes, esquire, on trust, *i.e.*, the manor of Bywell in Northumberlande, with my landes, &c., at Cockfielde, Keverston, Ingleton, Bollome, Forres of Langhton, Somerhouse and Haughton, wythin the Lordshipp of Raybye, to pay therefrom to ether of my two daughters Marye and Adelane, one thousande markes, and one hundrethe pounds yearly, unto Lady Margaret now my wyffe, and doughter of Sir Roger Cholmeley, knight, decessed, and late wyffe of Sir Henry Gascoigne, knight, also decessed, and sync that time maryed unto me the sayd Erle, and to my two doughters, Margaret and Elisabethe, begotten by me of her, ether of them one thousande markes provided that my two doughters do not marrye themselffes to any man, duringe the lyfe of their mother, wytheout her consent, and my sonne and hayre apparent, Charles Nevyll, after he hath accomplished the full aige of twenty-one yeares, to enter unto the said manner and landes, if he will bynde himselfe wythe sufficient suerties to pay the foresaid legacies. Also I wyll to my said feoffees my landes, &c., at Shotton, Woodlande, Stryckley Parke, Wakerfeilde, Langton, Ulnebie, Hylton, Manfield, Medomsley, Woodyfeild, Path-rawe, Nettlebedde, Sunderlande, Gaitesyde, Cletlam, and Stillington, in the Lordshipp of Rabye, for xxi yeares, together with landes, &c., in Newcastell-upon-Tyne, to the yearlye value of 30l., on trust to pay out of the same, to my sayd fowr doughters, the sum of fower score poundes yearlye, tyll they be maryed, and to pay all my debts, legacies and funerals, and yf the sayd charges be payd before the foresaid terme be expyred, then I will that my sayd sonne, Charles, shall enter into the same, and I gyve him my hooll interest and leas of the Collaige of Stayndropp. To my sayd wyffe I gyve my hole interest in Blandsbye Parke in Yorkshire, and in the parsonaige or tythe of Kyrkeby Mysperton, and in the personaige or tythe of Sehame, and all my goods at Kyrkeby Moreshead, Keldehome, Rockbarghe and Blandsbye Parke. To the said Ladye Margaret, now my wyffe, all the plaite belonging to the foresaid Sir Henrye Gascoigne, knight, or my said wyffe, at or before the day of our maraige, and the rest of all my playte, to be equallye deyded betwixte her and my sonne Charles. To my sayd wyffe all my householde stuffe at Kyrkeby Moreshead and Kelhome. To Thomas Gascoigne yongest sonne of the said Syr Henry Gascoigne, my fermeholde called Carleburye, after the expiracion of a lease granted by me to John Kyllinghall, for his lyffe, payinge the accustomed rent. To my basterd doughter, Margaret Watson, otherwyse called Margaret Nevyll, my two farmeholdes called Newesham and Westholme, after the expiracion of the leases granted by me to John Cholmeley and John Dowthaite decessed, for fourtye-one yeares. To my servannte William Lee, the offyce of the generall receyvorshipp of all my lands in the counties of Duresme and Northumberland, durynge the mynorytie of my sonne Charles, wythe a yearlye fee of 40s durynge his lyffe. To my servannte Francis Burton, the office of the generall receyvorshipp of all my lands in the countye of Yorke, wythe the yearly fee of 40s durynge his lyffe. To my servannte, Robert Cholmeley, gent., a yearlye fee of 20l., durynge his lyffe, and to my servante Nicholas Fetherstonhaughe the offyce of the kepershipp of my west parke of Brauncpith, with the yearlye fee, to have the same unto the deathe of Lyonell Fetherstonhaughe, hys father, and that he to enter into the one halfe of Standley, whereof I have made hym a lease, and after the deathe of the sayd Lyonell, I gyve the sayd offyce, wythe the said fee, unto my servante, George Bisham, for his lyffe. To my chaplayne, Sir Nicholas Forster, parson of Brancepith 20l., I wyll that all my servannts, having offices of me, and no leases or pattantes, do enjoy the same as well as if they had thereof leases and patentes. All my other goodes I gyve to my sayd sonne, Charles Nevyll, and I make my executors my sonne Charles Nevill, Sir Richard Cholmeley, knyght, Robert Bowes, and Jerrarde Salven, esquires, and for ther paynes and travell I do gyve unto them, over and besides their costs and charges, every one of them xl. markes.

Memorandum, thys present testament was reede, publyshed and declared before the within named right honorable Erle to be his true and last will, and all other former wylls by hym maide to be voyde, frustrate and nichillate, by hym confessed in the presence of Robert Dalton, bacheler in the dyvynitie, Jerred Salven th' elder, esquire, Christofer Chayter, George Fennye, George Cowper, Thomas

I

Gybson. Also I wyll and ordayne, that at what place soever yt shall please God
to call me to Hys mercy, that my householde beynge ther, the same house and my
servantes, shal be kept together and the house kepte in suche order as hathe bene
in tymes past, accordinge to my honor, by the space of thre monthes after my
decesse.

H. WESTMERLAND.

And whear I have gyven to my servant Robert Cholmeley ane annuytie of £20
duryng his lyffe, I charge it upon my landes, &c., in the countye of Durham and
Northumberland. To Margaret Gascoigne, doughter of Syr Henrye Gascoigne,
late of Sadburyne, decessed, my intereste in the deanrye and tythe of Darlington.
To Ladye Margaret, now my wyffe, one geldinge, called Gray Wycliffe. To my
brother-in-lawe, Syr Richard Cholmeley knight, one bay geldinge, which I bought
of my servannte Rauffe Newbye. To Roger Dalton one blacke geldinge, whiche
Thomas Watson bought at Malton. To my servannte William Constable my
greate gresselde geldinge, whiche I had at Hebburn. To all my householde
servantes gyving daylye attendans, every one of them one halfe yeares waiges, over
and besydes ther ordynarye waiges. I wyll that myne executors paye unto Syr
Robert Brandlinge of Newcastell upon Tyne, knight, c. marks which I do owe hym,
and also £80 to my sayd brother-in-law Sir Richard Cholmeley, whiche I do owe
to hym, and also to Thomas Nicholas, merchante talier of London, £18 whiche I
am indebted to hym. Item wher before thys tyme I did gyve by dede unto my
doughter Elenor my manor of Bolbecke in Northumberland, till she were paid
£1,000, now I will that yf she be of the said manor lawfullye evicted, then my
executors shall pay to her £1,000, to be taken out of all my landes and tenementes.
—H. WESTMERLAND.

And where I have gyven unto my now wyffe my interest in Blandesbye Park,
nowe knowe you that I wyll the said gyfte to be voyde, and gyve it to my sonne
Charles Nevyll.—H. WESTMERLAND.

*From the Registry at York. Proved Sep. 22, 1564. Printed in Wills and
Inventories, Vol. II., edited by Canon Greenwell for the Surtees Society, 1860.*

The Featherstonhalghs of Brancepeth mentioned in this will assisted the 6th
Earl to make his escape to Flanders. Douthwaite and Lee were retainers of Earl
Henry. The former lived at Westholme, the latter in East Brandon. The old
Nevill hostel at Newcastle has since been occupied as Nevill Hall by the Newcastle
Medical College.—*Vide notes by Canon Greenwell in Wills and Inventories.*

NEVILLS OF WEARDALE.

Sir Thomas Nevill, third son of Lord John Nevill (son of 1st Earl), married Elizabeth,
daughter of Henry Lord Beaumont.

Sir Humphrey Nevill, born at Slingsby Manor, Co. York; taken after battle at Hexham;
beheaded at York, 1463—attainted.

Arthur Nevill of Scole Acle.

Ralph Nevill of Scole Acle and Coveshouses in Weardale.	*Lancelot Nevill* married Anne, daughter of Rowland Tempest of Holmeside.
Arthur Nevill of Whesnopburn. Inquis. p. m. 1591.	

"The will of Anne, widow of Arthur Nevill, is interesting, as showing to what a low estate a relation of the proud and wealthy Earls of Westmoreland had fallen even before the attainder of the last Earl. Arthur Nevill could only be ranked among the yeoman, in spite of gentle blood and an historic name."—*Vide Wills and Inventories. Surtees Society*, Vol. II.

WILL OF ANNE NEVILL.

Feb. 16, 1597-8. Anne Navell, of Whesnupbourn, in Wardaill, in the parishe of Stanop, and within the countye of Durham, wedow. To be buryed in the churche or churcheyearde of Stanop. To my sonne Railfe Navell one kowe, and one fether-bed, and 6s. 8d. of money. To my man Railfe Navell one kowe. To Railfe Dalavaillye one coopbord, one graet potte, and a paire of cob irens. To Jennet Navell, *alias* Whitfeild, one calf, and the third part of my household stoufe. All the reist of my goodes I give unto my man Railfe Navell, whom I maik my wholl executor. Witnesses, Edward Dalavaillaye, William Emerson, and Thomas Watson.—(Pr. Nov. 24, 1599.)

Inv., Oct. 27, 1599. One maire 46s 8d, ij. kyne and calves £3 13s 4d, j. farawe kowe 36s 8d, ij. stirckes 30s, iij. dynmond sheip 10s, ix. lambs 20s. j. quy 22s. Hir houshold stufe 50s. Hir apparell, 20s. The hay £6. Somma totalis £21 8s 8d.

NEVILLS OF THORNTON BRIDGE.

Sir Ralph Nevill of Condell, descended from Ralph, third son of Ralph, Lord Nevill of Nevill's Cross.—*Vide* Chap. V.

Sir Alexander Nevill of Thornton Bridge; will dated 1457 ; buried at York.

Sir William Nevill, knighted by Richard of Gloucester, 1482.

Ralph Nevill, married Annie, daughter of Sir Wm. Gascoigne.

Ralph Nevill, married daughter of Christopher Ward of Newby.

Clara, married Sir Thomas Nevill of Holt, *Joane*, married John Constable *Catherine*, married Sir
Leicestershire; circum. 1560. Thus the of Burton Constable. Walter Strickland.
Nevills of Thornton Bridge merged into
the Nevills of Holt.—*Vide* Chap. V.

CHAPTER VIII.

THE RISING IN THE NORTH.

"Listen, lively lordlings all,
    Lithe and listen unto mee,
And I will sing of a noble Earle,
    ·The noblest Earl in the North Countrie.

Earle Percy is into his garden gone,
    And after him walkes his faire ladie:
I heard a bird sing in mine eare,
    That I must either fight or flee.

Now Heaven forfend, my dearest lord,
    That ever such harm should hap to thee:
But goe to London to the court,
    And faire fall truth and honestie.

Now nay, now nay, thou lady faire,
    The court is full of subtiltie;
And if I goe to the court, lady,
    Never more I may thee see.

Yet goe to the court, my lord, she sayes,
    And I myselfe will ryde wi' thee:
At court, then, for my dearest lord,
    His faithfull borrowe I will bee.

Now nay, now nay, my lady deare;
    For lever had I lose my life,
Than leave among my cruell foes,
    My love in jeopardy and strife."
           —*Percy's Reliques.*

On the morning of the 8th of October, 1569, a vast multitude of people lined the banks of the river Thames between Westminster and London Bridge. The greatest man in England, the man who should have married Mary of Scotland, was passing by to prison. Many hopes had hung upon him, but he was now known to be a coward. "Faint heart never won fair lady," or fair kingdom, and the heart of the Duke of Norfolk had been faint indeed. "He had sped," as he himself said, "like a mired and startled jade, and the further he plunged the more was he mired." Few felt pity when the traitor's gate closed behind him. The same day Don Guerau wrote to Philip of Spain, "The Earls of Northumberland, Westmoreland, Cumberland, and Derby—the whole Catholic body—are furious at the timidity which the Duke has shown. They intend to take forcible possession of the Queen of Scots. They will then make themselves masters of the northern countries and re-establish the Catholic religion.—*MSS. Simancas.*

After the horrors of the Popish persecution it may seem strange that any persons should have been left in England to care much for the Catholic faith ; but it must be remembered that the great diocese of Durham had been administered by a man of large and liberal mind. Cuthbert Tunstall, though a Catholic, had lodged with Erasmus at Brussels, and he thought for himself on every subject. "With mild and scholar-like scepticism he refused to persecute others for opinions on which he himself had felt doubt and indecision; *and during the heat of the Marian persecution not a single victim bled within the limits of Tunstall's jurisdiction.*"

It should be remembered also that Queen Mary restored to the Church, *so far as she was able*, the property of which it had been despoiled in her father's time, and of which it was again despoiled by her parsimonious sister.

The Reformation "broke with unwelcome lustre" in the North of England, for the old faith "lay like lees at the bottom of men's hearts, and if the vessel was ever so little stirred it came to the top." The people, doubtless, were ignorant and superstitious, but "ye olde popish doctryne" was the faith of their fathers, and they loved it with a blind devotion. "There be not," says Sir Ralph Sadler, "in all this countrie ten gentlemen that do favour and allow of Her Majestie's proceedings in the cause of religion." "Ecclesiastical arrangements everywhere were in extreme confusion." A document, produced in December, 1569, relative to the diocese of Chichester, says :—"In many churches they have no sermons, not one in seven years, and some not one in twelve years, as the parishes have declared to the preachers that lately came thither to preach. In Boxgrave is a very fair church, and therein is neither parson, vicar, nor curate, *but only a sorry reader.*"

In many places, images and other popish ornaments were hidden, ready to be set up mass again within twenty-four hours' warning.— (*S.P. Dom. Eliz.*, quoted in *Froude*, Vol. IX.)

But whatever the church services might be like, the people were commanded to attend them.

In the first year of Elizabeth it was required that laymen or women should pay one shilling for every time they did not attend their parish churches; and that if they should speak against the Book of Common Prayer, for the first offence they should be imprisoned six months, and for the second time they should suffer a year's imprisonment, and for the third time imprisonment for life. And if anyone, after April 1st, 1563, should maintain in writing the Pope's supremacy in the Church, he should be guilty of high treason; *i.e.*, if a man, he should be hung, cut down alive, his breast and stomach sliced open, his heart, still palpitating, be drawn out, and then, while yet warm, his limbs should be hacked off, dipped in boiling pitch, and exposed over the gates on the spikes; but if a woman she should be burnt alive.*

These "proceedings in the cause of religion" failed to increase the love of the Catholics for their Queen, even as the proceedings of her late sister had failed to win the Protestant heart.

Indeed they loved her not; but what they required was a leader. Had Norfolk, Northumberland, or Westmoreland, possessed the spirit of their ancestors, the pages of English history would have been greatly altered. Pembroke, Arundel, Throgmorton, and Lumley, had been quickly placed under arrest by the bustling Elizabeth; but the whole country was unsettled. The Queen refused to marry; the question of succession was, therefore, left to agitate the nation. Everywhere popish emissaries fanned the flame of rebellion, and the beautiful captive Queen of Scotland brought fuel to the fire. "Every high-spirited young gentleman, whose generosity was stronger than his intelligence, had contrived in some way to catch a glance from her eyes, and to hear some soft words from her lips, and from that moment became her slave body and soul." They would lie in wait "for a glimpse of her as she passed hunting, surrounded by her guards, or watch at night

---

* The Rack seldom stood idle for all the latter part of Queen Elizabeth's reign. —*Hallam.* Two hundred and four died the horrible death of hanging, drawing, and quartering, for their religion. Few incidents in the history of religious persecution are more revolting than the martyrdom of Margaret Clitheroe, who was slowly pressed to death in the Tolbooth, York, March 25th, 1586.—*Vide Baring-Gould's Yorkshire Recusants.*

among the rocks and bushes for the late light of the taper which flickered in her chamber window."—*Froude*, Vol. IX., p. 111.

The rugged ruin of Bolton Castle still stands among the wilds of North Yorkshire, bringing to the mind of the beholder sad thoughts of young Christopher Norton, who "got himself admitted" into Lord Scrope's Guard.

"A gallant youth he seemed to be."

"He held her skeins of worsted, and her soft eyes looked upon him. Scrope told him harshly that he should watch no more, for that the Queen would make him a fool." But the warning came too late. Two short years brought a sad awakening to his dream of chivalry. The gallant youth "stood on Tyburn, beholding the hanging of his uncle, and his quartering; being well assured that he himself must follow in the same way. He desired the people to pray with him, saying that he forgave his enemies. Being hanged a little while, and then cut down, the butcher opened him; and, as he took out his bowels, he cried, and said, 'O Lord, Lord! have mercy upon me!' and so he yielded up the ghost."—(*Howell's State Trials*.) But he was only one among many victims to the loveliness of one queen and the jealousy of another.

Let us return to the autumn of 1569. The whole scheme of rebellion had been broken by the irresolution of Norfolk. To the northern earls he sent a message, begging them, "for the brotherly love they bore him, not to stir, or he would be in danger of losing his head." He was not wrong about the fate of his head, for Elizabeth "swore that law or no law she would have it," and so in the end she did. When the Duke's message reached Northumberland's house at Topcliff, several gentlemen, who followed the royal example in the use of strong language, declared that, whether Norfolk lived or died, "they were resolved to stir notwithstanding." But they differed greatly about the conditions of their stir, and the meeting at Topcliff dispersed in indecision.

The Earl of Westmoreland is stated to have been twenty-one years of age at the time of his father's death. He would therefore be in his twenty-eighth year at the time of "The Rising." He loved field sports, and possessed none of the martial spirit of the old Nevills. Lord Hunsdon's letter to Lord Burleigh, touching the confession of Northumberland, states that "the earl" (Northumberland) "doth greatly excuse my Lord of Westmerland and sayeth playnly that they could never gett any howld of hym, tyll the last

ower, and that by procurement of hys wyfe. Yf hys confession be
trew, the rebellyon was one of the strangyst matters that hath byn
hard of, and pryncipally procured by old Norton and Martyngfelde,
and ernestly followde by the two wyves, the Countessys." But it
cannot be supposed that the Countess of Westmoreland instigated
this rebellion, for, although own sister to Norfolk, she was a "very
zealous Protestante." "The Lord Henry Howard did always main-
taine and defend ye Catholick religion against his sister of Westmerland." Her father, Henry Howard, Earl of Surrey, was beheaded in
1547, at the age of 29; and his children were brought up by the
Duchess of Richmond. Jane, who afterwards became Countess of
Westmoreland, was one of the most learned ladies of a learned age.
"She made such a surprising progress in the Latin and Greek
tongue under the tuition of Mr. Fox, the martyrologist, that her
skill in those languages was such that she might well stand in
competition with the greatest men of that age."—*Ballard's
Learned Ladies.* Westmoreland was very fond of his clever and
beautiful wife, and commonly called her "Twinkes," a curious
term of endearment. "Twinkes" was certainly innocent of any
evil designs against the Queen's government, and the Earl himself
for a long time remained unsuspected of treason.

The Earl of Bedford who met him at Morpeth, Aug. 18th,
1565, on *Border business*, writes:—"My Lord of Westmerlande
and the rest were so honourable and so forward for that service as
could be desired.—*Cott. MS.* Among the *Bowes MSS.* there is a
most friendly letter, written by Westmoreland to Sir George
Bowes :—

> " I recommende me hartely to you, and have sent you herewith a letter from the
> Duke's grace, which he prayed me to convey to you who hath also spoken to me
> that my man might take the hawkes which [you] doo gyve him, and keape the
> same till they be redy to sende him, which I must see conveyed as I dyd the last
> he had there. And thus, with my commendacons unto my Lady, trusting sone to
> see you and hir. I bid you hartely farewell. From London, the ijde of July, 1568.
>
> Your loving freinde, and assured to hys power,
>
> C. WESTMERLAND."

On the 17th of May, 1569, as one of the Commissioners under
the Great Seal, he attended, with Sir George Bowes, the musters,
taken from Hamilton Hills, of all the inhabitants of the wapentake
of "Langbarughe," from the age of sixteen and upwards. In September following he was still holding hospitable house to loyal
hearts at Brancepeth; as on the 7th, Lord Hunsdon, having finished

his warden court at Alnwick, writes to Cecil from Newcastle :—"I rode to my Lord of Westmerland too be mery."

On the 26th of September, Sir George Bowes writes :—"I met the Earl of Westmerland of Saturday next after St. Matthew's day (21st Sept.) or thereabout, as our ways crossed his to Brancepeth, and mine to the Isle (Sedgefield), and appointed then to meet the said Earl of Westmerland of Wednesday next after our hawking, which appointment I kept, but he came not, nor sent, though he were not far thence."

On the 12th of October, the Earl of Sussex writes to Sir George Bowes from York :—"All ys yet quyet here, and I trust wyll be, and yet I wyll not be neclygent."—*Bowes MSS.*

During the autumn fairs in Yorkshire men gathered in groups, and the air was full of uneasy expectations of change. Sussex, who was established at York as President of the Council, was anxiously watching the condition of the northern districts. At the beginning of October he invited the two earls to Council. They came, having some idea that Sussex, being friendly to Norfolk, would also be friendly to rebellion, but they found in him "not the slightest disposition towards disloyalty." They assured him of their own anxiety for the Queen's welfare; and returned home. Reports soon after reached him that they had taken arms, but he refused to believe it. A plan had been formed for Northumberland with a small body of cavalry to seize York city, during "Sunday sermon time," and take the Council prisoners in cathedral, but it "passed over;" and Sussex, knowing that the stables at Brancepeth, Raby, and Alnwick were more than usually empty, gave little credit to the "bruits of rebellion."

On the 7th of November, Westmoreland wrote, from Brancepeth, to Sussex, praying to be excused attendance at the York Council.

" To deale plainely with your lordship I ame not ignorant what false rumor, and moste untrewe tailes are surmised and spred abrode of me, and what evill reports the Bishop of Duresme (Durham), and others have made of me, and this contrie (without cause I take God to recorde) at London, whereupon as I am credibly informed the Quenes Majestie hath conceyved displeasure against me. And yet I can not think the bishop hath this done of himself, for that I never gave him occasion, but rather by procurement of others, who wishe the overthrow and decaye of me and my house. Which things considered I dare not adventure myself to come unto you, where I knowe my enemys to be, onless I should come with such a companie for the saftie of my persone as I feare, I wolde be mislyked of, and peradventure otherwyse enterpreted upon than my meaning and intention is; and

J

therefore my duty and allegiance reserved, I have thought it more mete to staye at home, where, God willing, I meane to use myselfe as an humble obedient subject and faithful servant to the Quenes Majestie, rather than by comyng with a nomber to give anie occasion of offence."—*State Papers, Domestic, Eliz.*

Northumberland's answer was more brief. Writing from Beamish, on the 6th November, he says, "I would most willingly repair to you as required, but my business does not admyt of so hastie departure. I will so order it as to come in a few days. Meanwhile if the matter be urgent praye send it by letters."

Sussex sent back word that they could not be excused; and on the 8th he wrote from York to Sir Wm. Cecil :—

"These Earls deal so fondlie that I feare they will forget their duty to the Queen. I will perform myne to the uttermoste, if she will have them chastysed. There is gret lacke of armour here, and some should be sent. If much cannot come speedily there should be a few cartloads of arquebuses and powder without which it would be hard to win any castle. I have sent for some from Newcastle. I feare some practice for religion whereto the earles give great suspicion."—*State Papers, Dom., Eliz.*

During Norfolk's examination it transpired that the Northern earls had been in correspondence with Spain. They were then immediately called to Court.

"Windsor Castle, Oct. 24th, 1569.—*The Queen to the Earl of Sussex.*—We will that you send for our cousins the Earles of Northumberland and Westmerland, and let them understand that for consideracions of our service wherein we mean to confer with them we would have them to repaire hither to our Court, and so in our name we require you to command them so to do without delaye."—*State Papers, Dom., Eliz., Add.* Vol. XV., 100.

The order came to Westmoreland at Raby. Had he gone to Court, and flattered the Queen—as Leicester did—and lied to her sufficiently, it is quite likely that, after having had his ears smartly boxed by her most irate Majesty, he would have been sent home again to "Twinkes," safe and sound.

Sussex had not neglected to send him sound and friendly advice. On the 9th November, he wrote from York, as follows (except that the orthography is here altered) :—

"I exhort you to perform the truth you have promised to her Majesty, and the word which, upon your faith, I have by my writing delivered to her: and to follow the good counsel I have oftent'mes given you, and take heed of the counsel of such as would show you honey and deliver you poison, and stand as a nobleman upon your honour, and truth: for it will stand by you. Let not vain delusions abuse you with fear of your own shadow; if you have neglected any duty, and abused me with fair speech, submit rather with humility to her clemency, that never sought to use extremity; than by wilful disobedience put in danger the destruction of your house; and force her to give you a sharp taste of that which in her heart she never meant to any."—*State Papers, Dom., Eliz., Add.* Vol. XV., 18.

Westmoreland replied from Brancepeth, Nov. 14th:—

"My Lord,—I am sorie that my happe is so harde that I can not obey the Quenes Majesties letter in coming up to her presence. Howe greate a grefe it is to my harte, God knows who ever loved her, and will do during lyfe, never meninge anie thing prejudiciall to her Majesties person, but have bene and ever will be, her faithfull and trewe subjecte. Althoughe I be now forced to thos extremities, contrarie to her plesure and your counsell, to remain here, seeking to strengthen myself against the malice of myne enemies, which daily seke my destruction; from which cause I am compelled to gather my frends, by anie meanes I think would beste serve my torne; nevertheless mayning faithfully to her highnes, althoughe I knowe it shall be otherways taken. If the Quenes Majesties letters had come before this day, I had been more clere from offence than now I ame; because my going to Duresme hathe made the pepell which I have been the stay of, all this while, till I feared to have bene plukt out of my howse; which unlawful means I never ment to yelde to, rather choosing to dye, then thus cruelly to have bene sent up. But, if her Majestie had, before this extremitye, preparyed for me, I would willingly have obeyed, but not to avoyde those dangers I have presumed so far, as I dare not venture to kome in [her] Majesties presence. But, good, my lord, for the frendship sake before tyme profeste, cease not to be a frende for me to her Majestie, though I look you will be otherwyse. Thus wyshing you much honor and helth, and trusting you will advertise her Majestie of this my excuse, I will make an ende."—*State Papers, Domestic, Elizabeth.*

Sussex sent his secretary to Topcliff to persuade Northumberland to act loyally. Northumberland answered that he "had not been well used." When the Queen of Scots landed within his liberty, Northumberland had claimed her as his prize. He went to Carlisle and demanded that she should be delivered to him, but Mr. Lowther, being warden of that march, refused. Northumberland called him a *varlet*, saying he was altogether too low a man to pretend to such a charge. Sir Francis Knollys wrote to the earl desiring him not to press his pretensions till they were settled by Elizabeth. The earl's disappointment on this occasion was one of the ingredients forming the mass of discontent that induced this ill-fated noble to engage in rebellion.—*Vide Chalmer's Life of Mary.*

But the chief incitements came from itinerant priests, who never ceased to stir up the people against the Protestant government. Pius V. exhorted the earls to "persevere, being assured that the God, who had inspired them so far, would help them until the end." "If," said he, "death should happen to you, and your blood be poured out, it is much more honourable to attain eternal life for the confession of God through a glorious death, than by living shamefully and ignominiously, in obedience to the caprice of a weak woman, with detriment to your souls."—*F. Gobau, Apost. Pii. Quinti. &c.*

Anne, Countess of Northumberland, "loved ye old religion." The first stroke of rebellion probably came from her, though this supposition runs in the face of the poetical license of the old ballad.

"The Countess Anne," says Froude, "was made of harder stuff than her husband. At midnight a message came to Sussex's secretary bidding him haste away, or it might be worse for him; while a servant, who had come probably no further than the countess's apartment, woke Northumberland from his first sleep, with the news that, 'within an hour his enemy, Sir Oswald Wolstrop, would be upon him to carry him muffled to Elizabeth.' The earl sprang from his bed, ordered his horses to be saddled, the bridge over the Swale to be broken, and the church bells to be wrung backwards. The jangled sound broke on the ears of Sussex's emissary as he rode out of the town. His guide, when asked what this meant, 'sighed, and answered, he was afraid it was to raise the country.'"

The Pope was the head of the Church, and the Pope had blessed this "glorious enterprise." The country was up. The roads were filled with companies of cavalry, "scattered bands of insurgents searching for weapons, and flying peasants driving their cattle before them for fear of plunder." Northumberland, Richard Norton and his sons, Reed, Markenfeld, Swinburne, and a hundred other gentlemen made their way northwards to join the Earl of Westmoreland.

> " The Nevill sees
> His followers gathering in from Tees,
> From Were, and all the little rills
> Conceal'd among the forked hills.
> Seven hundred knights, retainers all
> Of Nevill, at their master's call
> Had sate together in Raby Hall;
> Such strength that earldom held of yore;
> Nor wanted at this time rich store
> Of well appointed chivalry."—*Wordsworth.*

ADDENDA.—ABSTRACTS FROM STATE PAPERS.

York, Oct. 30th, 1569.—*Thomas, Earl of Sussex, to the Queen.*—The persons suspected to have been evil councillors to the Earls of Northumberland and Westmoreland, are Leonard Dacre, Mr. Markenfeld, Fras. Norton, Chris. Danby, Robt. Bowes, John Swinburne, Robt. Tempest, and Captain Reed; and that my Lord Talbot is acquainted with their councils; it is thought these men can declare the truth of all that has been intended. The motive of their counsels seem of divers natures; some specially respect the Duke of Norfolk, some the Scottish Queen, some religion, and some perhaps all three, yet use my Lord of Norfolk as a cover to the rest.—*Cal. S. P., Dom., Eliz., Add.* Vol. XIV., 100.

York, Nov. 8th, 1569.—*William, Lord Ure, to the Council.*—Yesterday night, John Horne, a servant of mine, who is with my wife at Wilton, in the Bishopric of Durham, brought me the following reports, from my house at Malton, in Yorkshire:—That a man of the Earl of Westmoreland's asked Thomas Lawe, another servant of mine, whether he knew that I and Sir Henry Percy, Sir Henry Gate, and Thomas Gower, from Newcastle, were to meet and come to Brancepeth Castle, with power to pull the Earl out of the same; that the Earl had received a letter from the Lord President, to come to York, but that it was only to entice him in, and then make him fast as the Duke is, and therefore he would not come, nor the Earl of Northumberland, as they had both vowed to abide together till death. Upon my man asking how they could do that, he replied that Brancepeth Castle was well furnished and strong, and they trusted to keep it until help came by sea or land. Colson, servant to the Earl of Westmoreland, told John Vase, another man of mine, that Brancepeth Castle is watched every night by horsemen, and by day by footmen. Francis Burton, one of the Earl of Westmoreland's men, told my brother, Thomas Ure, that the Earl of Westmoreland with his horsemen, and one Claxton of Winyard, co. Durham, rode several times into one of the Earl's parks at Brancepeth in the night, and there trained themselves in skirmishing and mustering. —*Cal. S. P. Dom., Eliz., Addenda.* Vol. XV., 16.

The Earl of Sussex to the Queen.

It may please your moste excellent Majestie:

I receyed, this morning, letters from the Erles of Northumberlande and Westmerlande; whereapon, calling together your counsell; now here, viz: Mr. Deane of Yorke, Sir Thomas Gargrave, Sir Nicholas Fairfax, Sir Henry Gate, Mr. Rookesby, and Mr. Vaughan; we all conceyved upon the good consydering of the letters, that the one dyrectly refused to come, and the other more covertly seemed to deferr his comyng. And therefore, perceyving, as well by the reporte of the pursuyvant that went with the letters, that he colde receyve no answer of ether of them, untell the Erles had met together at Bransbaye; where also olde Norton the Sherif, and Martenfield then were; as also by other circumstances, that they be at this present, both apon one councell; and that there entent is not in dede to come hether, we resolved that I shoulde presentlye advertise your Majestie herof, and therwith to send the coppies of both letters, which herewith your Majestie shall recyve.

I entend also, by there advyses, to wryte to the Erles, to-morrowe, your Majesties commandement, for their repaire unto your Corte, according to th effect of your letters.

I do certenlye feare that seing they have geven this answer they will not repaire to your Majestie; and considering the sequell herof, I fynde but these two wayes in the ende,—eyther that your Majestie should, upon there submission, forgyve that is paste, and call them home to your favour; or with force porsewe them; and so ether take them, or drive them owte of the realme.

It should appere, by all the intelligence I can gett, that they entende not to sturr present rebellion, but rather for feare to withrawe themselves for theire defence, if anie force be offered against them; so as I trust there shall be no actuall rebellion before the returne of your Majesties pleasure.

It maye also please your Majestie to appoint new Sherifes, in all those partes, whose truthe your selfe knowethe by proofe.

In the meane tyme, untell your pleasure be signifyed, I will, withe the advyse of your counsell here, consider what numbers of horsemen and fotemen shal be fit to be levyed for this service, &c.

God preserve your Majestie in long lyfe and prosperous rayne, and send all that wolde the contraye, shame and shorte lyfe. From Yorke, the 8th of November, 1569.—*S.P., Dom., Eliz.*

CHAPTER IX.

THE GATHERING OF THE CLANS.

"Now joy for you and sudden cheer,
    Ye watchmen upon Brancepeth towers,
Looking forth in doubt and fear,
    Telling melancholy hours!
Proclaim it! let your masters hear
    That Norton with his band is near.
The watchmen from their station high
    Pronounced the word, and the Earls descry
Forthwith the armed company,
    Marching down the banks of Were.

                    From far and near,
From every side came noisy swarms
    Of peasants, in their homely gear;
And mixed with these, to Brancepeth came
    Grave gentry of estate and name,
And captains known for worth in arms;
    And pray'd the Earls in self-defence
To rise and prove their innocence.
    Rise, noble earls, put forth your might
For holy church, and the people's right!"
                    —*The White Doe of Rylstone.*

THE story of the "Northern Rising" will be told best in the words of eye-witnesses.

From Barnard Castle, on the 10th of November, Sir Geo. Bowes writes to the Earl of Sussex:—

My bounden dewty premised; pleaseth your good lordship to be advertised, that this daye in the afternoon, the Erle of Northumberland, armed in a previe cote, under a Spanishe jerkyn, being open, so that the cote might be seane, and a stele cappe covered with grene velvet, is returned to Bransbeth, with viii with him, all armed with previe cotes and daggs; and in another company returned to Bransbeth, Francis Norton, and divers of his brethrene, and Captaine Rede, with twenty-nine horse, all armed; and in a third companye returned Markenfield, with òne which is supposed to be the Sheriffe of Yorkshyre, and ther company thirty horse [men], all armed in corslets, under jerkins."—*Bowes MSS. Published in Sir Cuthbert Sharpe's Memorials of the Rebellion.*

Sir George Bowes to the Earl of Sussex.—12th Nov.—My bownden dewtye premised; pleaseth your lordshipe to be advertysede, that for sewrtye the Erlles of Northumberlande and Westmerland ar together at Branspethe, and with them, or at Tyrsdell, hard by, at Francis Bullmer's howse, ar the Sheryve of Yorksher and Mr. Markenfeld, whose companye ridethe armed with corsletts and speares, and hathe ryden to and fro betwixt [Brancepath] and William Norton's hows twyse, so that they occupye the streets in [a] maner daye and nyght, butt delleth with no man. There [are] sundry tropes of twenty, or thereabouts, latly come forth of Yorkshyer, and direct their course to Branspethe, but yt ys nott as yett knowne what theys are; but I truste, by tomorowe at nyght, to understand and knowe the names of all the jentylmen that kepethe the Erlles, or anye of the others' companye. And yett ther ys verye strayt watche and ward; and this daye ys appointyd to be at Branspeth all that anye of them in [any] manner can make in ther armor; but what actyon they intend I know not, but ytt shall not sooner be uttered to any nomber, but I truste to be advertysed. But sewer yt is loked verye generally that tomorowe, or this daye, they will sett forthe what soever they pretend to doye, and shewe ther force, which is nott when yt is wholly gathered, but that I can lerne, above six hundred men, and thereaboutes. They will be together this daye or nyght, but dowting what myght happen to my selfe, whom theye greatlye menace, I have put my selfe and my howsehold only, into Barnard Castel.

Your Lordship's wholly at commandment.

Bowes MSS., No. 4. Vol. II.

Sir George Bowes to the Earl of Sussex.—Nov. 15th, 1569.—The doynges off th Erles of Westmerland and Northumberland. Yesterdaye at iiii of the clocke in the afternoone the sayd Erles accompanyed with Rychard Norton, Francys hys sone, with dyvers other of hys sayd sones, Xpoferr Nevell, Cudbert Nevyll, uncles of the sayd Erle of Westmerland, and Thomas Markynfelde, wythe others, to the nomber of three [score] horsemen, armed in corsletts and coytts of playt, with speares, harquebusses, and dagges; and entred the mynster theyr [at Durham], and theyr toke all the bokes, but one, and theyme and the comunyon table defaced, rentt, and brok in peces. And after made a proclamatyon in the Quenes name, that no man, before theyr pleasur knowne, shuld use any servyce; and callying the cetezens before theyme, told theyme how they had done nothyng but that they wold avowe, and was after the Quenes procedynges. And so taryinge abowt the space off one hour, they departyde; puttyng a watche of twenty-four townsmen to the towne, whiche tooke a servante of myne, which I sent thither, and hyme caryed to hys lodgynge, and theyr he was kept tyll this morninge, and so came away. In haste, at Barnard Castle, the xvth of November, at xii of the cloke, 1569. Your Lordships wholly at commandment.—*S.P., Dom., Eliz.*

This hasty letter is addressed "to my singular good Lord, the *Erle of Westmerland,*" instead of to the Earl of Sussex. Did Westmerland get hold of it, and have a good laugh over it with Twinkes, I wonder?

The events which it describes happened on Sunday, 14th. Sussex had sent his pursuivant from York with a last message of warning, and an earnest exhortation to the earls to return to their allegiance. The pursuivant was carried *nolens volens* to Durham "*that he might see the answer.*" The two earls, Sir Christopher and Sir Cuthbert Nevill, Richard Norton, and sixty men at arms, went with him. Old Norton was the Patriarch of Rebellion,

> "Of stature undepress'd in size,
> Unbent, which rather seem'd to rise
> In open victory o'er the weight
> Of seventy years, to higher height."

A massive gold crucifix hung from his neck, and his still stalwart arms grasped the banner of the five wounds, the banner round which all good Catholics had rallied in the "Pilgrimage of Grace."

> "He took the banner, and unfurl'd
> The precious folds. 'Behold,' said he,
> 'The ransom of a sinful world.
> Let this your preservation be,
> The wounds of hands, and feet, and side,
> And the sacred cross on which Jesus died!
> This bring I from an ancient hearth.'"

The people raised a shout of joy. "They overthrew the communion board, they tore the English Bible and Prayer Book to pieces, the ancient altar-stone was taken from a rubbish heap where it had been thrown, and solemnly replaced, and the holy water vessel was restored at the west door; and then, amidst tears, embraces, prayers, and thanksgivings, the organ pealed out, the candles and torches were lighted, and Mass was heard once more in the long-desecrated aisles."—*Froude*, Vol. IX.

"Tell your master what you have seen," said Northumberland to the pursuivant. "Bid him use no further persuasions; our lives are in danger, and if we are to lose them, we will lose them in the field."

"On Monday morning the rebels moved southwards to Darlington, gathering force like a snowball, and with herald's voice and written proclamation, at cross road and village green, in town hall, and pulpit, they made known their intentions to the world, and appealed to the religious conscience of the people."—*Froude*, Vol. IX.

K

The form of proclamation has been preserved:—

PROCLAMATION OF THE TWO EARLS.

"We, Thomas, Earl of Northumberland, and Charles, Earl of Westmoreland, the Queen's true and faithful subjects, to all the same of the old and Catholic religion. Know ye, that we with many other well-disposed persons, as well of the nobility as others, have promised our faith to the furtherance of this one good meaning; forasmuch as divers disordered and evil disposed persons about the Queen's Majesty have by their subtle and crafty dealings, to advance themselves, overcome in this realm the true and Catholic religion towards God, and by the same abused the Queen, disordered the realm, and now, lastly, seek and procure the destruction of the nobility. We therefore have gathered ourselves together to resist by force, and the rather, by the help of God, and you good people, to see redress of these things amiss, with the restoring all ancient customs and liberties of God's church, and this noble realm, lest, if we should not do it ourselves, we might be reformed by strangers, to the great hazard of the state of this our country, whereunto we are all bound.—*God save the Queen.*"

Sussex now began to feel "the solemnity of the occasion." "He sent out a Commission to assemble the force of the shire, but he feared they would not fight. He had not the money to pay them with, and Sir George Bowes declared that the men of the shire would never serve without wages." It was evident that unless the Queen could send down a little hard cash to York all must be lost. Sussex wrote to London to this effect.

York, Nov. 20.—*Thomas, Earl of Sussex, to Sir Wm. Cecil.*—"He is a rare bird that hath not some of his with the two Earls, or in his heart wishes not well to their cause. I heartily wish that her Majesty would quench this fire at the beginning, either by pardon or force; if by the latter, then not to trust these parts only, lest, by one foil taken, much be hazarded. The Earls are old in blood, and poor in force in any other cause than this; but it is not to be believed of them that see it not what is done directly and underhand to serve them for this cause. *Give advice that the sparing of a little money in the beginning be not repented of hereafter,* and send some good force that you may surely trust in these parts; for I fear meantime this country will hardly match them with-horsemen, and they think the greatest number will strike faintly against them."—*Cal. S.P. Dom. Eliz. Add.* Vol. XV., 32.

Meanwhile the earls advanced steadily southwards, their numbers being variously reported at from eight to fifteen thousand, among whom were two thousand horse, well armed and appointed. They had issued a proclamation, and Sussex, not knowing what better to do, issued one also.

Proclamation by Thomas, Earl of Sussex, Lord-Lieutenant of the North, by virtue of Her Majesty's warrant to him of the 15th Nov., 1569. Whereas, Thomas, Earl of Northumberland, and Charles, Earl of Westmoreland, being commanded upon their allegiance to repair to Her Majesty, have contemptuously disobeyed her command, and have, with Christopher Nevill, Rich. Norton of Norton Conyers, Thos. Markenfeld of Markenfeld, John Swinburne, Robt. Tempest, Fras. Norton, and others, committed divers offences, levied great numbers of horse and foot, and put them in armour, and do daily draw to them great forces, abusing her name and authority to further their wicked purpose, and intend to proceed further in their rebellious enterprise, if not resisted in time. We, therefore, in Her Majesty's name, and by her warrant, denounce the said Earls, and the others named, to be rebels and disturbers of the peace, and in her name, command that they henceforth be reputed rebels. And we, in Her Majesty's name, do command all faithful subjects to flee from the company or aiding of rebellious persons, and do by these presents receive to her grace and free pardon all such persons, other than hereafter be exempted, as have accompanied the said Earls and others, if before the 22nd inst., they repair to their dwelling-houses, and there remain quiet, and do not abide in company of the said persons aforesaid, after 21st Nov. Her Majesty's pleasure is that the said Earls, and the others named, and Thomas Jennings, be exempted from this pardon, and also any person adhering to or accompanying any of the before exempted after 21st Nov., and she commands all her subjects to repute them rebels. 19th Nov., 1569.—*Cal. S.P. Dom. Elis.* Vol. XV., 30.

But the rebels declined to take any notice of the Lord Lieutenant's good advice. They would not "repair to their dwellings and remain quiet," and Sussex grew more and more uneasy. "The only regular troops in the Presidency were on the Border, in garrison at Berwick or Carlisle, or in the Middle Marches, with Sir John Foster. Both Sussex and Cecil wrote pressingly that some of these soldiers should be sent to York, but they could not be spared from their posts. Northumberland had been in communication through the autumn with all the dangerous lords and gentlemen between Forth and Tweed, and the powder of general conspiracy had been laid throughout the island, wherever Mary Stuart had a friend."—*Froude*, Vol. IX.

ADDENDA.

York, Nov. 13.—*Thomas, Earl of Sussex, and six others of the Council of the North, to the Queen.*—Yesterday we heard, by letters from Sir Geo. Bowes, that the Earls of Northumberland and Westmoreland, old Richard Norton, Sheriff of Yorkshire, and his sons, Thomas Markenfeld, and some gentlemen of the bishopric are assembled at the Earl of Westmoreland's house at Brancepeth in the bishopric, with all their servants in armour; that the Earl of Northumberland, with such of his men as fled with him on the night of the 9th, rode armed with privy coats, and Norton, Markenfeld, and others in corselets and other white armour; and that they ride daily in that sort, and have warned all their tenants and friends to repair thither to them, yesterday, to-day, and to-morrow.—*Cal. S.P. Dom. Eliz. Add.* Vol. XV., 20.

Nov. 13, 1569.—[——*Lowther to the Earl of Westmoreland.* (?)]—I was to make my immediate repair, according to your letter, but being taken by Sir Geo. Bowes, and losing my horse, I am stopped at Barnard Castle. Bowes has a near spy about you, which must be cut off; for he could tell me of all meetings and conferences, and used to enjoy some of your land. Let nothing persuade you to the contrary but that Lord Wharton and Rich. Lowther are, and always will be, your own, and join with you until death.

Endorsed by Sir Wm. Cecil. "A letter of one that was taken with Sir Geo. Bowes."—*Dom. Eliz.* Vol. XV., 22.

Nov. 15, 1569, 3 A.M., *York.*—*Earl of Sussex to Sir Wm. Cecil.*—I have just received letters from the Earl of Northumberland to the Queen, which I send with speed, as he required. They are dated at Topcliff, but he is indeed at Brancepeth. The Queen's letters were delivered him two hours after these were sent. When the bearer of them returns I will write you further.

ENCLOSURE.—*Earl of Northumberland to the Queen.*—God and my conscience know that I never intended any disloyal act towards you, but shall be found ready, whilst I live, to spend life and lands, and all that I have, against all persons whatsoever; nor have I done anything offensive to law as all the country can testify, yet as the maintainers thereof are in these parts in some credit with some of your private councillors, who—as experience has taught me—have been willing to hear matters to my discredit, I durst not adventure to your presence till I had craved your pardon, if I have, through lack of skill, liked that which may not content you, and till time had shown how untrue those slanders are.—Topcliff, 13 Nov., 1569.—*Cal. S.P. Dom. Eliz.* Vol. XV., 23.

York, Nov. 15, 1569.—*Earl of Sussex and four others of the Council of the North to the Queen.*—The Earls of Northumberland and Westmoreland refuse to obey your commands to repair to your presence. They have been at Durham with their force in armour, to persuade the people to take their parts; some of their company have thrown down the communion table, and tore the Holy Bible in pieces. They intend to make religion their ground, they know their offences to be such that without your pardon, they must do their uttermost for surety of their lives. We request your instructions how to proceed, and want money and munition.—*Dom. Eliz.* Vol. XV., 24.

Nov. 15, 1569.—York.—*Thomas, Earl of Sussex, to the Queen.*—These simple Earls are now at Bransby [Brancepeth] with their wicked counsellors, where, under colour of defence, they assemble forces. I have prepared to assemble a force to suppress theirs, lest seeing no resistance, might carry them to further mischief; I mean to be within 16 miles of Brancepeth by the 21st.

Let me know your pleasure before the 21st; if it comes to a fight, either God shall give you the victory, or if any man will stand with me you shall find my carcase on the ground, whatsoever the rest of my company do; for I would for conscience' sake spend a thousand lives against all that shall draw sword against our religion.—*Dom. Eliz.* Vol. XV., 25.

Nov. 16, 1569.—York.— *Thomas, Earl of Sussex, to Sir Wm. Cecil.*—The Earls appear to have 500 horse, all serving men, and most furnished with a coat of plate, spear, and one or two daggers; they say they look for further force out of Northumberland, Westmoreland, and other places. They have as yet no show of footmen. They pay for all they take, and suffer no spoil.—*Dom. Eliz.* Vol. XV., 27.

Sir George Bowes to the Earl of Sussex.—Nov. 16th.—Yesterdaye Sir John Nevell, as one who seemeth to knowe hym very well sayethe, departyd forth of the Erles troup with iii horsemen in great haste, rode over thys river at . . . . towards Westmerland to what end God knoweth.

I humble beseche your L. to send me fifty pounds, for I have great layeings owte for many servyces, and now begynnethe to lacke money; and I shall aunswer yt agayn within one monethe.—*Bowes' MSS.*

Sir George Bowes to the Earl of Sussex, Nov. 17th.—Christopher Nevill is gone into Kirby-more-side to raise people, and comethe thorowe Cleaveland. The matter groweth very hot, and sure in my opinion requireth to be expedited; as what with feare, of faire speche or moneye, they drawe awaye the harts of people; and sure besydes my owne, and those apperteyning such of my friends, as will with me adventure all, ther eis not heare as yet above seventy men, and manye of them not the best furnished.—*Bowes' MSS. Printed in full in Memorials of Rebellion.*

CHAPTER X.

ONWARDS FOR CONSCIENCE' SAKE!

> "'This meeting, noble lords, looks fair;
> I bring with me a goodly train;
> Their hearts are with you: hill and dale
> Have helped us: Ure we cross'd, and Swale,
> And horse and harness follow'd—see
> The best part of their yeomanry!
> Stand forth my sons! These eight are mine,
> Whom to this service I commend:
> Which way soe'er our fate incline,
> These will be faithful to the end:
> These are my all!' voice fail'd him here."
>
> *The White Doe of Rylstone.*

THE rebellion was now fairly afloat. "Sir George Bowes flung himself into Barnard with a few score servants. Lord Darcy held Pomfret, and trusted faintly that, *if the Queen would send him money*, he might be able to stop the passage over the Don.

"There was no force anywhere which could meet the rebels in the field. On the 19th they were at Ripon, on the 20th at Knaresborough, and on the 23rd they had passed York. Their main body was at Wetherby and Tadcaster, their advanced horse were far down across the Ouse.

"The barns were full, the farmyards well stocked, and food was abundant. They moved on at leisure, intending to make first for Tutbury and release the Queen of Scots, and then either advance to London or wait for a corresponding movement in the south. To make the ground sure and to open a port through which expected succours could reach them from the Duke of Alva, by a side movement they secured Hartlepool. Misinterpreting the inaction of Sussex, they supposed that he was waiting only for a plea of constraint to join their party. They had avoided York on their advance, to prevent a collision, and they wrote to beg him to make common cause with them."—*Froude*, Vol. IX.

To Lord Derby they also wrote as follows :—

"Our very good Lorde, we have thought good to make you privie to our good and virtuous intent, for what cause we have assembled ourselves in armes, and howe we proceede, for the benefitt of our state and the Crowne of Englande, which we send you here inclosed the very forme of our Proclamation; and for the great confidence and trust we have in your Lord'pes virtuous meaning and religion, with the care your Lordship hath of the preservation of the Queen's Majesty, and the quiet of the comon wealth, the mayntenance of God's true religion, and the conserving of the antient Nobilitye, with the safetye of your frends and your howses; we are most hartilye to require you, for the causes aforesaid, to rayse your Lordship's powers, to joyne with ours, as also to procure such aide and assistance in all parts of your Lords'ps terrytories as may be more terror to effect our Godly and honorable enterprizes; and because we know your Lordship is wyse, we forbear to persuade with you howe necessarie this war is, which indeed is a peace to the performance of our duties, and therefore, good my Lord, let us, according to the hoape we repose in your Lordship, receyve an assurance of your good meaning and forwardness herein, and to hear from you agayne with speede. And so we most hartily take our leave of your good Lordship, at Ripon, this 27th Nov., 1569.

Your good Lordship's assured loving friends,

T. NORTHUMBERLAND,
C. WESTMORELAND.

"To our Right Honorable and our very good Lorde the Erle of Derby."

—*Burghley Papers*. Vol. I.

Lord Wharton and the Lowthers had arranged to give assistance in the storming of Tutbury Castle. The arrival of the Scotch Queen in the camp of the northern earls would have been the signal for the rising of Southampton, Montague, Morley, Worcester, and Derby. "Alva had a fleet already collected in Zealand, with guns and powder on board, and he was understood to be waiting only to hear that she was at liberty to launch them upon England."— *Froude*.

Meanwhile the Earls had a friend at court in the person of Leonard Dacres. Elizabeth at first viewed him with suspicion, but his ways were winning; and having ingratiated himself into the Queen's favour, he easily persuaded her that the fears of Sussex were groundless, and that no extra forces would be required to overthrow the power of the northern Earls. He obtained a commission to raise the men of his own county, and act under Lord Scrope at Carlïsle *against the rebels*. Meanwhile, Mary of Scotland was receiving "hartye commendatyons, and friendlye advyces from Dacres with the croked bake," and Northumberland had a message from Naworth Castle, saying, "If my company be greate enough, I will set upon hym (Scrope) and overthrow hym in the feld; and if I thinke myselfe not hable to medle with his lordship, I will then retorne to my Lord of Northumberland, with my whole power."— *S. P. Dom. Eliz.*

Whilst Dacre was hoodwinking friends and enemies all round, Sussex was writing piteous letters to London for help. But Elizabeth grudged all expense, and distrusted the earl's loyalty. Egremont Ratclif, younger brother of the half-blood to Sussex, had joined the rebels at Brancepeth. Westmoreland had won his heart, and given him "a small ring of gold upon condicions and promises that he would be to hym as to himselfe in all hys fortunes." "Nothing was more grievous to Sussex than the trayterous deling of his unnatural brother, upon whom he would in some sort be revenged." But vengeance came from another quarter, for the unhappy man afterwards entered the service of Don John of Austria, and being accused with others of an attempt to murder the Governor of Flanders, "his head was stricken off in the market-place of Namur, 1578."

During the third week of November, Lord Hunsdon was "sent to assist" Sussex in the command of the miniature army of the north. On the 20th he wrote from Doncaster to Cecil:—"The earls intend to go through withal. Their meaning is to take the Scottish Queen, and therefore, for God's sake, let her not remain where she is, for the greatest force are horsemen."

It was now Elizabeth's turn to feel the "solemnity of the occasyon." A commission was addressed to the Earl of Huntingdon for the removal of the Queen of Scots to Coventry. But the Earl of Shrewsbury, irritated because the commission had not been addressed to him, refused to resign his prisoner, therefore the two earls, being of "sour vysage," rode into Warwickshire together, with Mary in the middle, followed by a guard of four hundred men.

The southern Catholics now waited for the arrival of Alva's troops at Hartlepool, and Alva waited for the Scottish Queen to be set at liberty. Lord Derby, by way of self protection, sent on the letter he had received from the northern earls to Elizabeth. With their friends in this mood, the rebellious noblemen thought it prudent to turn their faces northward. "They had no money; the road to London was open, but they were unwilling to irritate the people by feeding their men upon plunder; and even could they reach London, they doubted their power to carry it by a *coup de main*, and to besiege it would be impossible."

Lord Pembroke now declared loudly that he had ever been a true subject, and the Queen with graceful confidence made him General of the Army of Reserve at Windsor. Southampton and Montague took ship, but were driven back by a storm. "The Queen heard of it; to disarm treason by not affecting to see it, she gave Montague the command of the south coast, and joined Lord Bedford in commission with him, as a security against his betraying his trust. A proclamation was now sent down and issued at York, promising a free pardon to all the rebels, except the two earls and ten others, on condition of their immediately laying down their arms. Lord Clinton went into Lincolnshire, Lord Warwick and Lord Hereford into the Midland Counties, to collect a force to relieve Sussex; and by the end of November two bodies of 4,000 men each were converging rapidly upon Doncaster."—*Froude*, Vol. IX.

The earls now parted. Northumberland marched home to Alnwick to fortify it, whilst Westmoreland, who felt "the necessity of doing something," besieged his old friend, Sir George Bowes, in Barnard Castle. In this, his only passage of arms, he was successful. The garrison surrendered, and the earl went on to Raby, confident of success. He suspected the loyalty of the royal troops, and vainly imagined they would come over to him. He expected Dacre also, but Dacre came not. The Raby exchequer was empty.

No one can help feeling pity for Westmoreland. "His own familiar friend whom he had trusted, had lifted up his heel against him." Elizabeth had sent a traitor into his camp, in the person of Sir Robert Constable, his own kinsman.

The Queen, who grudged every penny that had been sent to Sussex, was well pleased that "the good Constable should sow sedition among the rebels, discourage, divide, and disperse them, and spare no money in it." Of Sir Robert Constable we shall hear more anon.

Elizabeth placed great confidence in spies. A certain Captain Strelley undertook "to spy about Brancepeth." "The Queen," it was said, "conceyveth well of him. He is not unlike to achieve this his purpose; in hope whereof she hath promised him a suite which he hath bene a long suyter for."—*Sadler Papers*. This was probably the man who brought young Christopher Norton to the scaffold.

ADDENDA.

Extract from letter of Sir George Bowes to the Earl of Sussex.—Barnard Castle, Nov. 29th.—They have certeyne ordenance in Branspeth, which ys, as the knowledger advertysed me, a fawcon and two slyngs (and noo other) which ys said shall come hether; and was yeasterdaye beinge well carted, sett furthe at Bransbeth gayts, and a greate number of caryage horses prepared. They reporte to come thys waye, but I suppose to passe to Hartlepoyle, for here those things wyll stand them in noo steade. I have a prisoner here, Lockwodde, layte Secretary of th Erle of Westmerland, and two gentlemen of Wardell, taken goinge towards the Erles campe.— *Bowes' MSS.*, Vol. II.

York, Nov. 24, 1569.—*John Vaughan to Robert Owenson.*—To satisfy you touching our troubled estate, the Earls of Northumberland and Westmoreland, being sent for to repair to Court, refused; put themselves in armament at Brancepeth, in the Bishopric of Durham, with all their servants, tenants, and friends, and have entered Yorkshire, levying soldiers in the Queen's name to maintain their actions, which they have put forth to be for religion. They have Mass daily, yet they commit great spoil. They have passed all this part of Yorkshire, viz., Richmond, Ripon, Wetherby, Knaresborough, Tadcaster, Cawood, Selby, and now are returned towards Topcliff. The gentlemen in the action are old Richard Norton, with most of his sons, Thos. Markenfeld, Chris. Nevill, Robert Tempest of the bishopric, and John Swinborne, but no more of value. My Lord Lieutenant, Lord Hunsdon, and Sir Ralph Sadler are assembled to take order herein. The gentlemen here stand dutifully to the Queen.—*Abstract from State Papers, Eliz. Dom.* Vol. XV., 37.

York, Nov. 26, 1569.—*Sir Ralph Sadler to the Queen.*—The force and power assembled here for you is 2,500 foot and 500 horse; the rebels have 6,000 foot and 1,000 horse well appointed, a great number being serving men, servants, and tenants to the two Earls and to the other gentlemen; their associates are pistoliers, furnished with shot, which argues that this matter has long been prepared for by the rebels. It has, therefore, been wise in my Lord Lieutenant to forbear until he can take the field with some security. He neither lacks will nor courage, and spares no charge of his own, which I perceive is very great to him.—Vol. XV., 46.

York, Nov. 26, 1569.—*Henry, Lord Hunsdon, to Sir Wm. Cecil.*—I am sorry to hear of Westmorland's wilfulness in refusing to follow the advice of those who, for his house's sake, wished him well. The other is very timorous, and has meant twice or thrice to submit, but his wife encourages him to persevere, and rides up and down with their army, so that the gray mare is the better horse.—Vol. XV., 49.

York, Nov. 28, 1569.—*Thomas, Earl of Sussex, Henry, Lord Hunsdon, and Sir Ralph Sadler to the Council.*—The rebels are now retired to Richmond, and intend lying in the bishopric, either to stop the passage of such forces as we look for out of Northumberland, Cumberland, and Westmorland, or to seek means to fly out of the realm. We want power to follow them; they are much stronger than we both in horse and foot. Pray send money; without that we can do little, and the small number we now have here call upon us in vain to satisfy their wages.—Vol. XV., 51.

York, Nov. 30, 1569.—*Thomas, Earl of Sussex, to Sir Wm. Cecil.*—The rebel Earls, with all their confederates and horsemen, are returned to Brancepeth, and have ordered their footmen to follow them, who be so wearied with lagging from place to place, and deceived by the promises made to them—sometimes of pay, sometimes the spoil of this city, Newcastle, and Barnard Castle—that many have fled from them, and the rest, with winter travel, remain miserable. The horsemen, being serving men and their own tenants for the most part, and finding the sweet of the spoils, will not leave them but by force. They begin to be odious to such as at the beginning liked them, and, therefore, it were good to set on them in time; if I might have about 500 to 600 horsemen, and 400 or 500 arquebusiers from my Lord Admiral, I would not doubt their speedy overthrow.—Vol. XV., 53.

York, Nov. 30, 1569.—*Sir Ralph Sadler to Sir Wm. Cecil.*—The gentlemen of this country show themselves very forward in this service, but I cannot assure myself of such as be Papists, for if the father come to us with 10 men, his son goes to the rebels with 20. I would we had the said number of horse and foot out of the South, and then we should do well enough.—Vol. XV., 54.

York, Nov. 30, 1569.—*Henry, Lord Hunsdon, to Sir William Cecil.*—Nicholas Errington came to York yesterday from Berwick, and on the way was taken by rebels, and carried to the Earl of Northumberland at Richmond, where he was detained three days. He says they are better than 1,000 horse, well appointed, but that their foot are simple creatures, and nothing so well as they have been accounted, so that if we had 300 or 1,000 horse here, and 300 shot, we would nothing doubt their overthrow, for all their strength is in their horsemen.—Vol. XV., 55.

York, Dec. 1, 1569.—*Thomas, Earl of Sussex, to Sir William Cecil.*—This day I hear that Christopher Nevill has entered Hartlepool with 300 men, and keeps it for rebels. I advertise you that if Her Majesty has any ships abroad, one or two might be directed to that coast. Help me with some horsemen, arquebusiers, and money, and that will make an end of the whole quickly.—Vol. XV., 65.

York, Dec. 2, 1569.—*Sir Ralph Sadler to Sir William Cecil.*—The rebels are now at Raby, and yesterday or to-day are doing with Sir George Bowes at Barnard Castle. They have got Hartlepool, and have put 300 men into it. I gather that they mean to keep that town for their refuge, and to seek their escape by the sea, or else hope to receive some foreign aid. One or two of the Queen's ships should lie on this coast to prevent it.—Vol. XV., 66.

York, Dec. 2, 1569.—*Thomas Cecil to his father, Sir Wm. Cecil.*—Since my last of the 25th inst., we have remained at York. The army stays the arrival of band from Berwick and the West Riding towards Wakefield and Halifax, without which it is not thought meet to venture battle, this power being far weaker in horsemen than the enemy, and the foot very weakly armed. My armour has arrived, with one case of pistols, which were very ill-chosen by those you committed the buying of them to, being neither of good bullet nor long enough, and there is only one instead of two cases, as promised.—Vol. XV., 70.

Doncaster, Dec. 2, 1569.—*John, Lord Darcy, to the Council.*—This instant I hear by a spy who came from the rebels, that yesterday all the horsemen mustered on

Gaterley and other moors and wastes near Raby, where two Earls remain; that there are 1,500 or 1,600 horsemen, well furnished, who disperse themselves nightly about Percybridge, Caterigg, Richmond, Gretabridge, Bowes, Darlington, and some to the Spitte of Stainmore, from 8 to 12 miles distant from the place of their assembly.—Vol. XV., 71.

Newark Castle, Dec. 3, 1569.—*Sir F. Leek to the Council.*—The Earls remain at Raby; the people are dispersed, as well horse as foot, so that he could not judge of the number, but he was informed that there are 2,000 light horse, whereof 1,500 are very well furnished; the others after the order of Riddesdale. Last Thursday he met 500 horsemen a mile from Percybridge, with Christopher Nevill, their captain, better furnished than the northern horsemen, for besides their staves, few were without a case of pistols; he thinks he saw Wm. Norton in their company. The same day, between Percybridge and Northallerton, he met three bands of foot lying in several villages, who were so badly furnished of armour, weapons, and their own persons, that he never saw such unlikely soldiers; these rascals are supposed to number 10,000. Those foot who were promised wages and not paid have returned home, and say they would rather be hanged than serve the Earls any more. The bruit amongst the rebels was that their first voyage should be to Barnard Castle, whither the whole force should approach this day; yet he could hear of no artillery that the Earls have, other than hagbuts and a croke, but only three small brass pieces at Brancepeth. All their force, both horse and foot, wear red crosses, as well the priests as other.—Vol. XV., 73.

York, Dec. 3, 1569.—*Sir Ralph Sadler to Sir Wm. Cecil.*—If we feared nothing more than the loss of our own lives we would take the field with these untrusty soldiers; but if we should receive the overthrow, the sequel may be so dangerous, that it were better for Her Majesty to spend a great deal of treasure than we should give that advantage; wherefore so devise for our strength and furniture, that we may go to it with some security, and that with speed.—Vol. XV., 75.

York, Dec. 3, 1569.—*Thomas, Earl of Sussex, to Sir Wm. Cecil.*—Pardon me for writing what I think, but if I had been supplied with 500 horsemen and 300 shot in time, it would have ended these matters without further charge.—Vol. XV., 76.

York, Dec. 6, 1569.—*Sir Ralph Sadler to Sir Wm. Cecil.*—There are not ten gentlemen in all this country that favour her Majesty's proceedings in the cause of religion. The common people are ignorant, superstitious, and altogether blinded with the old Popish doctrine, and, therefore, so favour the cause which the rebels make the colour of their rebellion, that, though their persons be here with us their hearts are with them. And no doubt all this country had wholly rebelled at the beginning, if my Lord Lieutenant had not wisely and stoutly handled the matter. If we should go to the field with this northern force only they would fight faintly; for if the father be on this side, the son is on the other; and one brother with us and the other with the rebels. My Lord Lieutenant's charge is very great. He feeds all the noblemen and gentlemen assembled; therefore, in reason his diet is to be increased for the time of this service. Consider this, and whether of the treasure which shall come to my hands he shall have allowance thereof. He never spoke any word of it, nor seemed to make any account of the charge; but I write of myself, thinking it great reason that he should be considered, as all other noblemen supplying that place have been before.—Vol. XV., 77.

Cesawe-by-Topcliff, Dec. 12, 1569.—*Thomas, Earl of Sussex, Henry, Lord Hunsdon, and Sir Ralph Sadler to the Council.*—This day, Sir George Bowes, Robert Bowes, his brother, and divers of the gentlemen that were with him in Barnard Castle, came hither to us, by whom we understand that the soldiers in the castle daily leaped over the walls in great numbers to go to the rebels and that last Friday above 80 did so at one time; since which they have grown to such mutinies, as upon Saturday seven or eight score of them were appointed to guard the gate, and had always been of the best disposed, suddenly set it open and went to the rebels, whereupon Sir George was driven to a composition, and came away with all his men in safety. He has had long lack of drink, and was scanted of bread, and yet if his men had been true, he would have kept it until he had been relieved.—Vol. XV., 88.

Midnight, Newcastle, Dec. 19, 1569.—*Thomas, Earl of Sussex to Sir Wm. Cecil.*—I understand from Sir John Forster that the rebels, upon a skirmish between their scouts and his, returned to Hexham, and remained there this day at one o'clock; so that I shall set forward towards Hexham to-morrow, at 4 a.m., and will remove them or make them pay dearly, and follow their footsteps wheresoever they fly, over hills, wastes, or water, until I have either given them the overthrow, or put them out of the world. I have this night despatched to the Regent to hasten him to the Borders.

P.S.—*Remember to send the money which Mr. Sadler has so often written for.*—Vol. XV., 109.

Hexham, Dec. 20, 1569.—*Sir Ralph Sadler to Sir William Cecil.*—Coming to Newcastle on Monday, we heard from Sir John Forster that the rebels, having marched the day before out of Hexham, six miles towards Alnwick, were so impeached with hot pricking and skirmishing by his company that they retired back to Hexham; and, further, that they departed yesterday morning from Hexham, with 1,500 horsemen, their number having increased since coming into this country. Thereupon we came hither this night, with a number of weary horses, for the weather is extreme of frost and snow, so that we are forced to rest to-morrow, which can be no hindrance to this service, as we do not know where the rebels are. P.S.—Pecunia est nervus belli, and here be a great many calling for it, and we have not wherewith to satisfy any of them.—Vol. XV., 111.

PROCLAMATION OF THE TWO EARLS.

To all the Bailiffs and Governors of Richmond and to every of them:—These are to will and require you, and, nevertheless in the Quenes Majesties name, to command you that, ymediately upon the sight hereof, you make your repair to Stayndrope; to be there before us, the Erles of Northd. and Westd., and other the worshipfulls there, upon Monday nexte, before xii. of the clock none; bringing with you all and every such able men betwixt the age of 16 and 60 yrs of age as be within Richmond, with such furnitor of horse, armor, and weapon, as any of you have. Faile you not hereof, as you tender the settyng forwards of our proceedings, and will answer at your uttermost perell. Given at Durham, the 9th Dec., 1569. Let every man bring victualls for six days to serve with all.

Signed—T. NORTHUMBERLAND,

CHAS. WESTMORELAND.

PROCLAMATION ISSUED FOUR DAYS AFTERWARDS AT DURHAM.

Thomas, the Erle of Northd. and Charles, the Erle of Westd. do wyll and commande in the Quenes Majesties name, all and everie the tenants belonging to the *layte supposed* Bishop of Durham, that they make ready all suche rents as were due at Martynmas last, so as they may be undelayedlye payd in the accustomed place within the Exchequer of Durham before Satterdaye next, as they will answer to the contrarye at their perills.

Harl. MSS., 6990.

FORM OF PASS ISSUED BY THE EARLS.

Their shalbe to will and commaund to permytt and suffer this bearer to passe and repasse from place to place wher his busyness lyeth, without lett or truble of you or any of you, as you will answer the contrary at your perell.—From Durham, this 15th Dec., 1569.

T. NORTHD., C. WESTD.

To all and every the servants, tenents and adherents of the Erles of Northd. and Westd., ther frynds, confederats, and allies.

According to Hollinshed, "diverse excursions were made foorth of Newcastell into the Bishoprike, where the two Earles were incamped; and sundrie skirmishes chanced at that time (Dec. 14th) betwixt the two parties, though no great hurt followed thereof. The Erles yet one day came from Durham, and with their armie marched towards Newcastell. Sir John Forster and Sir Henrie Persie having intelligence thereof, issued foorth of Newcastell with all their forces, and certain peces of ordnance. They had also with them certeine bands of the souldiers of Berwike, meaning verelie to have joined battell with the Earles; Sir H. Persie shewing himself as willing and forward thereto as anie other of all the companies. At Chester Deane, midwaie betwixt Durham and Newcastell, the armies approached the one neere to the other, a small brooke running in a hollow dividing them asunder, so that there was no passage for them to convey their ordnance over and the bankes on either side being so steepe and cumbersome. Whereupon the Erles, perceiving that they were disappointed of their purpose, after some skirmishes betwixt the horsemen they returned to Durham; and from thence the next day they went to Hexham, and after being in utter despair, fled into Scotland."—*Hist. Scot.*, p. 397.

CHAPTER XI.

BACK FOR YOUR LIFE.

" Nevill is utterly dismay'd,
   For promise fails of Howard's aid;
   And Dacre to our call replies
   That he is unprepared to rise.
   My heart is sick : this weary pause
   Must needs be fatal to the cause."
         —The White Doe of Rylstone.

THE rebel garrison of Hartlepool, annoyed by the shots which the
Queen's ships sent among them, evacuated that town during the
second week of December. The Royal forces under Clinton and
Warwick met at Wetherby on the 13th.

Lord Scrope marched out of Carlisle to intercept the rebels in
their passage across the Borders, but here again the ingenuity of
their "croked bake" friend came to their assistance. Leonard
Dacre suddenly discovered a plot to seize the castle, and Scrope
thought it prudent to retire on Carlisle. "On the 17th, the
Queen's army was at Ripon. Lord Westmoreland still held the
fords and bridges of the Tees, and there, if anywhere, a stand was
to be made. He had some courage, and sufficient sense to know
that insurrection, if it meant anything, meant battle. In the Earl
of Northumberland the blood of Hotspur had cooled to the passive
temperature which could suffer, but could not act. In Percy's
weakness the hope of the rebellion ended."—*Froude,*Vol. IX. The
rebels dispersed. "Having lost that tide which taken at the full
leads on to fortune, all their after voyage was bound in shallows
and in miseries." The leaders escaped towards Hexham. "The
smaller gentlemen made for their homes, trusting to their insigni-
ficance to save their lives." In the face of biting wind the earls
pressed on towards Scotland. The ladies suffered much from the
blinding sleet that swept across the moors. Sir John Forster barred

the way to Berwick. A brief refuge was found in Naworth Castle, but Leonard Dacre offered only a frigid welcome, and the fugitives went on faintly into the deep darkness and the snow. "The iron entered into Northumberland's soul." It was indeed a pitiful sight when Thomas Percy gave his fair wife into the hands of Black Ormiston, one of the murderers of Darnley, and when Lady Northumberland's women were supported by Jock o' the Syde.

> "He is weel ken'd, Jock o' the Syde,
> A greater thief did never ryde."

But there was no help for it. They were now in the land of the outlaws. They were outlaws themselves. So they spent their Christmas "among the caves and peat holes of Harlaw." The Earl of Westmoreland was clothed "in the greasy breeks and jerkin of Jock o' the Syde to be more unknown." The Countess of Northumberland lay in Jock's house, "a hole not to be compared to any English dog-kennel." But even there they could not rest, for the betrayer was "smelling them out." Lady Westmoreland had been left behind at Brancepeth. There she prayed and wept alone, and, lest her lord, "being hard pressed should have scant tyme for prayinge," she repeated his Latin prayers after her own Protestant ones, "sayinge them fondlye." Then she asked that if he had erred he might be forgiven, and spared for the children's sake. The peace and goodwill of a holy season came upon her, but the snow drove wildly, and the wind howled dismally around the old towers of Brancepeth and Raby; and Northumberland's little children, left alone at Topcliffe, cried out for their father. And when the common people heard no ringing in of the new year they remembered how strangely the bells sounded when they rang them backwards, to raise the country, on the night of the 9th of November.

It soon became known in England that the Earls had found refuge in the house of Sir Thomas Ker of Farnihurst, near Jedburgh. Elizabeth sent a message to the Regent Murray that they must be taken and sent back. Murray was a rigid Protestant, and "one who walked uprightly." He had acted for Elizabeth against his own sister, the Queen of the Scots, when "assured that she was wicked." He was, therefore, not likely to have any sentimental eccentricities when dealing with the Northern Earls.

Northumberland was soon taken. He wished to see his wife, who had been left behind at the house of Jock o' the Syde. Hector

Armstrong of Harlaw volunteered to be his guide, and betrayed him. There was a short, sharp struggle. The borderers fought for Northumberland, but Murray's soldiers overpowered them, and brought the Earl to Jedburgh. The moss troopers carried their code of morals in the easiest possible fashion. Few things touched their conscience, and when they did it was not tender. But the troopers had their opinions as well as the Regent. They held that when a bird takes refuge in your bosom, it is an infamous thing to hold it out to the hawk. They were for killing the hawk, and petting the frightened bird. Into the question of the merits or demerits of the bird they did not enter. The hawk wanted it. The hawk should not have it. Westmoreland, the Nortons, Markenfield, Edward Dacre, Sir John Nevill of Leversege, and others had flown to the feudal Castle of Fernihurst. The Regent sent for them in the Queen's name. The laird of Fernihurst had only a hazy idea of all the majesty that lay in that name, but he had made up his mind with the stolidity of a true Scot; he would not give up "hys freends." Fernihurst was as sacred an asylum as any consecrated sanctuary. Murray set out with a numerous band of soldiers. As he approached Fernihurst his force dwindled "till it seemed like to go altogether." The Scottish people would not take the bird to the hawk. Murray turned back hastily, with a few faithful followers, and rode rapidly to Edinburgh, carrying Northumberland with him. The earl was sent to the island prison of Lochleven, where the Queen of Scots had been before him. But Murray, by his efforts to deal justly, had made himself odious in the eyes of the turbulent people he strove in vain to govern. Elizabeth was told by Lord Hunsdon (her dear Harry), that "the Scottish people do think it a great reproach, and ignominy to the whole country, to deliver any banished men to the slaughter; accounting it a liberty and freedom to all nations to succour banished men." Elizabeth thought them a little inconsistent, since they made no great stir for the return of their own banished Queen. It seemed as if they had had quite too much of her; but, however that might be, their ideas about extradition saved the life of Westmoreland.

Not being able to lay hands upon the Earl, Elizabeth executed her vengeance upon the unfortunate peasants of Durham. Sussex had served her well, as his own poor purse could testify, yet she suspected him as privy to Westmoreland's flight; and she now

M

requested him to give valid proof of his loyalty by stringing up
the rascal rebels on the green or gathering place of every disaffected
village. " The bodies must not be taken down, but abide till they
fall to pieces at the hanging place." Sussex, stung to the quick by
repeated ratings and undeserved taunts of disloyalty, resolved to
carry out his instructions thoroughly. At his bidding, Sir George
Bowes went on "circuit." The "minutes" of these "proceedings"
have not been preserved, but the trials were brief, and the executions expeditious, "the Queen being impatient of expense."

A thin paper book, preserved among the Bowes MSS., concludes
with the following summary :—

The totall nombre which joyned theymselves with the rebells within the liberties of Richmond and Richmondshyre ...	1,241
The totall nombre appointed to be executed	213
Servyinge men appointed to be executed in Richmondshyre ...	18
The totall nombre appointed to be executed in Richmondshyre...	231

A *facsimile* of the following fearful letter is given in Sharpe's
Memorials of the Rebellion. (The original is written on the last
page of the aforesaid "thin book.")

Jan. 10.—*The Earl of Sussex to Sir George Bowes.*—Sir George Bowes,—I have
sett the nombers to be executed in every towne, under the name of every towne, as
I did in your other book, which draweth nere to two hundred ; wheryn you may use
your dyscretyon in takyng more or lesse in every towne as you shall see just cause
for the offences and fitness for example, so as in the hole you passe not of all kynd
of such, the nomber of two hundered : *amongst whom you maye not execute eny that
hathe freholds, or noted welthye ; for so is the Quene's Majesties pleiser by her specyall
commandment.*—10th January, 1569.

—*Bowes' MSS.*, Vol. XIII., p. 33.   T. SUSSEX.

Another letter, of which the following is an extract, had some
time before found its way to London :—

Hexham, Dec. 25, 1569.—*Thomas, Earl of Sussex, to Sir Wm. Cecil.*—I find that
all forfeitures that by this late rebellion should grow to Her Majesty in the bishopric,
will by law fall to the bishop, which will be too great for any subject to receive ;
therefore, before I proceed against the offenders that have estates of inheritance or
great wealth, Her Majesty should either compound with the bishop for his royalties,
and keep them still in her hands, or translate him to some other bishopric, whereby
sede vacante all might grow to her.—*S. P., Dom. Eliz.* Vol. XV., 125.

Poor Pilkington made some show of resistance to this suggestion,
but the lawyers soon told him that, by virtue of the 25th Edward
III., all forfeitures of escheats by high treason, in all places and
under all circumstances, belonged to the Crown; and Elizabeth
gave him to understand that it was high time for him to "look

not after that bread which in the using perisheth, but after the immortal souls of his miserable people," from whom he had precipitately fled at the first rumours of rebellion.

Pilkington, though a prince bishop, was not a Puisset or a Bek, and therefore he set off for the North, "much murmuringe, and withal depressed." But the old priest found many "pickings," and left to his daughters fortunes, which Elizabeth described as "far too large."

Sussex was fully prepared to act out his instructions, but the Queen still distrusted him. On the 11th January, the day after he had sent his sanguinary programme to the Sheriff, he received a letter from Elizabeth saying that she "somewhat marvelled she had as yet heard of no execution done by martial law as was appointed." "If the same was not already done," he must "proceed thereto with all the expedition he might," and he must "certify her of his doings therein."

Goaded thus, all the bad blood in the veins of the Earl of Sussex was set in motion. "He went into it with a will."

The "good Constable" had also commenced his operations. Arriving at Fernihurst, as a visitor to his "most unfortunate and beloved cousin," he was welcomed by the whole household. If we are to credit the words of so infamous a man, it would appear that before the time of his arrival his "dear cousin" Westmoreland had been beguiling the hours of his enforced exile in the company of "the Laird's new wanton ladye." The Laird was jealous, and "the house was none so quiet." Constable thereupon began to be very eloquent. He reminded his cousin of his noble house and ancestral honours. He suggested that the Earl might find some better employment nearer home. He drew a picture of the Countess of Westmoreland pining in Brancepeth Castle for her absent lord. The weak Earl was moved. "The tears overhailed his cheeks abundantly." Constable waxed more eloquent. He urged the penitent to hide in a *really safe place*, his (Constable's) own house for instance. Perhaps Westmoreland thought that his kinsman manifested more anxiety than the nature of the case warranted; he certainly decided that for "the present" he would rather commit himself to the company of the "new wanton ladye," than to the care of his cousin Constable. The Laird and Lady of Fernihurst had been most kind, he said. He would not leave them without imparting some pledge of his esteem. His cousin might go, if he liked, to Brancepeth, and inform the Countess that " by God's grace he hoped to recover the Queen's favour," meanwhile "she (the Countess) should send one of her best jewels in a token to my Ladye Carr of Farneyhurst, and the fairest gelding she could get to the Laird."

Constable could get no further than this, for both Westmoreland and old Norton had resolved "it were better for them to abyde." He, therefore, went over to a house of entertainment at Jedburgh. The place was thronged with borderers. The good Constable made himself agreeable, and sat down at cards with them. They drank hard and blasphemed. They breathed the direst vengeance and hatred against spies and betrayers. They told him the story of Northumberland's capture through the treachery of Hector of Harlaw. They wished they had his head to eat at supper. Constable, admiring neither their zeal nor their appetite, went away, and wrote a letter to Sir Ralph Sadler. "He felt very uncomfortable," he said, "in fact, just like Judas. He hoped the Queen would spare his cousin's life, *after he had been trapped*, otherwise his conscience would be troubled all the days of his life. Sooner than his doings should be known, he would rather be torn every joint from another. A little money—about a thousand pounds—would be useful. He would spend it well."

The Queen was very accommodating. The money she thought might be forthcoming, and "rather for the coveringe of the enterpryse," Constable was informed that he might himself be apprehended, and be outwardly charged with offences against Her Majesty. "Her Majesty doth take your services in good and thankful part. Her Highness's pleasure is that you proceed in that you have begun. Her Majesty is very desirous to have these noysome vermin taken." So Sadler wrote.

The good Constable flushed with hope, posted off to Brancepeth, "the extremest day of wind and snow that ever he did ride in. He had a charming interview with 'Twinkes.' She was passyng joyful, and gave him a diamond ring, and a little cheyn, to be delivered to the Laird of Farneyhurst, and a 'little ring' for her own Lord."

The plot thickened, but unhappily there had been too many cooks in the royal kitchen. Dacres, of the "croked bake," once again came to the help of Westmoreland, and putting his hand into Her Majesty's broth, spoiled it.

ADDENDA.

List of Prysoners remaininge in the jayle at Durham on the Fyrste of Januarye, 1570, in the custodye of Sir George Bowes, Knyghte, Marshall.

Symond Dickby of Bedall, esquier; John Fulthorpe of Iselbeck, esq.; Henrye Johnson of Walton Head, esq.; John Markenfeyld, esq.; Asculte Cleaseby, gent.; Leonard Metcalfe of Bereparke, gent.; Robert Claxton of Wynyard, esq.; Jarrett Salven of Croxdayle, esq.; Jarrett, hys sonne; Anthony Bulmer, esq.; Robert Conyears, esq.; Robert Eden of West Auckland, gent.; George Gray of Branspeth, gent.; Oswald Ogle of Branspeth, gent.; Christopher and Marmaduke Norton, Cuthbert Claxton, Wylliam Claveringe, gent.; &c.

The list includes six gentlemen of Northumberland's household, 28 of his servants, and 12 tenants. Three household servants and 50 tenants of Westmoreland; three servants of Christopher Nevill, and one of Cuthbert Nevill, eight of Sir John Nevill, 19 of Thos. Markenfeld, 14 of Rich. Norton, with "sundry other gentlemen," and "39 retainers of none."—*Bowes' MSS.*, Vol. XIII., and *S.P., Dom. Elis.* Add., Vol. 17, 1.

Several of these names occur also in the list of prisoners at Carlisle.

A COPPIE OF SOME LETTERS WCH WERE FOUND IN RABIE CASTLE AFTER THE REBELLION, TO SHOWE THE FASHION OF THOSE TIMES.

To the ryghtt onerabayll and my very good lord and master, my lord off Wyastmorland, yeve thys wt sped.

I have resavyd yor Lordcheps later, wherin I do parsave yor Lordchep's rateryn (return) will nott be so soyn as I wolld wyche god ytt wyer: for thys shortt days and yll wyther henders the wyrkemayn sore, so thatt ytt gose nott so fast forwyard as I wolld wyshe ytt dyd: allso her ys bott ij qtrs off wyahtt wyntyng v pakes, and I knowe off no more to be had, and for maltt ther came in iiij qrs, and that ys all brawd (brewed) wher to have ane more I knowe nott; and all the moyne (money) I had will be gone yes wyke in housolld charges, and other neseserys; wherfor I beshe yor gud Lordchep I may know yor plesor, and I shall be gllad to acoumplys ytt to the otermost off my small pour, as my bounded dowte ys to do wth the hallpe of God, whome have yor Lordchep in hes bllysed kepyng. From yor Lordcheps maner off. Kerkbemorsyd.—ix off november, be the yll hand off yor Lorcheps pour servntt, OSWYNE OGLE.

To the right honourable Lord, my Lord the Erle of Westmland.—I comaunde me unto yor Lordship, And accordyng unto yo. Lordship comaundement for propayryng for such stuff as yor Lordship shuld occupy At yor home comyng nowe. As for wyne, my Lord, their cane none be gotten sayvyng one hogissr heid, whiche was gotteyn at Newcastill of reid wyne, which I trust yor Lorship will thynke wonderous deir. And also my Lord, as for wheit and mawte and other fresshe decatis, what appon yor awne and of other Provision, I trust ye shall be well servied, besuchyng yor Lordship that ye wold be content for to send over yor Clerke of your kechyng and your Coke for sleyyng of suche beveiss and muttons as must be occupyed at yor Lordships home comyng. Lowed be God their is any other svice that yor Lordship wold comaunde me withall, I besuch yor Lordship that I knaw yor ferther pleasoure theirin, writtyn at Brauncepath, xviijth Septembre, by yor faithful servant, R. CLAXTON.

The following plaintive letter from *Lady Westmoreland to the Earl of Sussex* will be read with interest :—

Good my Lord,—Have consideration of my desolate and comfortless estate, lackyng both quietness of mynd and helth, neyther beyng able to flee to any place, nor knowyng where to have any refuge ; and besides all other miserys, I am in great fere of the cruelty of the rude souldiers, and therefore, albeit my trust is that your lordship and other of the nobilitie wyll not, of your honours, deale otherwyse with me than semely : yet I most hartely beseche your good lordship that such order may be given that neyther I nor my children, nor such poore servants as are left about me, may be put in fere, or have any bodely harm. And as for this house and the stuff thereyn, and lykewyse the goods of such poor tenants and servants as are left about me, the same are and shall be at commandment But I beseech your good lordship that some way may be appointed to save and defend the same from common spoil, and that none thereof be taken but by direction and appointment ; for other-wyse shall innocent persons be utterly undone, and constrained to beg, or starve for hunger. Thus trusting, although your lordship has come to be my lord's mortal enemy in the field, you will not seek revenge on me and my poor children, I leve to troubble your lordship.

Your lordship's poor and unfortunate cousin,

JANE WESTMORELAND.

From Branspeth, this 16th day of December, 1569.

Howard Collection, 281.

Hexham, Dec. 21, 1569.—*Thomas Cecil to his father, Sir William Cecil.*—I have twice lost the opportunity of writing being commanded to remove with certain light horsemen to Brancepeth, to protect Lady Westmoreland from the spoiling of our own horsemen, that did nothing but spoil and rob in all places they came to. I found my Lady a marvellous sorrowful creature, whose misfortune is much pitied, being altogether undeserved. Nothing is more feared than the escaping of the two Earls, yet their flying has so discredited them where they were well-beloved, that should they assay the like wicked enterprise again they will be deceived of most of them that would otherwise have ventured their lives.—*Abstract, State Papers, Dom. Eliz.* Vol. XV., 114.

Hexham, Dec. 22, 1569.—*Thomas, Earl of Sussex, Henry Lord Hunsdon, and Sir Ralph Sadler to the Queen.*—We hear that the rebel Earls, with their principal confederates and the Countess of Northumberland, fled to Liddesdale on the night of the 20th with 100 horse, and there remain, under the conduct of Black Ormston, one of the murderers of Lord Darnley, and John of the Side, and the Lord's Jock, two notable thieves of Liddesdale.

Hexham, Midnight, Dec. 22nd, 1569.—*Sussex to Sir William Cecil.*—" I have intellygens of suche as were present, and sawe it, that the next morning after the erles came into Lydysdale, Martyne Elwood, and dyvers others of the pryncypall men of Lydysdale, dyd rayse ther force agenst the erles, Black Ormston, and the reste of ther company, and offered the fyght ; so as both partyes were lyghted, and in the end Marten Elwood sayd to Ormston he should be sory to enter deadly feude with him by bloodshed, but he would charge him and the reste before the Regent, for keeping of the rebells of England, if he did not put them out of the country ; and that yf they were in the country after the next day he would do his worste agaynst them, and all that mayntained them. Whereupon the erles were dryven to leave

Lydesdall, and to fly to one of the Armstrongs, upon the batable, or the borders betwyn Rydsdale and England. The same daye the Lydesdale men stole my Lady of Northumberlands horse, and her ij wemens horses and x other horses; so as when the erles went away, they left her, and all the reste that had lost their horses, on foote, at John of the Sydes House, a cottage not to be compared with any doge kennel in England. Such is their present mysery; and at their departing from her, they were not 50 horse, and my L. of Westmorland changed his cote of plate and sword, with John of the Syde to be the more unknowen."

Two days afterwards, Lord Hunsdon writes:—"The erles rebelles and their principall confederates (as I here) do lurke and hide themselfes in the woodes and deserts of Lyddesdale; but, if they tary on the Borders there, Sir Jo. Forster is in good hope to have som of them, or it be long. The erles have changed their names and apparell, and have made themselffes lyke to the outlaws of Liddersdale. We have to presume and to suspect gretely, that they shall receyve som helpe and comforte of the L. Hume and of the Carres in Tividale; but the greatest feare is of their escape by sea, eyther on the este or on the west coaste. Order is given here to the capteynes of the 2. Mates shippes, to attende well on the este coaste, and if you have done anything for the west coast, they shall the more hardly escape."

7th of January.—*Sir John Forster to Cecil.*—"Treuth it is, the Earl of Westmoreland presently lying in the overmost chamber in Farnyhurst Tower, and my Lady of Northumberland is lodged in the lowest chamber. Ther is in the erles companie Francis Norton and other six of the erles servants, the Welberries, Henry Ridley, and others; old Norton, Markenfield, Egremont Radcliffe, Swinborne, and Tempest. They are all presently with the Lord of Buckleugh, at Branxham."

Hexham, Dec. 22, 1569.—*Sir Ralph Sadler to Sir Wm. Cecil.*—You will perceive by our common letter what a fond and foolish end the rebels have made of their traitorous rebellion. They always fled before us after we came within 12 miles of them, and we followed as fast as we might without rest; nevertheless they escaped, which they might easily do in this waste and desolate country. We have now to devise how they may be trapped in Scotland.—*Addenda*, Vol. XV., 119.

Henry, Lord Scrope, to the Earl of Sussex.—I shall do my diligence for apprehension of Egremont Ratcliffe, who is in the Harlow Woods, with John of the Side, and Rowy Forster; Sir John Nevill and Ralph Conyers are also there.—Carlisle, 30th Dec., 1569.

The Earl of Sussex and Sir R. Sadler to Sir John Forster.—My Ladie of Westmerlande hathe made greate suete of us, to have licence to send a letter to her husbande, which we have perused, and finde that there is nothing in it but an advise to submitte himself to the Q. Ma. marcie. And althoughe we thinke little fruet will come thereof, yet for that we maye use the same to gett us some certen intelligence wher the Erle doth presentlye remayne, we have agreed to the sending of her letter, and do send the same to you enclosed, praying you to chuse suche a sufficient messenger for the carying therof to the Erle, as maye at his retorne bring you certen intelligence, where th Erle and all others of the rebelles remaine. And if th Erle will write anie answer, you shall will your servaunt to receive it and to bring it to you, and you shall send it to us, to th ende we may consider whether it be fitt to be delivered or deteyned, and so advertise the Q. Ma. of the hole. And so we bid you hartily well to fare.—Jan. 11th.

Countess of Westmoreland to her Husband.—I thought I could not discharge my duty towards you till I sued for leave to send you these few lines, to put you in remembrance of what you were always inclined to, had not the greatness of your offence to her Majesty been such as abashed you to come to her presence, and made you despair ever to obtain her pardon. I wish you most earnestly, as I am fully persuaded you will, to submit yourself, and to do it with speed, and crave her gracious pardon, lest your necessity be such as you shall be forced, being in a foreign land, to stand in need of their succour of whom perhaps you shall receive no benefit without incurring further danger: I mean in entering some practices that may aggravate her displeasure and cut off hope of recovering her favour. Therefore, my Lord, in good time perform your bounded duty to Her Majesty, and forget not the care that you ought to have to me and your poor children, now desolate and void of help, without the merciful clemency of the Queen, to which as I have often heard you say, she was naturally disposed. Do not fear, though your fault be very great, that her inclination can be so suddenly transformed from that, upon your submission and repentance, you shall find her accustomed mercy to remain, trusting she will consider that, as you have passed a few weeks in offending her, you have, I hope, many years to pass in her service, where I think you would willingly venture your life. As soon as I receive answer from you, I will not omit the duty of a true wife in being an humble suitor to Her Majesty for your life, lands, and liberty, that I may see your joyful return, and that she may once, by employing your service, find the true faith in you towards her which, for your late offence, I fear she will hardly believe. God preserve you in health, and bring you shortly to a more safe and quiet estate.

Henry, Lord Hunsdon, to the Earl of Sussex.—The Earl of Westmoreland is openly received and maintained at Fernihurst, where in outward show he was never merrier; and Swinburne and two others are with him. Richard Norton and two or three others with him are at Lord Buccleugh's at Branksom.—Berwick, 11th Jan., 1570.

Charles, Earl of Westmoreland, to his Wife.—I marvel that you, knowing my mind, besides duty, so well bent towards the Queen, should write so earnestly to me, as though I should both forget my duty towards her, which I will never do, and also you and my children. Which way has it been possible for me to send to you before? Now that I send, I pray you deal first with advice of Lords Sussex, Rutland, Hunsdon, and Sir John Forster, to know which way they think it best for me to make my humble submission to the Queen. My offence has been great in breaking the laws of the realm, yet not so heinous towards her own person, but if she be gracious unto me, I trust I might do her service in any place where she shall command me, to recompense this fault. Pray deal with Lord Sussex and the rest, that I may receive word from you and them by the last of this month; after that, God knows what shall become of me, for there will be no longer abiding here, for divers respects which I dare not write.

P.S.—Commend me to *Twinkes* and all her little ones.—*Add.* Vol. XVII., 37.

This letter was *inspected* by the "authorities." Hence its harsh tone. The postcript would be understood by the Countess.

Carlisle, Jan. 24, 1570.—*Henry, Lord Scrope, to Sir Wm. Cecil.*—I have here enclosed a letter from the Earle of Westmoreland in Scotland to my wife for that neither she nor I will have any doeings with him.

Syster Scrope,—As I have alwayes in tyme passed bene behouldenge unto you for your good wyll, so nowe I thinke myself most bounde unto you that doo nowe shew your good wyll unto me in thys myne adversytie. I praye you that you wyll send me some newes out of Englande, and some good wourde if you can, of my Four Graces, and of our oulde frend that roughte the plene and whyte sylver cheyne, which you sent my *Twinkes* for a token. I pray you that I may hear from you eyther by wrytinge or els by some trustie frende or servante; and I shall send you some wourde by them againe, more at large. *I truste that though your husbande be the Quenes Majesties officer yeat he wyll shewe some good wyll to me hys poure oulde frende*, for dyverse respectes which I dare not nowe wryte. Farewell good syster, and I truste to God, yeat for all that we shal be as merry as wee weare when you weare named Angelyca.—Your assured brother,　　　　C. WESTMERLAND.

State Papers, Dom. Elis. Add. Vol. XVII., 45.

[Henry, Lord Scroop, of Bolton, Governor of Carlisle, and Warden of the West Marches, married Margaret, third daughter of Henry, Lord Surrey, and sister to the Duke of Norfolk and the Countess of Westmoreland.]

Durham, Jan. 12th, 1570.—*Sir Ralph Sadler to Wm. Cecil.*—I send you herewith a long letter from Robert Constable, servant to my Lord of Leicester, and one of them that helped to steal his plate. He came to me and told me if I thought good he would go into Scotland, and doubted not but he could learn where they were, and entrap some of them, that they might be apprehended. I told him if he could do so, he would do Her Majesty a service that she would not leave unrewarded; upon this he has been in Scotland, and had conference with the Earl of Westmoreland and other rebels, as you perceive by his letter which I send you. I still animate him to proceed, and bring himself into credit with the rebels, the better to effect his purpose, which he has promised to do.—*Add.* Vol. XVII., 22.

12th January, 1570.—*Robert Constable to Sir R. Sadler.*—*Extract:* Then I pray'd my Lord (Westmoreland), that miserable estate that he had lewdly brought himself to, and to seke out the best way howe to recover himself again, and not to run wilfully upon his utter destruction to the overthrow of his house, which hath been honorable and of great antiquity, and never spotted till nowe by this woful fact. He looked at me, and took all patiently that I spoke; the tears overhalled his cheeks abundantly. I could not forbear weeping to see him sodenly fall to repentance. Neither of us could speak to another for a long time; at last he wiped his cheeks, and pray'd me to follow him. He went to his chamber in the tower, and commanded his men forth, and lookt to the door himself, and thus he began: "Cosin Robert, you are my kinsman, nere comed forth of my house, and one whom I duly love and trust. I must confess I have as lewdly overset myself as any man could do; not the less I pray you, let me have your counsel, what way you think were lyklyest for me to obtaine my pardone and favour of the Queen's Majestie." Then he told me that my Lady of Northumberland had received a favourable letter, and a frendly, from my Lords Hunsdon, willing her to come to him, and she should have all the friendship he could shew, and willed her not to doubt that the Queene's Majestye, who never was cruel to any, would begin to shew her cruelty upon her, being a gentlewoman. Howbeit, he would not promise her pardon, because he understood not the Queen's pleasure therein; and my Lord thought great unkindness, saying, that neither my Lord Lieutenant, nor my Lord of Hunsdon, nor my Lord Rutland, nor no nobleman nor friend that he hath in England, never one wrote to him, nor sent him any message yet since he came into Scotland, &c., &c. Then he asked me if I durst carry him a token to my Lady his weif: I promest, if the Lords and gentilmen were gone from Durham, I durst do that. He took a little ring off his finger, and pray'd me to deliver it to her, which she knew, and to will her to take no care nor thought for him, for all his care was for her and his children, which grieved him much more to consider the misery that he left them in, than any danger that colde happen to his own body, and that he hoped, by God's grace, to recover the Queen's favour again for all this; and to will my Lady to send by me one of her best jewels in a token to my Lady Carr of Farneyhurst, and the fairest gelding she could get to the Lord, because my Lord puts them to great charges, and they will take no money.—*Sadler Papers.*

Sir Robert Constable to Sir Ralph Sadler.—The Lord of Farnehurst is both poore and covetous, there is one there as covetous as he that may persuade him to do anything for profit, that he will say he may be lacless. Now what a golden hook may do, to a covetous man, if it be right laid, possibly he will bite, and it may catch him; besides that the Lord will soone be wary, with the cost he is at, and some part throw the jelousie he is entered in with my Lord of Westmoreland, and his (Fernyhurst's) new wanton Ladye.

I kyss'd my Lord's ryng and gave it to her (Lady Westmoreland). She was passyng joyeful. I told her how long I had wated to come to her speedyly; she excused her, and not the less asked me forgiveness divers times.

After she had enquired all things of my Lord, she told me that Sir J. Constable had been with her, from my Lord Lieutenant, and wylled her to wryte to my Lord her husband, and persuade him to make hys humble submission to the Queen's Majesty, both to win again the favour of God, of his natyve Prince, and all hys land and goodes again, which otherways were utterly lost, without hope of recovery; with such further instructions, by word of mouth, for me to say to my Lord, as is too long for me to wryte, wherein she hath shewed herself to be the faithful servant of God, a dutiful subject to the Queen's Majestye, an obedient, careful, loving wyfe to her husband, and for rypeness of wit, redyness of memory, and plain and pithy utterance of her words, I have talked with many, but never with her lyke. I have sent you herein enclosed a little cheyn, and a ring, with a diamond, to be delivered to the Laird of of Ferneyhurst; a tablet to the Lady, and a little ryng to my Lord.—*Sadler Papers.*

[It would appear that Sir Robert Constable was "overwhelmed with heped upp detts," and the estates which should have been his were held by the Crown, in consequence of the treasonable doings of his relatives, in the *Pilgrimage of Grace.* The unworthy conduct he pursued towards his cousin Westmoreland was probably the price fixed by Cecil for the restoration of his lapsed estate. Curiously enough his crest was a ship, and his motto,

> As to the ship is anchor and cable,
> So to thy friend be thou, Constable.

But Sir Robert Constable's principles must have been altogether very lax, for he married his second wife whilst the first was still living.]

CHAPTER XII.

VENGEANCE.

"Her grace she turned her round about,
　And like a royall queene shee swore,
I will ordayne them such a breakfast
　As never was in the North before.
　　*　　*　　*　　*
　　—Full many a gallant wight
　They cruellye bereav'd of life :
·And many a childe made fatherlesse,
　And widowed many a tender wife."
　　　　　　　—Rising in the North.

THE work of butchery went on steadily in the County of Durham. On the 23rd of January, Sir George Bowes loosely calculated that he had put to death about six hundred persons. Sussex had disposed of a great many more, and the people were now in " marvellous fear." Sir Thomas Gargrave wrote to tell the Queen that if it went on much longer " many places would be left naked and without inhabitant." A commission was appointed to try the principal rebels at York. The Court consisted of the Earl of Sussex, Lord Hunsdon, Sir Gilbert Gerrard (the Attorney-General), and Sir Thomas Gargrave. The following notes will give the reader a pretty clear idea of the way in which justice was meted out to the offenders :—

Henry Johnson.—He is very simple, was abused by his wife, who is Norton's daughter, and he hath made a state of his lands to her at the tyme of his marriage; so as by his life the Queen shall have his lands, and by his death his wife shall presently have them according to the state.

John Markenfeld.—Is very young, under twenty, and was attainted onely to bring his title to his brothers lands (if he have any) to the [Queen]; and it was not meant he should dye, for that he hath no lande, and is within the compass of the commission for compounding.

Astolphe Cleisby.—He being appointed for the first exequicon, was stayed at the request of the Lord Hunsdone, for such cawses as his lordship writed to Mr. Secretary.

Robert Claxton.—He was servant to the Earl of Westmerland, whom he followed in this accon. He hath many children, and hath married a widow, that hath children. He hath ever before this time been of honest behaviour, and is greatly lamented in the country; and as it is credibly informed, his land was assured to his wife at his marriage, so the Quene shall lose by his deathe.

Rauf Conyers.—He was servant to the Earl of Westmerland. He is of good religion, and, as it is affirmed, ther is some assurance made in his fathers life of his lands, whereby the Quene shold lose by his death.

Letter from the Queen to the 'Earl of Sussex, Lord Hunsdon, and Sir Thomas Gargrave.—We are pleased, that Henry Johnson, for his simplicity, and John Markenfeld, for his youth, and Ascolph Cleasby, at ye request of you, our cousyn of Hunsdon, shall be forborne from execution. And for the other four, Metcalf, Lambert, Claxton, and Conyers, we are in nothing moved to spare them, for any respect of the profit that might come to us by ther life; and yet knowing not of ye manner and circumstance of ther offence, how they have therein exceded in any mallice, we will not expressly command that they all shall suffer deth; but, although we thynk it good that som furder example be showed, we refer the same to your own judgment."

It fell out fortunately for Astolphe Cleasby that, at the time appointed for his *exequicon*, he happened to be acquainted with the three daughters of Lord Coniers; and Harry, son of Lord Hunsdon, being in love with one of these young ladies, besought his father to let Cleasby live that " he might help him withal." The poor boy was actually on his road to Knavesmire, there to be hanged and drawn, when he was suddenly summoned back to the small frivolities of earth. Lord Hunsdon's explanation of this singular occurrence is far too good to be omitted. He writes from York to Cecil:—

Sir,—The cause why I have requyred the stay of Askold Clesby, ys specyally, bycause he ys one that may doo very muche with one of my Lord Conyarsys dawghters and ayars (heirs) whom I am about to gett for my sunn Harry; whyche

wyll the better be browght to passe by hym, beyng yn grete credytt with all the
systers. He ys besyds no notoryus offendar, as ytt ys well knowne, and was followde
more of mallyce than otherwyse. He hathe nott one foote of land, and therfor good
Mr. Secretary move hyr Majestie for hys pardon; and so havying wrytten to youe
thys mornynge, I comytt ye too God.

What a revelation does this quaint note give us of the little
loves, and hopes, and fears, lying behind the more stirring scenes
of sixteenth century history! To help her dear Harry in an affair
of the affections was a cheap reward, which Elizabeth could well
afford to bestow. So the gallows were kept dangling before the
eyes of this poor boy, until "the Lord Conyarsys dawghter and
ayar" was gotten " for my sunn Harry."

There is a significant passage in Cleasby's will, proved in
1586 :—"To the care of my good Kate Conyers I leave my
daughter Elizabeth."

From York justice moved on her wondrous way to Durham.
The Protestant priests of that city were called upon to give an
account of their conduct on the day when the *oulde religion* was
re-established by the Earls.

George Cliff,[*] prebendary, aged 57, deposed (19 April, 1570)—That he was in
the Cathedral Church in the morning, at such service as was then done, on S.
Andrew's day (30th Nov.) ; and he was there on the Saturday next after (3rd Dec.)
at the even song, in his accustomed habit, and also on Sunday after. On 30th Nov.
one Robert Peirson, priest, sung mass at the high altar, at which mass he was
present, in the quire, and heard him ; he did not sing at it, nor look at the elevation,
and sat still in his stall ; and bowed not, nor knocked, nor kneeled, nor used any
open fact, nor reverend gesture.

Will. Headlam, curate of St. Nicholas, aged sixty-five. He was in the parish
church of St. Nicholas, the 10th day of December, being Saturday, and coming into
the quire he found Sir Robert Peirson saying mass, whereat he was not contented,
and tarried not, "but went his waies ;" he was at no other mass in any other place.

Oliver Ashe, curate of St. Giles, aged forty-one. Went to the Cathedral when
the said Holmes was at the " *hynder end*" of his sermon, and afterwards, he, the
said Holmes went to mass, and, when the sacring bell rung, he looked towards the
priest, but he could not discern the elevation ; whereupon he looked up to Mr.
Bromley, then in the loft over the quire door, and smiled at him.

William Smith, minor canon, aged 54. He was content and willing to do the
things herein confessed, being a "simple man and easye to be seduced ;" as for
books or any ornaments he knoweth not where they are, or from whence they came.

Robert Hutchinson, slater, aged 26. Helped to set up two altars in the cathedral,
at the commandment of Mr. Cuthbert Nevill, who sent for Henry Younger and him
to the castle, and kept them therein one day, because they refused to deal or meddle

*In the following year he was presented to the living of Brancepeth by pr. of the
Lady Adeline Nevill, which living he held till 1584.

with setting up of any altars; that he threatened them still to continue there, and that they at last consented. Various persons helped—rolling and lifting the stones into the church. The priest of Brancepeth was the overseer of all their working first and last, till the altars were finished, one being the high altar, the other set beside the clock. Many who assisted were soldiers. His labour was not cheerful, but sore against his will.

John Oliver, labourer, aged 60. He worked under Hutchinson and Younger in setting up the two altars; was commanded by Mr. Cuthbert Nevill, upon pain of hanging, to labour with them. Mr. Cuth. Nevill and Sir Rob. Peirson knew him to have been a workman and labourer at Brancepath.

. *Henry Younger*, of Durham, slater, aged thirty-six. He was commanded by Mr. Cuth. Nevill, and one Holmes, Mr. Grey, and the priest of Brancepath, to set up five altars; whereof he helped to set up two. He "gat him away" to his mother's at Egglescliffe, and there tarried. What he did was "sore against his will." He was in prison, fast in the castle, two days and one night, and sore threatened, or ever he consented.

Rowland Blenkinsop, minor canon, æt. 69. Is heartily sorry for his conduct; and was forced by the commandment of "my Lord of Northumberland to come to the church and do all that he did."

William Watson, chaplain to the chapel of the blessed Mary Magdalen, aged sixty. He took holy water, as others did. Is sorry, "and never intendeth to do the like again, by God's grace."

John Baxter, rector, So. Bailey, æt. seventy-four. Heard Holmes' sermon, and, when he gave the absolution, he kneeled down among the others; and afterwards, by the motion of Sir John Peirson, he came to Holmes in Peirson's chamber, where he was reconciled at last, and that was by the command of Mr. Cuthbert Nevill.

Tho. Richmond, church-warden. St. Margaret's, aged 60. He was especially commanded to do what he did by Mr. C. Nevill. He for fear obeyed, and not for any love of mass and mattens.

Robert Cornefurth, of Gilligate, tanner, says, that on the place green, Holmes and Mr. Nevill called him to them, to charge the church-wardens to burn the books.

Elizab., wife of Hen. Rutter, of Durham, says, she was delivered of a woman child in Elvet, the xvth day of November, being the morrow after the rebells left. Her child was born on Tuesday, and lay unchristened till Friday fortnight.

Hen. Rutter, her husband, says the child was born upon a Tuesday, the morrow after the Earles rose; he was sent for, to wait on his master, the Earl of Westmorland, on Wednesday, at Darlington. He has heard that Sir Robert Peirson, curate of Brancepath, christened his child, by commandment of Lady Westmarland.

John Lilborn, of Sheldon, gentleman, aged 31. He rent the Bible in pieces, in the church of St. Andrew, Auckland; and is heartily sorry therefore, and hath bought another Bible at his own charge.

Will. Harding, minor canon, was once at matins, and once at evensong; Cuthbert Nevill reviled him, saying he was of wicked living; and also two soldiers came to his chamber, and commanded him to come to the church, or else it would be worse with him.—*Depositions*, 1565-1573, *Durham Consistory Court.*

But as the days lengthened the northern sky did not clear for Elizabeth. Westmoreland was still free, and apparently enjoying himself. Leonard Dacres found that, notwithstanding all his precaution, his name had become hopelessly mixed up with rebellion. Compromising letters were discovered by Cecil's all-searching eye. The Queen was mightily indignant to find that Dacres had outwitted her with his oily tongue. She bade Sussex to take him alive. Sussex said he could not; Naworth Castle being too strong for his force. Elizabeth again bade him do as he was told. Lord Scrope was written to, and replied briefly that the Cumberland men would not fight *against* but *for* Dacres. Hunsdon complained that his men had not yet received their wages. Westmoreland waxing bold, threatened to burn Newcastle to the ground. In company with Buccleuch, he constantly harried Northumberland, "driving away great bodies of cattle." Rumour was rife that Dacres, Westmoreland, and Buccleuch would soon join their forces, and carry everything before them. Beacon fires blazed on every hill, the name of Dacres was in every man's mouth, but still the Queen sent neither soldiers nor money to support the loyal garrisons. Driven to desperation, Hunsdon left Berwick, on the 19th February, with 1,500 men, and met the Borderers beside the river Gelt. "They gave the proudest charge he ever saw," but the aim of his Berwickshire men was so true, and their front so firm that ere long Dacres "rode hard for Liddlesdale." The Queen was delighted. "It likes me not a little," wrote she, "that with a good testimony of your faith there is seen a stout courage of your mind that more trusted to the goodness of your quarrel than to the weakness of your numbers." *Beatus servus ille, quem, quum venerit dominus ejus, invenerit ita faciente.* I doubt not whether that the victory was given me more joyed me, or that you, my Harry, were by God appointed the instrument of my glory."—*Border MSS.*

She even promised "to increase his livelihood," but forgot about it afterwards.

I am carefully keeping along the line of history, so far as I can find it in documentary evidence. Elizabeth was undoubtedly a wonderful woman, and a great queen, but her strong points do not show themselves in the story of the Northern Rising.

Dacres fled to Scotland. He was received and honoured, and sat in "Cownsell" with Westmoreland, and with the rest of the lords. Throughout the spring Scotland maintained the rebels, and the spirit of revolt spread. The nobles assembled at Linlithgow informed Sussex that if he entered the country in a hostile manner they would not allow it; his mistress might not take upon herself to order the realm of Scotland. But on .the 17th April, 4,000 English soldiers marched through Northumberland. They burned Kelso, and passed up Teviotdale, "leaving neither tower nor town" undestroyed. Ninety strong castles, houses, and dwelling places, with three hundred towns and villages, were overwhelmed in an almost unopposed campaign.—*Froude*, Vol. IX.

Still Scotland shielded the refugees. Westmoreland, the Countess of Northumberland, Leonard Dacres, and the Nortons remained until August; but, as Elizabeth made their extradition a *sine qua non* in any treaty with Scotland, they then deemed it prudent to embark at Aberdeen for Flanders. On the representation of the Duke of Alva, King Philip of Spain allowed the Earl of Westmoreland a pension of fifty pounds per month.

"Le Conte de Westmorlant est aussi icy, en grande payne pour s'estre saulve avecq bien peu de moyen. En est personnaige de telle qualite qu'il merite respect, mais comme le moyen est par deca si petit, est ne scay l'intention de vostre majeste je la supplie tres humblement comme, j'ai fait du passe qu'elle me veulle advertir comme elle entend que a l'advenir je m'y doibve regler, et s'il luy plaist faire quelque bien principalement, a gens de telle ou aultre principale estoffe, qu'elle soit contente de la pourveoir de dela, piusque de ce costel icy, nous n'avons assez pour furnir seulement l'ordinaire."—*Alva to Philip*, Nov. 7, 1570.

Pensions were also allowed to other refugees.

"Los Caballeros Ingleses que residian en dichos estados con pensiones del rey Felipe, eran los siguientes Conde de Westmorland, 200 florines mensuales; Condessa de Nortumberland, 200; Leonardo d'Acre, 100; Egremond Radichiffe (Radcliffe, half brother to Sussex), 60; Richard Northon, 56; Francisco Northun, 36; Sanson Northon, 20; Christobal Namill (Christopher Nevill), 40; Entembert Nemill (Cuthbert Nevill), 40; Tomas Marchinfied (Markenfield), 36.—*Conzales* p. 131, *quoted by Sir Cuthbert Sharpe.*

ADDENDA.

Lord Hunsdon writes on the 31st January, 1570, *to Cecil.*—This nyght hathe Farneherst, and Bukklew, and Jhonston, with my Lord of Westmerland byn yn the myddel marche wythe 300 horse, as I am thys mornyng credably advertysed, and have byn as far as Morpett; but what spoyle they have dune I am not yett seure of, but ye may be seure yt ys too muche.

York, 1st Feb., 1570.—*Sir Thomas Gargrave to Sir W. Cecil.*—Yt ys here reportyd, that th Erle of Westmerland hayth, with a greet nomber of Scottes and rebelles, mayd a rode into Northumberland; and hayth burnyd houses, slane men, and taken prisoners. Yf this be trew, I doute not but yt ys certefyed to the Court. As before, I have wryttyn to your honor, I wold the propertye of the rebelles landes were altered; for that wold make the tenauntes and people depende upon the newe bandes, and alyenate theyr myndes frome the olde, and take awaye hope to have gaines at theyr handes.

Feb. 6.—*Sir George Bowes to Sir Thomas Gargrave.*—The Byshopryge is not so well, for I am advertised by a Justice of Peace that Xpofer Neyvell ys in or aboute Branspythe secretlye; and that he goyeth about to move new styrrs, or by secrett or open meanes, to kill my brother or me. And yt ys generally reported that theyr ys greater provysion maid at Branspeth then is convenyent; whereby the the people of that countrye ar much abasshed, and the evill boldened. But I intend to keape on my jorney and be at Durham of Wednesday; having with me many gentlemen, my frends, with the nombre of a hundreth horse, or ny there aboute.— *Bowes MSS.* Vol. XVIII., p. 13.

York, Feb. 4, 1570.—*Sir Thomas Gargrave to Sir Wm. Cecil.*—The Lairds of Buccleugh and Fernihurst, with the Earl of Westmoreland and Chris. Nevill, daily burn and spoil in Northumberland, and should be resisted. The Countess of Westmoreland should be removed, for resort to her does harm."—*Abstract S. P.* Vol. XVII., 69.

Berwick, Feb. 7, 1570.—*Lord Hunsdon to Sir Wm. Cecil.*—I understood my Lord of Westmoreland meant to surprise Newcastle, and it being easy to be done, and hearing he had been at Harbottle, and nearer, with 2,000 horse, and burnt divers houses, I repaired hither to take order with the Mayor for the better looking to the town. Now they keep watch upon the walls every night, and have made certain turnpikes without the gates, and bring the keys every night to the Mayor. Since my coming, Dr. Pilkinton and others have been with me, and reported that the Earl of Westmorland has threatened to take certain prebendaries and others of Durham, and hang them, whereof they are so afraid that they are ready to go out of the country; also, that the Earl's tenants are warned to be ready at an hour's warning. Some hold that he has been at Brancepeth of late, and say that there is great brewing there. The honest sort of the Bishopric, who are very few, are much perplexed, as they have nobody to repair to, whatever need should happen. The Bishop is in London, my Lord Ewre in Yorkshire, and will not dwell any more in the Bishopric; and Sir George Bowes and his wife gone to York, as they dare not tarry in the country, so that there is not one gentleman left but Mr. Hilton. Surely some man of credit should lie sometimes in the Bishopric, and sometimes at Newcastle, and so be both a surety to the town, a stay to the Bishopric, and a bridle to this part of Northumberland, which is as ill as the worst; as long as his (the Earl of Westmoreland's) wife lies at Brancepeth or in this country, he shall neither want relief nor intelligence.—*Add.* Vol. XVII., 76.

O

York, Feb. 8, 1570.—*Sir Thos. Gargrave to the Earl of Sussex.*—I hear that victuals are providing at Brancepeth, and that Chris. Nevill is resorting thereabouts, to move new strife; if so it is well that our troops are ready, but many of the horse will not be good.—*Add.* Vol. XVII., 81.

Feb. 9th.—*Sir George Bowes to Sir Thomas Gargrave.*—But sewer the people be not soo good here as in Rychmondshyre, for theye be moral lowse; soo that if I had not comed, ytt had bene dowtefull what wolde have folowed. Theys brewts was much forthered by the soden departure of the L. Ewrye, the Deane and some be gone from Durham, with there wyfes; and Nevell was here, and may be, but not in any showe of force. But I wyshe that the howse at Branspeth were skayled, for yt standythe perelowslye.—*Bowes MSS.* Vol. II., p. 43.

Hampton Court, April.—*The Queen to Sir Nich. Bacon, Lord Keeper.*—Warrant to the Sheriff of Durham to receive the said men—have them drawn on hurdles to the place of execution, hanged, cut down alive, their bowels cut out and burnt, beheaded and quartered, and their quarters placed over the gates and most public parts of the city."—Vol. XVIII., 40.

York, 10th Oct., 1573.—*Evidence concerning the Rebellion furnished by Sir George Bowes to Lord Huntingdon.*—They everywhere, and in every church and chapel where they came, pulled asunder the service books, paraphrases, and other books skripture, translated into Englishe. But the first spoile of goods they comitted was of the Lord Latymer; whose house of Snape they entred by force, and tooke from thence many articles of great valewe, as yt ys supposed; yet dyd not deal with any hangings or beds, but took all his horses and cattle, goinge only upon his parkes and grounds at Snape aforesayd. They did spoil Mr. Calverley, Chancellor of Durham, of all his moveables, Bartram Anderson, Francis Bainbridge, and Thomas Middleton, esquires, besides Franklin of Cocken; and also thrashed most of their corn. They did spoil all my house and grounds of Streatlam, the Isle, South Cowton, Stockton, and Evenwood, being then demesnes in mine own occupation; stocked with my own goods, and the Castle and Parks of Barnard Castle, whereunto I had drawn the greatest substance of all my moveables, except sheep. As for my corn about Streatlam and Barnard Castle, it did serve them for their horses.

In the besieging of Barnard Castle, they killed five men, three within and two without. That night the skirmish was, they hurt, with arquebus shot, three score and seven within the Castle.—*Harleian MSS.*, No. 6,991.

An Acte for the confirmation of the attaynders of Charles, Earle of Westmerlande; Thomas, Earle of Northumberland, and others.—xiii. Eliz., c. 16.

In theyr most humble wyse besechen your most excellent Majestie, the Lords spyrytuall and temporall, and al other your loving and obedyent subjectes, the Commons of this your most hyghe Court of Parlyament assembled, that where Charles, Earle of Westmerland, late of Branspethe, in the county of Durham; Thomas, Earle of Northd., late of Topclyfe, in the county of York; Anne, Countess of Northd., wyef to the said Earle of Northd.; Leonard Dacre, late of Harsley, in the county of York, esquire; Edward Dacre, late of Morton, in the county of York, esquire; Sir John Nevill, late of Leversedge, co. York, knight; John Swinburne, late of Chopwell, co. Durham, esquire; Thomas Markenfield, late of Markenfield, co. York, esquire; Egremounde Ratcliffe, late of the city of York, esquire; Christopher Nevill, late of Kyrby Moorside, co. York, esquire; Richard Norton, late of

Norton Coniers, esquire; Francis Norton, late of Baldersbie, co. York, esquire; George Norton, gentleman; Sampson Norton, gentleman; William Norton, gentleman; Christopher Norton, gentleman; Marmaduke Norton, gent.; Thomas Norton, gent.; Robert Tempest, late of Holmeside, co. Durham, esquire; Mychael Tempest, sonne of the said Robert; William Smith, late of Nunstanton, co. Durham, esquire; Bryan Palmer, late of Morton, co. Durham, esquire; George Stafford, esquire; Thomas Bishop, the elder, late of Pucklinton, co. York, gent.; Marmaduke Blakestone, gent.; Cuthbert Nevyll, esq.; Christopher Danby, late of Beiston, co. York, esquire; John Throllopp, late of Thornley, co. Durham, esquire; Anthony Hebborne, late of Hardwyke, co. Durham, esquire; Raulphe Conyers, late of Layton, esquire; John Gower, late of Richmond, gent.; Tristram Fenwick, late of Brinckborne, co. Northd., gent.; Anthony Welberie of Branspeth, gent.; John Saltmerslie of Rednes, gent., co. York; Henry Johnson of Walton Head, co. York; Symon Digbie of Aske; John Fulthropp of Islebeck; Leonard Medcalfe of Beereparke; Robert Claxton of Olde Parke, gent.; Robert Lambert of Owton, esquire; Raulphe Coniers of Cottam, gent.; Cuthbert Wytham of Bretonby; Robert Heighington of Richmonde; Thomas Jenny, gent.; Cuthbert Fenwick of South Sheeles; Cuthbert Ormarer of Belford; Rychard Dacre of Ayketon, co. Cumberd.; Wylliam Dacre of St. Bees; Robart Collingwood of Abberwicke; John Welbourn of Branspeth, gent.; George Horsley of Acklington Park; Thomas Greene of Tadcastra, yeoman; John Cowper of Keswyke; Raulph Swynnow of Thornhill, gent., most falsely and trayterously, by open rebellion in the north partes of this youre realme of England, have committed, perpetrated, and done many detestable and abominable treasons, against your Highnes, to the great peril and danger of your most royal person, and the utter destruction and overthrow of the good state, and publique peace of this your said realme, if God of his infinite goodness had not in due time opened and revealed to your Highness their traiterous intents and purposes, of and for which treasons, being most manifest and apparent, the said traitors and offendors aforenamed have been lawfully indicted, and some of them being fledd have bene and are lawfully and by due processe outlawed, and thereby justly attainted, and some of the said offendors have suffered paines of deathe according to their demerits.

Salvo to the Earl of Northumberland's brother; of others rights, except the offendors and their heirs; of the Bishop of Durham's right, except for this time as the Queen has "spent and consumed a great masse of treasure in repressing the said rebells."

Of all grants and leases made by the Queen since the rebellion; of pardons granted before; and salvo for the Countess of Cumberland and others for Edward Dacre's guift.

The bill was read for first time in the Lords April 10th, 1571, and was finally passed May 15th.—*Harl. MSS.* 73, *f.* 291. A copy in full was found among the Beamish Deeds attested, *Copia Vera, John Browne; Cleric Parliamentor, George Pearson, William Wilkinson.—June 29th,* 1699.

A survey of estates forfeited during the Northern Rising was made under a commission addressed to Wm. Homberston and others, forming two ponderous quarto volumes, which are still preserved in the Public Record Office. The first volume comprises the estates of the two Earls; the second those of Leonard Dacre, Sir John Nevill, and other persons attainted in Northumberland, Durham, Yorkshire, Cumberland, and Westmoreland. An abstract made by Dodsworth is printed among the Sadler Papers, edited by Sir Walter Scott.

CHAPTER XIII.

EXILED.

"But the flower is shed, and the spring is fled,
And he wanders alone at the close of the day :
And the sleety hail, in the moonshine pale,
Glistens at eve, on his locks of grey.

The sun shone bright and the birds sung sweet,
The day we left the North Countrie;
But cold is the wind, and sharp is the sleet,
That beat on the exile over the sea."
— *Claxton's Lament.*

"Che non ha doglia il misero maggiore,
Che ricordar la gioia entro il dolore."
— *Marino.*

IT now only, remains for us to follow the Earl of Westmoreland into his miserable captivity. Flanders swarmed with refugees, but none were safe from Cecil's eagle eye. His agents were abroad everywhere. They availed themselves of Westmoreland's friendly hospitality; and sitting at his board, laid traps to ensnare him. Charles Bailey (one among the many devotees of Mary, Queen of Scots) was arrested at Dover with letters in his possession from Westmoreland and the Countess of Northumberland, and also some perilous matter in cipher for the Duke of Norfolk. He was thrown into the Tower, and being put upon the rack would confess nothing. Lord Burghley, however, arranged that a man named Parker should personate Dr. Story, and appear to Bailey in the night. Dr. Story, whom the Catholics regarded as saint and confessor, was then a condemned prisoner in the Tower. Bailey, torn and discoloured by the rack, and weak with agony, saw the pseudo Story, who assured him that much was now known, and that by confessing certain things to Cecil he might even serve the Queen of Scots, and his other friends. Bailey, of course, confessed.

Months and years passed. Many a plot was hatched in Flanders, and strangled at its birth by Cecil. He seemed to be omniscient, and, in the light of his great knowledge, the throne of Elizabeth was safe.

Unsuccessful alike in his rebellion, and in his constant claims upon the royal clemency, Westmoreland dragged out a wretched existence. He was separated from his wife. He was overwhelmed in debt. At length he became an object of contempt. As the glories of Raby and Brancepeth slowly went to ruin, so did the mind of the once great Nevill. He seemed to sink into second childhood. A broken down old man, he yet posed as a suitor for Ricardot's daughter. He haggled over the conditions of marriage; and at last—his suit like all things else being unsuccessful—he died on the 16th November, 1601.*

"Thus perished on a foreign shore, after an absence of thirty years from his native land, subjected to every species of contumely and privation, and living on the precarious bounty of strangers— the last Earl of Westmoreland, of the noble house of Nevill."— *(Sir Cuthbert Sharpe.)*

Twinkes had long before gone to that better country where the weary are at rest. She lingered fondly for a while at Brancepeth, hoping to welcome back her lord to his ancestral home; but her residence there was viewed with suspicion. It was feared she would of her good nature encourage the rebels to make another

---

* The name of the Earl of Westmoreland appears amongst the pilgrims at Rome, in the records of the English College there.—*Collect Topog.*

In 1593, the year in which the Countess died, one Diaper gives an unfavorable account of the Earl's morality in Flanders, "He kepeth daily company with Sir Timothy Mocket; whose life and behaviour is either as bad or worse than my Lord's.—*Vide Strype*, Vol. IV., *quoted in Memorials of the Rebellion.*"

Who was Sir Timothy Mocket, I wonder?

Sir Cuthbert Sharpe also quotes, with a caution as to its authenticity, the *Estate of the English Fugitives*, in which it is stated that the Earl of Westmoreland commanded a regiment of English soldiers, and was present at the siege of Dermounde, and further, that being concerned in several brawls, he was suspended from the command by the Duke of Parma.

stir. On the 13th Feb., 1570, Sir George Bowes wrote to Lady Sussex :—" The Countess of Westmerland sayeth that she wyll in the beginning of the next week after thys, repayr to London, which I wyshe wer so."—*(Bowes' MS.*, Vol. XVIII.) She went accordingly. In May, 1577, the Queen granted her an additional annuity of £100, "during pleasure," for herself and three daughters, over and besides £200 allowed by a former warrant.—*(Privy Seal Records.)* Rowland remarks that "if the Queen did this it was very kind, as that sum would equal £3,000 at present value."

"There are," says Bloomfield, in his History of Norfolk, "four old stones in the nave of Kenninghall Church, in the shape of coffins, but no inscriptions or memorial of any kind; yet I find that on the 30th of June, 1593, here was buried Jane, Countess of Westmoreland, wife of Charles Nevill, Earl of Westmoreland, Lord of Raby, Staindrop, and Branspeth, Warkworth, and Sherryhutton and Middleham, daughter of Henry Howard, Earl of Surrey, and sister of Thomas, Duke of Norfolk."—*(Kenninghall Parish Register.)*

Peace to thy memory, gentle spirit ! Thy father beheaded at the age of twenty-nine, thy brother beheaded, thy husband exiled ! Thou didst deserve a better fate.

In the "*Memorials of the Howards,*" Lady Westmoreland is described as "a person of great virtue and acquirements, accompanied with such gentle feminine manners, sense, and affectionate love of her family, and her duties, that had her father lavished on her all his praise of the imaginary Geraldine, he could scarce have made her more interesting than what has been written of her by Robert Constable, the vile betrayer of the Earl of Westmoreland."

The daughters of the earl were attached to the "oulde religion," and for that reason got into trouble.

Margaret was five years old at the time of the Rising. In 1594, she was tried and convicted at the Durham Assizes, for having sheltered, and been found in company with, a seminary priest (John Bost), which thing, by 27th Elizabeth, was declared felony. Whilst she was under sentence of death, the Bishop of Durham interested himself in her case, and "strove hard" for her conversion. This Bishop (Hutton) was a worthy successor of good Tunstall.

He came from what is sometimes called a *mean extraction*. Who is your father? was one of the very few questions he could not answer. He thought the man came from Lincolnshire, but what did it matter? By his splendid ability he raised himself to a fellowship at Trinity, Cambridge. Then he became Regius Professor, Dean of York, Bishop of Durham, and finally Archbishop of York. He was one of the most learned and eloquent preachers of his day. He married three times, which Elizabeth thought very shocking, otherwise she liked him very much.

In all accounts of Durham, we are treated to a number of silly stories about St. Cuthbert; but few writers have troubled themselves to do justice to the memory of Dr. Hutton. I may therefore, perhaps, be excused if I go out of my way to tell a story far prettier than some I have heard told about St. Cuthbert.

Travelling one day along the rough country road between Wensleydale and Ingleton, Dr. Hutton suddenly dismounted, and, having delivered his horse to a servant, walked to a certain place at some distance from the highway, where upon the bare ground he kneeled down and continued a long time in prayer, "having tears upon his countenance, and yet a most blessed and celestial smile." He explained the act by saying that he remembered how, when a poor boy, without shoes or stockings, traversing this bleak mountain on a frosty day, he had disturbed a red cow, then lying on that identical place, in order to warm his feet and legs on the spot.—*Vide Whittaker's History of Richmondshire.*

I need make no comment upon the following letter, except that it was written in Dr. Hutton's house, and possibly under his supervision :—

"To the Quenes moste excellent Majestie— Most humblie with teares beseacheth your highnes, your Majesties most desolate poore subject, Margaret Nevill, one of the daughters of th' infortunate late Erle of Westmerland, to take princelie pittie upon my lamentable estate. With great greefe, I doe confesse (most gratious Sovereign) that sithins the death of my deare mother, having no part of that allowance, which it pleased your Majesty moste gratiouslie to bestow upon me, nor any of her maintenance, I was forced, by reason of great want, to receive reliefe of papistes, by whose subtiltie my needie simplicitie was allured from myne obedience and loialtie to their superstition and errors ; and so being drawne into the companie of a seminarie priest, I was condemned. At the assizes, the last somer, being destitute of help, it plesed the good bishop of Duresme, at the motion of my Lord President and the judges, to take me into his house, where he onelie hathe, and doeth yet wholie releeve me; and, by his godlie and sounde earnest instructions, he hathe (I moste humblie praise God) fullie reformed me in religion, which (by God's grace) I shall, with all obedience to your highnes, constantlie professe, while I live. And now (alas) seeinge this pittiful bishop, my onelie help, is verie shortlie to leave this countrie; and I know not how or where to be releeved. I commend my cause and woeful estate unto God and youre Majestie, most humblie beseaching your highnes, of your princelie and moste gratious wonted compassion, to be mercifull unto me, a moste distressed, poore maiden ; and to vouchsafe me your comfortable pardon for my life, and somewhat also for my releefe (which if I still want, my liefe will be no life, but mere miserie); so shall the enemies of true religion have no cause to rejoice at my woe; the repenting poore converts, by myne example, wil be comforted; and I (as most bounde) shall never cease with them to praie for your Majesties moste happie reigne, in all wished felicitie, long to endure. —Feb. 14, 1594.

"Your Majesties most woeful poore prisoner,
—*Lansdowne MS.*, No. 78, 12."   "MARGARETT NEVYLL."

The poor girl's letter appears to have made no great impression on Elizabeth.   Some days afterwards Dr. Hutton himself wrote to the Lord Treasurer.

" The Ladyie Margarett is descended of divers noble howses in the memorie of man: of the howses of Buckingham, Norfolk, Westmerland, and Rutland: and nowe (behoulde the instabilitie of all humane thinges) two of them are utterly overthrowne; onely one standyth unspotted, and shee herself a poore mayde, condemned to die.   Partly want did cause hir to wade to woe."—*Landsdowne MS.*, 78, 11.

In fact this girl had been in danger of actual starvation, in consequence of a fault committed by her father when she was only five years old.   The gates of her ancestral home were closed against her, and she wandered along life's unsheltered way, motherless and well-nigh fatherless, with the brand of the traitor and the heretic upon her poor innocent head, until, falling among Popish priests— the only people who had compassion on her desolate estate—she was declared guilty of felony.   Bost, the man who had befriended her, had already been launched into eternity by the hand of the Puritan, and "shee herself was a poore mayde condemned to die."

Very fortunate was it for this poore mayde that Matthew Hutton was just then possessed of more influence than fell to his lot on the day that he took shelter beside the red cow in Wensleydale.   His vigorous mind and warm heart, having entered upon the case of Margaret Nevill, became "resolute to carry the mayde into liberty."

On the 11th December, 1594, he wrote again to Cecil, as follows :—

" I sent up in the beginning of the term to sue for the pardon of the Ladye Margarett Nevill, taken in company with Boast, the seminary priest.   She lamenteth with tears that she hath offended God and her Sovereign.   She is wholly reclaymed from Poperye.   Dr. Aubrey hath had her pardon drawn since the beginning of the terme. If it come not quickly I fear she will dye with sorrow. It were very honorable for your good Lordship to take the case of a most distressed mayden, descended, as your Lordship knoweth, of great Nobilitie, the House of Norfolk, the House of Westmoreland, and the House of Rutland, in memory of man, and was but a child of five years old when her unfortunate father did enter into the rebellion ; and now she is a condemned person, having not one penny by year to live upon, since the death ot her mother, who gave her £33 6s. 8d. a year, part of that £300 which her Majesty did allow her. It were well that her Majesty were informed of her miserable state ; she is vertuously given, humble, modest, and of verie good behaviour. Thus committing her poor estate to your Lordship's honorable and charitable consideration, I humbly take my leave. From Auckland, the 11th Dec., 1594.

Your Lord'p's bound in Christ,
MATTH. DUNELM.

To the Ryght Honorable my especial good Lorde, the Lord Burley, Lord Tresurer of England."

—Lansdowne MSS.

In 1595 she was still a prisoner. Hutton was then Archbishop of York, and, having as he thought written letters enough on the subject, he went up to London for a personal interview with the Queen, and besought her Majesty that "she would have consideracon of the mayde's petition."

Three years afterwards Bishop Matthew speaks of her as " pardoned." She ultimately married Sir Nicholas Pudsey, Co. York, by whom, let us hope, she was made happy ever afterward.

Her sister, Lady Katherine Nevill, was married privately at Battersby Manor House, Co. York, to Sir Thomas Grey, of Chillingham, who died April 9th, 1590.

His will, dated 17th January, 1589, bequeaths to his sister-in-law, Lady Anne Nevill, 200 marks, to be paid by Sir Henry Constable, " which he oweth me for my wife, by his father's gift ;" and states that his wife is niece to Lady Catherine Constable, who owes him 500 marks. After the payment of various legacies, his wife inherits the residue of his fortune, and is appointed executrix."
—*Sir C. Sharpe.*

The following letter relating to her was written by Tobie Matthew (Dr. Hutton's successor) to Lord Burghley, and is dated May 27, 1598 :—

" Right Honorable,—Maie it please your good Lordshipp to be advertized, that I have lately caused the Lady Catherine Gray (widdow of Sir Thomas Gray) one of Westmoreland's daughters, to be apprehended by Mr. John Conyers, the sheriff of this countie, and Mr. Robert Talbois, one of the justices of peace, and have committed her to the safe custodie of Christopher Glover, gaoler of Durham Castle, to be kept forthcoming in his private house nighe the gaole. This ladie was many years sought by the late Earle of Huntingdon, was detected for the receiving and relieving of sundry seminary priests, as Stafferton, with the flesh mark in his face, (with whose too much familiaritie she hath been judge), Boast, who since was executed, Mushe and Patteson, besydes some others whose names come not presently to mind.   She hath alwaies illuded the processes and messengers of the Ecclesiastical High Commission by eloyning and withdrawing herselfe hitherto from all appearance of late tyme.   Somewhat since Martynmas last she took to farm a house and land called Grenecroft, nighe Lanchaster, in this countie, eight miles hence, North and by West, letten unto her by Mrs. Hall, a widdow conformable, and sister to Nicholas Tempest's wife, of Stella, that great Recusant, where the ladie hath been coming and going ever since, and sometimes made good cheere to twentye of her frendes at once, especially at Christmas, and where if I be truly informed, there was bad rule kept, both spiritually and carnally.   Within half a mile of that house, on this syde Lanchester, dwelleth at the Manor House one William Hodgson, an olde servant and follower of the Earle's, whose son, called Jock, is a special Recusant, and is reported (but how certainely I know not) to have married this ladie.   This William Hodgson is a perilous fellow, conformable to all her Majesties proceedings, and fermor to her Highness of the whole Deanery of Lanchester dissolved, worth as it is said, some 200 marks or better, above the yearly rent.   In Lanchester towne dwelleth Launcelot Hodgson, when he is at home, but he is now in prison for recusancy; a dangerous person, and not unlerned, who the last yere was married, as hymself confesseth, by an old Popish priest, but no seminarest, nor at a masse, as he alledgeth, to Marie Lee, daughter to another of the Earl's chief old servants and officers at Branspeth in those daies.   The manor of Lanchester belonging to me, and Branspeth lordship to her Majesty, by the Earle's attainder, doe adjoyn together, and therefore I thinke the Ladye Graye did there meane, for the tyme, to sett up her rest, soe nighe her father's olde tenants.   The house itself also (standing towards the Fells, and nighe a pretty wodde), strongly built of new, with many shifting contrivances, may yeld good opportunitie to lodge and intertaine not only other ill guests, but percase the Earl himself, *si et quatenus*. Now that she is in hands, I would from your Lordship be directed, with some expedition, how she shall be dealt with and used : 1st, Whether detayned in durance, or bail'd upon good bond for her appearance from tyme to tyme.   2ndly, Whether she shall be touched only for recusancie, or charged with any other matters that may occurre.   3rdly, Whether if any thinge amountinge to felonie shall arise against her, she shall be tried thereof at the next assizes here, or in Northumberland, as her sister Ladie Margaret was, anno 1593, and by her Majestye most graciously pardon'd, in hope of the continuance of her pretended conformitie (from which I hear she has relapsed since).   4th, Whether she shall be suffered to keep house for herselfe, with some of her own servants about her, and other frends sometimes resorting to her as she desyreth earnestly, or lyve as her keeper shall provide for her, in a more private and close manner.   5th, Whether she shall be permitted to ryde abroad and take aire, or continue within her lodging; with such other particulars as your Lordship in your wisdome shall think fit to impart unto me.   My health will not yet serve me either to send for her or go to her; but at the tyme of my visitation, about a fortnight hence, or eighteen days, I shall take occasion to speak to her and examine her, if your Lordship before that time shall so advise me, and if God will give me leave. The while, with humble thanks to your good Lordship for the allowance of my impost, I betake your Lordship to the grace of God. At Bishop Auckland, 27th March, 1598.

Your Lordship's most humble in Christ,

TOBIE DURESME.*

To the Ryght Honorable my singular good Lorde, Lord High Tresurer of England."

—*Strype*, Vol. IV., p. 343.

Mr. Surtees, in his *History of Durham*, has written a note on Greenecroft, the house mentioned in this letter. " The house," he says, " has been modernised, and I do not know that it is now remarkable for any shifting contrivances, of which, however, there are several in the county of Durham. At Binchester, which was a seat of the Nevills, is a private staircase for escape, concealed as part of the chimney, &c." The country between Branspeth and Lanchester is still comparatively wild and moorish. John Hodgson is denominated of Manor House (1615); but a confusion arises between this and Welhome Manor House, near Newcastle, both held by this family, one of whom certainly was the Hodgson mentioned in Constable's letter to Sir R. Sadler, though I know nothing of the scandal between Lady Catherine (who seems, by the by, not to have been quite so discreet and modest as poor Lady Margaret) and Hodgson.

In 1604, King James gave a warrant to pay to the Earl of Northampton, during the life of his niece, " the Lady Margaret Nevill, one hundred marks to her own use, as an enlardgment of a former pencon of £50, and to Katherine and Anne, two other of the daughters of the Earl of Westmoreland, 200 marks to each of them, and to the Lady Adeline Nevill, £50 yearly." *(Privy Seal Records.)* Lady Katherine died without issue. The Lady Anne

* *Tobie Matthew* succeeded Dr. Hutton on the recommendation of the Earl of Leicester. He had previously been made Dean, "though the Queen stuck a good while, he being such a young man, *and married*." Tobie was "exceedingly anxious" at the delay, knowing that in case of his non-residence, twenty-one days before Michaelmas, the whole tithe of the deanery would in accordance with the statutes go to the resident prebendaries. When the plague broke out in Durham he again became "exceedingly anxious," and fled to Stockton "to be rid of the horror." "He preached hard,"—1,992 times altogether. "Neither was there a pulpit in York or Durham diocese, where he preached not." Frances his wife had a bishop for her father, an archbishop for her father-in-law, four bishops her brethren, and an archbishop her husband. *(Vide her tomb in York Minster.)* Tobie himself declared of his sons, that, "the first, being a hectoring papist and knighted, had wit but no grace; the second had grace but no wit; the third had neither grace nor wit.—*Sloane MS.* Tobie was the archbishop, who alienated York House, in the Strand, from the See of York, disposing of it to George Villiers, Duke of Buckingham for lands in Yorkshire of inferior value.

married David, younger brother of Sir Wm. Ingleby, of Ripley. (She left an only daughter, Mary, who married Sir Peter Middleton of Stokeld.—*Dugdale Visit., Yorks.*) In the Brancepeth survey, 1614, she is named as having a lease of the East Parke from the Queen, at a rental of £40. Tobie Matthew describes her as "*obstinate.*" The Lady Eleanor died unmarried.

Christopher Nevill died in exile, at Louvain. He had been an active promoter of the rebellion, and his character appears to have been strongly tinctured with turbulence and immorality. He is mentioned as having gone to a horse race at Gatterly Moor, to assault and even to kill Christopher, son of Thomas Rokeby of Morton.—*Whittaker's Richmondshire.* On the discomfiture of the rebels, he took refuge at Fernihurst. Together with his brother Cuthbert, he was suspected of lurking about Brancepeth.

On 15th January, 1570, Constable writes to Sadler :—

"I understand that Mr. Cuthbert Nevill ys somtyms in Braunspeth lordship, and somtyms in Raby lordship ; resett somtyms with one, somtyms with another, but I cannot tell with whom : possyble in ye parsenage in Branspeth, but I am not seure thereof."

On the 8th February, Sir Thomas Gargrave writes to Sir George Bowes :—

"Yf ether Chrystopher or Cuthbert Nevyll be in the Bishoprick, I cold wyshe ye shuld practyse to take them, and yt wyll surely be well taken, and also yf the Lady (Westmoreland) provyde more provysyon then ys necessary, I wold wyshe she shuld be prevented by some menes and rather than evyll shuld chance I wold wyshe her removed hether ; and that I trust would make the country there more quyet ; but if she will not remove, then I wold have you to use, and to apply some force to stop soden entents there ; and call all the gentlemen, and men of welth, and wyll them at theyr perells to remain dewtyful subjects."—*Bowes' MSS.* Vol. XVIII.

The same day Sir George Bowes wrote to Sussex, saying :—

"The former rumours certyfied to your Lordship are sundry wise confirmed, but as far as we can perceive Christopher and Cuthbert Nevill are departed, and bestowed themselves in other places, where, or to what purposes, we can not yet certainly learn."—*Bowes' MSS.* Vol. II.

Both the brothers eventually escaped to Flanders. Sussex writes to Cecil, on April 10th, 1570, as follows :—

"The berer hereof Christopher Wandisford, that maryed a daughter of Sir George Bowes, and was with him in Barny Castell, and after, in all the siege against the Rebells. His mother was married to Chr. Nevell, who of long time *did deale very ill with her*, and now the land that was her joyntur is come to her Majesties hands by the offence of Nevell. Wandisford repareth thyther to be a Suter, that he may be fermor of the land that Nevell had, in the right of his mother; and that some porcyon of the rent might be allowed to his mother for her mayntenance."—*State Papers.*

In 1574, the Lord President ordered the houses of John Rudyard and John Ratcliff of Gisburne, to be searched, "who had been at Brancepath and only left the Earls on Friday before they rose." From the depositions of the parties, and the papers discovered, it appeared that Nevill had given the rectory of Kirkbymoorside to Wm. Barkley, *alias* Smith, "whose wife Katherine was the reputed concubine of Nevill." She had sent Elizabeth Fenwick, *alias* Alnwick, with a *ring of gold* to Farnihurst to Nevill, but she did not see him then. The Earl of Westmoreland gave her two shillings. She was sent a second time before Easter, and gave Nevill the ring at Hundelee. He sent no token in return, but desired Katherine Smyth "by word of mouth to lyve according to the laws, that he had left enough for her, and would never think well of them that were not good to hir."—*Sir Cuthbert Sharpe.*

Sir John Nevill of Leversege, Co. York (*vide Pedigree Table No. I.*) was another pensioner of King Philip, and died in exile. He was High Sheriff in 1560. After the Rebellion he took refuge in Hume Castle. On April 17th, 1560, Lord Hunsdon writes to Cecil :—

"Having occasion to send to my Lord Hume, I sent a servant of myne, who had been before acquainted with Sir John Nevyll; and whilst my man tarried for answer of my letter, Sir John had some talk with my said servant, and wished that himself with the rest might return into their country, and enjoy the benefit of the same."

Sir Thomas Gargrave says that he was "confirmed in Popery and false doctrine by Dr. Robynson in Queen Mary's days; and in King Edward's days was a Protestant. Sir Thomas, in company with Sir Hugh Saville, examined Lady Nevill, when the following painful evidence was taken :—

"Lady Nevill, Sir John's wife, is in poor case, *having only a white frieze gown, and ten children, and neither house, meat, nor drink.* Yf her husband might have his lyfe he would come in and submytt hymself to imprisonment, or otherwise, as shuld please the Queen's Majestie."—*Sir T. Gargrave to Sussex, York, Feb.,* 1570. *S.P. Elis., Add.* Vol. XVII., 87.

Sir John soon afterwards escaped across the sea, and was joined by his wife at Louvain. He also went on pilgrimage to Rome.— *(Murdin,* p. 191*).* The manors of Hunslett and Kellington, with lands in Holbecke and Knowlesthorpe "late parcel of the lands of

Sir John Nevill, attainted," were granted on lease to Edward Carey, in 1573. In the following year the Queen granted "Robert Nevill, Gent.," out of his father's possessions the *pittance of £20 a year during pleasure*, to be paid by the receiver of York, out of the lands of Leversedge.—*Privy Seal Records quoted by Sharpe.*

What became of the other nine children; with whom the "poore ladye" appeared before Sir Thomas Gargrave in her white frieze gown, is more than I can say. History has left us a piteous picture of Northumberland's little daughters. Their uncle, Sir Henry Percy, who remained loyal, passing by Topcliffe, three weeks after Christmas, reported to Sussex that he "founde the younge ladys in hard case, for neither had thay any provisione, nor one penny to relyve them with, but some lyttle thynge from me. They wolde gladly be removyde, ther want of fier is so grett whos yeres may nott well suffer that lacke."—*S.P.* There was "sharpe execution" done at Topcliffe before Percy's visit, and "the poor children as they looked shivering out of their window, must have seen scores of their father's servants hanging on the trees about the house."—*Froude, Vol. IX.*

We are now approaching the end of this miserable story. "On the 22nd of August, 1572, the Earl of Northumberland was beheaded on a scaffold, in the Pavement; his head being smitten off with a broad carpenter's axe. His head was set on a very high pole on top of Micklegate Barr, but his body was buried in Crux Church, by two of his servants and three women, in St. Thomas's quire, where he now lies without any memorial."—*MS. Hist. York, by Thomas Beckwith, F.S.A., quoted in Sharpe.* Into the harrowing story of the sufferings that Lady Northumberland endured in Scotland we need not enter here. She "tuke shipping at Old Aberdeen on August 23rd, 1570, in a ship, callid the *Port of Leith.*" Landing in Flanders, the Earl (Westmoreland) and Countess "had nether penny, nor half-penny." She was supported as we have seen, by foreign charity. One of her last letters expresses regret at the loss of Sir John Nevill. She died at Namur, October 17th, 1596. Her daughter Mary, "having vowed virginity," wept over her mother's grave, and forsaking this world's vanities, became the founder of the Benedictine Dames, at Brussels.

Richard Norton, "the old gentleman with a reverend gray head, bearing a cross with stremer" (*Camden*), also died in exile, and the demesne of Norton Conyers and Hereford was confiscated. He had married Susan Nevill, fifth daughter of Richard, Lord Latimer. His brother, Thomas, was hanged at Tyburn, a certain space, and was taken down and quartered in the presence of his nephew, Christopher, who then presently must drink of that same cup." Christopher was the bright boy whose ardent soul had been fired by the glance of the Scottish Queen. He was the seventh son of Richard. Francis, of Baldersby, was the eldest. He made abject entreaties to Cecil for pardon, but died in exile, "his hope being deferred." The third son, Edmund, does not appear to have been implicated in the Rebellion. The present Lord Grantley is descended from him. There were eleven sons altogether. The old ballad speaks of "eight good sonnes," all

"doom'd to dye, alas! for ruth."

Leonard Dacre died abroad, August 12th, 1573. His fall was great. "Though he were crook backt, yet had he behaved himself valiantly." His name had been "a strong tower in the North Countrie, so that verie fewe might be founde to lift hand against a Dacre." *(Lord Scroop to Cecil, Jan. 31st, 1570.)* A stone, formerly visible at St. Nicholas', Brussels, bore a record of his decease.—*Theatre Sacré de Brabant, quoted in Sharpe.*

Randal Dacre was buried at Greystocke, in 1634, and the register states that he was "the last male heyre of that line."

"Sic transit gloria mundi."

And now, if you are not quite tired out, my patient reader, let the Bishop of Durham give us his benediction.

Bishop Pilkington to Lord Burghley (S.P. Dom. Eliz., Vol. 77, No. 56).—Jesu Helpe!— Right Honorable, this 22 of Aprill, William Lee, the chefe mane about the late Erle of Westd., came here, and tolled me that yester night died the Lord Nevill (for so he and all that faction, with no litell glorying, term the earle's sone, which was borne and so catholicli christened in the late rebellion). This last week died the ladie Marie Nevill, the erle's sister, at Sir Joa. Constables, so there remanes onely of that generation the Ladie Adeline, another sister off the same nature that the rest be (obstinate). In the weke afore last died old Salvin who was godfather to the erle's son, and because he would die as he lived he willed his sone to buri him without priest or praier, and so in an evening they privatlie putt hym into a grave. Butt I have called his son, and will punish such disorder. Iff sharpe laws be not made there will be no feare of Godd left. William Lees request was that the child might be broght with solemn pompe, as a noblemanes sone, and be buried among his ancestors. For any solemnitie I willed him rather no, nor among his ancestors, butt at his jopardi, butt to be buried honestlie according to the laws, and though he was otherwise christened I liked well, and further I hadd not to doe.

When he cold have no better answer he said he would meddle no farther, untill he herd from mie ladie his mother. I wold gladlie know yor lordships pleasure. What shall I do iff they attempt ani such thing. These with many of their like practices declare their herts and their meaning. Butt Godd lives, who will give us his blessinge.—At your lordship's command,

J. DUNELM.

To the Right Honorable, and my verie good lorde, the lorde Burghley, one of the Quenes Majesties most honorable Privie Counsell.

HASTE, HASTE, HASTE, HASTE, HASTE! with all diligence for the Quenes Majesties weightie affaires.

Received the 20th off Aprell at one in the after.

Endorsed 23 Aprill 1571.—Bishop of Durham to my Lord.

ADDENDA.

Antwerp, January 27th, 1571.—*John Fitzwilliam to Cecil.*—"Yf my L. of West-merland be seure of your honor's friendshipe, he wolde be a suitor for the Quenes Majesties most gratious pardon, withe as muche humilitye as may be, and tourne to be a trew and obedyent subjecte;—he hath a grete good opynyon of your honor, and acknolegethe your honore to have byn alwaies his frende, before his offence, whereof, nowe, he muche repenteth."

October 21st, 1571.—*Deposition of Henry Sympson before Sir Thomas Gargrave.* —States that he has recently returned from Flanders—has seen the Earl of West-merland at Louvain. The Earl kepith a good house, and hath forty or fifty that came to meate with him, but there is not of his own livery, that be household servants, past twelve or thirteen."

[Sympson related the conversation that he heard whilst being entertained at the Earl's supper table. Sympson was a Darlington man, of reduced circumstances. He wanted a place at Newcastle, as a "hat maker;" but there is no record as to whether Mr. Secretary helped him to obtain this modest situation, in return for his valuable information.]

Lady Westmoreland to Cecil.—Right Honorable, I beseech you, bear with my importunitye, and let it not offend you that I earnestly crave your goodness to be a suter for me to the Queen's Majestye, to give me leave to come to her Royal Person; which although my Lord's doing have been such as they much abash me so to do, yet myne own innocence, and great desyre I have to do my humble duty to her Highnesse, somethynge emboldens me to continue this my sute, trustying more by youre friendship and good helpe to obtaine the same, otherwyse it would be a greater griefe unto me than all my other miserys. Thus beseeching you to take petie of my miserable and unfortunate estate. I cease to trouble you. From Howarde House, the 23rd Marche, 1570.—Your most humble suter,

J. WESTMERLAND.

To the Ryght Honorable Sir Willm. Cecil, Knt., Principalle Secret'y to the Queen's Majesty.—*Lansdowne MSS.*

ABSTRACTS FROM STATE PAPERS.—1571.

Antwerp, Jan. 26, 1571.—*John Lee to Sir William Cecil.*—The Earl of Westmore-land has talked with me on a report that I was here as an advertiser for England, but I persuaded him on the contrary, except that if I understood anything prejudicial to Queen or country, I was bound to reveal it. He showed himself repentant of his late undutiful proceedings, and would submit to Her Majesty and sue for pardon, but he despairs of it, notwithstanding her great clemency. I persuaded him to try to regain what he had lost, and told him he would find friends with Her Majesty. I asked what the Queen and Council thought of him before his rebellion, and which councillors would best aid him. He said all were inclined to him, but he was most beholden to you, and your friendship would stand him in most stead. His sister, Lady Elinor, Mr. Pelham's wife, has written him a friendly letter to submit to Her Majesty, and he seems wery willing if you will be his friend. —*Addenda*, Vol. XX., 6.

Antwerp, March 27, 1571.—*The Earl of Westmoreland to Sir William Pelham.*— Brother Pelham,—Thes shal be to lett you understand that for the great good wyll I have (my dewtye requiring no lesse) to obteyne the Quenes Majesties most gratious favour, by all honorable meane possyble that lyes in me to doo; and beinge voyde of a faythful frende to ayde and assyste me towardes the effectinge thereof; these shal be to desyer you, if you shall be moved therunto by any of the Quenes Counsell, that you wyll vouchsafe to come over hether, and to confer with me of summe pointes, which shall not onely tend to the princes safetye, and to the further advancynge of your credit and my honor, if I be not (as I have hetherto bene) altogether infortunate. If you refuse me I shall thinke myselfe voyde of any frende or kinsman in that lande, as knoweth the Almightie God, who preserve you and my syster, with your chyldren, to his pleasure.—Your assured brother to his small power and good harte.   C. WESTMERLAND.

Brother, as my truste is in you deale secretly in thys matter or I doo nothinge at all, nether mistrust the nobleman's secresye that sall deale with you, nor yeat the conveyer of my letter.

Antwerp, April 20, 1571.—*John Lee to Lord Burghley.*—Lord Westmoreland is at Louvaine, sick of an ague. The Earl would submit to any reasonable order, and this would so crack the credit of the rest here that the Queen would not need to fear their proceedings against her.—*Add.* Vol. XX., 21.

Antwerp, May 1, 1571.—*John Lee to Lord Burghley.*—The Earl is still sick. He wrote me lamenting Fitzwilliam's death, knowing not by whom to proceed in his suit for the Queen's favour, which he much desires. I pray stand his good Lord, and you will have no cause to repent it. His upright dealing makes me remind you of him.—Vol. XX., 30.

Antwerp, June 11, 1571.—*John Lee to Lord Burghley.*—Sir John Nevill, Chris. Danby, Robt. Tempest, and Marmaduke Blakestone have been earnest suitors at Brussells for pensions, of which they are assured. Lord Westmoreland remains at Louvaine, not wholly recovered of a broken leg.—Vol. XX., 46.

Antwerp, Feb. 4, 1572.—*John Lee to Lord Burghley.*—Dr. Saunders and Sir John Nevill, with five or six more, have departed from hence toward the Pope, expecting to find better entertainment there, than they have done here.—Vol. XXI., 18.

Antwerp, March 21, 1572.—*John Lee to Lord Burghley.*—I have tried to accomplish what Leicester and you gave me in charge at my last being with you; I have so persuaded therein that Westmoreland is wholly resolved to become a suitor to the Queen, and is content not only to deliver the whole grounds of the late rebellion, trusting thereby to purchase grace, but will discover all such practices as he knows to be at present in hand, the secrecy whereof he refuses for divers respects to commit to paper; so that his desire is to persuade Mr. Pelham, to whom he has written, to come over hither to confer with him, and he will deal so frankly and plainly that he trusts that neither he, the Queen, nor you shall mislike thereof.

P.S.—I have sent Earl Westmoreland £20; let it not be to my discredit; I did it simply to advance my services to the Queen.—Vol. XXI., 28.

Antwerp, May 4, 1572.—*The Earl of Westmoreland to Lord Burghley.*—I can but render unto your lordship my most hartye thanks for that it hath pleased you to travail towards helping my misery; I lament that time and other lets disable you to do me good; pray continue my good lord to Her Majesty, though I find the entry of my suit very hard. Touching the other two points of your letter to Lee, as soon as he has recovered I will discharge myself of all that I can say. I thank you also that 'it may |be lawful for my friends to relieve me, and pray that my wife or my sister Pelham may know it, lest I be constrained to entangle myself, which hitherto I have not done.—Vol. XXI., 41.

Antwerp, Nov., 1572.—*Westmoreland to Cecil.*—If among the heaps of my calamities ther appered any sparke of better fortune, wych may kepe lyfe in a restlesse body, almost consumed wyth continewall lamentyng, or, in great decaye of worldlye friendship, and any staye left unto me whereon I may repose my afflicted state, surely that hath only proceeded of the comfort which conveyed by one year's late advertizement, whereby I was not only assured of your lordship's noble and pitiful . . . . but also, upon the consideration of my present state, put in hope of your greter favour; not doubting but the innocence of my cause shall appear to be suche, as your lordship shall rather find occasion to encrease your goodness, than any offence to kindle Her Majestie's indignation.

The greatest matter wherewyth I am charged is the accusation of one who falling by presumption from the duty of his allegiance careth not how far by undue surmises he speaketh to all dishonour. But seeing of the dead we ought to speak but well, and the ripping up of his unjust and rash doings can breed me no security in this heavy plight; I will not again fret this festered sore but leave him to God's mercy, whose untrue speeches I would not have feared if I might have tried the cause with the person himself; not doubting but my plain and trewe defences should soon have put him to sylence, whose wrytings will remain perpetual witness of my evil behaviour. Nothing, in truth, God is my witness, I desyre so much as Her Highness's good and gracious opinion, which if the truth of all these deliverings might be revealed by their confession who in this tragedy play'd, I doubt not but I should soon recover, and the chiefest parts should be more apparent to the world. In the meantyme I wholly commytt myself to your lordship's protection wherein I am the more encouraged by your goodness the wych to my brother Henry, who otherwyse being surcharged wyth the malice of hys adversaries, must have yelded to hys own mysfortunes. Myne own heavy state is rather enforced to praye in aide, then my poore good will lyke to be commodious; yet your lordship, I hope, wil accept the same, because that shall be alwayes faithful. Thus most humbly beseeching God to preserve your lordship in all honour and prosperity, I humbly take my leve the last of this month.—Your Lordship's most devoted during lyfe,

                                                    C. WESTM'L'ND.

"The Right Honourable my very good Lord, the Lord Hygh Tresurer of England."—*Cotton Coll. Calig. C.,* 3,433.

Queen of Scots to her Ambassador in France, the Archbishop of Glasgow.—"To the English, and more especially to the Earl of Westmoreland, you will communicate my good intentions when I shall have the power; and with regard to his appointment, I should be very glad that he had it, provided that his safety were secured, of which I entertain doubts. In short, it is not easy for a good Catholic to continue here without danger to his life, or of what is still dearer to him—his conscience. Thus informing you of the offers which have been made to him, I shall, in my first despatch, state what I may hereafter discover. Certainly, I will not advise him to refuse a good offer, if it occurs, but I would admonish him, in accepting it, that he takes good care not to injure the service of God, his friends, and his reputation; and not to be certain of his life, except on dishonourable conditions.—*From the original cipher. Lingard.*

[This letter directs that a certain sum be paid to the Earl. In another letter, dated March 27th, 1577, Queen Mary says, "I esteem and honour his good will, and will not neglect whatever may be in my power, which let him understand from me, assisting him if necessary with two or three hundred crowns."

"Mary Stuart throughout life never lacked gratitude to those who had been her friends."—*Froude*, Vol. XII. Both friends and foes are carefully mentioned by name in the letter written to Philip of Spain, the night before her execution. The friends were to be sheltered, the foes punished. Westmoreland's name occurs as a friend.]

The Earl of Westmoreland to his Wife.—"My good wyfe and dearest beloved good creature,—You revive, by your letters, the remembrance of my long endured evil, by exile from my Countre, wherebye you saye I am subject to all slanderous reportes and perills. I confesse I feale the smart therof, and therefore arme myselfe agaynst the worste; not expecting better tyll it shall please God soo to qualifie the Quenes Majesties harte, as she maye thinke me worthy so muche of her favor as I maie be admitted to live and die under her protection, in that soyle that nature hathe soo manie wayes made sweet under me; as no condition elsewhere can equall the leaste of those comfortes I might enjoy there, and to recover her Majestie's assured favour. I could be contente to remaine a prisoner all my life in any place [it] shoulde please her to appointe, where I may enjoye her favour, your presence, and my countrye, with such condition onely as in conscience and honor I am bounde to regarde before my lyfe.—Louvaine, ix. Sep., 1574."

Lady Westmoreland to Lord Burghley.—"As I am bound, I give your Lo. most humble thanks; first, for my poore husband, whom your carefull frendshypp always sekyth to bryng to better estate, although it semyth that his own cruell fortune repughneth of good menes and endevours that may be used to do him good. For myne owne part, I hard not of hym a longe tyme; and which greves me not a lyttle. I fere he hath not receyved my last letter, because he makyth no answer; but I beseche your Lo. most humbly to continewe your goodnes, trustyng that, in the ende, a more happy effect maye follow. I have also most humbly to thanke your Lo. for your continuall goodnes to my selfe, and for the lese of the parkes of Branspethe, yt plesed you to procure me at the Quenes Majestys hand, yet am I forcyd, although I be very lothe so often to trouble your Lo. to be a suter to you, that my lese in one point may be amendyd; which is thoys that the Quenes Majesty hath ther grawnted yt to me no longer then yt plese her to kepe it in her own handes, so that if eyther her selfe, or successors shall eyther gyve yt or sell yt, my lese is of no valew. In consideration wherof I beseche your Lo. to shewe me so much favour as I maye have a newe lese grawnted for twenty yeres, in such sort as I maye enjoye it quietly, wher so ever her Majesty bestow the land; and that it maye passe in the name of thys berar, my servant John Emerson. Thus feryng to troble your Lo. I ende, remayning your poore frynd, and wyshing all good hap. to your Lo. and all yours. From Fremyngham, this 10 of October, 1574. Your Lo. most bownd, duryng lyef   JANE WESTMERLAND.

July 20th, 1577.—*Sir F. Walsingham to Sir Henry Sydney.*—The Queen being advertised, from her ambassador resident in France, that the Earl of Westmoreland should be privately repayred into Ireland about some practice; and though she fyndeth yt a matter unlykely, yet her pleasure is, that your Lordship should, in some secret sort, use some apt instruments in the discovereye whether he be there or not, and in case he be ther, to seke all the wayes you may for the apprehension of him."—*Sydney Papers.*

Brussels, March 10th, 1577.—*Dr. Wilson to Lord Burghley.*—The two Morleys was lately at Antwarpe, and is gone to Mastryke (Mastricht) in company of the Earl of Westmoreland."

(This Dr. Wilson was employed as a spy in Flanders, "to undermine the rebells' doeings. He afterwards received the Deanery of Durham, as a reward for his "long contynued efforts.")

The Earl of Westmoreland to the Earl of Leicester.—My very good Lord,— Whereas I wrote a letter unto my brother Pelham, with whom I would have conferred by word of mouth, onely as touching my submission unto the Queen's Majesty, for that I am an ill penman, I understand from a letter written by my Lord Burley to her who hath made me privy thereunto, that the Queen's Majesty by no means will grant thereunto, which grieveth me not a little, notwithstanding I do most willingly obey Her Majesty's plasure, as my duty requireth, whatsoever otherwyse is thought of me; beseeching your Lordshyp to stand my good Lord in this my banishment, and to forget all private . . . . that hath passed between us heretofore, and to aid me with your furtherance towards obteyning of the Queen's Majesty's favour, to the restoring again of my decayed House, whereby you shall bynd me and myne always to be yours; and I assure your Lordship wherewithall, that if it would please Her Majesty to pardon this my former youth, I shall not only remain her loial and duetiful subject for ever, but also I trust within a few years by services to recompénse any errors past. Thus desyring your Lordship to deal so favorably with me, as that I may be advertized by your letters wether your Lordshyp should refuse me herein, as I trust you will not, I do greatly dispare of the good success of my interest, as knoweth the Almighty God, unto whose protection I leave your Lordship.—From Antwerp, this 4th Maye, 1579.— Your Lord'p's assured in his small power,   C. WESTMERLAND.

The Ryght Honorable and his assured good Lord the Erle of Lecester.

ABSTRACTS FROM STATE PAPERS, 1572-1601.

Berwick, June 13, 1572.—*Henry, Lord Hunsdon, to Lord Burghley.*—Examination of Northumberland. His answers are very long, and yet not so long as he would have made discoveries of every trifling thing of no effect; but he seems unwilling to leave out anything. He greatly excuses my Lord of Westmoreland, and plainly says that they could never get any hold of him until the last hour.

P.S.—My wife prays that although you are greatly busied with the entertaining and the affairs of Montmorency, yet that you will despatch me of my prisoner, that we may make merry this summer at Brancepeth.

Westmoreland asked what the ground of the quarrel was to be. They said religion. He said no, for such quarrels were accounted rebellion in other countries, and he would not blot his long stainless house. This happened as my cousin and I looked for, that we might excuse ourselves to the rest. We ever judged Westmoreland was unwilling, but urged to the matter.—*Add.* Vol. XXI., 56.

Brussells, June ⅟₈, 1572.—*Thomas Jennings to the Countess of Northumberland.*— Your letter of June 8 [came?] at the arrival of the English gentlemen, who will be grateful for your courtesy, especially the Nevills. I have pawned my credit for their apparel, diet, and money.—Vol. XXI., 59.

Note.—Thomas Jennings is sometimes described as Jenny. His descendants preserved their property to sacrifice it to royalty in the cause of Charles I.—*Surtees.* Vol. I., 77.

Berwick, July 20, 1572.—*Henry, Lord Hunsdon, to Lord Burghley.*—If I hear not soon, I must carry him (Northumberland) with me to Brancepeth, where I can keep him safe. I do not believe in the rumour of making new officers, until I hear it from you.—Vol. XXI., 75.

Antwerp, Feb. 17, 1575.—*Edw. Woodshaw to the Earl of Westmoreland.*—I have been lately moved by a devilish man (Moffatt) to be an instrument to your utter undoing, and conjured to keep it secret. I warn you not to trust to evil men. If you will write me by the bearer, I will come to you, and give you such knowledge that, if you will be secret, you may entrap the layer of the traps, get £1,000, and rejoice your friends and shame your enemies. I will tell you more when we meet. I defy all the gold and silver in the world, and would lose all rather than seek your death, and be such an enemy to the King and the Catholic cause.—Vol. XXIV., 5.

Feb. 27, 1575.—*Edward Woodshaw to Lord Burghley.*—I trust you have received my letters from Sir Thomas Gresham, with one from the Earl of Westmoreland to me. I went to Louvaine to the Earl, who was very friendly; after much talk it was concluded that when I heard from you or my good Lord of Leicester, or had any news by Moffatt, who has gone to dwell at Bruges, I should repair again to him, and he would act as I counselled him.—Vol. XXIV., 7.

This Woodshaw was one of Cecil's "creatures." He escaped to Antwerp to be out of reach of punishment for a robbery in which he was concerned at Wakefield, and afterwards served under the Duke of Alva, "whom" (he assures Cecil) "I hate as the Devil himself." "If you could get my pardon for that offence (the robbery) and some living I could serve my country as few can."—*Woodshaw to Lord Burghley*, Sept. 3.

THE FOLLOWING LETTERS WERE WRITTEN BY SPIES.

"The Earl of Westmoreland beginneth to pursue again his sute for Richardot's daughter, and Richardot (as is said) standethe upon this—that he procure 200 crowns a month pension, more than he hathe alredie, which he will have to be assured of his daughter, which (if he get yt) must be had from the King.—Bruxelles, Oct. 15, 1600."

Nov. 20, 1601.—"Th' Erle of Westmerland fell sick here, at the campe, above three weeks agone; from whence he was caryed in a coach to Newport, and there continued sick till the 16 of this month, and then died. What benefit his heirs may reape by his lands in England, I knowe not; but I thinke his executors shall get little of his goods here, bienge in as many mens debt as he could borrowe moneye of; and to the King that he had gotten beeforehand of his entertaynment, which, as you know, was 200 crowns a month."—*State Papers.*

PART II.—CHAPTER I.

ISSUE OF JOAN BEAUFORT, COUNTESS OF WESTMORELAND.

"𝕱ilia Lancaster: Ducis inclyta, spousa Johannis
Westmerland primi subjacet hic comitis
Desine, scriba, suas virtutes promere, nulla
Vox valeat merita vir reboare sua
Stirpe, decore, fide, tum fame, spe, prece, prole
Actibus et vita pollnit immo sua
Natio tota dolet pro morte. Deus tulit ipsam
In Bricii festo, C. quater. M. quater. X.

Inscription on her monument in Lincoln Cathedral.

TWENTY-THREE children fell to the lot of Ralph, 1st Earl of Westmoreland. Nine of these were by his first wife, Margaret, daughter of the Earl of Stafford. They comprise the ancient house of Westmoreland, and have already been disposed of. Fourteen children by his second countess, Joan Beaufort, remain for our consideration. The following table will show their order and importance :—

1. RICH. NEVILL married Alice, d. of Earl of Salisbury. Lord Chamberlain of England, 1460. Created EARL OF SALISBURY by Pat. 4th May. 1448. Beheaded at Wakefield, 1461.	2. Sir *Wm. Nevill*, BARON FAU-CONBERG and EARL OF KENT.	3. GEORGE summoned to Par. as BARON LATIMER, 1432 to 1469 Died 1469	4. *Thomas*, married Alice d. of—Seymour.	5. *Robert*, Bishop of Salisbury 1427, of Durham 1438. Died 1457.	6. EDWARD married Eliz. Beauchamp, and became BARON OF BURGAVENNY, 1435. (See House of Abergavenny.)
7. 8. 9. *Cuthbert*, *Henry*, *John*, died young.	10. *Joan*, a nun.	11 *Catherine*, married, 1st Jno. Mowbray. Duke of Norfolk, and and Marshal of England; 2ndly John Wydville.	12. *Anne*, married 1st, Humphrey, Duke of Buckingham; 2nd, Walter Blount Montjoy.	13. *Eleanor*, mar. 1st, Richard Lord Spencer; 2ndly, Henry Percy, Earl of Northumberland.	14. CICELY married Richard Plantagenet, DUKE OF YORK, and was mother to Edward IV. and Richard III.

A sketch of the eldest son, Richard, Earl of Salisbury, will be found in the next chapter. William, the second son, married Jane, daughter and heir of Thomas De Fauconberg. At the siege of Orleans, 9th Henry VI., he won for himself a high celebrity as a soldier, and his valiant conduct at the battle of Towton, where he fought on the Yorkist side is noticed by all the old chroniclers. Edward IV. promoted him to the Earldom of Kent, and made him Lord High-Admiral of England, and Knight of the Garter. He died in 1464, leaving three daughters. Joane, the eldest, married Sir Edward Bethom, and died without issue. Elizabeth married Sir Richard Strangeways. Alice married Sir John Conyers of Hornby. The arms of Fauconberg were:—gules, a saltire argent; a mullet sable for a difference. In 1643 there was a fresh creation in the Belasyse family of a Viscounty of this title, but this also has become extinct.—(*Rowland.*) When Lord Fauconberg was sent into Normandy as an Ambassador, in the reign of Henry VI., he was taken prisoner. His letter to Henry requesting a safe conduct from the King to three merchants for two years, has been preserved. These merchants were probably instrumental in procuring his ransom.

Regi Domino nostro supremo.

Suplicat humiliter Willelmus Nevill dominus de Fauconberg prisonarius in servicio vestro in Francia, captus per adversarios vestros et ad magnam et excessivam financiam et redempcionem positus sibi quasi importabilem, quatenus placeat vestre Regie Majestati sibi dare et concedere unum salvum conductum pro tribus mercatoribus de regno Francie, seu factoribus attornatis et procuratoribus suis, cum tribus vel quatuor mercatoribus in societate eorundem, pro una navi portagii Centum doliorum vel infra, per duos annos duraturum in forma que sequitur. Et ipse Deum pro vobis exorabit.

George Nevill, Lord Latimer, and Edward Nevill, Lord Burgavenny, will be noticed hereafter as the heads of their respective houses.

Robert Nevill, fifth son of Earl Ralph, became Bishop of Salisbury in 1427, and of Durham in 1438. In the royal letter to the Pope requiring his translation he is styled " Consanguinem suum charissimum ex preclarissima familia oriundum." The city of Durham in his day was the seat of many conventions and negotiations between England and Scotland at which his mild disposition acted favourably. The Exchequer on the Palace Green, which is now part of the University Library, was built by him in 1438. His arms are over the door. It was constructed to contain the Palatinate offices, with halls for holding the Bishop's Chancery, and Court of

Pleas. Bishop Nevill appointed his brother George, Lord Latimer, his chief chamberlain. He retained the accustomed splendour and costliness of the Palatinate Court, but his sway was mild, and his vassals were never oppressed during his episcopate of nineteen years. He died July 8th, 1457, and therefore did not witness those terrible scenes of carnage and crime, by which his nephews, Edward IV. and Richard III. gained the English throne.

On the 26th September, 1448, Henry VI. visited the shrine of St. Cuthbert at Durham,' and remained at the castle four days as the guest of Bishop Nevill. On the feast of St. Michael he assisted at vespers. He afterwards wrote a letter expressive of the delight which this visit had given him. He was greatly affected by "the noble manner of divine service, the sumptuous and glorious churches, and the multitude of ministers, in the province of York and diocese of Durham." The people were "all radicate in the faith of God, as Catholike a people as ever we came among, and all good and holy," and their "hearty reverence and worship shewn unto the King" was "as good and better than ever we had in our life. Wherefore, we dare well say, it may be verified in them the holy saying of the Prince of the Apostles, St. Peter, when he sayeth, 'Deum timete, Regem honorificate. Wryten in our city of Lincoln, the morrow of St. Luke the Evangelist, 1448."—*Vide Low's Diocesan History*.

Unhappy, unsuspecting man—too gentle and too good to be a king in those dark days—from thy sweet dream of a loyal people, all good and holy, thou hadst indeed a rough awakening!

Bishop Nevill desired burial in the Galilee, near the shrine of Bede, but his executors placed him beside his ancestors in the Nevill chantry. A marble table monument, inlaid with brass, was placed over his tomb. Only the matrix of the brass now remains.

The name of this Bishop appears in several Commissions for negotiating truces with Scotland in 1449 and 1451, and the city of Durham was in his time the seat of many conventions of the delegates of the two nations.

Robert Nevill was translated from Salisbury to Durham by Papal provision, Jan. 27, 1437. He received the temporalities of the diocese, April 8, 1438, and was enthroned on April 11. His promotion was probably due to the fact that his brother, the Earl of Salisbury, had been appointed Custodian of the Temporalities of Durham.—*Fœdera.*

R

His mild character is proved by the fact that "to the heir of Emilden he freely returned the whole of his estates which had been escheated to the see in consequence of the forgery and collusion of his ancestor." He further "restored their ample possessions to the Grays of Northumberland in the person of his nephew, Sir Ralph Gray, representative of Sir Thomas, who suffered for treason under Henry V."—*Surtees' Hist. Dur.*

Besides the usual officers of the See, several grants of new and peculiar offices occur on the Patent Rolls of Bishop Nevill; amongst these are a Chamberlain, a Vice-Chamberlain, a Master of the Horse, and an Armourer.

CECILY NEVILL, DUCHESS OF YORK.

"From Lady Cecily Nevill, Duchess of York, are lineally descended seven Kings of England, three Queens of England, four Princes of Wales, four Kings of Scotland, two Queens of Scotland, one Queen of Spain, and one Queen of Bohemia; as also, one Prince Elector Palatine of the Rhine. The aforesaid Lady Cecily Nevill died in the 11th year of Henry VII., 1495, having lived to see three Princes of her body crowned, and four murthered. She was the youngest daughter of Ralph, Lord Nevill of Raby, Staindrop, Brandspath, Sherryhutton, Middleham, and Warkworth, first Earl of Westmoreland, and Earl Marshall of England, and of his wife Lady Joan Beaufort, daughter of John of Gaunt, Duke of Lancaster and Acquitane, and King of Castile and Leon, and the sister of King Henry the Fourth of England, and to Lady Philippa, Queen of Portugal, and to Lady Katherine, Queen of Spaine, from whom descended all the late Emperors of Germany, the Kings of Spain, the House of Austria, and most of the Princes throughout Christendom now living."—*Cole's MSS., Brit. Mus., date* 1642.

Lady Cecily was the youngest of twenty-three children of Ralph, the first Earl of Westmoreland. She married Richard Plantagenet, Duke of York, which induced the Nevills to interest themselves in placing him upon the throne. As three sovereigns, however, of the House of Lancaster had successively possessed the throne, there appeared but little probability that Cecily's husband would ever ascend it, his own father having been attainted and executed for treason. Notwithstanding circumstances so gloomy, she saw her lord, by the aid of her own family, and particularly by the heroic valour of Salisbury and Warwick, her brother and nephew, raised to the post of Governor of the Kingdom, and declared heir apparent to the Crown. She saw her own family, the Nevills, as great as subjects could be. She also saw her husband, when just ascending the steps of the throne, by his own rashness killed in battle, and his head, separated from his body, in derision crowned with a paper diadem.

Of her sons five died children. Edward, who survived, became King, as Edward IV. The second, Edmond, a youth of twelve years of age, was cruelly put to death after the battle of Wakefield. George, the third son, who had been sometimes true, and at others disloyal, to his eldest brother and sovereign, was convicted and put to death by the procurement of one, and by the order of another of his brothers. Richard, the youngest son, after usurping the regal power and honours, fell in the field of battle fighting against a Prince of the Lancaster line.

Cecily Nevill had four daughters. Ursula, the youngest, died unmarried. Ann, who had two husbands, was married to Henry Holland, Duke of Exeter, godson to King Henry VI. The Duke was greatly attached to that pious Prince, and refused to desert his interest, though contrary to his own. This so much displeased his Duchess that she procured a divorce from him. She afterwards saw him reduced to a state of abject wretchedness at the Court of Burgundy.*

He was found dead at sea, between Dover and Calais, in 1475, but during his lifetime Ann married Sir Thomas St. Leger, Knight. She survived this alliance only two years, dying January 14th, 1475. St. Leger was put to death at Exeter by King Richard III. for attempting to dethrone him. Elizabeth, second daughter of Cecily, married John de la Pole, Duke of Suffolk, whose descendants were so peculiarly unfortunate. Margaret, the third daughter of the Duchess of York, was married to Charles the Rash, Duke of Burgundy, slain in 1477. She was the only one of Cecily's children who survived her, and was the celebrated enemy of King Henry VII. and all the Lancastrians, spending her rich dower in projects to ruin that monarch, though the fate of Elizabeth his Queen, her own niece, must have been included in it.

Horace Walpole describes Cecily Nevill as "a princess of spotless character," and in that description he was probably correct, though Clarence accused his mother of adultery; and Dr. Shaw, the ignorant and officious partisan of Richard, in his eagerness to do

---

* "No common beggar could have been poorer. He concealed his name, but I saw him following the Duke of Burgundy's train bare-foot, begging his bread. He married King Edward's sister, Anne, and, being afterwards known, received a small pension."—*Philip de Commines.*

that Prince good service, overshot the mark by attacking the
Duchess of York during his malicious diatribe at St. Paul's Cross,
on the subject of the illegitimacy of Elizabeth Woodville's children.
Cecily Nevill was respected in her widowhood; her person was
safe amongst her enemies, and her reputation remained unsullied
at a time when it was very much to the interest of the Lancastrians
to have aspersed her character.

In the reign of King Edward IV. she was treated with the
respect due to his mother.   In 1461, he sent, under his sign
manual, a letter acquainting her of his having defeated Henry VI.,
with every particular of the bloody battle of Towton.   Fabian says
that in February, 1470, when the nobility strove to make up the
breach between King Edward IV. and Clarence, these royal
brothers met for that purpose at Baynard Castle, where the
Duchess their mother then lay.

She opposed the marriage of her eldest son, King Edward IV.,
with his subject Elizabeth, widow of Sir Richard Wydeville, Knight,
as highly impolitic and injurious to his dignity and interest.

All the private councils of her son Richard were held at
Baynard's Castle, her own residence.   He wrote to her accounts
of his proceedings, and from the tenour of his letters there can be
little doubt but that she favoured his usurpation, although, of
course, she was not cognizant of all his deep laid schemes.   The
letter written from Pontefract (June 3rd) after he became King
is very affectionate and respectful.

After Richard's fall at Bosworth, Cecily saw the Crown go to
an illegitimate stem of the Lancastrian line.   It was, however, some
satisfaction to her to have it settled in her issue by the marriage
of King Henry VII. with her eldest grand-daughter, Elizabeth,
the heir of King Edward IV.   She lived to see several children
of this union.

The Duchess appears to have had her general residence at Baynard Castle, in London, and Berkhamstead, in Herts.   The former
was given by King Henry Henry VI. to Richard, Duke of York,
her husband, upon the death of Humphrey, Duke of Gloucester.
In this palace, in 1458, the Duke of York lodged his train of four
hundred men and all his noble partisans, with their warlike suits,
to deliberate about the most effectual means of asserting his claim
to the Crown.   Here again in 1460 the friends of York met and
voted to crown him; here likewise Richard III., with seeming

reluctance, was prevailed upon to take the kingdom. King Henry VII. obtaining the castle upon the Duchess' death, rebuilt it, says Stow, in his history of London, more in the manner of a palace than a castle.*

In the reign of King Richard III., Cecily Nevill resided in London, but she died in her castle of Berkhamstead, and was buried at her own desire at Fotheringay, in Northamptonshire, beside the Duke of York her late husband, of whose splendid funeral Sandford gives a particular relation. It was all but regal. She died in more frugal times.

Many and great were the changes this unhappy lady saw. She lived in the reigns of five sovereigns; she saw the Crowns of France and England wrested from the brow of Henry VI. She saw her son, King Edward IV., crowned, dethroned, restored, and cut off by his intemperance at an early age. She saw her grandson, King Edward V., deprived of his sceptre, imprisoned, and murdered; by whom, and when, perhaps, she never knew. She saw her youngest son, King Richard III., usurp the regal honours, and lose them soon after with his life; and finally she saw the enemy of her father proclaimed by the name of King Henry the Seventh.—*Vide Cecily Nevill, a paper read before Society of Antiquaries, by Mark Noble, F.S.A.*, April 14th, 1796.

The Duchess of York was remarkable for her beauty, and still more so for her indomitable pride. In the north she was called the Rose of Raby, but in the neighbourhood of her baronial residence of Fotheringay Castle, the common people called her "Proud Cis." She had a throne room at Fotheringay, where she gave receptions with the state of a Queen. Curious portraits in painted glass of Cicely and her husband exist in the south window of the chancel of Penrith Church, and were engraved in Jefferson's Antiquities of Leath Ward. Cecily appears decorated with a garland of gems, and gives the idea of a very handsome woman.— *Vide Miss Strickland's Eliz. Woodville.*

Cecily Nevill is numbered among the direct ancestors of our most Gracious Queen. Her great grand-daughter, Margaret Tudor, was the grandmother of Mary of Scotland, the mother of James I., and James's grand-daughter, Sophia, was the mother of George I.

* Baynard's Castle took its name from its founder, a nobleman who followed the Conqueror. Here Richard Nevill, Earl of Warwick, came with 600 men, in "red jackets embroidered with regged staves." It was afterwards a palace, and then came to Herbert, Earl of Pembroke. The Earls of Shrewsbury resided in it until it was burnt in the great fire.—*Pennant.*

The Duchess of York was the patroness of learning in those wild days when literature was well nigh forgotten altogether. She was a great benefactress to Queen's College, Cambridge. "In her good she was not elated, in her evil day she was not cast down."

The will of the Duchess is short, and, considering her great rank, may be deemed curious.

"Cecily, late wife of Richard Duke of York, and mother of King Edward the Fourth, April 1st, 1495. My body to be buried near the body of my late husband, Richard Duke of York, in his tomb within the Collegiate Church of Fotheringay. To my daughter Ann, my largest bed of bandekyn, with a counterpoint of the same; to my daughter Katherine, a traverse of blue satin; to my daughter of Suffolk, my chair with the covering, all my cushions, horses and harnesses for the same, with all my palfreys; to my son of Suffolk, a cloth of estate; to my son Humphrey, two altar cloths of blue damask; to my son William, a traverse of white sarcenet; to my daughter Anne, Prioress of Syon, a book of Bonaventure. I bequeath all my plate for carrying my body from the Castle of Berkhamstead to the Castle of Fotheringay. To dame Jane Pesmershe, widow, mine Inn, called the George, in Grantham, for her life, with remainder to the College of Fotheringay. And I appoint Mr. Oliver King, Bishop of Bath; Sir Reginald Bray, Knight, and Sir Thomas Lovell, Knight, Councillors to the King's Grace, my executors. And I constitute Sir Henry Heydon, Knight, Steward of my House and supervisor of this my will. Proved 27th August, 1495."

Of the uniform manner in which the household of the Duchess of York was conducted, and of the moral and religious sentiments there inculated, we have substantial proof in a highly interesting document which has been preserved to the present day.

"She useth to arise at seven of the clock, and hath readye her chapleyne to saye with her mattins of the day and mattins of our Lady, and when she is fully readye she hath a low mass in her chambre; and after masse she taketh something to recreate nature and soe goethe to the chapelle, hearing the divine service and two lowe masses. From thence to dynner, duringe the tyme whereof she hath a lecture of holy matter. After dinner she giveth audyence to all such as hath any matter to shewe unto her by the space of one hower, and after she hath slepte she contynneth in prayer unto the first peale of evensonge. In the tyme of supper she recyteth the lecture that was had at dinner to those that be in her presence. After supper she disposeth herself to be famyliar with her gentlewomen to the seeac'on of honest myrthe, and one hower before her going to bed she taketh a cuppe of wynne, and after that goeth to her pryvie closette and taketh her leave of God for all nighte, makinge end of her prayers for that daye, and by eighte of the clocke is in bedde. —*Board of Green Cloth MSS., St. James's; quoted in Miss Halsted's Richard III.*

PART II.—CHAPTER II.

RICHARD NEVILL, EARL OF SALISBURY.

WARWICK.—What plain proceeding is more plain than this?
Henry doth claim the crown from John of Gaunt,
The *fourth* son ; York claims it from the *third*;
Till Lionel's issue fails, his should not reign.
Then, father Salisbury, kneel we together ;
And in this private plot be we the first
That shall salute our rightful sovereign,
With honor of his birthright to the crown.
My heart assures me that the Earl of Warwick
Shall one day make the Duke of York a king.
YORK.—And, Nevill, this I do assure myself:
Richard shall live to make the Earl of Warwick
The greatest man in England, but the king.

King Henry VI.—Second Part.

RICHARD NEVILL was the eldest son of Ralph, first Earl of West-moreland, by his second Countess, Joan Beaufort. He married Alice, sole daughter and heir of Thomas de Montacute, Earl of Salisbury; and in her right, upon her father's death obtained that title.

In the 9th year of Henry VI., he had a grant from the King of divers manors to enable him to support the great expenses he incurred in France. When Henry went to Paris to be crowned King of France, the Earl of Salisbury accompanied him.

In 1433, the Earl was constituted warden of all the west marches towards Scotland, and in the following year warden both of the east and west marches. By an indenture dated 1436 he was retained by the Crown to serve in the wars in France and Normandy, with three banneretts, seven knights, 249 men at arms, and 1,040 archers. In 1442, he was warden of the west marches and governor of Carlisle. The King then made him a grant of £9,083 6s. 8d. per annum for thirty years, an enormous sum in those days.—(*Rowland.*) All our historians agree that the Earl of Salisbury and his stout son, the

King-maker, were two of the most powerful nobles who ever flourished in England. As they were closely associated in their military career, much of the history of the father may be found in that of the son. The Earl of Salisbury was executed at Pontefract Castle, after the battle of Wakefield. His third son, Thomas Nevill, perished on the same field, December 30th, 1460.

THE WILL OF RICHARD, EARL OF SALISBURY.

" My body to be buried in the Priory of Bustelsham, in the county of Berks, which is under the patronage of me and my dear wife, in her right, among the noble lords, late Earls of Salisbury, her ancestors in the place which, with the advice of the Prior, I have fixed upon.   I will that 200 marks be expended by my executors for my tomb, and 100 marks upon my funeral.   Also that 40 marks be distributed amongst poor maidens at their marriages, and that £100 be spent in masses, alms, and other works of charity for my soul.   I ordain that on the day of my funeral there be offered two coursers, one of them completely harnessed, with caparisons of my arms, and that there be banners, standards, and other accoutrements, according as is usual for a person of my degree.   I will that my feoffees stand seized of my castle and manors of Sheriff Hoton, East Lilling, West Lilling, and Raskelf, to the use of my wife during her life.   Also I will that the covenants of marriage of Thomas, my son, with Maud, Lady Willoughby, his wife, be fully performed according to the agreement made between me and Ralph, Lord Cromwell.   Also, I will that the marriage covenants made for the marriage of Catherine, my daughter, with the son and heir apparent of William, Lord Harrington, the son of William Bonville, be performed.   To my son George twelve silver dishes and a cup with cover gilt.   To my daughter Alice a gilt cup with cover.   To Eleanor a silver bowl.   To my daughter Margaret 1,000 marks to her marriage, and a gilt cup with cover.   To my daughter, the Countess of Arundel, a cup of gold.   To my brother, Lord William Fauconberg —— To Alice, my wife, ——

I appoint Sir James Strangways, Robert Danby, Christopher Conyers of Hornby, John Wytham, John Ireland, and John Middleton my executors.

Dated May 10th, 1458.

THE ENTERMENT OF THE ERLE OF SALISBERY AT BUSHAME.

The enterment of the Erle of Salisbery at Bushame, in the schere of Bokingham, the 15th day of Janyur, the secund yere off the regne of Kinge Edward the Fourth; and off Sir Thomas Neville his son; there two coffurs in a chaire, wt six horse trappid in the chaire; the first wt Seint George's armes, the remynint coveryd in blake; a banerolle of Seint George befor, two behinde. Firste, befor the day off conveynge of the body of the said Erle, the Earle of Warwike, son and heyre of the said Erle of Salisbery, aftur the chaire on horsebake; the Lord Montague on the right sid on fote, the Lord Lattymer's sone withe many Knyghts and noble Squyers on fete, on every sid the nombro of sixteen; the Baner and Standard of the said Erle immediately next after the chare, befor the said Erle of Warwike, a mylle wtout the townn, metinge the corsse, first, two Haraulds and two Kinges of Arms wt the cotes of armes of the said Erle at every corner, conveying the same to the place where he was enterid; at whiche place ther he was reseived, the body and the bonys so coffured, the Bischop of Exetur, Chauncelere of Englond, the Bischop of Salisbery, the Bischope of Seint Asse, and two Abbots, all myterd, wt a solempne procession, accompanyd with the Lord Hastings, the King's Chamberleyne, the Lord Fitzhughe, and many other Knyghts and noble Squyeres in gret nombre. Item, on the morne aftur, the Estats, Princes, Lords, and Ladys come unto the highe masse, the said Kings of Armes, Heralds, brought out of the revestry honorably every of them, &c., then Garter of the cote of armes, Clarens the sheld, Windesore the Swerde, Chester the helme and tymbre, and converid, to the body of the said Erle's herse, holdynge the cote of armes and the swerd on the right side, the sheld on the lefte side, the helme and tymbre at the hede, in the mydst wth out the pale and the p' close unto the offeringe, &c. Item, aftur the Gospelle of the masse, the two Kings of Armes went ffurthe to the weste dore of ye chirche, where there was a man armyed on horsebak trappid wt an ax in his right hande, the point towards; the said Kings reseived hym, and conveid hym unto the quire dore of the chirche, where he did alight, holdinge, the said horse trappid in his hand, in the arms of the said Erle.

Item, at the offeringe tyme, the Erle of Warwik, conveid between two noble and worshipfull knyghts, offered the masse penny, and stood apart on the right side of the Biscope, &c.

Item, then offered the Duk of Clarens, convied between two Barons to the offeringe, and he offered 6s. and 8d. And the Ducheese of Suff. and the Duk together everyche of them offered a scute.

Item, the Erle of Warwike comynge agayne for himself, offered 20d. And the Erle of Worcestre for hymselfe, offered 20d.

Item, the Lord Montague, 20d.

Item, the Lord Hastings, 12d.

Item, the Lord Fitzhewe, 12d.

Item, the remnant of Ladys and Gentillwomen wt oyr Knyghts and Squyeres and Gentillmen offerid.

ISSUE OF RICHARD NEVILL, first son of Ralph, first Earl of Westmoreland, by his second wife, Joan Beaufort.
Richard Nevill = Alice, sole daughter and heir Thomas de Montacute, Earl of Salisbury.

1. RICHARD NEVILL, KINGMAKER = Anne, daughter of Richard Beauchamp, Earl of Warwick.	2. John Nevill, created MARQUIS MONTAGUE, and Chancellor of England, slain at Barnet; married Isabel, co-heir of Sir Edmond Ingle-thorpe. (See pedigree of Montague.)	3. Sir Thomas Nevill, slain at Wakefield with his father; s. P., married Maud, d. of Robert Lord Willoughby de Eresby.	4. GEORGE NEVILL, Bishop of Exeter and ARCHBISHOP OF YORK. Died 1478.
ISABEL, born 1451, married, 1469, George, Duke of Clarence, brother to Edward IV.; created Earl of Salisbury and Warwick; attainted 1477.	ANNE = Edward, Prince of Wales, son of Henry VI.; afterwards married Rich., Duke of Gloucester, (Richard III.)		
Edward Plantag., styled Earl of Warwick; beheaded 14th Henry VII., 1499. Last male heir of Plantagenet.	Margaret Plantag., restored Countess of Salisbury, beheaded on Tower Hill, by Henry VIII. She married Sir Richard Pole.		

5. Joane, married William Fitzalan, Earl of Arundel.	6. Cecily, married, first, Hen. Beauchamp, Duke of Warwick; 2nd, John Tipcroft, Earl of Worcester. She died 1450.	7. Alice = Henry, Lord Fitzhugh.	8. Eleanor = Thomas Stanley, Earl of Derby, K.G.	9. Catherine, married, first, William, Lord Bonville, and Harrington; second, William, Lord Hastings, of Ashby-de-la-Zouche. She is a prominent character in the Last of the Barons.	10. Margaret = John de Vere, thirteenth Earl of Oxford, who died 5th Hen. VIII.

S

PART II.—CHAPTER III.

THE HOUSE OF LATIMER.

"The good old rule
Sufficed them; the simple plan
That they should take who had the power
And they should keep who can."

WE have already shown that John Nevill, the son of Lord John Nevill of Raby, bore the title of Baron Latimer in right of his mother, *vide* Part I., page 34. He died without issue male, and his sisters were his co-heirs. Elizabeth, one of them, married Sir Thomas Willoughby. Many of the entailed estates came to Ralph, the first Earl of Westmoreland, being the elder brother of the half-blood; and Earl Ralph settled them upon George, his third son, and he accordingly, in the 10th Henry VI., was summoned to Parliament as Lord Latimer.

In the 13th Henry VI., 1435, George Latimer was one of the chief commanders of the King's forces, then raised in the north for the defence of those parts against the Scots. The same year he came to an accord with Maud, Countess of Cambridge (widow of his uncle John, Lord Latimer), viz., that if, by the advice of their counsel, they should grant unto Sir John Willoughby, Knight (to prevent lawsuits), any of those lands which formerly belonged the said John, Lord Latimer, of such lands she should give two parts, and he, the said George, one part.

In the latter part of his life, Lord Latimer became an idiot, wherefore the custody of his lordships and lands was committed to his nephew, Richard Nevill, Earl of Warwick. Lord Latimer married Elizabeth, third daughter and co-heir of Richard Beauchamp, Earl of Warwick (by his first wife Elizabeth, daughter and heir of Thomas, Lord Berkley).

Lord Latimer was summoned to Parliament from the 10th Henry VI., to 9th Edward IV., in which year he died.—*Rowland.* For his issue, see Table.

The following is an extract from the will of his consort, Lady Latimer :—

"In the name of the blessed hooly and Almyghty fforremour and maker of all thyngez, oure Lord God, Fader and Sonne and Holy Gost, in Trinite. The xx day of September, the yere oure seid Lord mcccclxxx., and of my sov'eign lord Kyng Edward the iiijth, the xx yere, I Dame Elizabeth Lady Latymer, the seid xx day loued and thonked be oure said graceous and blessed Lord God beyng in christen beleve and of hole mynde, though by the same oure goode and graceous Lordez visitacion. I be and have be right fervently greved in my body with seknesse to me most hertuly welkome of and by his sondez ordeigne make and declare this my will and testament that hereafter foloweth. First, I comytte and betake my soule to the m'cy and pitee of the most graceous and m'cifull Lord my Creatour and Maker my Lord God. My body to be entered in the Chapell' of oure Ladye withyn the the Collegiall' Church' of Warwyke which the right famous renouned honorable and Cristen Prynce of ,noble memorye my lord and fader, Sir Richard Beachamp, late yerle of Warrewike, caused and ordeyned to be made, and that my seid body be leyde even' beneth' the hed of my seid lord and ffadur betwene my naturaly borne sonne Harry Latymer and Olyv' Dudley late my sonne in the lawe. And I ordeygne and wull' that there be iiij., sev'all' stones of faire marbull' with images uppon theym of coper and gilted covenable and convenient for myn' astate and their degreez with the epitaffez of oure burthez decesses and other metely thyngez to such proposez wreten uppon the same stones be purveid and leid uppon us, and a like stone uppon my lord my husbond. And for so much' as my doughtor Dame Kat'yne hath' no livelode nor other substinance to fynde hur mete drynke clothes nor other necessariez duryng my liffe I wull' socour helpe and fynde her as I may and as I am naturally bound to do. And wull' that after my decesse she have the lordshippes and man's of Stowe with 'thapprtenancez in Northamton'shire, the man' of Tetecote, with' Pike, Holiwell', and Larkebeare, in the counte of Deyveinschire, the landez and ten'tez in Bruggewater, in the counte of Som's.—*Excerpta Historica.*

Sir Henry Nevill, the son of Lord George, being slain at Edgecote during his father's lifetime, RICHARD NEVILL succeeded his grandfather in the Barony of Latimer. Lord Richard Nevill became a very distinguished soldier. He held an important command in the King's forces at the battle of Stoke, near Newark, and vanquished John, Earl of Lincoln, who headed the Rebellion in the 1st year of Henry VII. In 1491 he had livery of all lands of which his grandfather died seized. In the following year he figured as an important character when the Scots besieged Norham Castle. He disputed the claim of Lord Brook to the Barony of Latimer so successfully that Lord Brook resigned his demand, and the matter was amicably settled by a marriage between the two houses.—*Vide Table.* Lord Latimer's name occurs in the famous letter of the Barons to Pope Clement the Seventh, 22nd Henry VIII.

But the most notable day in the life of this lord was that on which he appeared at the ever famous field of Flodden.

The challenge sent from Wooler on the 7th of November, 1513, by the Earl of Surrey to King James IV., was signed by Richard, Lord Latimer. James accepted the challenge. Every reader of history knows how this rash and headstrong monarch fought.

> " Till shades of death did close his eyes,
> Till then he did his soldiers cheer,
> And raise their courage to the skies."

His body was found on Flodden Field. There also lay the flower of Scottish nobility and 10,000 of the meaner sort—if any could be called mean—who so bravely had "fought around their King."

Lord Latimer married Ann, daughter of Sir Humphrey Stafford of Grafton, in the county of Worcester.—*For issue see Table.* He sat in Parliament from 7th to 12th of Henry VII., and from 1st to 21st of Henry VIII. He died in 1531.

JOHN NEVILL, eldest son of Lord Richard, succeeded his father in the Barony of Latimer.

He married Dorothy, daughter of Sir George Vere (brother of John, Earl of Oxford); but his name is famous in history, chiefly on account of his second marriage with Catherine, daughter of Sir Thomas Parr.

> "Oh! lucky looks that fawned on Catherine Parr,
>   A woman rare like her but seldom seen ;
> To Borough first, and then to Latimer,
>   She widow was, and then became a Queen."
> "For when the King's fifth wife had lost her head,
>   Yet he dislikes the life to live alone ;
> And once resolved the sixth time for to wed,
>   He sought outright to make his choice of one.
> That choice was chance, right happy for us all,
> It brewed our bliss, and rid us quite from thrall."
>   *Thockmorton MS.*

The last two lines denote the unfeigned delight of Sir Thomas Throckmorton at the marriage of his cousin, and the consequent elevation of his family; but they will be re-echoed for ever by all Cambridge men, as the name of Katherine Parr is sacred among us. When the University was in danger of being devoured by the rapacity of Henry VIII., the ready wit of Katherine Parr saved it.— *Vide MS. C. C. Coll. Cam.*, 206.

By the marriage of her progenitor—Ivo de Tallebois, with the sister of the Earls Eadwine and Morkar—Katherine Parr inherited both Saxon and Norman blood. Her ancestor, Sir William Parr, married Elizabeth, daughter of the Lord Fitzhugh, by Alice, daughter of Ralph Nevill and Joan Beaufort. Alice Nevill was sister to King Henry's great-grandmother, Cicely Nevill, Duchess of York. Katherine Parr was, therefore, fourth cousin to Henry VIII.

She was born at Kendal Castle, in Westmoreland. Among the Scroop MSS. there is a curious letter from her mother, Dame Maud Parr, to Lord Dacre, in which she (Dame Parr) assures Lord Dacre that "there can be no marriage until my lord's son (Scroop) *comes to the age of thirteen and my daughter to the age of twelve.*"

The letter concludes thus :—"My lord, it might please you to take so much as to help to conclude this matter, if it will be, and if you see any defect on my part, it shall be ordered as ye deem good, as knoweth Jesu, who preserve your good lordship."

In this matter Dame Parr was doomed to disappointment. Her next move was to marry Katherine to Lord Borough of Gainsborough, "a discreet widower, well advanced in years." Her labours in this instance were crowned with success. At the age of sixteen Katherine was left a widow, lovely and wealthy.

"How long she continued the widow of Lord Borough is uncertain, but she was probably under 20 years of age when she became, for a second time, the wife of a mature widower, and again undertook the office of step-mother. It is not unlikely that her residence with Lady Strickland at Sizergh Castle might lead to her marriage with John Nevill, Lord Latimer, as Lady Strickland was a Nevill of Thornton Briggs, and would naturally afford her kinsman every facility for his courtship to their fair cousin. Lord Latimer was related to Katherine in about the same degree as her first husband, Lord Borough."

The manors of Cumberton, Wadborough, and several other estates in Worcestershire, which Lord Nevill inherited from Elizabeth Beauchamp, were settled on Katherine, but she resided with her husband at his stately mansion of Snape Hall in Yorkshire. "There she pursued the noiseless tenor of her way, in the peaceful routine and privacy of domestic life, to which those talents and acquirements which afterwards rendered her the admiration of the most learned men in Europe, and the intellectual model of the ladies of England, were calculated to lend a charm. Fortunate indeed must Lord Latimer have felt himself in being able to obtain so charming a companion for his latter days, and at the same time one so well qualified to direct the studies, and form the minds of his children.

Lord Latimer was so strenuous a Catholic that he became one of the leaders of the northern insurrection, on account of the suppression of the monasteries, and the sequestration of the Church property by Cromwell in 1536. The Duke of Norfolk was empowered by the King to put down this rebellion. He prevailed upon the insurgents to lay down their arms, on condition of receiving free pardon, with a promise that their grievances should be discussed in Parliament. The pardon was dated Dec. 9th, 1536. In February the insurrection broke out again, but Lord Latimer did not join it. The prudent counsels of Katherine possibly deterred her lord from involving himself a second time in so rash an enterprise."—*Miss Strickland's Lives of the Queens.*

The will of Lord Latimer is dated Sept. 12th, 1542. It was proved March 11th, 1543.

He bequeaths the manors of Nunmonkton and Hamerton to his wife, and directs that his body be buried on the south side of the Church of Well, where his ancestors are buried, if he should die in Yorkshire. He appoints the Master of the Hospital and Vicar of Well, receivers of all profits of the parsonage of Askham Richard, as also of the parsonage of St. George's, York, wherewith to endow a grammar school at Well, and to pray for the soul of the founder.

Lord Latimer died in London, and was interred in St. Paul's Cathedral.

He evidently died in the communion of the Roman Church, and it was not until after his decease that Lady Katherine openly professed and supported the Reformed faith.

Surely no creature was ever so zealously and continually courted as this extraordinary lady. Scarcely was the breath out of her husband's body when she was wooed by Sir Thomas Seymour, the handsomest bachelor at Court, and brother of the late unhappy Queen Jane. Katherine owned that she loved him, but added, that, "her will was *overruled by a higher power*." On July 10th, 1543, some three months after the proving of Lord Latimer's will,

Cranmer issued a license for "the marriage of our Sovereign Lord the King with Katherine Latimer, in whatever church, chapel, or oratory he may please." The oratory that "pleased" our Sovereign lord was the Queen's closet at Hampton Court, and the ceremony was performed by Gardiner, Bishop of Winchester. At the words "till death us do part," the Queen's cheek blanched, so it was said; but be that as it might, King Hal had found his match at last.

The story of the way in which this truly wonderful woman "managed" the King's Majesty is a most refreshing piece of literature, but it belongs not to our present purpose of sketching the House of Nevill.

Suffice it then to say that Katherine made her step-daughter, Margaret Nevill, the only daughter of Lord Latimer, one of her maids of honour. Furthermore she wrote a book called "The Lamentations of a Sinner," in which she flattered and soaped her sovereign lord to such an extent that even his Tudor heart was satisfied. She greeted this irritable and voluptuous monarch with the most winning smile whenever he brought his swollen and enfeebled body into her presence, and when the progress of disease rendered locomotion no longer possible the King's ulcerated leg sometimes reposed serenely on Katherine's lap in the presence of the whole Court. She smiled, too, when the King, in the Act of Settlement, spoke of "our entirely beloved wife, queen Katharyne, *that now is, or of any other our lawful wife that we shall hereafter marry;*" and she smiled again, when Gardiner's funeral oration on the King's Majesty (text—"Blessed are the dead which die in the Lord") being finished, and the plots against her life being finished with it, and her "beautiful head standing safe at last," she gazed on the ring of her fourth betrothal; and soon after married her old and true love, Sir Thomas Seymour, Lord Admiral of England. Katherine was thrice a stepmother, and at last a mother.

"God rest her soul," exclaims a writer of the last century, "for her body reposed but little, either in life or death!"

(The embalmed body was buried at Sudely, but several times exhumed.)

"All honour," says another writer, "be unto this inestimable lady, the Lady Katherine, who, for the furtherance of the Protestant faith was permitted to live with and to outlive King Henry VIII., and by sowing in the hearts of her stepchildren, the Princess Elizabeth and Prince Edward, the pure seed of the kingdom, caused the fruits of righteousness and peace to spring up within these realms."

JOHN NEVILL, son of John, Lord Latimer, succeeded to the Barony of Latimer in 1542. He sat in Parliament from the 35th Henry VIII. to 19th Elizabeth. He married Lucy, daughter of Henry Somerset, Earl of Worcester. He was the last Lord Latimer, and died April 22nd, 1577.—*Vide chap., Nevill Monuments.*

EDMUND NEVILL, great grandson of Richard, Lord Latimer (see Table), claimed the title of Earl of Westmoreland. His right thereto is thus expressed by himself in a letter to James I. :—

"Richard the eldest son of Ralph the first Earle, by Joan, his second wife, was Earl of Salisbury, and his issue male expired in George, Duke of Bedford, who died in 1485, without issue male; George, the other son of Ralph and Joan, was Lord Latimer, to whom I am next heire male, and therefore pretend right to the Earldom of Westmoreland, by the grant of Richard the Second.

"The King's Majestie, besides the gracious promises made to me in the lifetyme of Queen Elizabeth, and since his own coming to the Crowne, hath both by word and writing allowed me the said title, the least of which is not only a full and sufficient investiture of a tytle of honor lawfully descended, but hath the power of a new creation, in the greatest honors in the realme. His Majesty hath also further promised me, on the word of a King, that if any defect of right grew by the attaynder of Charles, 6th Earl of Westmoreland, he would supply it out of his own grace and bounty: the occasion of the said Charles having fallen, being for his favour and affection to the Kings mother (Mary Queen of Scots).

"Signed,   WESTMERLAND.

—*Lansdowne MSS.*

In April, 1605, he wrote to James I., as follows :—

"I submit myne honor, my goodes, my life, and whatsoever I am, freely to be disposed as your Majesty's Royal judgement shall think meetest for your service; not seeking by standing upon the nice pointes of my right to urge unreasonable demands, as by myne enemies is suggested, but humbly beseeching your most Excellent Majesty to free me out of the labyrinth of the lawes wherein I have wandered up and down these many years unprofitably, and out of the lands and possessions of my House to shape me such a proportion of estate as may enable me to do your Majesty service worthy the name and House of my ancestors whom to exceed in loyal and honorable actions for my Prince and Country is the utmost end of my ambition."

After the discovery of the gunpowder plot he wrote again :—

"My dread Souveraige Lord,—Seeing your Majesty hath vouchsafed a gracious and benigne acceptance of the dutiful gratulations of many of your loveing subjects for your late happy escape and preservation, I find no cause to think it any presumption in myself to tender the lyke loyal testimony of my inward joy for your Majesty's safetye, wherein I know not whether the treachery of your disloyal subject, such as no age hath ever heard of give more cause of wonder, or that admirable Providence which hath ever seemed to watch for your special preservation, even before you were borne; an argument strong enough to teach all malicious men that in vain they seek to hurt that annoynted of God whom angels are appointed to guard; for whose safety and happiness I know not what subject should have more cause both to be thankful to God and gratulate with your Maiesty than my selfe, whose desyres and endeavours, both long before your happy coming to this crowne, and ever since, have been directed to that principal; and wherein, if those affectionate desires have not been accompanied with answerable effects, the fault lies not in my will but my fortune.

Wherefore I know not whom I should accuse for calling to remembrance with what love and liking your Maiesty entertained the first offer of my affections and services, with what continuance of favour and liberal promises you still sought to nourish the same, with what affability and princely kindness you received me, when first I came to kiss your Royal hand, giving me assurance not to hold what was mine own by due descent, but promising further additions of your own grace (and from that meeting, and during some tyme), shewing yourself easy in access, affable in pleasing, willing to my first demande, and thereby confirming unto me those titles of honor of my House which your Maiesty had before acknowledged both by word and writinge; and now on the contrarie side, being myself a stranger thus long, not only to your favour but to your Court, kept from my native inheritance, which your laws have cast upon me, called in question for the titles of my House, which your Maiesty had accorded unto me, turned to the law to plead with you, at whose feet I could lay my life and estate, without any suit, abandoned to the importunity of creditors for those debts which I entered into for your service, and in expectation of my rightful fortunes, what can I do, seeing this uncouth change (without any knowledge or conscience of just cause), but wonder (as all men doe), what interposition hath caused this dark eclipse, that your gracious favour no more shines upon me, whereby I am left desolate, and bare both from fruit and leaves, like the winter season, when the sun hath declined his course another way! Yet herein I am most miserable, that I neither see end of my misery, nor hope of redress; which lies only in the sacred breast, and is quite taken away by debarring my access to your Maiesty; yea, myself herein am consenting to mine own wrong, who being loth to interrupt your Maiesty's open pastimes and recreations (which should be free from care) with my said complaint, do ofter pretermit the occasion of my soliciting mine owne cause. And shall my modesty and good respect make me fare the worse? Alas! let your Maiesty at length take pitty of his heavy sufferings, whose hart to you hath been ever faithful; and if nothing else, yet let my ever tried loyalty move your heart to compassion. It is a kind of remedie to know the worst of evil; and then I humbly beg (that in recompence of all my constant affection) you will either relieve me by some speedy course of justice, or set an end to my tedious expecting by some certain composition, whereby I may be made so happy as to be enabled to serve your Maiesty and my countrie in that place whereto I am inheritable by birth."

This case was referred to the Judges by King James; and is reported by Lord Coke (Rep. 7, Mich. 7th James). It appears by this report to have been resolved by all the Judges that the ancient

T

Earldom of Westmoreland was forfeited by the attainder for treason of Charles, Earl of Westmoreland. The Crown certainly acted upon this resolution, by conferring a new Earldom of Westmoreland on Sir Francis Fane, in 1624, which is still in existence.

In a manuscript book which has evidently been in the archives of the King of Spain, having the arms of the King of Spain on the back, among other State papers, was the following in the Spanish language. It would appear from this document, that this same Edmond Nevill, as Earl of Westmoreland, had applied in 1621 to the Spanish Court for a pension, and the Memorial which he presented was forwarded to Count Gondòmar, the Spanish Ambassador in England, to report upon it.

"By the King.

"Count Gondomar, Member of my Councils of War and Affairs, my Chamberlain and Embassador in England. On the part of the English Earl of Westmoreland it has been represented to me, that he has served in the affairs and to the effect contained in the Memorial of which a copy is enclosed, praying me for those reasons to grant him a pension in Flanders suitable to his rank. I (charging you to send me your advice thereupon) will approve what decision it may be proper to make on this claim.—Madrid, Nov. 25, 1621."

Addressed on the cover,

"By the King.

"To Count Gondomar, Member of his Councils of War and Affairs, his Chamberlain and Embassador in England."

The Enclosure.

"To your Royal Majesty.

"The Earl of Westmoreland represents that persecution which he suffers on all sides may truly be called miserable. It is now forty-six years since he left England (flying from the persecution of Queen Elizabeth), in the time of Don John of Austria and the Prince of Parma, under whose command he served at the sieges of different places, namely, Maestricht, Oudenarde, Tournay, Dunkirk, Bergen, Neuport Dixmuyde, Ypres, and many other places, in which he gave satisfaction to the Duke of Parma, that he proposed to reward him; but of this the Queen of England being informed, she, jealous of his credit here, summoned him home under penalty of losing all the possessions of his house, as well honours as lands. Upon his return the Petitioner was well received by the Queen, who passed to him her Royal word that he should not be troubled for conscience sake, which mode of treatment she adopted to draw over the Petitioner to her party, and for this purpose she offered him the command of some ships destined for the West Indies, under the orders of Sir Francis Drake. From this service he excused himself by the pretext he was not accustomed to the sea, and her jealousy was increased by seeing he was not willing to serve against the Crown of Spain, so that she sought every ground for imprisoning him, which at last she did under colour of his keeping up correspondence with the Queen of Scotland, then a prisoner, the mother of the present King of England. A few months after his imprisonment, the Queen of England took under her protection the Low Countries, and declared open war against His Majesty who is now in glory, having levied for this purpose a powerful army under the Earl of Leicester, to whom its command was given, and who was made governor of the rebellious provinces, and she sent to the Petitioner, then in the Tower of London, Sir Philip Sydney, created governor of Flushing, with orders to set him at liberty, upon condition of his serving in the expedition against the Crown of Spain ; and that not only he should have an honourable command in the Queen's army, but also be put in possession of all the lands belonging to his family, which were then in the Queen's power. All this the Petitioner refused, declaring that the laws of hospitality would not permit him to carry arms against your Viceroy in his own country, who had there received him so kindly, and entertained him during his stay, which reply was so ill received on the part of the Queen, that she ordered the Petitioner to be more strictly confined than before in the said Tower of London, in which for fourteen years from that time he remained a prisoner, and sixteen years more in the country under the guarantee of many of his peers, that he should not leave the country without her licence. Since it is known to all, and confirmed by the King of England himself, the land of Neville, Latimer, and Westmoreland produced 400,000 doubloons per annum,* of which the Petitioner is the true and undoubted heir ; and he could afterwards, if it were necessary, give a more detailed account of his sufferings and losses in England, all which being taken into consideration, and the Petitioner having now no means of support for himself, his wife, and children, and having lost all his wealth in England to the amount above-named, on account of the affection he has always borne and will bear towards the Crown of Spain and the Holy Catholic faith, he humbly beseeches your Majesty, as an act becoming your Royal greatness, in consideration of the circumstances herein set forth, to grant to the Petitioner a pension suitable to his rank and the great losses he has sustained for the Crown of Spain and his Holy Catholic faith. And the Petitioner will ever pray, &c."

"There is one Nevill," says Wadsworth, in his *English Spanish Pilgrims*, printed in 1630, "who styles himself Earl of Westmerland, but his Earledome many times will scarce furnish him with a dinner, and were it not for his second wife (this Nevill's first wife is yet living in London) who playeth the *shee physitian* in the Archduchess Court, he might oft times be put to narrower shifts notwithstanding his 100 crowns pension a month."

If this somewhat scurrilous paragraph does not refer to Edmund Nevill, I am unable to attach any meaning whatever to it.

In 1639 there was an alarm of a Spanish Armada. Some of the English Catholic exiles were colonels in it, and "one Nevill who termed himself Earl of Westmerland had a great command." It was totally defeated by the Dutch.

---

* If this statement be correct, the income would be equivalent to £150,000 in modern money.

" At Green Street, in the parish of Eastham, in Essex, about a mile north-west of the church, is an ancient mansion, supposed to have been the residence of the Nevills. The church stands near the Thames. Behind the altar is a handsome monument of Edmund Nevill and his lady in kneeling attitude, with this inscription—

In memory of the right honorable Edmond Nevill, Lord Latimer, Earle of West-moreland, and Dame Jane, his wife, with the memoryals of their seven children; which Edmond was lineally descended from the Honorable blood of Kings and Princes, and ye 7th Erle of Westmerland of the name of Nevills.

By God's great power who doth command all powers,
　To us these seaven children were for blessings given,
Some do survive as images of owers,
　And some are gone from whence they came to heaven
Birth, blood, and beautie like to flowers still fade,
　Death turns each living thing to shade.

His title to the Earldom of Westmerland was evidently a matter which Edmond Nevill did not intend the world to forget, for we are treated to another verse—

" From princely and from honourable blood
　By true succession was my high descent,
Malignant crosses oft opposed my good
　And adverse chance my state did circumvent."

Edmund Nevill certainly had two wives, and both of them were called Jane." *Vide Lyson's History of Eastham*, 1820.

The first was Jane Martignis, Dame de Colombe; and the second, Jane, daughter of Richard Smythe, co. Warwick. By the latter he had issue, Ralph, Katherine, Dorothy, Jane, Margaret, Anne. Katherine was buried at Eastham, under an altar tomb of black marble, and the inscription styles her "the right, virtuous, fair, and noble ladie Katherine Nevill, first daughter of Edmund, Earl of Westmoreland, who died a virgin, Dec. 1st, 1613, being of the age 23 years." Dorothy married Arthur Hill, Esq., who died 1645.

Lysons states that Jane, widow of Edmond Nevill, died at Mile End, 1647. In her will she styles herself "Dame Jane Nevyll, Countess of Westmoreland, relict of the Right Honorable Edmund Nevyll de Latimer, claiming of right to be, and generally reputed to be Earl of Westmoreland." She directs that her body should be decently buried at Eastham, and that a hearse of velvet should be put in the Church, and covered with escutcheons. She bequeathes £100 per annum out of the pension granted her by King James, to her daughter, Dame Dorothy, wife of Arthur Hill, Esq., her only surviving child.

The date of Edmond Nevill's death is not known. As he assumed the title of the Earl of Westmoreland, notwithstanding the attainder of the 6th Earl, he was several times summoned to appear before the Lords' Commissioners for executing the office of Earl Marshal. The last record of these appearances is March 2nd, 1605.

Upon an old survey of the estates which belonged to the Lords Latimer, there is an entry in the handwriting of Edmund Nevill, with reference to the decease of his father, Richard Nevill of Wyke, Worcestershire. "My Lord, my father departed this world, May 27th, Anno Domini 1590."

By the marriage of Dorothy, daughter of John, last Lord Latimer, with Thomas Cecil, first Earl of Exeter, the manors of Snape and Well,. in the honour of Richmond, were carried into the Burleigh family.

Well Church is mentioned in Domesday. Turchil was the last Saxon lord of Well. Snape is not mentioned by Dugdale. By what means the manors of Snape and Well passed to Ribald, first Lord of Middleham is not recorded. They descended from him to Mary de Middleham, and so passed to the Nevills.

In 5th Edward III., Ralph Nevill obtained charter of free warren for these manors. In 38th of same reign he gave eleven messuages and 2½ acres of land in Well, and ten acres in Snape to the Hospital of Well for the celebration of divine service there, according to a special ordination made by him for three priests to pray for the good estate of himself when living, and for the souls of himself and ancestors thereafter.

"On the 12th April, 1343, William, Archbishop of York, appropriated the Church of Well with all its rights to the master of the hospital. The original endowment of this hospital by the Nevill family was rational and judicious, and the engrafting of a grammar school upon the first foundation was an improvement adapted towards the end of Henry Eighth's reign, when classical literature was spreading in every direction."—*Whitaker's Richmond.*

Leland describes Snape as "a godly castel in a valley longing to the Lord Latymer, and two or three parkes welle wooded about it. It is his chefe house, and standith a two mile from Great

Tanfeld." When the Cecil family succeeded that of Latimer they transformed the castle of Snape into a commodious quadrangular house suited to the taste of the period. This work bears date 1587.

Snape Castle was sold at the commencement of this century, by the then Marquis of Exeter. It is now the property of Sir Frederick Milbank. The ancient chapel still remains; and is used by the Vicar of Well, for Divine Service. The south side of the castle quadrangle is kept in repair; and contains lofty apartments, which are let as farm houses. The remainder of the castle has been roofless and dismantled for more than one hundred and fifty years.

PEDIGREE OF LATIMER.

GEORGE NEVILL, third son of Ralph, first Earl of Westmoreland, by Joan Beaufort. Summoned to Parliament as BARON LATIMER, 10th Henry VI. Married Elizabeth, daughter and co-heir of Richard Beauchamp, Earl of Warwick. Died 1469.

1. *Sir Henry Nevill*, slain at Edgecote, V. P. 1469; married Joan, daughter of John Bouchier, Baron Berners; buried in Beauchamp Chapel, Warwick.   2. *Jane*, mar. Oliver Dudley.   3. *Katherine*.

1. RICHARD NEVILL, succeeded his grandfather as BARON LATIMER. *Fought at Flodden.* Married Anne, daughter of Sir Humphrey Stafford. Died 1531.   2. *Thomas Nevill*, of Mathon, Worcester, married Anne, daughter of Robert Greville, of Charringworth, Gloster. Founder of the NEVILLS OF CHENSTON.   3. *Jane*, married Sir James Radcliffe.

1. JOHN NEVILL, succeeded his father as BARON LATIMER; married, first, Dorothy, daughter of Sir George Vere, brother of John, Earl of Oxford; second, Katherine, daughter of Sir Thomas Parr, afterwards Queen to Henry VIII. Died 1542.

JOHN NEVILL, last LORD LATIMER, married Lucy, daughter of Henry Somerset, Earl of Worcester; buried at Well, 1577. Wife buried at Hackney, 1582.

2. *William Nevill*, of Wyke, married Elizabeth, daughter of Sir Giles Greville.

Richard Nevill, of Wyke, married Barbara, daughter of Thomas Arden, of Park Hall, Co. Warwick. Died 1590.

3. *Sir Thos. Nevill*, of Pigotts Ardley, Essex, mar. Mary, eldest daughter of Sir Thomas Tey.

4. *Marmaduke*, m. E. izabeth, youngest d. of Sir Thomas Tey.[*]

5. *Dorothy*, married Sir Christopher Danby, of Swinton.

6. *Susanna*, born 1501, married Richard Norton, Esq. of Norton Conyers, the patriarch of the rebellion of 1569.

7. *Elizabeth*, married Edward Lord Willoughby de Broke.

1. *Katherine*, m. Henry Percy, Earl of Northumberland, 19th Elizabeth.   2. *Dorothy*, mar. Thomas Cecil, Earl of Exeter.

Edmund Nevill 16c6 claimed Earldom of Westmoreland without success.

3. *Lucy*, m. Sir William Cornwallis of Broome, Co. Suffolk.   4. *Elizabeth*, married, first, Sir John Danvers; second, Sir Edmond Carey, the third son of Henry Lord Hunsdon.

* An inscription in the Tower of London is supposed to refer to this Marmaduke Nevill, but there is no record of his incarceration.

PART II.—CHAPTER IV.

THE HOUSE OF WARWICK.

"This I dare boldly write,
No man could better love, or better fight."

Who has not heard of Guy—"Sir Guy, of Warwyke, flower and honor of knighthode, sonne to Sir Seywarde, Baron of Walingford, by his Lady and wyfe, Dame Sabyne, a florentyne in Italy of the noble bloode of the countrey, translate from Italy unto this Lande?" And who has not heard of fair Felys, daughter of Roband, Earl of Warwick, with whom Guy fell in love—Felys, who had the hair and eyes, the roses and lilies of Venus, without her mole? Who has not heard how Felys cared not for Guy because he had lost his estates in the Mercian quarrel, and, though valiant and magnificent, he was a poor man withal?

May I again relate the story?—how, though Felys despised him exceedingly, yet for her sake Guy went forth to make himself a name before which even the haughty Felys might bow down—how unceasingly he fought, being ever the strong victor, yet ever just and gentle—how in great battle he won an Emperor's daughter, and, though she was passing fair and loved him, he left her for the sake of Felys; but Felys bade him depart. Then Guy went forth again to foreign lands, his arm being so strengthened by fierce desire to subdue all things, even Felys herself, that none could stand against him. Covered with glory he came again to Angleland; and, at Lincoln, Felys met him, and married him, in the presence of King Athelstan. Thus Guy became Earl of Warwick. But when the new moon came, Guy remembered that one enemy was left unsubdued, therefore for the crucifying of the flesh he departed from Felys "to her greate hevynes, and never knew her after, and all the while she kept her clene and trew Lady and wyf to him, devout to Godward, and by way of Almes greatly helpinge them that were in poor estate."—*Rous. Asmolean MSS.*, 839.

Guy journeyed to the Holy Land, "where Jerusalem's fair city stood, and where the Lord was crowned with thorns, and, having in that land done many mighty deeds, he came once more to Angleland" in disguise. He put the Danes to flight; but none knew him save Athelstan, who kept his secret.

Then Guy lived as a hermit in a cave near Warwick, and, in the guise of a pilgrim, often asked alms of the Lady Felys at the Castle gate. Thus he viewed her whom he loved so well, and heard her ask all palmers if ever in their travels they had seen the Earl of Warwick. Having seen her truth and tears, creeping back to his cell, he placed a dead man's head before him, and sought in prayer to overcome the love of earth.

At last he sent a ring to Felys, and bade her seek him in his cell; and when she came, he said, "O Felys, I have spent my youth upon the love of thee; for thy sake I have waded in blood; and for my God I have kept old age, the night of nature; yet let me die beside thee!" Felys, stricken with severest sorrow, died fifteen days after her lord.

Early in the present century, the following Anglo-Saxon inscription was discovered by Mr. Daniel Lysons, on the south wall of the cell at Guy's Cliffe.

Y. D.   .   ,
CHRIST-TU   ICHNIECTI
THIS I-WIHTTH
GUHTHI.

Translation :—"Cast out Thou Christ for thy servant this burden."

("The characters may be safely referred to the tenth century, and to the lifetime of Guithi or Guy himself."—*Vide Account of the Saxon Inscription at Guy's Cliffe by R. Carr Ellison. Published by Cooke and Sons, Warwick.*)

Should you ever go to see Guy's hermitage, you will be disposed to agree with Dugdale when he says, that, "For one who desireth a retired life in a delicious place, the like of Guy's Cliffe is not to be found." But you must go to the porter's lodge at Warwick Castle if you want to see fair Felys' slippers, and Guy's sword, Guy's helmet, Guy's tilting pole, and Guy's porridge pot (warranted to contain one hundred and twenty gallons); and the porter will tell all that I have told you—with additions.

Turchill, described as a descendant from Guy, was Earl of Warwick at the time of the Conquest, but was dispossessed by Henry de Newburgh, whose family held the earldom for two centuries, when it passed by marriage to the noble line of Beauchamp. "Richard Nevill, eldest son of the Earl of Salisbury, married Anne, daughter of Richard Beauchamp, Earl of Warwick, who was the cousin and heir of Henry, Duke of Warwick." On the death of Lady Anne, he had, by a patent dated July 23rd, 1449, 26th Henry VI., confirmed to him "the dignity of Earl of Warwick, and to his wife's heirs with all pre-eminences that were used prior to the creation of the dukedom of Warwick." They had entailed the castle of Warwick, with divers lordships in that and sixteen other counties upon their own issue, and in default of such issue, upon the issue of Anne, with remainder to Margaret, eldest daughter to the same Richard Beauchamp, the late Earl of Warwick, and her heirs."—*Rowland.*

The marriage of Cecily Nevill (sister of the Earl of Salisbury, and youngest daughter of Ralph Nevill, first Earl of Westmoreland) with the Duke of York, will explain why Salisbury and Warwick, Fauconberg, Latimer, and Abergavenny fought on the Yorkist side in the Wars of the Roses.

On the 21st of May, 1455, Henry VI. left London for the north, where his partisans were most numerous. The day following he entered St. Albans, and found the force of York advancing to meet him. The talking was bold on both sides. The King was requested to deliver up to York and Salisbury "*such as we will accuse*" (the Earl of Somerset and his associates), and he answered, "rather than you shall have any lord here, I will this day in this quarrel myself live and die." The fight began in the evening. Clifford gallantly defended the barriers of the town, but the younger Richard Nevill broke through them; loud cries of "*A Warwick! a Warwick!*" filled the air; panic seized upon the Royal troops; Somerset, Clifford, and Northumberland were slain; and at the very commencement of the war Henry found himself wounded, and a prisoner in the hands of Warwick. The rebel lords, however, knelt before him, explaining that their quarrel was not against him, but against those who had influenced him. They led him back to London in triumph. On the 9th of June, Parliament declared the Yorkists innocent of any disloyal practices, and Henry assured them of his forgiveness.

U

The life of this unhappy King was seldom illumined by any bright gleams of intelligence; but on the 12th of November he was voted altogether insane. York became Protector; Salisbury, Chancellor; and Warwick, Governor of Calais. In the spring the King felt himself better; York was allowed to pose no longer as Protector; and the friends of the slain lords loudly called for vengeance.

Henry sat at Coventry, February, 1457, as umpire between the unquiet Roses; and the Nevills were told that they must found a chantry at St. Albans, where priests might pray for the soul of the slaughtered Somerset; and the house of Nevill must also make full satisfaction to all claimants. This the Nevills were quite prepared to do, but not in the way which the King expected. There was, however, some show of reconciliation; and, after further conferences at Blackfriars, all parties marched in procession to St. Paul's Cathedral on the Feast of the Ascension, which Fabyan describes as a "dissimilated love day." The leading members of the adverse factions walked hand in hand together, "being paired according to the degree of deadly animosity that had previously divided them." The Duke of Somerset with the Earl of Salisbury headed the procession, followed by Exeter and Warwick, walking together in unwonted fellowship. The King walked alone. Then came the Duke of York, leading Queen Margaret by the hand, being apparently on the most affectionate terms with her.

Warwick brought with him 600 retainers in red coats (his livery), embroidered with white ragged staves before and behind. They were lodged at the Erber. "This vast palace stood near Dowgate Hill. Edward III. granted it to one of the noble family of the Scroopes; from them it fell to the Nevills. Warwick and Salisbury lodged here with 500 men, in the famous congress of barons in the year 1458, in which Henry VI. was virtually deposed. Richard III. repaired it, and in his time it was called the King's Palace. It was rebuilt by Sir Thomas Pullison, Mayor, in 1584, and was afterwards the residence of Sir Francis Drake."—*Pennant.*

To Warwick the pacific ceremony of Ascension Day was specially meaningless. In his breast all the old Nevill love of battle seemed to be concentrated, and he delighted in war for its own sake.

His little ships, sailing out from Calais in utter disregard of international law, engaged a fleet of twenty-eight vessels, freighted with merchandise belonging to the rich citizens of Lubeck. "There was not so great a fight upon the seas these forty winters."—*Fenn's Letters*, Vol. I. The Hanseatic League complained; and Warwick was recalled, May, 1458, to give an account of his singular proceedings. It was reported that Queen Margaret meditated an arrest of all the Nevills. The air was full of rumour and suspicion. Relationships were everywhere strained to their utmost tension. A spark sufficed to kindle the full flame of war.

One day as Warwick left the Council at Westminster, a quarrel arose between some of his servants and certain men of the Royal retinue.* The Earl, suspecting that his own life was aimed at, withdrew from the metropolis, and sought his father. In the old Yorkshire stronghold of Middleham they formed their plans. Warwick returned to Calais and collected the veterans who had served in the French campaigns. To them the name of Nevill was sacred. In that name they found all the law, and the loyalty, and the love they cared to know.

Salisbury moved out of Middleham with 5,000 men, and encountered the Queen's forces under Lord Audley, at Bloreheath, in Staffordshire, Sept. 23rd, 1459. Nevill shrewdness once more triumphed. Salisbury feigned flight; but when half the Royal army, eager for pursuit, had crossed a foaming torrent, the Yorkists suddenly faced round, and obtained an easy victory over a confused and isolated foe. At Ludlow, Salisbury was joined by York and Warwick. There the confederate lords awaited the coming of Henry, who approached from Worcester, with an army of 60,000 men. On October 13th, Sir Andrew Trollop, Marshal of the Yorkist army, went over to the King with the best part of the insurgent troops. The rebel leaders, daunted by such unexpected and wholesale treachery, broke up their camp in the night. York made for Ireland, and the Nevills, passing through Devonshire, sailed first to Guernsey, and from thence to Calais.

They were all attainted at the Coventry Parliament, held in November; but Warwick was still Admiral of the Fleet, and

---

* According to Fabyan the dispute commenced whilst Warwick was in the Council Chamber, and originated in an assault made by one of the loyal servants on a person belonging to the Earl's retinue. Stow and Polydore Vergil assert that Warwick's man was the aggressor, and that he severely wounded the King's servant; whereupon the *black guard* (as the scullions, cooks, and kitcheners were called), armed with clubs and cleavers, rushed forth to avenge their comrade. In the midst of the fray the Council broke up, and, Warwick, emerging, was fiercely attacked, and with difficulty fought a way to his barge.

Governor of Calais. The Duke of Somerset was instructed to take the command of the fleet from him, but Warwick soon gave that young gentleman to understand that possession meant nine points of the law. Somerset's own sailors hauled down the Royal colours, and gave up their ships to Warwick, who used them for his own purposes. He sailed over to that country which has ever been the congenial home of conspiracy, and, after laying deep schemes in Dublin with the Duke of York, he turned again towards his favourite Calais. The Duke of Exeter made a feeble attempt to intercept his passage, but was too frightened to engage the Nevill fleet.

In June, 1460, the Yorkists again crossed the Channel. With them came the benediction and the ghostly presence of Coppini, Bishop of Terni, and Papal Legate. Bouchier, Archbishop of Canterbury joined them. Their forces grew to 30,000 men. London opened its gates to them. The king met them at Northhampton, July 16th, 1460. Treachery was found in the royal camp in the person of Lord Gray of Ruthyn; and the House of Nevill was once more victorious.

It was the policy of Warwick to spare the people, and refuse quarter to the nobility. This accounts for the large number of knights left on the battlefield of Northampton. The Queen escaped to Wales. Henry was led captive to London.

ADDENDA.

THE BATTLE OF BLOREHEATH was fought on the morning of Sunday, September 23rd (S. Tecla's Day). Bloreheath is in the parish of Drayton, on the high road leading from Drayton to Newcastle, but the heath has long been enclosed and cultivated. At the time of the battle Henry was lying dangerously ill at Coleshill. Margaret witnessed the fight from the tower of Mucclestone Church, and when Audley's banner fell, she fled to Eccleshall Castle. She was bitterly disappointed at the result of this battle, for, in her progress through Warwick, Stafford, and Cheshire, she had given away a vast number of little silver swans, the ancient device of Edward III., which she had adopted as the badge of her son Edward. The young prince was extremely popular in those counties, and 10,000 men are said to have worn his badge on Bloreheath. Indeed the force of James Touchet, Lord Audley, was superior to that of Salisbury. The latter, after having attacked the Lancastrians with a copious discharge of arrows, feigned flight. Audley had that day received an imperious command from the Queen to bring Richard Nevill dead or alive to her, and in his eagerness to obey this mandate he pressed after the crafty Earl. A stream, now called Mill Brook, a tributary of the Tern, lay between them. It flows through a narrow valley and its banks are steep. When half the Lancastrians had crossed, and before they had time to fall into proper array, Salisbury turned upon them; and, from the tower of Mucclestone Church, Margaret saw the heath dyed with the blood of 2,400 of her too eager troops. Among the slain were Lord Audley; Hugh Venables of Kinderton; Thomas Dutton of Dutton; Richard Molyneux of Sefton; William Troutbeck; John Legh of Booths; John Done of Wickington; and John Egerton of Egerton, Knights; with Richard Done and John Dutton, Esquires. Lord Dudley was wounded and taken prisoner.

Sir John Nevill, afterwards Lord Montague, and Sir Thomas Nevill (afterwards slain at Wakefield), were also wounded, and were, with Sir Thomas Harrington, travelling to the north, when they were taken prisoners by a party of Lancastrians and sent to Chester, but were soon after set at liberty.—*Vide Battle of Bloreheath. Paper read before the Society of Antiquaries, by Richard Brooke, Esq., F.S.A., Dec. 8th, 1853.*

Another reason for the Lancastrian disaster is found in the fact that although Lord Stanley had promised his assistance to the Queen he continued inactive, "nor did he in anywise resist" the Yorkists, "in accomplishing their fals and traiterous purpose, in the which they slough James Lord Audeley, and many other Knightes and Squiers, and other your liege people, and more despite didde many of their throtes cutte, which were sent thither by youre commandement. . . . . The seid Lord Stanley, notwithstondyng youre commandement came not to you, but William Stanley his brother went, with grete nombre of people to the Erle of Salesbury. Also the seid Lord Stanley sent his servant, Richard Hokesley, to Egglesshall, certifying to oure Soverayne Lady the Quene that he wold come in all haste, which notwithstondyng was not perfourmed, but in defaute thereof, youre people were distressed at Bloreheth aforesaid, as is well knowen. Howe be it that the said Lord Stanley was within VI. mile of the seid Heth, the same tyme accompanyed with two thousand men. Also when the seid Erle of Salesbury and his felysship had distressed youre seid people at the said Heth, the seid Lord Stanley sent a letter to the seid Erle to Drayton the same nyght, thankyng God of the goode spede of the seid Erle, rejoysing him gretely of the same, trustying to God that he shuld be with the same Erle in other place to stond hym in as good stede, as he shuld have doon yef he had been with theym there; which letter the seid Erle sent to Sir Thomas Haryngton, and he shewed hit openly seying, Sirres be mery, for yet we have moo frendis."—*Rot. Parl.* 38, *Hen.* VI., Vol. V.

As Lord Stanley married the Lady Eleanor Nevill, Lord Salisbury's own daughter, his conduct need not appear surprising.

In the *Natural History of Staffordshire*, printed in 1686, mention is made of a stone set up on Bloreheath in memory of James, Lord Audley, there slain.

Mr. Brook refers to a square pedestal apparently of great age, with a rude and battered cross standing thereon, and bearing the following inscription :—

On this spot
Was fought the battle of
Blore Heath
In 1459 ;
Lord Audley
Who commanded for the side of Lancaster
Was defeated and slain.
To perpetuate the memory
Of the action and the place
This ancient monument
Was repaired in
1765
At the charge of the Lord of the Manor,
Charles Boothby Schrymsher.

BATTLE OF NORTHAMPTON.

" There was a great bataille fought in Henry 6th tyme at Northampton on the Hille without the southe gate, where is a right goodly Crosse, caullid as I remembre the Quene's Crosse, and many Walschmen were drounid yn Avon (Nene ?) ryver at this conflict. Many of them that were slayn were buried at De la Pray and sum at St. John's Hospitale."

" The Lord Fanhope toke King Henry's part. The Lord Gray of Ruthine, did the same in countenance. But a litle afore the feeld he practised with King Edward, and other, saying that he had a title to the Lord Fanhope's landes at Antehill (Ampthill), and there aboute, or depraving hym with false accusations, so wrought with King Edwarde, that he with all his strong band of Walschemen felle to King Edwarde's part, upon promise that if Edwarde won the feelde, he shaul have Antehill and such landes as Fanhope had there. Edward won the feelde, and Gray opteinid Antehil *cum pertinentiis*, and still encreasing in favour with King Edwarde, was at laste made by hym Erle of Kent."—*Leland's Itinerary*.

"The Queen caused her army to issue out of the towne and to passe the ryver of Nene, and there in the newe felde between Harsyngton and Sandifford, the capitaynes strongly emparked themselfes with high bankes and depe trenches."—*Hall*.

By Harsyngton is meant Hardingstone. Sandiford was probably a ford over the Nene.

The battle commenced at seven in the morning. By nine the Royal army became a rout. The Lancastrians had taken up a position with the Nene in their rear, consequently when they fled towards Northampton great numbers of them were drowned. There is reason to believe that a bridge existed near Northampton Castle from a remote date, but the early bridges were too narrow to afford much assistance to a fugitive force. The Duke of Buckingham, the Earl of Shrewsbury, Sir Christopher Talbot, Viscount Beaumont, Lord Egremont, and Sir William Lucy were counted among the fallen Lancastrians. The total number of the slain and drowned is placed as high as 10,000. The body of Buckingham was buried at Grey Friars, Northampton. The site of the monastery has been built upon, but Grey Friars *Street* remains. Shrewsbury was interred at Worksop.

The Queen and Prince Edward watched the battle from a distance till they saw the wild rush across the Nene, when they fled towards the Bishopric of Durham, but subsequently passed into North Wales. Dafyd ap Jeuan ap Einion received them with Cambrian honours in the rocky fastness of Harlech. Worcester states that they were captured near Chester by one of Lord Stanley's servants, and that, after being rifled of her jewels, Margaret escaped, and joined the Duke of Somerset, who was also most energetically engaged in flying for his life.

Stow mentions a heavy fall of rain on the day of the battle. The Lancastrians could not keep their powder dry, and their cannon proved only a hindrance. During the short time that it lasted the battle seems to have been very fiercely and obstinately contested, but Lord Grey's treachery decided the day for the Yorkists. Holinshed states that he actually assisted them to pass the entrenchments. The position of the Yorkist leaders is given in *Drayton's Polyolbion*.

> "The Earl of March, who sought
> To prove by dint of sword, who should obtain the day,
> From Towcester trained on his powers in good array.
> The vaward Warwick led (whom no attempt could fear),
> The middle March himself, and Falconbridge the rear."

Delapie Abbey, mentioned by Leland, Stow, and others, was a house of Cluniac Nuns near Hardingstone. The hospital of St. John, also mentioned by Leland as the burial place of "sum of the slain," still exists in Bridge Street, Northampton. Despite the unpleasing odour imparted to it by shoes, secularists, and other modern innovations, this old town, with its circle of quaint and beautiful villages, must be reckoned among the most delightful haunts of the archæologist.

PART II.—CHAPTER V.

RICHARD NEVILL, THE KING-MAKER.

WARWICK.	Then let the earth be drunken with our blood—
	I'll kill my horse, because I will not fly.
	Why stand we like soft-hearted women here
	Wailing our losses, whiles the foe doth rage?
	(Enter a son that has killed his father, dragging in the dead body.)
SON.	Who is this? O God! it is my father's face,
	Whom in this conflict I unawares have killed.
	O heavy times, begetting such events!
	From London by the King was I pressed forth;
	My father, being the Earl of Warwick's man,
	Came on the part of York, pressed by his master;
	And I, who at his hands received my life,
	Have by my hands of life bereaved him—
	Pardon me, God, I knew not what I did!
	And pardon, father, for I knew not thee!
	(Enter a father that has killed a son, bringing in the body.)
FATHER.	Thou that so stoutly hast resisted me,
	Give me thy gold, if thou hast any gold,
	For I have bought it with a hundred blows.
	But let me see: is this our foeman's face?
	Ah, no, no, no, it is my only son!
KING HENRY.	O that my death would stay those ruthful deeds!
	O, pity, pity, gentle heaven, pity!
	—*King Henry Sixth, Third Part.*

On the 16th October, 1460, the Duke of York, standing in the House of Lords, openly claimed the throne. The claim was compromised by a declaration that he and his heirs should succeed to it after the King's decease. To this decision the meek monarch made no objection; but Margaret could not brook the setting aside of her son. Her friends gathered round her. Northumberland, Clifford, and Dacres came to her standard. Nevill went to war with Nevill. " This conflict was in maner unnaturall, for in it the sonne fought against the father, the brother against the brother, the nephew against the uncle, and the tenant against the lord."—*Hall*.

York and Salisbury spent their Christmas in Sandal Castle; and Margaret, accompanied by the Dukes of Exeter and Somerset, the Earls of Devonshire, Wiltshire, and Northumberland, with the Lords Clifford and Roos, marched from York towards Wakefield.

Hall says that, when the Duke of York was shut up in Sandal, Queen Margaret provoked him by many grievous taunts for his lack of courage in allowing himself to be besieged by a woman. Hall's account of the battle of Wakefield Green is especially interesting, because the historian's grandfather, Sir Davy Hall, was the Duke of York's favourite and confidential servant. The old man represented that, as the Queen commanded 18,000 men, it would be prudent to keep within the Castle until assistance under the Earl of March arrived; but York replied, "Ah! Davy, Davy, hast thou loved me so long, and wouldest have me dishonoured? Thou never sawest me keep fortress when I was regent in Normandy, where the Dauphin himself, with his puissance came to besiege me, but like a man, and not like a bird in a cage, I issued and fought with my enemies, to their loss for ever, and if I have not kept myself within the walls for fear of a great and strong prince, nor hid my face from any man living, wouldst thou that I, for dread of a scolding woman, whose only weapons are her tongue and her nails, should incarcerate myself?"

It is quite likely, however, that the difficulty of provisioning an army within Sandal Castle in mid-winter, when no commissariat arrangements had been previously made, was the chief reason why the Duke resolved to fight at once. On the last day of the year, he entered upon the last action of his eventful life. Sandal Castle stood upon a slight eminence, commanding a view of the surrounding level country. It seems somewhat strange, therefore, that unseen by the Yorkists, Margaret placed two large companies in ambush under the Earl of Wiltshire and Lord Clifford; and that York, on descending the hill and engaging the vanguard, was caught "like unto a fish in a net;" and, in less than half an hour, manfully fighting, he was slain. When his head was brought to the Queen, "she turned pale and shuddered, then laughed long and violently."

v

Two thousand eight hundred Yorkists perished, among whom were Lord Harrington, Sir Thomas Nevill (Salisbury's third son), Sir John Mortimer, Sir Hugh Mortimer, Sir Hugh Hastings, Sir Davy Hall, Sir Edward Bourchier. Monstrelet states that for Richard Nevill the worst indignities were reserved, as the mob was incited to break into his prison and execute him after a rude fashion. This scene was perhaps never enacted except in Monstrelet's imagination. Salisbury was certainly beheaded at Pontefact, and his head appeared beside that of his brother-in-law on the gates of York. Margaret ordered that "between the two, room should be left for the heads of the Earls of March and Warwick." *

The place where York fell is about 400 yards from Sandal Castle, close to the old road from Barnsley to Wakefield, a road which, in more modern times, became known to the inhabitants of Wakefield by the euphonius name of *Cock and Bottle Lane*. The exact spot was marked by a triangular piece of ground with a fence around it, which the tenant of the place was bound by his lease to maintain. In the Parliamentary wars Sandal Castle was held for the King by Colonel Bonivant, but surrendered in October, 1645, and was dismantled in the following year. Portions of the walls still remain, and, being of enormous thickness, show what the strength of the fortress once was.

Crowned with a paper diadem, the severed head of Richard Plantagenet appeared upon the gates of York, and the snow fell softly and sadly upon it. Meanwhile Edward, Earl of March, prepared to avenge his father's death. Being of the lineage of Mortimer, with immense patrimonial possessions in Wales, the Welshmen flocked to his standard. He entered Shrewsbury at the head of 23,000 men. There he was menaced by Jasper Tudor, Earl of Pembroke, the half brother of King Henry. On the 2nd

---

* The beautiful little chapel on Wakefield Bridge was long supposed to have been erected by Edward IV. to mark the spot where his brother, the young Earl of Rutland, was struck down by the dagger of Clifford, but architectural evidence points to the age of Edward III. or earlier.—*Vide Journal Archæol. Instit.* Vol. II. The will of William de Bayley of Mitton, in Craven, who died in 1391, contains conclusive evidence of the existence of a chapel on Wakefield Bridge 70 years previous to the battle; and an old MS. among the Hatfield Papers states that William Terry del Wakefield founded a chantry, by license of Richard II., in the Chapel on Wakefield Bridge, *lately* built. The chapel is an architectural gem, although it *has* been an old clothes shop, a warehouse, a flax-dresser's shop, a newsroom, a cheese-cake house, and a tailor's shop. It is now reverently cared for by my old friend, the Rev. H. G. Parrish, Vicar of St. Mary's, Wakefield; but in consequence of the soft stone used for its restoration, the work of decay has already re-commenced.

of February, 1461 (Candlemas Day), he found himself at Mortimer's Cross, in what is now the parish of Kingsland, Herefordshire. Edward was ever a giddy youth, and on this particular day he saw, or thought he saw, a prodigy, or rather what more scientific and less superstitious people would call a parhelion :—

> "Three glorious suns, each one a perfect sun,
> Not separated by the racking clouds,
> But sever'd in a pale, clear, shining sky.
> See, see! they join, embrace, and seem to kiss,
> As if they vow'd some league inviolable:
> Now are they but one lamp, one light, one sun."

Edward looked upon the phenomenon as a compliment from heaven to himself. "He fiercely set on his enemies, and them shortly discomfited." The main results of the battle are related upon a monument set up on the road between Leominster and Wigmore :—

> "This pedestal is erected to perpetuate the memory of an obstinate, bloody, and decisive battle, fought near this spot, in the civil wars, between the ambitious houses of York and Lancaster, on the 2nd day of February, 1461, between the forces of Edward Mortimer, Earl of March, and afterwards Edward IV., on the side of York, and those of Henry VI. on the side of Lancaster. The King's troops were commanded by Jasper, Earl of Pembroke. Edward commanded his own in person, and was victorious. The slaughter was great on both sides, four thousand being left dead upon the field, and many Welsh persons of the first distinction were taken prisoners, among whom was Owen Tudor (great grandfather to Henry VIII., and a descendant of the illustrious Cadwallader), who was afterwards beheaded at Hereford. This was the decisive battle which fixed Edward IV. on the throne of England, who was proclaimed King in London on the 5th of March following.
> Erected by subscription
> In the year 1799."

The individual who composed this inscription was probably a Welshman, otherwise he would have remembered that it was the battle of *Towton*, which "*fixed*" Edward on the throne.

In seeking to avenge his father's death, Warwick was less fortunate than his kinsman of March. On the 17th February, Warwick moved out of London, carrying with him the captive King. For the second time in his life he took possession of S. Albans. When Margaret entered the town she was greeted with showers of arrows; but she forced the archers back upon the main body of the Yorkist army, which lay on Barnet Heath. Lovelace, who commanded a large body of Londoners, remained inactive, secretly favouring the Queen; and the remainder of Warwick's troops were unable to cope with the stout northern soldiers who fought under Margaret's banner.

Henry and his spouse were now re-united.   A solemn service of thanksgiving at the Abbey of S. Alban's; and the execution of Lord Bonville and Sir Thomas Kyriel concluded the Queen's proceedings for that day.   Her northern friends carried fire and spoil in every direction.   The interference of the pious Henry saved the Abbey of S. Alban's from being sacked by the rude soldiery. London refused to open her gates to the lawless Lancastrians, and a large convoy of provisions was stopped in Cripplegate by the citizens.   Margaret hated the metropolis for its disaffection, and its base insinuations as to the legitimacy of her son.   The northerners were instructed that they might plunder up to the gates of the city. The city accordingly retaliated, and its retaliation struck a deadly blow from which the fortunes of the Queen never recovered.

" In three great political struggles the suffrages of the city of London turned the balance.   The Empress Maud, Margaret of Anjou, and Charles I. lost all with the goodwill of the Londoners." —*Strickland's Margaret of Anjou.*

The bereaved kinsmen, Richard Nevill and Edward Plantagenet, were now drawing near each other.   They met at Chipping Norton, near Cotswold, and marched towards London with an army of 40,000 men.

Each had lost a father through Queen Margaret, and each had a hundred memories to keep alive the bitterest animosity against her.   Margaret did wisely to turn her face northwards.   Metropolitan ideas were distinctly Yorkist.   On the 2nd of March, the Londoners gathered in S. John's Field; and when they were asked whether they would have the Earl of March for their king, loud cries of " *Yea, yea; Long live King Edward!*" filled the air.   On this occasion the Nevills' were very conspicuous.   William Nevill, Lord Fauconberg, reviewed the troops; and George Nevill, Bishop of Exeter, harangued the multitude on the incapacity of Henry, and the extraordinary abilities of Edward.   The red coats of Warwick's men, and the badge of the bear and ragged staff were everywhere visible.   In a solemn service before the high altar at Westminster Abbey, Edward was that day accepted as King of the English people.   But a greater victory awaited him.   Let the reader go back with me to the morning of the 29th of March, 1461.

We stand on Towton field. It is Palm Sunday. In many a Yorkshire abbey holy men are singing Hosanna hymns to Christ, the Prince of Peace. The crisp snow is not yet reddened with the blood of the slain.

"It is morning, yet the sun rises not! The air is dark; thick clouds obscure the sky. A storm is gathering in the heavens and upon earth. There is active preparation for the work of death. The Red Rose and the White are about to be bathed in blood. Fauconberg confronts the army of Henry with young Edward's vanguard. The archers are measuring the distance with their eyes, knowing how far their feathered shafts can carry death. Suddenly the south wind, in a roaring gust, rushes down with a storm of snow; the flaky tempest drives full in the faces of the Lancastrians and blinds them."—*Grainger's Yorkshire Battle-fields.*

The wily Nevill (Fauconberg) instantly gives the command— "Send ye each an arrow against the foe; then retire three strides and stand." The whistling shafts, swifter than the tempest, rush against the distant foe, who knowing nothing of the stratagem, bend their bows and ply their strings until their quivers fail. The Yorkists in grim quiet stand idle; not one Lancastrian shaft has reached them. Now the forces of Fauconberg advance; and, with loud derisive shouts, send their thick volley like lightning upon the Lancastrian line."

"They do not see, and cannot shun the wound;
The storm is viewless as death's sable wing,
Unerring as his scythe."

The Yorkists empty their own quivers upon the unresisting foe; then they gather Lancastrian arrows from the field, and send them winged with death to their former owners.

Impatient of the deadly shower, Northumberland, Somerset, and Trollop urge on their men to close combat; now the only hope of victory. Their bows are cast aside, that the sword, spear, and battle-axe may decide the contest. A fearful scene of close and deadly fight ensues; no military skill is employed; no manœuvring of forces; nothing but brute force and physical endurance can avail. Each man fights as though the battle depended upon himself alone—the determination of all is to conquer or to die.

"None from his fellows starts,
But playing manly parts,
And like true English hearts,
Strike close together."—*Drayton.*

"Ten hours have passed, yet the deadly struggle is maintained ;
sometimes ebbing, sometimes flowing, like the ocean tides."

A reinforcement of fresh men comes to Edward from the Duke
of Norfolk about three o'clock in the afternoon, and the battle is
turned once more against the brave Lancastrians. They give way,
at first in good order ; not flying, but retreating as they fight, and
making a bold stand now and then; but as the day wanes the
Yorkists fall upon them with fresh fury, and at last they fly in
utter rout and confusion. The ghastly dead are everywhere—

> "Heaped and pent,
> Rider and horse, friend and foe, in one red burial blent."

For ten miles the land is strewn with corpses, up to the very gates
of York.

"The place where this sanguinary battle was fought is a ridge
of high ground extending between the villages of Towton and
Saxton. Towards the east and south-east, it commands a fine view
of the immense vale which is watered by the Wharf, the Ouse, the
Aire, and the Derwent, and comprises a part of both the East and
West Ridings; the churches of Selby and Howden, the spire of
Hemingbrough, and the hills of Brayton, Barf, and Hamilton
Haugh all come within the prospect. Towards the north-west
there is also a pleasant view over Bramham Park, and the vale of
the Wharf, as far as Harewood. The small river Cock, which rises
to the south-west of Aberford, runs with a tortuous course on the
back of this ground on the north-west side, and flows into the
Wharf, about a mile to the south-east of Tadcaster. Towton is two
miles to the south of Tadcaster, and in the great road from London
to York. Saxton is about two miles nearly south from Towton."

"The Duke of Somerset began his operations in the morning
of the previous day (28th), by sending Lord Clifford to dislodge the
Yorkists from their post on the north side of the Aire ; and the
attack was so successful, that they were driven across the river with
great slaughter; the commander of their detachment and several
eminent officers being slain in action. Richard Nevill, Earl of
Warwick, on hearing of this disaster, was under great consternation,
fearing that it might discourage the troops. But to show that his
fears were not for his own safety, he stabbed his horse ; and, kissing
the hilt of his sword, made in the form of a cross, swore that if the
whole army should take to flight, he alone would defend the cause

in which he was engaged. Edward, perceiving the Earl's concern, judged it necessary to prevent the ill effects which this check might have on the minds of the soldiers. He therefore issued a proclamation, informing them that those who desired it might depart ; that he would liberally reward those who should do their duty ; but that no favour was to be expected by any that should fly during battle. At the same time he detached William Nevill, Lord Fauconberg, to pass the Aire to Castleford, between three and four miles above Ferrybridge, with orders to attack those who guarded the post lately lost. Fauconberg executed his orders with such secrecy and promptitude, that he passed the river at Castleford before the enemy had the least notice of the transaction. Then marching along the north side of the river, he suddenly attacked Lord Clifford, who was at the head of a body of horse, which was completely routed. Clifford was killed by an arrow ; and the brother of the Earl of Westmoreland was also slain. The post of Ferrybridge being thus recovered, Edward passed with his whole army over the Aire, and marched northward towards Tadcaster, in quest of the enemy. Such were the operations preliminary to the bloody and memorable battle of Towton (the Pharsalia of England), which was fought on Palm Sunday, 29th of March. Henry's army consisted of 60,000 men, commanded by the Duke of Somerset ; that of Edward amounted to 48,660, and was led on by himself in person. The principal slaughter began when the Lancastrians retreated in confusion across the Cock in order to reach Tadcaster bridge. The Cock is a very small river, or rather a rivulet, over which a man might easily leap, its breadth being in most places less than four yards."—*Allen's Hist. Yorks.*

The old road from Towton to the river Cock was so steep and perilous, that little imagination is needed to conjure up the fearful scene that must have been enacted when, in one wild disordered mass, the Lancastrian cavalry, with horses wounded and ungovernable, plunged among the flying foot soldiers, who were crowded together in this precipitous lane. In a few moments hundreds of human beings were trampled to death beneath the snow ; hundreds more were thrown headlong into the river, and became a bridge over which their comrades passed recklessly, to be in their turn struck down by the infuriated Yorkists, who pressed ever upon them from the rear, and gave no quarter. The blood of the slain lay caked in the snow, which, slowly dissolving during the days that followed, ran for several miles in a horrible stream among the furrows of the fields, until it gained the channel of the Wharf.

This terrible tale of carnage, unequalled in all the annals of England, is told by Biondi, in the soft plaintive language of his native country.

"Quei che restarono vivi presero la strada del ponte di Tadcaster, ma, non potendo arrivarvi, e credendo guadabile un picciolo rio detto Cocke vi s'annegarono la maggior parte: affermatosi costantemente essersi passato sopra il dosso de' corpi morti, l'acque del detto rio, e del fiume Vuarf in cui eglisgorga, tinte in maniera, che parvero di puro sangue."

A contemporary historian assures us that, besides those who perished in the waters, thirty-eight thousand men remained dead on the field. Edward, in a confidential letter to his mother, while he conceals his own loss, informs her that the heralds employed to number the dead bodies, returned the Lancastrians alone at twenty-eight thousand. Among the dead were found the Earl of Northumberland; the Lords Dacres and Welles; Sir John Nevill, and Sir Andrew Trollop. The Dukes of Somerset and Exeter had the fortune to escape; but Thomas Courtney, Earl of Devonshire, was taken.

There is a meadow to the west of Towton Dale called the Bloody Meadow, celebrated for producing rich rank grass. It formerly contained extensive patches of dwarf rose trees, which bloomed red and white. Tradition points to North Acre Field as the scene of the severest slaughter.

> "The Lord of Dacres
> Was slayne in the North Acres."

Lord Dacres was buried in the church of All Saint's, Saxton, "under a meane tombe" (i.e., one of medium size) of dark marble.*

Lord John Nevill is said to have been buried at the chapel of Lead, half-a-mile from Saxton, but there is no monument to his memory. On the north side of Saxton church a huge trench was exposed to view in 1848, containing a vast quantity of bones. The

---

* The inscription styles Henry of Windsor, King Henry VI. The tomb was, therefore, probably erected after the fall of the House of York. Drake says that when the tomb was violently wrenched open to admit the body of Mr. Gascoyne, Dacres' remains were found in a standing posture. He does not inform us who Mr. Gascoyne was, when alive; but whoever he was, whether a gentleman or some rag merchant, it evinced very bad taste on the part of his relations to violate a soldier's grave.—Vide Mr. Brook's Paper on Towton, read before the Soc. Antiq. Jan. 18, 1849.

skulls possessed very sound teeth. They probably represent young men of the Yorkist faction. So many Lancastrian bodies would scarcely be honoured by interment in consecrated ground.

It is remarkably that three of the battles in the Wars of the Roses were fought on the Sabbath day, viz., Blore Heath, Towton, and Barnet. It is remarkable also that the elements seemed to fight against the Lancastrians. There was snow at Towton, a dense mist at Barnet, and heavy rain at Northampton. At Mortimer's Cross there was a parhelion. At Blore Heath, Northampton, and Towton, rivers contributed to the Lancastrian overthrow.

In old documents Towton Field is variously described as Saxton-feld, Tawtonfeeld, Palm Sunday Field, and Sherburn. Leland speaks of a "great Chapell begon by Richard III. but not finished, in which chapell were buried many of the slayne." Tiles and worked stones have been discovered in that part of Towton known as Chapel Garth. Drake describes his visit to the battlefield in 1730, when some excavations were going on. He saw vast quantities of bones, some broken swords, and five groat pieces dated in the reigns of Henry IV., V., and VI. A gold ring, figured with a lion, and the inscription, "Now ys thus," meaning probably "This age is fierce as a lion," was afterwards discovered. Dr. Whitaker concluded that it belonged to the Earl of Northumberland. Together with several other relics, it is described in his *History of Leeds*.

The field of Towton was a fearful spectacle for any woman to witness.

> " Cressy was to this but sport,
> Poictiers but a pageant vain,
> And the work of Agincourt
> Only like a tournament."

It was well, then, that Margaret remained at York during Palm Sunday. With her consort and her son, she fled thence to Newcastle. Alnwick Castle opened its gates to her in sorrow, for the Lord of Alnwick had been slain for her sake. But nothing could daunt this Queen. She recovered her spirits, shot a buck with a broad arrow in Alnwick Park, and went on to Berwick. Leaving her husband and her son at the Scottish Court, she sailed from Kirk-cudbright, April 8th, 1462, and landed in Bretagne, with the view of stirring up her Continental friends. Nothing could daunt *her*. In October, 1463, she was back again ; and, with the aid of Scottish and French allies, took Bamborough, Dunstanborough, and Alnwick. But when the Kingmaker appeared with an army 20,000 strong, the Frenchmen took to their ships. Many of these were dashed to pieces on the wild Northumbrian rocks. Five hundred foreigners perished on Holy Island. Bamborough and Dunstanborough sur- rendered, after a brave and obstinate resistance; but Alnwick still defied the storm.

An army of Lancastrians advanced apparently to its relief. Warwick drew up his forces to receive them; but Lord Hungerford and a few knights, having cut a passage to their friends, in a sally from the walls, the Queen's army retired; and the garrison, deserted by its leaders, capitulated. "Alnwick was given to Sir John Ashley, to the great offence of Sir Ralph Grey, a partisan of York, who had formerly won it for Edward, and now expected to possess it again. Being disappointed, he forthwith became a violent Lancastrian."— *Lingard.*

Henry now hid himself in Merionethshire, and his intrepid wife wandered in the woods round Hexham. Monstrelet's story of the Queen and the robber, whether true or not, is known and admired by every schoolboy. The Queen's cave is still pointed out, though, of course, that proves nothing; for in Damascus they point out the "street called Straight," and the window from whence S. Paul made his exit in a basket from that inhospitable city. It is certain, however, that Margaret escaped to Flanders, and afterwards to her father's duchy in Lorraine.

The triumph of Edward in the north was entirely due to Warwick, for though the young king came himself as far as New- castle, he was incapacitated by disease, brought on by indulgence.

When the Kingmaker turned his back upon the north, the Scots came down to Bamburgh and retook it. Sir Ralph Percy and Sir Ralph Grey did the same to Berwick. Somerset hurried from Wales into Northumberland; and the ex-king also appeared on the Borders with a small force. On April 25th, 1464, the battle of Hedgeley Moor was fought. Sir Ralph Percy, deserted by his comrades, the Lords Hungerford and Ros, led his forces single handed against John Nevill, Lord Montague, warden of the east marches. Percy fell with the well known words on his lips, "I have saved the bird in my breast," words which have become pro- verbial as an expression of unsullied honour. These words are generally supposed to mean that he had kept fealty with Henry VI., but as Percy had only five months before taken part with Edward against Henry, it may be that the allusion points to Margaret. *Vide* an interesting paper by George Gray Bell, in *Archæologia Æliana*, 1st series, Vol. IV., p. 35, relative to a cave near North Sunderland, discovered in 1844. From the neat state of the interior, its paved floor, and the small size of the entrance, the writer concludes that it was not devoted to smuggling, but was a place of concealment; and in all probability the spot where the Queen lay hidden, and was maintained by Percy; and to which she again fled after the battle of Hexham, until she could procure a ship to convey her to the Continent. A rude column stands to Percy's memory, seven miles south of Wooler. Nevill's force is estimated by Warkworth at 10,000; by William of Worcester at 4,000. On the 15th May, he surprised and destroyed Somerset's camp on the banks of Dilswater. The Earl fled, but was pursued by the servants of John de Middleton, and beheaded at Hexham. His body was buried in the Abbey. Sir Edward Fyshe and others were executed at the same time. Three days after, Lords Ros and Hungerford, Talboys, Earl of Kyme, and Sir Thomas Finderne were found in the woods near Hexham, and executed on the Sandhill, Newcastle.

Sir Ralph Grey fled to Bamburgh, and was there besieged *cum maximis bombardis* by Warwick. The Kingmaker brought with him two huge cannon, one of which he called *London* and the other *Newcastle*. Sir Ralph Grey's chamber was "smitten through oftentymes," and at last he fell with a portion of the falling wall. He was executed at Doncaster in the following July. John Nevill was rewarded with the earldom of Northumberland.

Henry fled from Hexham before John Nevill arrived there;* and, after wandering in Westmoreland and Yorkshire, was betrayed by a monk, and carried to London. Warwick conducted him to the Tower.

* King Henry was the best horseman of his company that day, for he fled so fast no one could overtake him. Three of his bodyguard, with their horses trapped in blue velvet, were taken ; one of them wearing the King's cap of state.—*Hall.*

PART II.—CHAPTER VI.

WHITE, OR RED?

"Hath not thy rose a thorn, Plantagenet?"
Henry VI., Act 2, Scene 4.

"From the first battle of St. Alban's Warwick had been foremost amongst the assailants of the Lancastrian line. It was to his counsel that men ascribed the decisive step by which his cousin Edward assumed the throne. The death of his uncle and father, and the youth of the King, placed the Earl at the head of the Yorkist party. His services were rewarded by a grant of vast estates from the confiscated lands of the Lancastrian baronage. The command of the northern border lay in the hands of his brother John, Lord Montague. George Nevill was raised to the see of York, and post of Lord Chancellor; and lesser rewards fell to Warwick's uncles, the minor chiefs of the House of Nevill, the Lords Fauconberg, Latimer, and Abergavenny. The vast power which such an accumulation of wealth and honour placed at the Earl's disposal was wielded with consummate ability. A Burgundian chronicler, who knew him well, describes him as 'le plus soubtil homme de son vivant.'

"In the three years which followed Towton the power of the Nevills overshadowed that of the Crown. While Warwick was winning triumphs on the battle-field, the young King seemed to abandon himself to voluptuous indolence, to revels with the city wives of London, and to the caresses of mistresses like Jane Shore.

Tall in stature, and of singular beauty, his winning manners and gay carelessness secured Edward a popularity which had been denied to nobler kings. When he asked a rich old lady for ten pounds towards a war with France, she answered, ' For thy comely face thou shalt have twenty.' The king thanked her, and kissed her, and the old lady made her twenty forty. But Edward's indolence and gaiety were mere veils thrown over a will of steel. From the first his aim was to free the Crown from the control of the baronage. Yet even a king as bold as Edward might well have shrunk from a struggle with Warwick. The Earl was all-powerful in the State ; the military resources of the realm were in his hands. As captain of Calais, he was master of the one disciplined force at the disposal of the Crown ; and as Admiral he controlled the Royal fleet. The strength he drew from his wide possessions, from his vast wealth (for his official revenues alone were estimated at 80,000 crowns a year), from his warlike renown, and his wide kinship, was backed by his personal popularity. The Yorkist party, bound to Warwick by a long series of victories, looked on him rather than on the young and untried King, as its head."—*Green's Hist. Eng. People*. Vol. II.

Whilst the Nevills were fighting for Edward in Northumberland, the King himself was spending his energy in licentiousness. The vast estates of the slain and exiled Lancastrians he had given away with a wild liberality. The coinage was now changed and debased to supply his own extravagance. As he journeyed northward with the avowed intention of putting down an insurrection, which the Nevills had already quelled, he turned aside to hunt in the forest of Grafton. In the neighbourhood of this forest there dwelt a lonely and lovely widow, whose husband, Sir John Grey, for King Henry's sake, risked and lost both his life and estates in the second battle of St. Alban's. The Lady Elizabeth Grey lived with her mother, Jacquetta of Luxembourg. The admirers of Lord Lytton will not fail to remember Jacquetta, in the "Last of the Barons," as the widow of the Duke of Bedford, the wife of Sir Richard Wydville, and the friend of alchemists and astrologers. What took place in the forest of Grafton is more a matter for the novelist than historian. The Lady Elizabeth pleaded for her fortified estates ; and pleaded to some purpose, for she was married, upon the 1st of May, 1464, to the King of England. From that day the decline of the Nevill power must be dated.

If John Nevill, as he chased the rebels through the woods of Hexham, had known what was taking place at Stony Stratford, perhaps his arm might have proved less strong against the Lancastrian insurrection.

King Edward, having married a poor and pretty woman with a number of needy relations, at once set to work in his unscrupulous way to make them all rich. Warwick had solicited the hand of the daughter and heiress of the Duke of Exeter for his own nephew. That hand, however, was bestowed on one of the Queen's family. The Lady Catherine Nevill, eldest daughter of the first Earl of Westmoreland, (by Joan Beaufort) and widow of the Duke of Norfolk, was now a dear old creature of eighty *(juvencula fere* 80 *annorum.* Wyrcest); and was, of course, the King's aunt. *Her* hand was bestowed on John Wydevill, a blooming boy of some twenty summers. William of Worcester calls this a devilish match ; or, if you don't like the plain English, his exact words are *maritagium diabolicum.* The expression doubtless originated in the old English proverb that "the marriage of a young woman and a young man is of God's making, *e.g.,* Adam and Eve; an old man and young woman of our Lady's making, *e.g.,* Mary and Joseph ; but that of an old woman and a young man is made by the author of evil."

In the month of May, 1467, the Nevills and the Wydevilles met together at the King's Council. Both France and Burgundy sought alliance with England. The Burgundian Duke was a Lancastrian ; and so far had been Henry's friend, and therefore Edward's foe ; yet the Wydevilles favoured him and pressed for the marriage of his son with Margaret, the King's sister. Warwick had been to the Burgundian Court, and cordially disliked its Duke. Warwick's policy was a strict and cordial alliance with France ; for he knew that "while Margaret of Anjou could look for aid from that country, the house of York could hope for no cessation of civil war." In Lewis XI. Warwick thought he saw the elements of a great king, resolute to reanimate the depressed monarchy of France, and vindicate the independence of her Crown over the too powerful vassal states of Burgundy, Brittany, and Bourbon.— *Gairdner's Lancaster and York.*

Edward however was heartily tired of Warwick's tutelage. Warwick had fought for him; built up and strengthened his throne ; and he was now to be rewarded by perfidy, insult, and humiliation.

Assuming a feigned adherence to Warwick's counsel, Edward sent him on a fool's errand to the French king at Rouen, bidding him treat for peace. He was received in France with enthusiasm. Noblemen and bishops paid court to him; the richest robes were presented to the men of his retinue. " The magistrates of Rouen, in their formalities, were ordered to go out to meet him upon his landing at the Key Gate of St. Eloy, with abundance of pomp and ceremony, bearing before him crosses, banners, holy water bottles, and the relics of several saints, attended by the priests in their copes; and after this manner he was conducted to the church of Notre Dame, where he made his offering ; and from thence to a magnificent apartment prepared for him in one of the religious houses. The King presented him with valuable and rich presents, and a huge gold cup set with precious stones. The Duke of Bourbon presented him with a fine diamond. The King, the Queen, and the young Princesses remained with him a fort-night; the Admiral of France, and the Bishop of Laon attended him."—*Jean de Troyes' Chronicle.*

Such conduct on the part of Lewis XI. was quite remarkable, for never was there a king in Europe whose manners were less courtly. He always detested show, and despised the pomp of State. His dress was invariably slovenly, and his favourite associates were men of humble origin. The unusual parade, which he thought fit to make over the arrival of Warwick, highly incensed Edward. " Surely not I, but Richard Nevill must be accounted King of England!" he exclaimed. The work of humiliating Warwick was at once begun. When Parliament assembled the Chancellor (George Nevill) was too ill to attend; but Edward, suspicious of his loyalty, went to his house with an armed force, and compelled him to deliver up the seals. Two manors which had been previously granted him by the Crown were likewise taken away.

Warwick was represented as a false Englishman, and a friend to France. The London merchants supported the King, as they wished for an alliance with the master of Flanders and the Lower Rhine. A marriage treaty between Charles of Burgundy and the Princess Margaret proved the triumph of Warwick's rivals. The French ambassadors returned to their native land, carrying with them some hunting horns and leathern bottles, as a present from Edward to the King of France; a meagre and insolent return for all the valuable gifts that had been sent into England.—*Jean de Troyes' Chronicle.*

Warwick withdrew to Middleham Castle, and formed plans for future action, while Edward sought to entrap and overthrow the man who had raised him to the throne. The few miserable people who were suspected of remaining loyal to the Lancastrian cause were everywhere hunted down. A poor shoemaker was nipped to death with red hot pincers for assisting Margaret of Anjou to carry on a correspondence with her friends in England; " but, basely born as he was," he refused to betray the Queen's adherents. But at the taking of Harlech Castle in Wales, a man was found willing to accuse Richard Nevill as a secret partisan of the exiled Queen. The man was Margaret's own emissary, and swore that Warwick had spoken in her favour at the Court of France. The Earl replied with brief scorn that all the world saw in him the bitterest foe Lancaster had ever known. As he refused to quit Middleham Castle his accuser was dragged thither.—*Stow.* " The charge against the Earl was declared groundless; but Edward selected a body guard of 200 archers, who were ordered to attend always upon his person. Everything seemed to threaten a rupture when the common friends of Nevill and Plantagenet interfered. The Archbishop of York and Earl Rivers met at Nottingham to settle terms of reconciliation. The prelate conducted his brother to Coventry, where he was graciously received; and the Archbishop, as the reward of his services, recovered possession of his two manors."— *Vide Worcester quoted in Lingard.* Warwick appeared in Court. The King conducted the Princess Margaret to the coast on her way to Flanders, "the Erle of Warrewyke riding before hur on hur hors."—*Cot. MSS.* On the discovery of a conspiracy in favour of Henry, Warwick sat among the judges at the trial of the accused. But other influences were at work to fan the fire that was smouldering in the home of "the Last of the Barons." The brother of Edward loved Warwick's eldest daughter, and cordially hated Elizabeth Wydeville, whose issue he greatly feared would set aside his claim to the throne. The King was violently opposed to the match which Clarence desired, and earnestly laboured to prevent its accomplishment. He even wrote to the Pope imploring his Holiness to withhold his sanction on the ground of relationship. This was quite too much for Warwick's pride; and, therefore, George Plantagenet and Isabel Nevill were married in the Church of S. Nicholas, Calais, July 11th, 1469; the ceremony being performed by the bride's uncle, George Nevill, Archbishop of York.

At the time of this marriage an insurrection broke out in Yorkshire, headed by Robin of Redesdale. The insurgents demanded the removal of the Wydevilles from the King's Council, and the abatement of taxes. Warwick's name has been freely mentioned as the instigator of this movement, in which great numbers of his tenantry were involved. But Robin of Redesdale was defeated and slain at York by Lord Montague, Warwick's own brother. The place of the border hero was, however, quickly supplied by the son of Lord Fitzhugh, and Sir Henry Nevill, the son of Lord Latimer. It should be remembered, however, that the *Latimers were Lancastrians.* Lord Montague did not further oppose the insurrection, consequently it gathered strength.

A Royal army was defeated at Edgecote; and Earl Rivers, the Queen's father, with his son, Sir John Wydeville, were beheaded. From Nottingham, Edward sent a letter to Calais, craving once more the help of the man he had insulted. "We do not believe," said he, "that ye should be of any such disposition towards us, as the rumour here runneth, considering the trust and affection we bear you. And cousin, ne think but ye shall be to us welcome." Warwick, accompanied by his brother and Clarence, accordingly crossed the Channel; but, distrusting the King's disposition, they gathered some force at Canterbury. Popular opinion was still on the side of Warwick, and Edward found his soldiers rapidly deserting. The King and the Kingmaker met at Olney. At a word from Warwick the insurgents returned to their homes, and Edward went as Warwick's guest to Middleham. The King afterwards represented this visit as a forcible detention. The Croyland historian, and De Commines, both of whom were the King's confidants, speak of it as an imprisonment. In the attainder of Clarence it is stated that "the King's persone and life" were held "in straite warde, putting him thereby from all his libertie." —*Rot Parl.*, VI., 193.

"The Duke of Burgundy," says Commines, "was greatly concerned at the King's imprisonment." He "practised secretly" for his escape, and threatened to break off the English trade with Flanders. So alarmed were the London merchants at these threats that they demanded the King's release. It is probable that Edward found it extremely convenient to remain under the shadow of Richard Nevill's wing just at this time. It is probable also that in the halls of Middleham the merry monarch received a little

x

good and sober advice, of which he stood in great need. But it is *not* probable that the Kingmaker, who by a mere word and a smile had just dismissed a great army of men only too eager to execute his wishes, should be frightened into submission by the mere threats of a few London merchants. Hall fixes the scene of the King's imprisonment at Cawood, and says that the Archbishop of York (George Nevill) allowed him to hunt, and while engaged in the chase he was carried off by his friends. Supposing it to be a case of imprisonment at all, England had then two rival captive Kings, one lying in the Tower, the other in Yorkshire.

But in the Fenn collection (1, 294), there is a letter which says that "the King hath himself good language of the Lords Clarence and Warwick, saying they be his best friends." Lord Lytton shrewdly observes that " he would scarcely have so said if he had just escaped out of their prison."

There is a far weightier reason for believing in Warwick's integrity. Sir Humphrey Nevill, the zealous Lancastrian, of whose cavernous retreat near Hexham we have already spoken, now raised the banner of the Red Rose in Scotland. *He was defeated and taken prisoner by Richard Nevill, Earl of Warwick, who handed him over to Edward, by whose order he was executed at York.* About the same time the King's eldest daughter, a child of four, was betrothed to George Nevill, the son of Lord Montague, Earl of Northumberland. This alliance was viewed by many as a safeguard against any designs that Clarence, with the help of Warwick, might make upon the throne.

Thus far had Warwick followed Edward through good and evil report.

But suddenly the world witnessed an inexplicable termination to the Earl's loyalty. Three months before, he had by a word dismissed thousands of enthusiastic insurgents. He is now an insurgent himself. The men of Lincolnshire rose against the King. At Erpingham, in Rutlandshire, they were completely defeated by Edward, March 12th, 1470.*

The confession of their leader, Sir Robert Welles, is extant. It shows that Clarence and Warwick instigated the insurrection, the real object of which was to place Clarence upon the throne. The King repeatedly offered terms of reconciliation to his brother

---

* Sometimes called the battle of Lose-Coat Field, because, when the Royal artillery opened fire, the greater part of the insurgents flung away their coats, and took to their heels, leaving their leader to his fate.

and Warwick, but his overtures were refused. The Duke and the Earl fled westward, and sailed from Dartmouth for Calais.

The great guns of Calais were turned upon them; and, amidst the greatest possible commotion, the Duchess of Clarence gave birth to a son. "There are good and bad people in the world," says Commines. The Governor of Calais (left there by Warwick as his deputy) was "one of the bad." He sent two flagons of wine to the Duchess for her comfort; and informed her father that, if he persisted in entering Calais, he was a lost man, for the garrison would betray him. At the same time this deceitful deputy-governor sent word to Edward that the town should be held for the King of England. He was, therefore, appointed sole governor by Edward. The Duke of Burgundy sent him a letter of thanks and a promise of a pension of a thousand crowns. Meanwhile Warwick sailed away to Harfleur, where he and all his company were honourably received by the Admiral of France, who lodged them in his own palace, and took care to have their ships laid up safely in the harbours of Honfleur and Harfleur. A little after, the ladies and their attendants removed to Valognes, where very beautiful apartments were prepared for them.—*Jean de Troyes Chronicle.*

And now took place that remarkable alliance between the Lady Anne Nevill and the exiled Prince of Wales, which reconciled Warwick to the House of Lancaster, and estranged him from the interests of Clarence. Strange indeed are the world's mutations. Margaret of Anjou now posed as Warwick's friend, and Clarence practised secretly as his foe. The Kingmaker, aided by Lewis XI., prepared to invade England. The Duke of Burgundy, more active than Edward, despatched his fleet to blockade the mouth of the Seine.

The Burgundian ships were dispersed by a storm; and, on Sept. 13th, Warwick landed unmolested at Dartmouth, where men flocked to his standard. Meanwhile his brother-in-law, Lord Fitzhugh, raised a pretended rebellion in the North. Edward was thus drawn away from the southern coast, and Fitzhugh quietly retired before him into Scotland. The Archbishop of York and Lord Montague were the King's confidants. He seemed to forget that they were Warwick's brothers. "As he sat at dinner, word was suddenly brought to him that Lord Montague and many other men of quality were mounted on horseback, and were causing the soldiers to cry, 'God bless King Henry.' There was with the King at that time a very prudent gentleman, the Lord Hastings, High Chamber-lain of England, who, although he had married Warwick's sister (Catherine Nevill) remained faithful to the King. It happened by God's grace that the King's quarters were no great distance from the sea (Lynn), and some ships that followed with provisions for the army lay at anchor, with two Dutch merchants hard by. The King had but just time to get aboard one of them, and thus he made his escape in the year 1470, attended by some seven hundred men of his own, without any clothes but what they were to have fought in, no money in their pockets, and not one of them knew whither they were going. It was very surprising to see this poor King, for so he might justly be called, run away in this manner, and be pursued by his own servants. He had indulged himself in ease and pleasure for twelve or thirteen years together, and enjoyed a larger share of them than any prince in his time. His thoughts were wholly employed upon the ladies, and upon hunting, and upon the adornment of his beautiful person, far more than was in reason. In summer hunting he had several tents set up for the ladies, where he treated them after a magnificent manner; and, indeed, his person was as well turned for love intrigues as that of any man I ever saw in my life, for he was young, and the handsomest man of his time. I mean when he was in this adversity, for afterwards he grew passing corpulent. But see now how suddenly he is fallen into the calamities of this miserable world!"—*Commines.*

The character of Edward gives some show of reason to the explanation which Hall gives of the sudden spirit of rebellion manifested by the Earl of Warwick.

"And farther it erreth not from the truth that the King did attempt a thing once in the Earl's house, but whether it was unto the daughter or niece was not for both their honours openly known, but surely such a thing *was* attempted."

This assertion is credited by several historians. I have no desire to enter into any discussion as to its probability.

PART II.—CHAPTER VII.

THE FALL OF WARWICK.

> " Thus yields the cedar to the axe's edge,
> Whose arms gave shelter to the princely eagle,
> Under whose shade the ramping lion slept,
> Whose top-branch overpeer'd Jove's spreading tree,
> And kept low shrubs from winter's powerful wind.
> These eyes, that now are dimm'd with death's black veil,
> Have been as piercing as the mid-day sun,
> To search the secret treasons of the world :
> The wrinkles in my brows, now fill'd with blood,
> Were liken'd oft to kingly sepulchres ;
> For who lived King, but I could dig his grave ?
> And who durst smile when Warwick bent his brow ?
> Lo, now my glory smear'd in dust and blood !
> My parks, my walks, my manors that I had,
> Even now forsake me, and of all my lands
> Is nothing left me but my body's length.
> Why, what is pomp, rule, reign, but earth and dust ?
> And, live we how we can, yet die we must.
> *Henry VI. Part III. Act V., Scene 2.*

IN eleven days from his landing at Dartmouth, Richard Nevill was once more the master in England. In eleven days he had destroyed a throne. The house of York, built up by the costliest sacrifice of human life, was overthrown; and the Red Rose of Lancaster blossomed again. According to Oliver de la Marche, Warwick gained his success in three ways, "The first by flattery and feigned humility to the Londoners, who loved him. Secondly, he was master of the five ports in England, where he allowed great injury to be done, and never in his time was justice done in England to any foreigner who had suffered loss, wherefore he was loved by the freebooters, whom he thus contributed to support.

And thirdly, he kept the city of London on his side by always owing 300,000 crowns to the citizens, wherefore they desired his life and prosperity, that they might be paid." In this feeble *résumé* of Warwick's abilities there is, no doubt, a slight element of truth.

But the thread of this narrative had better be continued in the language of Philip de Commines, who was the Duke of Burgundy's emissary to Calais, and therefore actually witnessed much of what he relates. "At Westminster, King Henry was restored to his royal prerogative in the presence of Clarence, who was not at all pleased at the sight. The Duke of Burgundy heard that King Edward was dead; and for this he was in no wise sad, for his love was greater for the House of Lancaster than for York; but he dreaded the Earl of Warwick. When I went to Calais, no man came out to meet me as formerly; all were in the Earl's livery. At the gate of my lodgings and the door of my chamber, the people had made more than a hundred white crosses with certain rhymes underneath, signifying that the King of France and the Earl of Warwick were all one, which I thought very surprising. The Lord Wenlock sent to me to dine with him. I found him well attended, with a ragged staff of gold upon his bonnet, which was the cognizance of the Earl of Warwick; all the rest had ragged staffs likewise, but they who could not be at the expense of gold, had them of cloth. I was informed at dinner, that within a quarter of an hour after the arrival of the news from England the whole town got this livery, so hasty and sudden was the change; and this was the first time I had ever seen such an instance of the instability of all human affairs. Those whom I formerly endeavoured to have turned out of the town, as being faithful to the Earl, were now in great reputation, yet they knew not that I had ever spoken against them. I told them upon all occasions that Edward was dead, though indeed I knew well to the contrary. I added likewise that even if he were not dead, it was of no importance; for the Duke of Burgundy's alliance, though he had married Edward's sister, was with the King and kingdom of England, so that this accident could in no wise infringe it, for whomsoever they declared their King, should be so to us; and in consideration of such revolutions in times past, the words *king* and *kingdom* had been used. It was thus arranged between us that the alliance we had made with England should stand good, which accommodation was welcome to the Duke of Burgundy, for the Earl of Warwick was sending troops to make war upon him; albeit the London merchants diverted him from that undertaking.

" The Duke tried much to pacify the Earl of Warwick, declaring himself of the House of Lancaster, and using all such expressions as he thought would best serve his turn. In the meantime Edward arrived at his court, and pressed very hard for supplies to enable him to recover his kingdom, and entreated him for God's sake not to abandon him, since he had married his sister. The Dukes of Somerset and Exeter violently opposed it, and used all their artifice to keep him firm to King Henry's interest. The Duke was in suspense, and knew not which side to favour, fearing to disoblige either, because he had a desperate war at home. However, finding King Edward bent upon his return to England; and being unwilling, for several reasons, absolutely to displease him, he pretended publicly that he would give him no assistance; and issued a proclamation forbidding any of his subjects to go along with him; but privately and underhand he sent him 50,000 florins with St. Andrew's Cross, and furnished him with ships, which he ordered to be equipped for him at La Vere (Flushing), a free port open to all comers."— *Commines. Scroble's Translation.*

" On the xj. daye of Marche he made saile, and so did all the shipps that awayted on hym, takyng theyr cowrse streyght to the coste of Norfolke, and came before Crowmere, the Tuesdaye, agayne even, the xij. of March, whithar the Kynge sent on land Syr Robert Chambarlayne and Syr Gilbert Debenham to have some knowledge how the land inward was disposed towards hym, and they browght hym knowledge that it might not be for his well to lande in that countrye. Then fell great stormes, wynds, and tempests upon the sea, so that in great torment he came to Humbrehede, where the othar shipps were dissevered from hym. The Kynge with his shippe aloone, wherein was the Lord Hastings, and other to the nombar of vc. chosen men, landyd on Holdernes syde at a place callyd Ravenersporne. The Kyng's brothar Richard landyd at anothar place iiij. myle from thens."

" The people of the countrie in greate nombar in dyvars placis were gatheryd in harnes, redye to resiste hym in chalenginge the crowne, wherefore the Kynge said openly that *hys entent was only to claime to be Duke of Yorke,* and to enjoy the inheritaunce that he was borne unto, wherefore the people were content in noo wyse to annoy hym."

"He toke his waye towards Wakefielde, leving the Castell of Pomfrete on his lefte hand, wher abode the Marqwes Montaqwe (John Nevill) that in no wyse trowbled hym. Wherefore the Kynge sayde, as Julius Cesar (*sic*) sayde, *he that is not agaynst me is with me.* Abowte Wakefylde ceme som folks unto hym, but not so many as he supposed wolde have comen, nevarthelesse his nombar was encreasyed. And so from thens he passyd forthe to Doncastar, and so forthe to Notyngham."—(*Historie of the Arrivall of Edward IV.*—an official Yorkist document.)

It was a march of deceit. He wore in his bonnet an ostrich feather, the device of Edward, the Lancastrian Prince of Wales; and in every village caused his followers to shout, "*Long live King Henry !*" Before the high altar of York, he swore that he came only to recover his father's dukedom, and renounced all claim to the throne.—*Polydore Vergil, and Fabyan.* "As he passid through the countery he shewid the Erle of Northumbrelande's lettre and seale that sent for hym."—*Lelana's Collectanea.* This "lettre" was a forged document, but the supposed signature of the feudal lord of Yorkshire proved a signal success.

The Lancastrian Earls of Exeter and Oxford were posted at Newark, but withdrew at Edward's approach. Warwick had left London for his own shire; and, after hurriedly collecting an army, threw himself into Coventry. On the 29th of March, "the Kynge (Edward) desyred him to come owte to determyne his quarell in playne fielde, which the same Erle refused to do at that tyme."— *Historie of the Arivall.* Warwick would have fought, but that "he had receyvid a lettre from the Duke of Clarence that he should not fight ontil he cam."—*Leland, Coll. II.*, 504. Having now sufficiently deceived his father-in-law, Clarence went over with his whole force to his brother's side; and at Warwick "they met togethar with as hartyly lovinge chere and countenaunce as might be betwix two sooch bretherne."

Clarence then sent over to Coventry an offer of "mediacon and good condicions," which "condicions" were indignantly rejected by Warwick. Richard Nevill never wavered in the cause which, for reasons best known to himself, he had so recently taken up; and even had he been so disposed, the presence of Exeter and Oxford must have bound him to the Red Rose. London had been left to the care of his brother George, Archbishop of York; and, therefore, he trusted that Edward would be kept out of the capital until he could march to its relief. But Warwick had yet to drink the dregs of his cup of treachery. On Friday, April 5th, Edward left Warwick; and, on Palm Sunday, attended service at the Parish Church of Daventry, when the priests took good care to make the image of St. Anne perform some very remarkable evolutions, "whereat all that sawe worshipped, thanked God and Seint Anne, and toke good hart for theyr good spede."

On the 9th of April, the Archbishop of York, having received letters from his brother urging him to keep Edward out of London, "cawsed Henry, called Kynge, to take an horse and ryde from Powles thrwghe Chepe, and so made a circute abowte to Walbrook, and so returned agayne to Powles (St Paul's) to the Bysshopes Palays, where the sayd Henry at that tyme was lodged, supposynge, that whan he had shewyd hym in this arraye, they shuld have provokyd the citizens to have comen to them and fortified that partye. But they of the citie in great nombar, the maior, aldarmen, and othar of the moaste worshipfull were fully disposed to favour Kynge Edward, and to have the citie open unto him at his comynge."—*Historie Arivall.* The Archbishop was probably almost as helpless as was King Henry, in the hands of an excited population, and found it utterly impossible to obey Warwick's injunctions. On Thursday, April 11th, Edward arrived unopposed, and "rode streight to Powles, and from thense went unto the Byshops palays, where the Archbyshope presented hymself to the Kynges good grace." It is stated that he swore allegiance to Edward on the Sacrament the morning before the King left London for Barnet, but was committed to the Tower for a few days, probably because Edward mistrusted him.—*Fenn, II.,* 64. *Rymer, XI.,* 709. Commines gives three reasons for Edward's friendly reception in London. "The first was the loyalty of the multitudes remaining in sanctuary, and the birth of a young prince of whom the Queen was in sanctuary brought to bed. The next was the great debts which he owed in the town, which obliged all the tradesmen who were his creditors to appear for him. The third was that the ladies of quality and rich citizens' wives, with whom he had formerly intrigued, forced their husbands and relations to declare themselves on his side."

On the strength of the second reason a great number of ladies and gentlemen might have claimed an extreme amount of metropolitan popularity. La Marche gave a like reason for Warwick's enthusiastic reception. **Y**

Warwick, having joined his forces with those of Lord Montague, marched rapidly after Edward, "but the Kyng was well advertised of this yvell and malicious purpose, and therfore, with a grete armye he departyd out of the citie of London towards hym upon the Saturdaye, Ester's even, the xiij day of Aprell. And so he tooke in his companye to the felde Kynge Henrye, and so that aftar noone he roode to Barnete."—*Historie of the Arrivall.*

The Battle of Barnet was fought on Easter Sunday, April 14th, 1471, at a place formerly called Gladmore Heath, now a mere suburb of London. The Heath lay a little to the north-west of Barnet, and upon it Warwick encamped during Easter Eve. On that evening his advanced guard encountered the army of Edward, and was driven back upon the main body. Edward, after passing through Barnet, "drewe towards his enemies, without the town, when it was right derke, and disposed his people in good arraye all that nyght, and so they kept them still without any mannar of langwage or noyse. The Erle of Warwike had many moo goons and ordinaunce than the Kynge; and, weninge gretly to have annoyed the Kinge and his hooste, the Erl's fielde shotte gunes almoste all the nyght. It so fortuned that they alway ovarshote the Kyng's hoste, and hurtyd them nothinge, for the hoste lay much nerrar than they demyd."—*Historie of the Arrivall.*

Easter Day opened with a dense fog. Fabyan evidently had his doubts about the origin of this fog. ' Of the mystes and other impedimentes which fell upon the lordes partye, by reason of the incantacyons wrought by Fryer Bungey as the fame went, me lyst nat to wryte." ·

The allusion is to the Friar Bungey whose character is so admirably drawn in *The Last of the Barons.*

The forces of Edward were greatly superior to those of Warwick, owing to the reconciliation which Clarence had effected with his brother. The van was led by Gloucester, the main body by Edward and Clarence, whilst Hastings commanded the rear.

The Lancastrian right wing, consisting chiefly of cavalry, was commanded by the Lords Montague and Oxford; the left wing, also largely composed of horse, was led by Warwick himself with the Duke of Exeter; and the middle body of archers and billmen was placed under the care of Somerset.

"The Kinge betymes, betwyxt four and five of the clock, notwithstandynge there was a great myste, advancyd bannars, and set upon them firste with shotte, and sone they came to hand strokes, wherein his enemies manly and coragiously receyved them, as well in shotte as in hand strokes when they joyned because of the myste, which myste cawsed the bataile to be the more crewell and mortall. This battayle duryd, some tyme in one place and some tyme in another ryght dowbtefully, because of the myste, by the space of thre howrs, or it was fully achivyd."—*Historie of the Arrivall.*

The dense fog caused inaccuracy in the line of battle. The Lancastrian right wing, under Oxford, outflanked the Yorkist left wing, under Hastings. Oxford had thus an advantage, which he quickly used in making a. most intrepid onslaught against the astonished Yorkists, who turned and fled for London with the news of Edward's defeat.—*Hollinshed.* The troops of Oxford for a brief season took to pillaging; and when again they appeared as combatants, the badge of Oxford, a star with rays, was in the mist mistaken for Edward's Sun in splendour, a device he had adopted in consequence of the famous parhelion at Mortimer's Cross.* The Lancastrian archers shot at Oxford's company; loud cries of treachery filled the air, and Lancastrian fled from Lancastrian.— *Cont. Croyland, Fabyan.*

Accompanied by his esquires, John Milwater, and Thomas Parr (both of whom were slain), the boy Duke of Gloucester in this battle gave proof of coming valour.

"Warwick at the head of his troops attacked the part of the Yorkist army where Edward was, and the battle was for a long time obstinate and bloody. Edward, however, brought up his reserve at an opportune moment, and at length Warwick was slain." His brother Montague also lay dead upon the field, with Sir William Tyrrel, and many other knyghts, squires, and noblemen. "The Duke of Excestar was smytten downe and sore woundyd, and lafte for dead; but he was not well knowne, and being lafte a lytle oute of the field he escapid afterwards." He lay upon the field from seven in the morning until four in the afternoon, when he was brought to the house of one of his servants named Ruthland, where he was attended by a surgeon. He was then conveyed to sanctuary at Westminister; and afterwards went abroad. The Duke of Somerset and the Earl of Oxford fled in the company of some northern men, towards Scotland; but changing their plans, Somerset made for Wales, in order to join Jasper, Earl of Pembroke; and Oxford escaped to France, from whence he not

---

* The Silver Star of the De Veres also had its origin in superstition. One of the ancestors of Oxford in the Holy Land saw a falling star descend upon his shield.

long afterwards returned, with some men; and seized the fortress of St. Michael's Mount on the coast of Cornwall, which he held for several months against King Edward's forces.

On Edward's side there were slain at Barnet, Lord Cromwell, Lord Saye, Sir Humphrey Bourchier, son of John, Lord Berners, Sir John Lisle, and about 1,500 men; but the loss on the Lancastrian side is said to have amounted to about double that number; Edward having given orders not to allow any quarter. Most of the slain were buried on the plain where they had fallen, and where, according to Stow, a chapel was built afterwards, in memory of them, of which there are now no remains; but he states that, when he wrote, it was a dwelling house, and the upper portions remained. Some of the bodies of the persons who had been of a higher rank, are said to have been removed and interred in the church of Austin Friars, London.

An obelisk of stone called Hadley High Stone, was erected near Hadley village, a mile beyond Barnet, by Sir Jeremy Sambroke, Bart., in 1740; and upon it was cut the following inscription:—

> Here was
> Fought the
> Famous Battle
> Between Edward
> The IVth and the
> Earl of Warwick
> April 14th
> ANNO
> 1471
> In which the Earl
> Was defeated
> And Slain.

"On the morrowe aftar the battayle the Kynge commandyd that the bodyes of the dead lords, the Erle of Warwicke and hys brothar, the Marques, should be brought to Powles, in London; and in the Churche there openly showyd to all the people, to the extent that aftar that the people shuld not be abused by feyned seditiows tales, and that no pretens of their being alive shuld stir up rebellion aftarwarde."—*The Arrival.*

"They were then carried down to the Abbey of Bisham, in Berkshire, where among their ancestors by the mother's side, the two unquiet brothers rest in one tomb. The large river of their blood, divided now into many streams, runs so small they are hardly observed as they flow by."—*Habington's Life of Edward IV.*

The tomb in Bisham Abbey remained till the dissolution of monasteries, when the abbey was destroyed; and all knowledge of the exact spot where the Nevills were interred is now for ever forgotten.

To Henry VIII. belongs the glory of utterly destroying many of England's greatest monuments. "His own statue," says Bernard Burke, "still stands in the Palace of Westminster, but grateful should we be that not one drop of his blood taints the Royal line which now occupies the throne; and, as far as we know, Providence has not permitted any of it to linger on the earth, even through an illegitimate channel."

The following letter written by the Earl of Warwick, in 1452, was discovered in the British Museum, and was first published in Miss Strickland's *Life of Elizabeth Woodville.* When the fair Elizabeth was maid of honour in Queen Margaret's Court, she was seen by a brave young knight named Sir Hugh Johns. Though forward in battle, he was very bashful in the presence of ladies; and not daring to tell the Lady Elizabeth that he loved her, besought Warwick to inform her of that fact, which the Earl immediately proceeded to do. Miss Strickland observes that no one can read the letter without being convinced of Warwick's ambition to become a match-maker as well as a king-maker:

To Dame Elizabeth Wodeville.—Worshipful and well beloved. I greet you well, and forasmuch my right well beloved Sir Hugh John, Knight (which now late was with you unto his full great joy, and had great cheer, as he saith, whereof I thank you), hath informed me how that he hath for the great love and affection that he hath unto your person as well for the great sadness (seriousness) and wisdom that he hath found and proved in you at that time, as for your great and praised beauty, and womanly demeaning, he desireth with all haste to do you worship by way of marriage, before any other creature living (as he saith). I (considering his said desire, and the great worship that he had, which was made Knight at Jerusalem, and after his coming home, for the great wisdom and manhood that he was renowned of, was made Knight Marshall of France, and after Knight Marshall of England unto his great worship, with other his great and many virtues and desert, and also the good and notable service that he hath done and daily doth unto me), write unto you at this time, and pray you effectuously that ye will the rather (at this my request and prayer), to condescend and apply unto you his said lawful and honest desire, wherein ye shall not only purvey right notably for yourself unto your weal and worship in time to come, as I hereby trust, but also cause me to shew unto you such good lordship as ye by reason of it shall hold you content and pleased, with the grace of God; which everlastingly have you in His bliss, protection, and governance.   WARWICK.

The Duke of York also wrote in Sir Hugh John's behalf, but the young knight is described as *portionless*, and not having sufficient spirit to speak for himself, was rejected by the fair Elizabeth; who, after marrying a rich Lancastrian cavalier, eventually became the spouse of Edward IV.

Love and money are said to be the principal powers of this world. I therefore append a letter about money, written by Warwick, three years later than the date of his affectionate epistle to Dame Elizabeth. It belongs to the Fenn collection :—

" *To our right trusty and well beloved friend, Sir Thomas Todenham.*—Right trusty and well beloved friend, we greet you well, heartily desiring to hear of your welfare, which we pray God preserve to your heart's desire; and if it please you to hear of our welfare, we were in good health at the making of this letter, praying you heartily that you will consider our message, which our Chaplain, Master Robert Hopton, shall inform you of; for as God knoweth, we have great business daily, and have had here before this time, wherefore we pray you to consider the purchase we have made with one John Swythcote (Southcote), an Esq., of Lincolnshire, of 88*l.* by the year, whereupon we must pay the last payment, the Monday next after Saint Martin's day (11th Nov.), which sum is 458*l.* Wherefore we pray you with all our heart, that you will lend us 10*l.* or 20*l.*, or what the said Master Robert wants of his payment, as we may do for you in time for to come, and we shall send it to you again afore new years, with the grace of God, as we are a true knight; for there is none in your country that we might write to for to trust so well as unto you; for as we be informed, ye be our well willer, and so we pray you of good continuance; wherefore we pray you, that ye consider our intent of this money, as ye will that we do for you in time to come, as God knoweth, who have you in his keeping. Written in London in All Souls Day, within our loggings in the Grey Friars, within Newgate. "RICHARD, EARL OF WARWICK.

"London, 2nd Nov., 1455, 34 Henry VI."

The seal on this letter is of red wax, on which is the bear and ragged staff, with the Nevill motto, and around it a braid of twine. "The sum required was about £7,000 of present money. It is to be regretted the whole purchase money is not mentioned, as it would have distinctly shown the value of a rent of £88 in land in those days."—*Rowland.*

"Richard, Earl of Warwick, was so popular that every man wore his badge; no man esteeming himself gallant whose head was not adorned with his ragged staff; nor no door frequented, that had not his white cross painted thereon."—*Commines.*

"He was ever in great favour of the Commons of the land, because of the exceeding household which he daily kept in all countries wherever he sojourned or lay; and when he came to London, he held such a house that six oxen were eaten at a breakfast; and every tavern was full of his meat. For who that had any acquaintance in his family, should have as much sodden and roast as he might carry upon a long dagger."—*Stow*.

The same Earl of Warwick had a grant of pre-eminence above all the Earls of England; and a peculiar officer at arms was assigned him for his service in martial exploits, called Warwick Herald. He was Captain of Calais and the Tower of Risebank, and Lieutenant of the Marches there; also Governor of the Castle of Guyesnes; General Warden of the East Marches towards Scotland; Lord Great Chamberlain of England for life; Constable of Dover Castle; and Lord High Steward of all England. He had a grant of divers manors in Warwickshire from the Crown, and was afterwards made Constable of the Castle of Hampness, in the Marches of Picardy, for life.

His revenues were valued at four score thousand crowns per annum, *besides his own inheritance;* a sum not much short of three hundred thousand pounds in our money.—*Dugdale—Rowland*.

"Besides all this, the Erle of Warwycke, as one to whome the Commonwelthe was much beholden, was made Ruler and Gouvernor of the Realme, with whom as felow and compaignon was associated George, Duke of Clarence, his sonne in-law."—*Hall, Polydore Vergil*. This was in the Parliament which met Nov. 26th, 1470. In the *Arrival* Warwick is mentioned as styling himself Lievetenaunte of England.

The Earl's Countess, after his death, lived in great penury. All her vast inheritance was taken from her by Parliament, and settled upon Isabel and Ann, her two daughters.*

In the reign of Henry VII., the great possessions of the Countess were restored to her, but only that she might re-convey them to that avaricious monarch, who entailed them upon his own issue.

The Earl of Warwick styled himself Lord of Glamorgan and Brecknock. From the Conquest the Clares and Spencers, Earls of

---

* After the battle of Barnet the Countess took sanctuary at Beaulieu, where she remained two years. " The Countess of Warwick is out of Beaulieu, and Sir James Tyrrel conveyeth her northwards, but the Duke of Clarence liketh it not. The world seemeth queasy for all the persons about the King have sent for their armour, on account of the quarrel regarding the inheritance of Anne."—*Paston Letters*, 1473.

The award made in Council by order of the King, assigning a division of the estates between Clarence and Gloucester, was of course unjust to the Countess of Warwick, she being true heiress to the vast property of De Spencer and Beauchamp. " The Countess of Warwick was no more to be considered in the award of her inheritance than if she were dead."—*Carte*.

Rous actually accuses Gloucester of incarcerating "the venerable Countess Anna, the rightful mistress of the Warwick patrimony, when in her distress she fled to him as her son-in-law for protection."—*Vide Miss Strickland's Anne of Warwick*.

Gloucester, were Lords of Glamorgan ; afterwards the Beauchamps and the Nevills; and by Anne Nevill the title came to Richard III. When he died, it devolved on Henry VII., who granted it to his uncle, Jasper, Duke of Bedford, who died without issue, and left it to Henry VIII.—*Rowland.*

Penrith Castle was built by the Nevills as a protection to the town against any future attacks of their hostile neighbours. By the death of the Earl of Warwick the same reverted to the Crown, and was granted by Edward IV. to his brother Richard, Duke of Gloucester.—*Lyon's Cumberland.*

Daniel's " History of the Wars of the Roses," published in 1609, describes Warwick as

> —— " That blazing star of fight.
> The comet of destruction, that portends
> Confusion and distress, what way he tends."

The day before Towton, at the battle of Ferrybridge, the great warrior is represented as slaying his favourite charger in the presence of the King; exclaiming, " Let him flee that flee will ; I will tarry with him that will tarry with me ; and so he kissed the cross of his sword to confirm that resolution."

Yet his contemporary, Commines, and not a few more recent writers—including the late lamented John Richard Green—have overshadowed the memory of the hero of Towton with imputations of cowardice ! But as Commines was the agent of one of the Earl's bitterest foes—the Duke of Burgundy—his estimate of Warwick's character should be taken with the usual grain of salt. Nor need we be surprised at the little parenthetical libel to be found in the pages of *The Arrival*, which was a purely Yorkist document, written by one of Edward's own suite, and approved by that monarch.

It is most difficult to form accurate ideas about any of those strange characters that appeared in the wars of the Roses. Writers of the period are few ; and these few, divided by Yorkist or Lancastrian sympathies, contradict each other. " No part of English history since the Conquest," says Hume, " is so obscure, so uncertain, so little authentic or consistent as this." This, as Sir John Fenn observes, " is a truth known to and lamented by every man of historical knowledge, and may be partially accounted for by the invention of the art of printing. Those who first practised that art were solicitous to perpetuate things *already* committed to

writing, relative to past times and occurrences; not regarding
recent transactions as of equal consequence.   This art likewise
probably prevented the writers of manuscripts from multiplying
their copies; they foreseeing that the new invention would in time
supply a sufficient number, at a much less price, by which means
the value of their manual labour would be greatly diminished."—
Preface to Fenn's Letters.

From the midst of that dim period no figure looms out with so
much majestic grandeur as that of the ONE man round whom, and
for whom, Yorkist and Lancastrian fought alike.   We surely need
not lay upon his shoulders all the sins of that most sinful season;
yet we may fitly regard him as the beginning and the ending of
the Wars of the Roses, for without him York had been weak
indeed, and after his death it scarcely needed Tewkesbury to
destroy the hope of Lancaster.*

I cannot better close this chapter than by the *résumé* of Hume.

"The King-maker had distinguished himself by his gallantry in
the field, by the hospitality of his table, by the magnificence, and
still more by the *generosity* of his expense, and by the spirited
and bold manner which attended him in all his actions.   The
undesigning frankness and openness of his character rendered his
conquest over men's affections the more certain and infallible; his
presents were regarded as sure testimonies of esteem and friendship;
and his professions as the overflowings of his genuine sentiments.
No less than thirty thousand persons are said to have daily lived at
his board in the different manors and castles which he possessed
in England; the military men, allured by his munificence and
hospitality, as well as by his bravery, were zealously affected to his
interests; the people in general bore him an unlimited affection;
his numerous retainers were more devoted to his will than to the
Prince or to the laws; and HE WAS THE GREATEST, as well the last,
of those mighty barons who formerly overawed the Crown."

* The last attempt on behalf of Henry of Windsor was made by Thomas, the
natural son of William Nevill, Lord Fauconberg.   This Thomas Nevill is usually
distinguished as the *Bastard of Falconberg.* He had been Warwick's vice-admiral,
and a week after the battle of Tewkesbury he landed at Blackwall, and burnt
Bishopgate, and held Aldgate until, after a long and bloody contest, he was driven
back to Stratford.   After hearing of the death of Henry he submitted, and obtained
a pardon for himself and followers, by the delivery to Edward of his fleet of 47 ships.
By the order of Gloucester he was subsequently beheaded at Middleham, and his
head was fixed on London Bridge, "looking Kentwards," Sept. 28th.—*Vide Fenn II.;
Archæologia, Vol. XXI.; Lingard, Vol. IV.*

PART II.—CHAPTER VIII.

THE LADY ANNE NEVILL.

Enter the Ghost of Lady Anne.

GHOST (*to Richard)*—"Richard, thy wife, that wretched Anne, thy wife,
That never slept a quiet hour with thee,
Now fills thy sleep with perturbations:
To-morrow in the battle think on me,
And fall thy edgeless sword; despair, and die!"

Richard III., Act 5, *Scene* 3. *Bosworth Field.*

"I have heard that when he went abroad his eyes whirled about, his body privily fenced, his countenance and manner like one always ready to strike again. He took ill rests at night, lay long waking and musing, sore wearied with care and watch, rather slumbered than slept, troubled with fearful dreams, suddenly sometimes started up, leapt out of bed, and ran about the chamber; so was his restless heart continually tossed and tumbled with the tedious impression and stormy remembrance of abominable deeds."—*Moore* 69.

"IF" ——! Ah, that haunting, irritating, implacable, "if"! The life of Anne Nevill, like so many other sad lives, hung upon the "if," and the "if" went against her. If there had been no mist at Barnet, her father had not died. If there had been no baffling breeze—no sorcery, as the Norman sailors said—the voyage between Harfleur and England might have ended in twelve hours instead of sixteen days, and then the terrible tale of Tewkesbury had not been told. "If," says Commines, who always loved to point the moral, "If the Earl of Warwick had stayed till he had been joined by the forces of Margaret, in all probability he had won the day. But the hatred he bore to the Queen induced him to fight alone. By this example we may observe how long old animosities last, how highly they are to be feared in themselves, and how destructive and dangerous they are in their consequences." "If," says another old chronicler, "the stars in their courses had not fought against Sisera, the tent peg of Jael had not been driven into his unlucky head, and if the elements had not fought against the house of Lancaster it had remained until this day." If the Lady Anne Nevill had not married into the house of Lancaster in the day of its decline, and if the Lady Isabel Nevill had not married "false, fleeting, perjured Clarence," things might have been very different; but enough of this—we cannot unmake history.

Anne Nevill was born at Warwick Castle in the year 1454. Richard Plantagenet was her senior by two years, and the cousins appear to have been playmates.[*]

At the enthronement of George Nevill as Archbishop of York, Richard was a guest at York Palace. He sat under a splendid canopy with the Countess of Westmoreland on his left hand, and his cousins, the Lady Anne and the Lady Isabel opposite to him. The position of the young ladies was probably arranged specially for his entertainment, as the Countess, their mother, sat at the second table, a place of inferior dignity.—*Vide Miss Stricklana's Anne of Warwick.*

Clarence appears to have been disappointed that the Lady Anne could not fall in love with her cousin of Gloucester. He assured Warwick that this only was necessary to complete the victory of the Nevills over the Wydevilles. "By sweet St. George, I swear," said he, "that if my brother Gloucester would join me, I would make Edward know we were all one man's sons, which should be nearer to him than strangers of his wife's blood."—*Hall.* If the appearance of Richard in the least answered to the description which Rous has given of him, we cannot wonder that the Lady

---

[*] According to the laws of chivalry the young warrior knight should spend seven years in the company of some great baron, in order that he might be well tutored in all chivalrous accomplishments. There seems good reason for supposing that the Duke of Gloucester was trained in the home of Warwick. The Exchequer rolls show a record of money "paid to Richard, Earl of Warwick, for costs incurred by him on behalf of the Duke of Gloucester, the King's brother." "This Richard Plantagenet lived for the most part in the Castle of Middleham." *Buck. Bk.* I, p. 7. The partiality of Richard for Middleham is well known. *Whittaker's Richmondshire.*

The heir of Lord Lovell was a ward at Middleham during the same period, a fact which resulted in a lifelong friendship, unpleasantly alluded to in the old song—

"The Cat, the Rat, and Lovell the dog
Rule all England under the Hog."

The fate of one of Anne Nevill's playmates was very horrible. After the battle of Stoke, Lord Lovell hid himself in an underground cell. The person who was entrusted with his secret, allowed him to die of starvation in the place of his seclusion. At least so the story goes, and a skeleton was found in the subterranean chamber at Minster Lovell, in Oxfordshire, towards the close of the seventeenth century.

Anne could not bring herself to regard him as a lovable person. "Verily the Duke had no reason to bless his stars, for at his nativity the scorpion was in the ascendant, he came into the world with teeth and with a head of hair reaching to his shoulders. He was of small stature, with a short face, and unequal shoulders, the right being higher than the left."

"By sweet S. George," repeated Clarence, "if the Lady Anne could but fancy my brother we might "——; but the "if" was still against Anne. She could *not* fancy him. It seemed very unfortunate, for Majerus, the Flemish chronicler, declares that Richard favoured his cousin with a very strong affection. If so, Anne was probably the only person upon whom that distinguished honour descended, for the Duke seems to have been strangely like those disagreeable people, who troubled the first Bishop of Ephesus— "truce breakers, false accusers, traitors, fierce, covetous, *without natural affection.*"*

Anne spent much of her life with her mother at Calais. "When the Duke of Clarence had sworn on the sacrament ever to keep part and promise with the Earl, he married the Lady Isabel, in the Church of our Lady at Calais, in the presence of the Countess of Warwick and the Lady Anne Nevill."—*Hall.*

In May, 1470, we find Lady Anne in the court of Lewis XI. at Amboise. She was then "sweet seventeen," "quiet and of good countenance." Another wooer favoured her with "a strong affection," and he at least was handsome.

> "A sweeter and a lovelier gentleman,
> Framed in the prodigality of nature,
> Young, valiant, wise, and, no doubt, right royal,
> The spacious world cannot again afford."

The marriage between Edward Plantagenet, Prince of Wales, and the Lady Anne was proposed by Lewis XI., on the 15th of July, but the Queen would not in anywise consent. "She saw never honour, nor profit, *ne* for her, *ne* for her son the Prince. She besought the King to leave off speaking for the pardon of the Earl

---

* Miss Halsted, who sometimes suffers her admiration for Richard to run away with her sense of justice towards other people, asserts that Warwick "discouraged all growing attachment between Gloucester and the Lady Anne, because he was unable to detach him from the interest of his Royal brother, or make him the passive tool of his ambition."

Miss Halsted further assures us that "the final ruin of the House of York, and the foundation of all the crimes imputed to Edward IV. and his brothers of Clarence and Gloucester, may be traced to the one all absorbing passion of Warwick."

of Warwick and the said alliance, for that in England she and her
son had certain friends which they might likely lose by this means,
which would do them more hindrance than the Earl and his allies
could do them good."—*Manner and Guiding of the Earl of Warwick. Harleian MS. Edited by Sir Henry Ellis.*

But Prince Edward had something to say in the matter; "for
that he fain would take unto himself the Lady Anne Nevill."
"They loved each other exceedingly."—*Prevost.* Queen Margaret
opposed the match resolutely for fifteen days; and then, "seeing
that her father, King Renè, and her son himself wished it, she was
content that so it might be." The marriage contract was signed
in the presence of Lewis XI. and his brother Charles, Duke of
Guienne, at Angers, July 30th, 1470.

"The Earl of Warwick swore upon the true cross at Angers, in
St. Mary's Church, that without change he shall always hold the
party of King Henry, and serve him, the Queen, and the Prince,
as a true and faithful subject oweth to serve his sovereign lord."

"The King of France and his brother, then clothed in canvas
robes, in the said church of St. Mary, swore they would help and
sustain, to the utmost of their power, the Earl of Warwick, in the
quarrel of King Henry. Queen Margaret then swore to treat the
Earl as true and faithful to King Henry and the Prince, and for
his deeds past never to make him any reproach."

"After the recovery of the Kingdom of England, the Prince was
to be regent of all the realm, and the Duke of Clarence to have all
his own lands, and those of the Duke of York. *Item*—From that
time forth *the daughter of the Earl of Warwick shall be put and
remain in the hands and the keeping of the Queen Margaret, but
the said marriage not be perfected till the Earl of Warwick had
been over with an army into England, and recovered the realm in
the most part thereof for King Henry.* The Earl of Warwick
affirmed at the same time that if he were once over the sea he
should have more than fifty thousand fighters at his commandment;
but if the King of France would help him with a few folk he would
pass the sea without delay, wherefore the King gave him subsidy of
forty-six thousand crowns, besides two thousand French archers."—
Harl. MSS.

Prince Edward plighted his troth to the Lady Anne in the presence of the King of France, King Renè, Queen Margaret, the Duke
and Duchess of Clarence, and the Earl and Countess of Warwick.

Warwick fulfilled his part of the contract by recovering, during a brief season, "the Realm for King Henry;" but whether the Lady Anne was ever *actually married* to Prince Edward must remain a matter for doubt. A great degree of importance was attached to betrothments at the period under consideration; *indeed, they may almost be said to have constituted a portion of the marriage ceremony, so sacred was the pledge that bound the persons affianced to each other.—Sharon Turner, Hist. Vol. III. 457.* In the 15th century a betrothment entered into by both parties with their full and free consent was as binding and valid as a marriage solemnised before the Church, for *marriage, according to the doctrine of the ancient Canon Law, held good however informally administered, provided the consent of the parties concerned was previously obtained.*

By all the Tudor chroniclers the Lady Anne is represented as having been actually married to Prince Edward, but no instrument is now known to be in existence to show that she was so married. The Croyland chronicler says that the marriage *was contracted,*[*] but Warkworth plainly speaks of the Lady Anne as *Prynce Edward's wyf.*

One thing seems certain. Anne's first match was emphatically a *love* match, whatever the second one may have been.

Warwick left Angers on the 4th of August, his wife and daughter remaining with Queen Margaret as pledges of his fidelity. They were entertained with princely hospitality by King Renè till the autumn, when Margaret, her son and his bride, and the Countess of Warwick proceeded to Paris with a guard of honour. They arrived in November; and the Archbishop of Paris, the university, the parliament, the officers of the Chatelet, the provost of the merchants, all in their habits of ceremony, received them, by command of Lewis XI., with all the honours due to French royalty. The streets of Paris were gaily dressed to welcome them; and in their lodging at the palace they received tidings that King Henry was freed and in possession of his kingdom, upon which the Queen with all her company resolved to return to England.— *Felibien. Histoire de Paris, quoted in Miss Strickland's Margaret of Anjou.*

---

[*] "After the son of King Henry, to whom the Lady Anne was *betrothed*, fell in the Battle of Tewkesbury, Richard, Duke of Gloucester, besought that the said Anne should be given to him *to wife*."

With the assistance of her father, Queen Margaret continued her preparations; and by February, 1471, she had a large force ready to embark; but it was not until the 24th of March that the wind allowed her fleet to set sail. After a weary struggle with the adverse elements the unhappy Queen arrived at Cearne Abbey in time to hear of the fall of Warwick, "whereat she fell into a swoon and desired to die." The Countess of Warwick, who had previously landed at Portsmouth, took sanctuary in Beaulieu Abbey, where she was soon after joined by her daughter with the Queen and the Prince of Wales.—*Fleetwood*.

Margaret then attempted a march towards Wales, to join, if possible, her forces with those of Jasper, Earl of Pembroke. The Duke of Somerset and the Earl of Devonshire came to her help, and her army gathered strength, but Gloucester closed its gates against her. It was the city of Richard Plantagenet, and the dark Duke had no intention of winking at the escape of the husband of the Lady Anne. The Queen offered large bribes to the governor, who simply replied that he was bound by the Duke to oppose her passage. "There is noe bridge on Severne beneath Gloucester," says Leland. On Friday, May 3rd, the Queen arrived at Tewkesbury, having travelled that day 36 miles. Her troops were exhausted with the heat and lack of food. They had toiled for hours through dense tangled woods. Edward was close upon them. To attempt the passage of the Severn with the enemy so near was perilous. It certainly meant destruction to the rear part of the army. They encamped therefore "in a close hard at the Townes end, having the towne and Abbeie at their backes, and directlie before them and upon each side of them they were defended with cumbersome lanes, deepe ditches, and manie hedges, beside hils and dales, so as the place seemed as noisome as might be to approach unto, and right harde to be assailed."—*Hollinshed*.

The next day, Edward made a fierce attack upon this position, which was eventually carried by the craft of his brother Gloucester. The Duke pretended to retreat, and the impetuous Somerset was lured to follow him into the open field. So were the unhappy Lancastrians "beaten downe, slaine, or taken prisoners." Somerset and several others fled to the Abbey; Edward entered the church with his sword drawn; but the priest holding aloft the host charged him not to stain the holy place with blood.

The fugitives were dragged forth, and beheaded in the market-place. The King had issued a proclamation that whosoever should bring to him Edward, called Prince, should receive £100 a year for life, and the Prince's life should be spared. "Sir Richard Crofts *nothing mistrusting* the King's promise, brought forth his prisoner, being a goodly well-featured young gentleman, of almost feminine beauty.—*Hall.**

"The Lady Anne was with her husband, Edward of Lancaster, when that unfortunate Prince was hurried before Edward IV., after the battle of Tewkesbury. The Duke of Gloucester was the only person present who did *not* draw his sword on the Royal captive out of respect to the presence of Anne, as she was the near relative of his mother, and a person whose affections he had always desired to possess."—*Joan Majerus, Annal. Flandr., quoted by Bucke.*

If this statement be correct, it assists us in giving credence to the fact that the Lady Anne afterwards accepted Richard as her husband.

The body of the slaughtered Prince was interred in Tewkesbury Abbey, in a common grave, together with the bodies of some soldiers slain in the battle.—*Leland's Collectanea.* Near the centre of the choir, under the tower, a brass plate is let into one of the stone slabs of the Abbey floor. The inscription upon it was written by the Rev. Robert Knight, Vicar of Tewkesbury, in 1796.

Ne tota pereat memoria
Edvardi Principis Walliæ
Post prælium memorabile
In vicinis arvis depugnatum
Crudeliter occisi
Hanc tabulam honorariam
Deponi curabat
Pietas Tewkesburiensis
Anno Domini
MDCCXCVI.

In Gough's edition of Camden, published in 1789, it is stated that there was a monument in the chancel to the memory of George, Duke of Clarence, and Isabel, his wife; and that near the entrance of the choir, under a large grey marble slab stripped of its brasses, Prince Edward was interred; and in an examination of the grave, his bones were discovered deposited in a stone coffin, which was broken during this examination.

* Hall is a very poor authority in his additions to Polydore Vergil, whose record he translates. There does not appear to be any existing document to prove that Sir Richard Crofts ever received the annuity. The statements of the chief authorities with reference to the death of the Prince will be found in the chapter on Sheriff Hutton.

On Monday, 6th of May, Queen Margaret was found in a religious house. She was carried to London, and made a gazing stock in the midst of the King's triumphal procession. The Lady Anne, who in one short fortnight had lost her father, husband, and uncle, rode with her.—*Prevost.* Edward might well have spared the gentle lady this last indignity.

Margaret was taken to the Tower. "The same night betwixt xi and xii of the clok, was King Henry, being prisoner yn the Toure, put to Deth, the Duke of Glocestre and dyverse other beyng there that night.*—*Leland Coll.*

Sheltered by the darkness of that same awful night, Clarence spirited away the Lady Anne Nevill. The reason is given by the Continuator of the Croyland Chronicle. "The Duke of Gloucester desired to find the Lady Anne, that he might marry her, but the Duke of Clarence, not wishing to share with him the inheritance of the Nevills, disapproved of this match. But the Duke of Gloucester, being of crafty and cunning mind, found out the Lady Anne, who was in the city of London, disguised as a cook-maid in a mean household, and forthwith he carried her to the sanctuary of S. Martin."—*Croyland Chron. Trans.*

She was afterwards placed under the care of her uncle, the Archbishop of York. Prevost, the French biographer, states that she was compelled by violence to marry the Duke. On account of affinity, a papal dispensation was necessary to legalise the marriage. The free consent of the contracting parties was indispensable to the procurement of such a bull; and as the bull was never granted, it has been supposed that Anne refused her consent. It is probable also that the arch schemer, who pressed so earnestly for her hand, had really no objection to leave the way open for a prospective divorce. There is a curious clause among the parliamentary rolls of 1474, empowering the Duke "to continue full possession and enjoyment of the Lady Anne's property, *even if she were to divorce him.*"—*Rot. Parl.*, Vol. VI.

The marriage was celebrated at Westminster, by George Nevill, Archbishop of York, in 1474, according to the Sprott Fragment;

---

* The *Arrivall* states that this unhappy King "dyed of pure displeasure and melencholy," but another hand has written on the margin of the manuscript, "*was mordered.*" Fabyan relates the common rumour that "he was stykked" by Gloucester's dagger. Margaret was ransomed by her father. Her mental agonies had been so great that they developed an aggravated form of leprosy, and she became a spectacle of horror — *Villeneuve.* In the prayer book of the once beautiful Queen, the significant words, "*Vanité des vanités, tout la vanité!*" were found written.

but this is really the date of the Act dealing with Anne Nevill's property in consequence of her marriage. Hutton gives 1473 as the date. Sir John Paston's letter to his brother proves that Gloucester was not married on February 17th, 1472, but another letter, written April 15th, 1473, speaks of his "late marriage." Sandford states that the Duke's son was born in 1473, and we have good authority to show that he was ten years of age at the York coronation in September, 1483.

Being warden of the Northern Marches, Gloucester took up his residence at Middleham, and the Lady Anne found herself once more in the old home. Gloucester was much occupied with the Scots, and the Duchess spent much of her time alone in the halls of Middleham. Her little son was the one solace in all troubles.

There is an entry in the Middleham Castle account of one hundred shillings, as being the annual wage of Jane Collins, the boy's nurse; and one Dirick, a shoemaker, is allowed thirteen shillings for his shoes.—*Harl. MSS.*

The death of Edward recalled Gloucester from Yorkshire to London. Soon afterwards a hurried summons came to the Duchess that her presence was required in the metropolis. On Monday, July 5th, 1483, she passed in state, as Queen of England, from Baynard's Castle to the Tower. Four thousand "gentlemen of the north," under the command of Ratcliffe, appeared in procession, probably with the view of preventing any demonstrations of disapproval on the part of the citizens. Piers Curteys, the King's wardrober, created an impression also. He furnished velvets, satins, and damasks of every hue, with cloths of gold richly embroidered; ermine, minever pure, and other costly furs; mantles trimmed with Venice gold; canopies, banners, pennons, and horse furniture, all of the most dazzling appearance and costly material. "The King wore a doublet and stomacher of blue cloth of gold, wrought with netts and pine-apples, and a long gown of purple velvet, trimmed with ermine. The Queen appeared in her still radiant beauty, clothed in a kirtle and mantle of pure white cloth of gold, trimmed with Venice gold and ermine, the mantle being wrought with seventy annulets of silver and gylt, and the people loved to behold her exceedingly."

The next day, the splendour of religious ritual was added to the pomp of the secular Court. The King and the Queen came down out of Whitehall into the great hall of Westminster, where they were met by a great company of bishops, abbots, and priests with mitres and crosiers. The Bishop of Rochester bore the great cross before Cardinal Bouchier, two Earls following with St. Edward's staff. The Earl of Northumberland carried the pointless sword of mercy, the Earl of Kent and the Viscount Lovell the naked swords of justice, the Duke of Suffolk bore the sceptre, the Earl of Surrey the sword of state, the Duke of Norfolk the crown, and my Lord of Lincoln the ball and cross.—*Harl. MSS.*

"The King and Queen went into the great hall of Westminster, directly to the King's Bench, where they sat some time; and from thence the King and Queen walked barefoot upon striped cloth unto King Edward's shrine; all their nobility going before them, every lord in his degree. The Earl of Huntingdon bore the Queen's sceptre, Viscount Lisle the rod with the dove, and the Earl of Wiltshire her crown. Over the head of our sovereign lady was a canopy, at every corner a bell of gold, and on her head a circlet of gold, with many precious stones set therein, on either side of the Queen went a bishop, and my Lady of Richmond bore the Queen's train. So they went from S. Edward's shrine to the seats of state by the altar, and when the King and Queen were seated, there came forth their Highnesses priests and clerks, singing most delectably, Latin and pricksong, full royally. Then the King and the Queen put off their robes, and stood all naked from their waists upwards, till the bishop had anointed them.* The bishops of Exeter and Norwich stood on each side the Queen; the Countess of Richmond was on her left, and the Duchess of Norfolk knelt behind the Queen and the other ladies. Then the King and Queen came down to the high altar and kneeled, and anon the cardinal turned him about with the holy Sacrament in his hand, and parted it between them both, and so they received the good Lord."—*Excerpt. Hist.* 381.

Afterwards, at the banquet in the Hall of Westminster, on the Queen's right hand stood my Lady of Surrey, and on her left the Lady Nottingham, holding a canopy of state over her head. The King sat at the middle of the table, the Queen at the left hand of the table, and on each side of her stood a Countess, holding a cloth of pleasance when she listed to drink. The champion of England after dinner rode into the hall, and made his challenge without

---

* At the coronation close fitting tunics of crimson satin were worn, having apertures on the breast and between the shoulders, which were drawn aside when the consecrating prelate traced the sign of the cross, as ordained in the pontifical. The passage therefore means that the royal pair divested themselves of their regal mantles, and opened their tunics that they might be anointed. The Queen was anointed on the forehead and chest only, so that one opening sufficed in her dress, which was unlaced and relaced by the lady-in-waiting.

being gainsayed. The Lord Mayor served the King and Queen with iprocras, wafers, and sweet wine, and by that time it was dark night. Anon came into the hall great lights of wax torches, and torchettes, and as soon as the lights came up the hall, the lords and ladies went up to the King and made obeisance; and anon the King and Queen arose up and went to their chambers, and every man and woman departed and went their ways, where it liked them best.—*Harl. MSS. Grafton.*

On the 23rd of July, Richard commenced his Royal progress, quitting Windsor for Reading, where he granted to Lady Katherine Hastings, formerly Lady Katherine Nevill (see Part II., Chap. 1), "his full and entire pardon, restoring her estates, and promising to protect and defend the widow, and *to suffer none to do her wrong.*" And there, for the sake of her children, the proud Nevill knelt in abject gratitude to him who had sent her husband, the gallant Hastings, to a taitor's death. Then the King went to Oxford, where the University hastened to pay him reverence. He passed through Woodstock, Worcester, and Gloucester, proceeding westwards as far as Tewkesbury, for the *suppression of crime and the reformation of manners.* He granted bequests and charters to the towns, and endowments to the churches. He founded the Herald's College. For "the completion of that unparalleled ornament of all England, the King's College, Cambridge, he paid £700." He ratified the privileges of the University, remitted fees, and altogether spent a vast amount of money. Thus Richard strove to redeem his faults, and a solemn service was commanded "to be held annually, on the 2nd of May, by the whole congregation of regents and non-regents of the University aforesaid, for the happy state of the said most renowned Prince, and his dearest Consort, Anne."

At Warwick Castle, the Court was for a short time kept up with great magnificence. The Queen brought with her the young Earl of Warwick, the son of her sister Isabel. It was doubtless owing to her influence that this ill-fated Prince was treated with comparative kindness during the major part of Richard's reign.

The re-coronation of the King and Queen, and the re-investiture of their son as Prince of Wales, took place at York, August 31st, 1483. The Queen walked in procession through the city, holding the Prince of Wales by the right hand, upon whose head there was the demi-crown appointed for the heir of England. Five marks were paid to Michell Wharton for bringing the boy's jewels from York to Middleham.—*Middleham Household Book, Harl. MSS.*

An insurrection under Buckingham to release the children of Edward, whom Richard himself had (in another way) already released, called the King into Lincolnshire. A second conspiracy of Buckingham's to marry the Princess Elizabeth (Edward's daughter) to Henry, Earl of Richmond, was defeated by Richard's ingenuity. By promises and threats he lured the Princess out of sanctuary. She was kindly received by Queen Anne, and appeared in the Christmas festivities at Westminster Hall. It is highly probable that Richard intended her to marry his son,* but that ill-fated boy died on the last day of March, 1484. A mystery hangs over his death; indeed mystery hangs over all the events of his father's reign. His parents were at Nottingham when the child died at Middleham. Rous calls it an "unhappy death." To the audit of expenses paid for his son's clothing, Richard added in his own handwriting the words "*whom God pardon.*" What had the little boy done that he should be prayed for by so sincere a sinner as Richard III.?

In the north aisle of Sheriff Hutton Church there is an alabaster monument, known to the villagers as the little "Crumpling." "Crumpling *may* refer to the crumply, *i.e.* wrinkled, folds of the dress, but the exact word occurs for a diminutive or deformed person. The affix *ing* has a definitive meaning (*e.g.* gosling from goose); and we know that Richard was called Crouchback by the Yorkshiremen, though of course it does not follow that the Little Crumpling was himself deformed. The tomb has the Trinity and a shield with a plain cross, which may either be that of St. George, or that of Burgh, represented by the House of York."—*Longstaffe.*

Several very competent judges have decided that this little effigy must represent the son of the Lady Anne Nevill.

The head rests on double cushions, and is surmounted by a coronet. Underneath the recumbent figure there is a curious Gothic sculpture, divided into seven richly canopied compartments.

Todd, in his work on Hutton, describes the monument as that of "a young *female.*" The disposition of the robes possibly gave him that impression.

* He even offered to marry her himself if the Queen should die. From the letter of the Princess to the Duke of Norfolk it would appear that the idea of this incestuous connection inspired her with no feelings of horror. She declared that she was the King's in heart and thought. He was "her joy and maker in this world, but she feared 'the Queen would never die.'"—*Bucke.* Even Ratcliffe and Catesby opposed the marriage. In the great hall of the Temple, Richard was induced to declare publicly that no such marriage had ever been contemplated, and he wrote a letter to the citizens of York to contradict the slander.—*Croyland Chron. Drake's Eboracum. Lingard.*

The life of Queen Anne was bound up in the life of her boy. "Neither the society that she loved, nor the pomp and festivity of the Court, could cure the languor or heal the wound in the Queen's breast for the loss of her son."—*Croyland Chron. Contin.*

"She fell into a weary, lingering decline, and died at Westminster Palace, March 16th, 1485, in the midst of the greatest eclipse of the sun that had happened for many years."

The funeral of this queen was extremely magnificent, for Richard loved magnificence in everything. He shed tears at the grave, but the chronicler intimates that the King's smiles and tears were always at command as expediency required.—*Baker's Chron. Grafton.*

"The body was interred near the altar of Westminster, not far from the place where the monument of Anne of Cleves was afterwards erected; but no memorial marks the spot where the broken heart of the hapless Anne of Warwick found rest from as much sorrow as could possibly be crowded into the brief span of thirty-one years."—*Miss Strickland's Anne of Warwick.*

Long before, there had been "dyverse tales" of poison, and rumours that "Richard's Queen would suddenly depart from this world." Hollingshed treats us to a terrible picture of how this strange rumour was propagated among the Royal servants, until at length it reached the ears of Anne, who lay in her chamber in the last stage of decline. Stung by the cruel report, she rushed into the presence of the King with dishevelled hair and disordered dress, and sobbing piteously, urged him to tell her "what she had done to deserve death; whereat the King soothed her with fair words and smiles, bidding her be of good cheer, for, in sooth, she had no other cause."

"On each side of the faded, melancholy portrait of this unfortunate lady, in the pictorial history of her maternal ancestry, called the Rous Roll, two mysterious hands are introduced, offering to her the rival crowns of York and Lancaster; while the white bear, the cognizance assumed by her mighty sire, the Kingmaker, lies muzzled at her feet, as if the royal lions of Plantagenet had quelled the pride of that hitherto tameless bear, on the blood-stained heath of Barnet."—*Miss Strickland's Lives of the Queens.*

The portraits of both the husbands of Anne, with her father and son, appear in this roll, and they well agree with the descriptions which historians have left us. Rous was a priest who lived under the protection of the Nevill family at Guy's Cliff.

Queen Anne survived her sister Isabel eight years, as that Princess died Dec. 12th, 1476.

The Duchess of Clarence was interred in a stone arched vault, near the high altar of Tewkesbury Abbey. The entrance to the vault is covered by a large blue stone, under which is a flight of eight steps leading to the vault, which was opened and examined in 1826, on the occasion of some repairs, when the skulls and some bones of a man and a woman were discovered in it, besides which there were also six large stones at the south end of it, which had apparently been placed there in order to support two coffins abreast. Sandford expressly states that the Duke was buried at Tewkesbury, near the body of his Duchess. It was evident that the vault had been once previously entered, probably at the time of the dissolution of monasteries, or during the Parliamentarian wars, and rifled of everything worth taking away. The floor of the vault was paved, and extending nearly the length and breadth of it was the representation of a cross, formed by the insertion of bricks, some of which contained the arms of England, and others contained representations of *fleurs de lis*, and ornamented letters. Under the belief that the mortal remains so discovered were those of the ill-fated Duke of Clarence and Isabel his wife, the skulls and bones were collected, placed in an ancient stone coffin, and the vault again closed up.—*Paper read before Soc. Antiquaries by R. Brook, Esq., March 8th,* 1855.

I append a letter written by the husband of the Lady Anne.— *Fenn Collection.*

To my Lorde Nevyll in hast, &c., &c.—My Lorde Nevyll, I recomaunde me to yoe as hartely as I can, and as ever ye love me and yor awne weale and sewrty, and yhs Realme yt ye come to me wt yt ye may make defensably arrayde in all the hast yt ys possyble; and yt ye wyll yef credence to (Sir) Richarde Ratclyff, thys berrerr, whom I nowe do sende to you enstructed wt all my mynde and entent: and my Lorde do me nowe gode vyce as ye have always befor don, and I trust nowe so to remembre you, as shalbe ye makyng of you and yours. And God sende you goode fortunes. Wrytten att London, the xjth day of June wt the hande of yor hertely lovyng Cousyn and master, R. GLOUCESTRE.

The date of the letter is probably Wednesday, June 11th, 1483. 1 Ed. V. It may have been addressed to Ralph Nevill, the second Earl of Westmoreland, or possibly to his nephew, Ralph, son of Sir John Nevill. If to the latter, the address "to my *Lorde* Nevyll" must have been used out of courtesy.

PART II.—CHAPTER IX.

THE BROTHERS OF THE KINGMAKER.

> "Fill high the sparkling bowl!
> The rich repast prepare."

WHEN only a boy of fourteen, George Nevill, the brother of the Kingmaker, had a papal dispensation to enable him to hold a canonry at Salisbury as well as a stall at York. At three and twenty he was appointed Bishop of Exeter, the Pope issuing a bull which enabled him to receive the income of his bishopric during the period which elapsed between his nomination and his attaining canonical age for consecration. He was translated in 1465 from Exeter to York, and was enthroned with astonishing expense and pomp. The Duke of Gloucester, and almost all the nobility, bishops, and great men of the kingdom were present at the magnificent feast given on that occasion; indeed, from far and wide, the whole country

> "Gathered then
> Her beauty and her chivalry, and bright
> The lamps shone o'er fair women and brave men."

The Queen's relations alone were absent, because they were jealous of the prodigious power of the Nevills.

The following particulars concerning this extraordinary feast will afford some idea of 15th century magnificence:—

The goodly Provision made for the Installation Feast of George Nevill, Archbishop of York, A.D. 1465.

In wheat, quarters	...	...	300	In bittors 204
In ale, tuns ...	...	...	300	In heronshaws 400
In wines, tuns ...	...	...	100	In pheasants 200
In ipocrasse, pipes	...	...	1	In pertridges 500
In oxen	...	...	104	In woodcocks 400
In wild bulls ...	...	...	6	In curliews 100
In muttons ...	...	...	1,000	In egrits... 1,000
In veals	...	...	304	In geese... 2,000
In porkes ...	...	...	304	In cappons 1,000
In swanns ...	...	...	400	In piggs 2,000
In cranes ...	...	...	204	In plovers 400
In kidds ... - ...	...	...	204	In quailes 1,200
In chickens ...	...	...	2,000	In fowles called rees 2,400
In pigeons ...	...	...	2,000	In peacocks 104
In connies ...	...	...	4,000	In mallards and teales... ... 4,000

In staggs, bucks, and roes ... 500 and more
In pastries of venison (cold) 4,000
In parted dishes of jellies... 4,000
In plain dishes of jellies 3,000
In cold tarts, baked 4,000
In cold custards, baked 3,000
In hot pastries of venison 1,500
In hot custards 2,000
In pikes and breams 308
In porpoises and seals 12
Spices, sugared delicates, and wafers, plenty.

The Great Offices.

The Earl of Warwick, as Steward.
Earl of Northumberland, Treasurer.
Lord Hastings, Comptroller.
The Lord Willoughby, Carver.
The Lords Greystock and Nevell, Keepers of the Cupboard.
Sir John Brecknock, Surveyor in the Hall.
Lord John of Buckingham, Cup Bearer.
Sir Richard Strangewich, Sewer.
Sir Walter Morley, Marshall, and eight other Knights, for
    the Hall.
Also eight Squires, besides other two Sewers.
Sir John Malvery, Panter.
The Serjeant of the King's Ewery as Ewerer.

Estates sitting at the High Table in the Hall.—First, the Archbishop in his Estate. Upon his right hand the Bishop of London, the Bishop of Durham, and the Bishop of Ely. Upon the left hand the Duke of Suffolk, the Earl of Oxford, and the Earl of Worcester.

B B

At the second Table in the Hall.

The Abbot of Saint Maries.	The Prior of Durisme.
The Abbot of Fountaunce.	The Abbot of Whaley.
The Abbot of Salley.	The Abbot of Kirkestall.
The Abbot of Rivals.	The Abbot of Bylande.
The Abbot of Whytby.	The Abbot of Selby.
The Abbot of Meux.	The Prior of Bridlyngton.

The Prior of Gisbrough, and other Priors, to the number of eighteen, sytting at the table.

At the third Table in the Hall.

The Lorde Montague.	The Lorde Ogle.
The Lorde Cromwell.	With forty-eight
The Lorde Scrope.	Knyghts syttinge at the
The Lorde Dacres.	boorde.

At the fourth Table there.

The Deane of Yorke Mynster, and the Deane of Saint Savior, with the brethren of the sayde Mynster.

At the fyfth Table in the Hall.

The Maior of the Staple of Calice, and the Maior of Yorke, with all the worshipfull men of the sayde Citie.

At the sixth Table.

The judges of the Lawe, four Barons of the Kinge's Exchequer, and twenty-six learned men of the Lawe.

At the last Table in the Hall.

. Threscore and nyne worshipfull Esquiers, wearing the Kinge's lyvery.

Estates sytting in the Cheefe Chamber.

The Duke of Glocester, the Kinge's brother. On his ryght hand the Duches of Suffolke; on his left hande the Countesse of Westmerlande, and the Countesse of Northumberlande, and two of the Lord of Warwicke's daughters.

At the second Table there.

The Barronnesse of Greystocke, with three other Barronnesses, and twelve other Ladies.

At the third Table there.

Eighteen Gentlewomen of the sayde Ladies.

Estates syttyng in the Seconde Chamber.

The Elder Duches of Suffolke.	The Lady Hastynges.
The Countesse of Warwike.	The Lady Fitzhewe.
The Countesse of Oxford.	

At the second Table there.

The Ladie Huntley, the Lady Strangwicke, and eight other Ladies, syttynge at the table there.

Estates syttyng in the Great Chamber.

The Bishop of Lincolne.	The Bishop of Exeter.
The Bishop of Chester.	The Bishop of Carlile.

At the second Table there.

The Earle of Westmerlande, the Earle of Northumberlande, the Lord Fitzhewe, the Lord Stanley, and ten Barons more there.

At the thirde Table there.

Fourteen Gentlemen, and fourteen Gentlewomen of worship.

In the Lowe Hall.

Gentlemen Franklins, and head Yeomen, four hundred and twelve, twice fylled and served.

In the Gallery.

Servauntes of noble men twice fylled and served, four hundred and mo.

Officers, and servauntes of officers, one thousand.

Cookes, in the kitchen, sixty-two.

Of other men servaunts, with broche turners, one hundred and fifteen.

" The inverted proverb," says Fuller, "found truth in this man —*one glutton-meal makes many hungry ones*—for some years after he was slenderly dyetted, not to say famished, in the Castle of Calis; and, being at last restored by the intercession of his friends, he died broken-hearted at Blyth, and was buried in the Cathedral of York, 1476."

During his episcopate the See of York was abridged of a large part of its ancient jurisdiction. St. Andrew's in Scotland, was made an archiepiscopal see by Pope Sixtus IV. The Tweed henceforward became the northern boundary of the Province of York. Nevill resisted this arrangement, but the Pope was strong enough to carry his point. The near relationship of the Archbishop to the Earl of Warwick involved him in the great political struggles of his day; consequently George Nevill appears more in the light of a great temporal prince, rather than as the Christian pastor of a diocese. Yet he was not unmindful of the duties which he owed to those who were under his spiritual charge. A provincial council was held at York, in 1466, at which the archbishop promulgated certain constitutions, by which he enjoined every parish priest to expound to his people, in their mother tongue, the fourteen articles of faith, the ten commandments, the two evangelical precepts, the seven works of mercy, the seven deadly sins *cum suâ progenie*, the seven principal virtues, and the seven sacraments of grace. The priests were favoured with a long explanation of these several points, so that they might know how to teach the people.— *Ornsby's York.*

The Archbishop officiated at the marriage of the Duke of Clarence with the Lady Isabel Nevill, and also at the marriage of her sister, the Lady Anne, with Richard III.

I have already alluded to the supposed imprisonment of Edward IV. at Middleham Castle in 1469. *Vide Part II., Chapter* 6.

Warkworth says that "the kynge scaped oute of the Bisshoppes handes by fayre speech and promyse"—presumably the promise was that the King's infant daughter should marry George Nevill, the Archbishop's nephew—but the Croyland historian declares that Edward escaped *pene miraculose*.

Many writers treat this story of the imprisonment as incredible.

Fabyan relates that early in the following year, the Archbishop invited the King to meet Clarence and Warwick, at his seat at the More, in Hertfordshire. As Edward was washing his hands before supper, John Ratcliffe, afterwards Lord Fitzwalter, whispered in his ear that one hundred armed men were lying in wait to surprise and convey him to prison. The King stole to the door, mounted a horse, and rode home in hot haste to Windsor. This story also rests on a somewhat slender foundation.

Archbishop Nevill brought Henry VI. out of the Tower, and continued to hold the seals during that King's brief restoration.

Later on, says the writer in *Leland's Collectanea*, "he was doble to King Henry, and kept hym at London, when he wood have beene at Westminster, for he had lettres of King Edward to kepe King Henry out of sanctuary." On the 9th of April, 1471, in obedience to the earnest exhortations of his brother Warwick, the Archbishop endeavoured to make some show in favour of Henry, but it was a poor show indeed. Hoping to rekindle loyalty to the Lancastrian cause, George Nevill conducted the King in procession through the city. He was disappointed. The excitement was too much for Henry. He was attacked by one of his epileptic fits. With vacant eye, haggard face, and drooping head, the impotent monarch rode from Walbrook to St. Paul's. Some men who thought of his great father and Agincourt, pitied him, the rest ridiculed the unhappy man. The city merchants and the city wives cried out for Edward. The Archbishop of Canterbury, and Urswick, the Recorder, also called for Edward. Sir Thomas Cook, the Mayor, too timid to call either for Henry or for Edward, took fright, and fairly ran away. Warwick had left six thousand soldiers with the Archbishop; but two thousand armed gentlemen, headed by the Earl of Essex, issued out of the sanctuaries, and the city bands joined them. It was no time to waver, but George Nevill wavered. Letters came to him from Edward with assurances of affection and reward. The tower was surrendered to Edward's friends. Carried away by the tumult, he went out to welcome his brother's foe, and thus sealed his brother's fate.

His life after the battle of Barnet was not happy. Though he had rendered the King many services, Edward could not feel easy on his throne as long as a Nevill remained at liberty. "They had hunted together at Windsor; and the King in return had promised to hunt with the prelate at the Moor, in Hertfordshire. The most magnificent preparations were made for his reception; all the plate, which the Archbishop had secreted since the death of his brothers, had been collected, and the principal nobility of the neighbourhood were invited to partake of the entertainment. But Edward sent for the Archbishop to Windsor, and arrested him on a charge of having lent money to the Earl of Oxford. The revenue of his bishoprick was seized, his plate confiscated, his mitre converted into à crown, and his jewels divided between the King and the Prince of Wales. The prelate lingered in prison for three years, partly in England, and partly in Guisnes, and did not recover his liberty till a few weeks before his death in 1476."—*Lingard*, Vol. IX.

Of *John Nevill, Lord Montague*, the brother of the Kingmaker and the Archbishop, not much remains to be said. He was first summoned to Parliament as Baron Nevill of Montacute, 38th Henry VI., 1460. In the third year of Edward IV. he was advanced to the title of Earl of Northumberland; Henry Percy, the real heir, having fled into Scotland with King Henry.

"Then the Lord Montague, the Earl of Warwick's brother, which the King had made Earl of Northumberland, was mighty and strong by the same, and for so much as the King and his Council thought he would hold with the Earl of Warwick, therefore the King and his Council *made* the country to desire that they might have the rightful heir Percy, son to Henry Percy, that was slain at York Field, to be the Earl of Northumberland, and so it was done. And after this the King made the Lord Montague Marquis Montague, and made his son the Duke of Bedford, which should wed the Princess, the King's eldest daughter, which by *possibility* should be King of England. And so he had many fair words and no lordships, but always he promised he would do."— *Chronicle of Warkworth*.

Lord Montague's own words, as reported by the same authority, are that the King having made him a marquis, "gave him a pie's nest to maintain his estate with."

We have already related how Montague fought for the King at Hedgeley and Hexham. As he remained inactive at Pontefract

Castle, when Edward passed through Yorkshire to recover his kingdom, it has been surmised that the Marquis was false to his own brother, but remained true to Edward until the battle of Barnet. The real reason of Montague's fatal supineness is given in Stowe's Chronicle. "The Marquis Montacute would have fought with King Edward, but that he had received letters from the Duke of Clarence that he should not fight till he came." "Your brother the Earl hath had compunctious visitings, and would fain forgive what hath passed for my father's sake, and unite all factions by Edward's voluntary abdication of the throne—at all hazards, I am on my way northward, and you will not fight till I come." So wrote Clarence, and as Edward had only a small force when he passed through Pontefract, and had taken oath to Henry, swearing on the sacrament that he came to England only as Duke of York, Montague let him pass, for the love he once bore him.

There is no reason to suppose that John Nevill was false to his brother. His gallant conduct on the field of Barnet should clear him of such a baseless charge.

George, the eldest son of the Marquis, was in the lifetime of his father created Duke of Bedford, by Edward IV., as the King intended he should marry his daughter Elizabeth. Owing to the revolt of his uncle, the Earl of Warwick, and his subsequent attainder, the Duke was degraded by Parliament of all his honours and dignities, in the 17th Edward IV. He died without issue in 1483, and was buried at Sheriff Hutton.

ISSUE OF JOHN NEVILL, MARQUIS MONTAGUE, SECOND SON OF
RICHARD, EARL OF SALISBURY.

John Nevill=*Isabel*, daughter and co-heir of Sir Edmund Inglethorpe of Borough Green, Co. Cambridge, by Jane, sister, and eventually heir to John Tiptoft, Earl of Worcester. She re-married Sir William Norreys.

1. *George Nevill* created Duke of Bedford, 1469; succeeded as Marquis Montague, 1471; degraded by Act of Parliament, 1477; ob. s.p., 1483.	2. *John Nevill*, died young, 1460; buried at Sawston, Cambs.	3. *Ann*, daughter and co-heir, married Sir Wm. Stonor. Oxon.	4. *Elizabeth*, daughter and co-heir, married Thomas, Lord Scrope, of Masham, who died 1493. She re-married, before 1496, Sir Henry Wentworth, who died in 1500. She died 1515.
5. *Margaret*, daughter and co-heir, married, 1st, Thomas Horne; 2nd, Sir J. Mortimer; 3rd, Chas. Brandon, Duke of Suffolk.	6. *Lucy*, married, 1st, Sir Thos. Fitzwilliam, of Aldwark; 2nd, Sir Anthony Browne.	7. *Isabel*, married, 1st, Sir William Huddlestone, of Sawston; 2nd, William Smith, of Elford, Co. Stafford.	

PART II.—CHAPTER X.

THE HOUSE OF ABERGAVENNY.

"The Lord of Burgavenny is one of the ancyentest Barons of the realme."— *Leland*.

After the Conquest divers princely baronies were granted for the purpose of guarding the country against the incursions of the Welsh. The Earl of Chester was planted on the north border of Wales; and the barons of the middle part of the south marches possessed a palatinate jurisdiction, having a Court of Chancery, with their own writs and pleadings. The castle and lands of Abergavenny, then comprised under the description of Gwent Land, or Higher Gwent, were granted to be holden *per Baroniam*, or Grand Sergeanty.

By a writ of 1st Edward I. it is proved that the barony of Burgavenny was a very large seignory, and had petty barons holding under the same.

Hamelyn de Baalum, a companion of the Conqueror, was the first baron. He built the castle and founded the priory of Abergavenny. He was buried at the priory in the reign of William Rufus; but the barony he held was not styled the Barony of Burgavenny until granted to Sir William Cantilupe in the reign of Henry III.

Bryan of Wallingford, the nephew of Hamelyn de Baalum, became second baron. Both his sons were lepers. He therefore went on pilgrimage to Palestine, and left his barony to his cousin-german, Walter of Gloucester. Seized by the spirit of the time, *he* also left his barony, and the post of High Constable of England, to assume the habit of a monk in the priory of Llantony, where he died in the reign of Henry I. The barony then descended to Henry of Hereford, who was murdered by one of his fierce Welsh neighbours. His successor, Sissilth ap Jago, was disposed of in the same way. Hugh Beauchamp, the supposed ancestor of the great Earls of Warwick, who was made Warden of Higher Gwent by Henry II., then received the barony; but Syssell ap Dyfnewall, who had slain his predecessors, dispossessed him. Syssell was in his turn murdered in a midnight carousal by William Braose, the nephew of Henry of Hereford, the fifth baron. This was an act of vengeance, as Henry had previously fallen by the hand of Syssell. Braose entered upon his uncle's inheritance, but was driven out by King John, and died a beggar in France. His son, Gyles Braose, Bishop of Hereford, ingratiated himself into the favour of John, and received livery of his father's land. He is known as the ninth baron, and being a wise and excellent person, and contrasting very favourably with his predecessors, he died lamented in 1216. The bishop was succeeded by his brother Reginald, also a good man. His son William acted against the Welsh with Henry III., and was hanged by Llewellyn, Prince of North Wales. Leaving no male issue he was succeeded by William Cantelupe, the husband of his daughter, Eve. Eve survived her lord a year, and during the minority of her son, George, the barony was held by the Earl of Pembroke. George Cantelupe, 14th baron, died in 1273, without male issue. His daughter Joane married William, Lord Hastings, who held the barony in her right. After this, until the year 1390, the barony descended regularly from father to son.

Lawrence Hastings (great-grandson of William), 18th Baron Burgavenny was created Earl of Pembroke by Edward III., in the thirteenth year of his reign. He was a great favourite with that monarch, and married Agnes, daughter of the famous Roger Mortimer, Earl of March. His son John, 19th baron, was the first English subject who imitated Edward III. in quartering arms; and his grandson John, 20th baron, who was "exceeded by none in beauty and urbanity of manner," unhappily fell in tilting with

Sir John St. John, during a Christmas festival at Woodstock, 1390. As he had no issue the title of Earl of Pembroke ceased; but the baronies vested in him devolved upon Reginald, Lord Grey of Ruthyn, as descended lineally from Elizabeth, sister of John de Hastings, father of the before-mentioned Lawrence, the first Earl of Pembroke.

The death of this popular young nobleman was attributed to a judgment on the family, on account of Aymer de Valence, Earl of Pembroke, his ancestor, having been one of those peers who passed sentence of death on Thomas, Earl of Lancaster, at Pontefract; for it was remarked, that after that sentence, not one of the succeeding Earls of Pembroke ever saw his father,* nor any father ever took delight in seeing his child.

John Hastings was buried in Grey Friars, London, under a splendid monument which remained until the dissolution of religious houses by Henry VIII., when, of course, it was destroyed.

Lord Grey, of Ruthyn, is known as 21st Baron of Burgavenny; but the estates were under litigation during twenty years, and by compromise, Sir William de Beauchamp became 22nd Baron. He married Joane, daughter of Richard, Earl of Arundel; and his son, Richard Beauchamp, married Isabel, daughter of Thomas le Despencer, and had livery of her lands. He was created Earl of Worcester by Henry V., as a reward for valour. *His sole daughter and heir, Elizabeth, married Edward Nevill, who became Lord Burgavenny in her right.* The marriage took place in 1435, but Edward Nevill was unable to possess the barony until 1450; as, by special entail made by Sir William Beauchamp, 22nd Baron, for failure of issue male, it descended to Thomas Beauchamp, Earl of Warwick, and his heirs male.

Richard, son of Thomas Beauchamp, therefore, became 24th Baron Burgavenny, besides being Earl of Warwick. He married Isabel, widow of his first cousin, Richard Beauchamp, Earl of Worcester, of whom we have just spoken. This lady, therefore, married two gentlemen bearing the same name, both of them being Barons of Burgavenny. The name of Richard Beauchamp, Earl of Warwick, is specially great in English history. He was Knight of the Bath at nineteen; Knight of the Garter at twenty-three. In

* Lawrence Hastings, 18th Baron Burgavenny, died when his son John was a year old. John, 19th Baron, died at Calais, presumably by poison, when his son, the last Earl of that line, was three years old.

Jerusalem, in Venice, in Russia, Poland, and Prussia, he figured as a hero. He was a distinguished leader at Shrewsbury. He was Captain of Calais, and Regent of France. The Emperor of Germany told King Henry that "no Christian Prince had another such a knight for wisdom, nurture, and manhood, and if all courtesy were lost yet it might be found again in him." He founded a chantry at Guy's Cliff, rebuilt the chapel, and set up the statue of Earl Guy. His son Henry succeeded him ; and, as to his daughters, Anne married Richard Nevill, Earl of Salisbury; Margaret married the renowned John Talbot, Earl of Shrewsbury; and Elizabeth married George Nevill, Lord Latimer, from whom the Willoughbys and Grevilles, Barons of Brooke, and Percies of Northumberland are descended.

The lands of which this Earl died siesed were, according to Dugdale, "vast." The yearly value was 8,306 marks 11 shillings 11 pence. Dugdale says that at the time he wrote, that sum would be augmented in value sixfold, and would be about £40,000 per annum. Now it would be not less than £100,000 per annum.

The magnificent chapel adjoining the Collegiate Church of St. Mary, Warwick, was built by his executors, pursuant to his will. He ordained that three masses should be sung every day as long as the world should endure. To the church of St. Mary he gave an image of our Lady, in pure gold, to remain for ever ; and ordained that four images of gold, each weighing twenty pounds, like himself, in his coat of arms, holding an anchor between his hands, should be delivered at the shrines of St. Alban's, St. Thomas of Canterbury, St. Winifred in Shrewsbury, and the shrine at Bridlington, in Yorkshire. His tomb is described by Dugdale as inferior to none in England, save that of Henry VIII., in Westminster. It was twenty-one years in constructing, and cost about £30,000. I shall have occasion again to refer to it in my chapter on the Nevill monuments.

The Earl died at Rouen, April, 1439. The Lady Isabel, who married two Barons of Burgavenny, and outlived them both, left a will so curious that its introduction here may be excused.

"Isabella Beauchamp, Countess of Warwick, December 1st, 1439. My body to be buried in the Abbey of Tewksbury; and I desire that my great templys, with the bayleys, be sold to the utmost, and delivered to the monks of that house, 'so that they grutched not with my burial there.' Also, I will that my statue be made, all naked, with my hair cast backwards, according to the design and model which Thomas Porchalion has for that purpose, with Mary Magdalen laying her hand across, and St. John the Evangelist on the right side, and St. Anthony on the left; at my feet an escutcheon, impaling my arms with those of the Earl, my husband, supported by two griffins, but on the sides thereof the statues of poor men and women in their poor array, with their heads in their hands. To our Lady at Caversham, I bequeath a crown of gold, made of my chain, weighing twenty-five pounds, and other broken gold in my cabinet, and two tablets, the one of St. Katherine, and the other of St. George, the precious stones of which tablets to be set in the said crown. I will that my tablet, with the image of our Lady, having a glass for it, be offered unto our Lady of Walsingham, as also my gown of green alze cloth of gold with wide sleeves, and a tabernacle of silver, like in the timber to that over our Lady at Caversham. To our Lady of Worcester, my great image of wax, now in London. To the Abbey of Tewksbury, my wedding gown, and all my cloths of gold, and cloths of silk, without furs, except one of russet velvet, which I bequeath to St. Winifred."

Henry Beauchamp, son of the famous Earl of Warwick, was created Duke of Warwick, and, as 25th Baron, continued to hold the Burgavenny estates, though Edward Nevill still claimed them. He had a grant in reversion of the islands of Guernsey and Jersey, and was *crowned King* of the Isle of Wight by Henry VI. He married Cicely, daughter of Richard Nevill, Earl of Salisbury, and by her had issue, a daughter, who for some time held the estates as Baroness of Burgavenny. She died 27th Henry VI., and Edward Nevill* then had livery of the castle and lordship in right of his wife, although he was afterwards dispossessed by his nephew, the Kingmaker.

Edward Nevill, 6th son of the 1st Earl of Westmoreland, being a younger brother of a large family, sought his own elevation by selecting a wife, who brought him an ancient barony, and made him Peer of the Realm. Lady Elizabeth Beauchamp, as we have already seen, was daughter and heir of the celebrated Richard Beauchamp, Lord Burgavenny, by Isabel, his wife, which Isabel was also daughter and heir of Thomas, Lord le Dispencer. Elizabeth Beauchamp, therefore, as her heir, carried that ancient title also (being the Premier Barony of England) to her husband, Edward Nevill.

* "Sir Edward Nevill, Lord of Burgavenny and De la Spencer, was summoned to Parliament in the 29th Henry VI., 1450, and he married his first wife (1435) Lady Elizabeth Beauchamp, the sole child and heir general of Richard Beauchamp, Lord Abergavenny, and Earl of Worcester, and the half-sister to Henry Beauchamp, Duke of Warwick, and to Lady Ann Beauchamp, the wife of Sir Richard Nevill, the great Earl of Warwick; and this Lady Abergavenny was cousin-german to Henry V., and to Lady Blanch Plantagenet, Empress of Germany, and to Lady Philippa Plantagenet, Queen of Denmark, and she died in 1448. Her husband, Sir Edward Nevill, was brother to John, Lord Nevill of Raby, to Richard Nevill, Earl of Salisbury, and to George Nevill, Lord Latimer."—*Harl. MSS.*

In 1460, Edward Nevill accompanied Edward, Earl of March, with an army of 25,000 men, and being refused admittance to King Henry VI., the battle of Northampton ensued, when the Royalists were vanquished with loss of 10,000 men.

After Edward the Fourth attained the Crown, Edward Nevill was one of the lords who faithfully adhered to him, and in the second year of his reign went with him towards Scotland, when several places were reduced to obedience in the North. In the 10th Edward IV., anno 1471, he was commissioned to muster and array all men fit to bear arms in the county of Kent, and to march and oppose George, Duke of Clarence, and his own nephew, the famed Earl of Warwick.

Elizabeth Beauchamp, his first wife, who was born at Hanly Castle in Worcestershire, in December, 1415, died in 27th Hen. VI., anno 1448, and was buried in the church of the Carmelites, at Coventry.

Edward, Lord Burgavenny, departed this life on Thursday, 18th October, 16th Edw. IV., anno 1476, and was buried, it is believed, in the Priory Church at Abergavenny, where his tomb is to be seen.—*Rowland.*

Edward Nevill was dispossessed of his barony by the Kingmaker, who held the lordship as 28th Baron. He was followed by Richard, Duke of Gloucester, who held the estates by right of his wife, Anne Nevill, but after he came to the Crown he allowed the *title* to George, second son of Edward Nevill. By the death of Richard, the barony came to Henry VII., who in the first year of his reign granted it to his uncle, Jasper, Duke of Bedford.

Edward Nevill, and George, his son, were certainly summoned to Parliament as Barons Burgavenny, and as such we must therefore consider them; but the castle and lordship were not re-granted to the Nevills until Henry VIII. granted them to George, the grandson of Edward. The following table will make the succession clear:—

ISSUE OF EDWARD NEVILL, 27TH BARON BERGAVENNY, SIXTH SON
OF 1ST EARL OF WESTMORELAND, BY JOAN BEAUFORT.

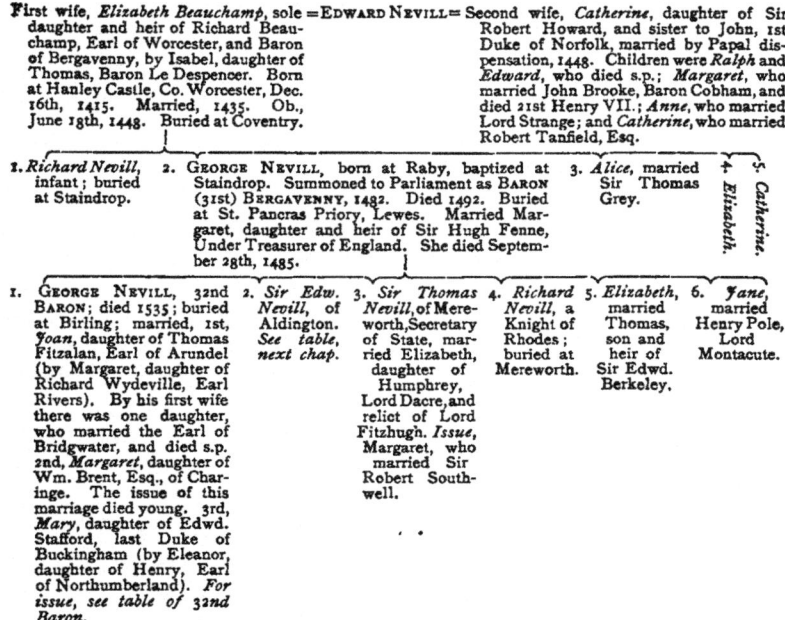

First wife, *Elizabeth Beauchamp,* sole =EDWARD NEVILL= Second wife, *Catherine,* daughter of Sir daughter and heir of Richard Beauchamp, Earl of Worcester, and Baron of Bergavenny, by Isabel, daughter of Thomas, Baron Le Despencer. Born at Hanley Castle, Co. Worcester, Dec. 16th, 1415. Married, 1435. Ob., June 18th, 1448. Buried at Coventry. | Robert Howard, and sister to John, 1st Duke of Norfolk, married by Papal dispensation, 1448. Children were *Ralph* and *Edward,* who died s.p.; *Margaret,* who married John Brooke, Baron Cobham, and died 21st Henry VII.; *Anne,* who married Lord Strange; and *Catherine,* who married Robert Tanfield, Esq.

1. *Richard Nevill,* infant ; buried at Staindrop.

2. GEORGE NEVILL, born at Raby, baptized at Staindrop. Summoned to Parliament as BARON (31st) BERGAVENNY, 1482. Died 1492. Buried at St. Pancras Priory, Lewes. Married Margaret, daughter and heir of Sir Hugh Fenne, Under Treasurer of England. She died September 28th, 1485.

3. *Alice,* married Sir Thomas Grey.

4. *Elizabeth.*

5. *Catherine.*

1. GEORGE NEVILL, 32nd BARON; died 1535; buried at Birling; married, 1st, *Joan,* daughter of Thomas Fitzalan, Earl of Arundel (by Margaret, daughter of Richard Wydeville, Earl Rivers). By his first wife there was one daughter, who married the Earl of Bridgwater, and died s.p. 2nd, *Margaret,* daughter of Wm. Brent, Esq., of Charinge. The issue of this marriage died young. 3rd, *Mary,* daughter of Edwd. Stafford, last Duke of Buckingham (by Eleanor, daughter of Henry, Earl of Northumberland). *For issue, see table of 32nd Baron.*

2. *Sir Edw. Nevill,* of Aldington. *See table, next chap.*

3. *Sir Thomas Nevill,* of Mereworth, Secretary of State, married Elizabeth, daughter of Humphrey, Lord Dacre, and relict of Lord Fitzhugh. *Issue,* Margaret, who married Sir Robert Southwell.

4. *Richard Nevill,* a Knight of Rhodes ; buried at Mereworth.

5. *Elizabeth,* married Thomas, son and heir of Sir Edwd. Berkeley.

6. *Jane,* married Henry Pole, Lord Montacute.

In this table I have not noticed the second marriage of the 31st Baron. Of the second wife not much appears to be known, except that her name was Elizabeth, and after the death of Lord George Nevill, she married one Richard Naylor, a citizen of London. Her will, dated April 14th, 1500, directs her body to be buried in the church of St. Martin, Bishopsgate, in a vault in the chapel of our Lady there, beside the body of the said Richard Naylor. She gives her lands in Chatham, Chilham, Peckham, Sellinge, and Boughton under the Blore, in Kent, to her son, John Naylor, and desires that a priest should be found to pray for the souls of her four husbands, George Nevill, Richard Naylor, Robert Bassett, and John Stokker. The first husband died in 1492, therefore this gay widow must have been thrice married in eight years, as her will was proved in 1500.

The will of her first husband is as follows :—

"George Nevill, Knight, Lord of Abergavenny, July 1st, 1491. Being sick, I desire my body to be buried in Monastery of St. Pancras, called the Priory of Lewes, on the south side of the altar, where I have late made a tomb for my body. I will that twenty-four poor men clothed in black, shall carry torches burning at my funeral, and at the celebration of masses for my soul, and that they receive eight pence for their pains. Also, I will that my executors pay 200 marks to the Priory to cause mass to be sung at the altar, near the place of my burial, every day; and to keep my obit yearly in that church."

Then follow bequests of the manors of Bergnorth, in Norfolk, to his son John, the manor of Hokham to Edward, Claxhall to Thomas, and Otteley to Richard. The son, John, mentioned in this will, died without issue. There was also a son, William, who took orders, and died abroad.

GEORGE NEVILL, 32ND BARON, had livery of his father's lands in 1492. He was summoned by King's writ at the Tower of London, June, 1483 (Edward V.), to prepare himself to receive the honour of knighthood previous to the coronation. He afterwards attended Richard III. into the north. In 8th Henry VII. he was one of the principal persons with the King at the siege of Bolloyn. In 1497, a rebellion broke out in Cornwall, headed by James, Lord Audley. The rebels were defeated at Blackheath by Lord Berga-venny and Lord Cobham, and 2,000 of them were slain.

After the departure of King Philip from England, and in the 21st year of Henry VII., Hall relates:—" That the King of England began to suspect Sir George Nevell, Lord Burgavenny, and Syr Thomas Grene of Grenes Norton, Knight, that they were con-federated and partakers, in the beginning, with Edmonde De la Pole, and so upon this suspicion they were commanded to the Tower. But shortly after, when they had been tried and purged of that suspicion and crime, he commanded them both to be set at liberty. But Syr Thomas Grene fell sick before, and continued in the Tower, in hope to be restored as well to his health, as he was to his liberty, and there died. The Lord of Burgavenny, for his modesty, wit, and probity (because the King found him like himself), always true, faithful, and constant, was of his Sovereign Lord more esteemed, favoured, and regarded, than he was before."

In the 2nd Henry VIII. he was made Constable of Dover and Warden of the Cinque Ports, and in the fifth year of the same reign was elected Knight of the Garter, and installed in the eighth stall on the Prince's side, May 7th.

He was present at the Battle of the Spurs, and had command of the right wing of the King's army in France. His name is mentioned as a prominent spokesman in the celebrated interview between Henry VIII. and Francis I. at the Field of the Cloth of Gold.

In 1519, he was out of favour with the King and imprisoned for a short time in the Tower.

Shakspeare, in his play of Henry VIII., introduces him with Buckingham and Norfolk. The conversation turns on Cardinal Wolsey, of whom Lord Abergavenny says—

> "I cannot tell
> What heaven hath given him,—let some graver eye
> Pierce into that; but I can see his pride
> Peep through each part of him, whence has he that
> If not from hell?

In the 21st Henry VIII., George Nevill was summoned to Parliament as Premier Baron of England. In the following year he signed the letter of the Peers to the Pope, informing his Holiness that he would lose his supremacy if he did not grant the divorce between the King and Queen Katherine.

Lord Abergavenny died 27th Henry VIII., and was buried at Birling. By his will dated June 4th, 1535, he entailed the castle and lordship of Burgavenny on himself and the heirs *male* of his body, by Mary, his wife, with remainder to his brother Thomas, and the heirs male of his body, with remainder to his brother Edward and the heirs male of his body, with a remainder to his own right heirs.

This will is frequently referred to in the Acts of Parliament relating to the family, and is indeed the foundation of the title to the family estates.

Lord Abergavenny's brother, Sir Thomas Nevill, was of the Privy Council, and Secretary of State to Henry VIII. He was member of the House of Commons in 1514, and probably represented the county of Kent.—*Willis's Notitia Parliamentaria*, Vol. III. In the sixth Parliament of Henry VIII., he was chosen Speaker of the Commons. The following eulogium appears in the *Lords' Journals* concerning him :—

"This day Thomas Nevill, descended of a noble house and family, being own brother to the Lord Bergavenny, having been nominated and elected Speaker of the Commons' House of Parliament, was presented to the King's Majesty, in full Parliament; and conducted himself with so much ability, good taste, prudence, and discretion, in the office intrusted to him, that he obtained the greatest praise to himself, with the approbation and satisfaction of all who heard him. To which praise the King's Sacred Majesty added no small accession of distinguished honours; for in the face and presence of the Lords Spiritual and Temporal, and the Commons of the Realm, he advanced him to the rank and dignity of a Knight, to the honour of God and St. George; a distinction which we have never heard to have been conferred on any other man at any former period."—*Lords' Journals. Translation.*

In Mereworth Church, Kent, there is an ancient monument bearing the following inscription:—

"Here under this tombe lyeth buried the body of Sur Thomas Nevell, Knt., one of the most honorable counsell unto oure souverain Lord and Kyng, Henry the 8th, wych Sur Thomas decessed the 29th daye of Maye, in the Year of oure Lorde God 1542, on whose soul and all Christian souls Jesu have mercy."

The arms are engraved on brass: Nevill quartering Warren and Beauchamp, a rose.

Elizabeth, his wife, the daughter of Lord Dacre and Dame Ann Graistock, was buried at Narden in the diocese of Canterbury, and her tomb was embellished with the following extraordinary inscription:—

𝔒 𝔏𝔬𝔯𝔡 𝔪𝔶 𝔖𝔞𝔟𝔦𝔬𝔲𝔯 𝔞𝔫𝔡 𝔥𝔢𝔟𝔢𝔫𝔩𝔶 𝔐𝔞𝔨𝔢𝔯,
𝔥𝔞𝔟𝔢 𝔪𝔢𝔯𝔠𝔶 𝔬𝔫 𝔈𝔩𝔦𝔷𝔞𝔟𝔢𝔱𝔥 𝔊𝔯𝔞𝔦𝔰𝔱𝔬𝔠𝔨 𝔞𝔫𝔡 𝔇𝔞𝔨𝔢𝔯.
—*Weever's Funeral Monuments.*

We have now to speak of another brother of the 32nd Baron, Sir Edward Nevill, of Adlington. His name is conspicuous in the accounts of sundry jousts and Court festivities in England and France.

Hall relates that in 1522, he was confined to the Tower with Lord Montacute by Henry VIII., for favouring the Duke of Buckingham, and after they were released Sir Edward was forbidden the King's presence.

On the 4th of December, Sir Geoffrey Pole was indicted for holding correspondence with his brother the Cardinal; and Sir Edward Nevill, for saying "The King was a beast, and worse than a beast." George Crofts, Chancellor of the Cathedral of Chichester, for saying, "The King was not, but the Pope was Supreme Head of the Church." John Collins was indicted for saying, "The King would hang in hell one day, for the plucking down of Abbeys." All these persons except Sir Edward Nevill, pleaded guilty, and were condemned; and they were all executed but Sir Geoffrey Pole, who had discovered the matter.

Sir Edward Nevill was arraigned before Thomas, Lord Audley, Lord Chancellor, the Lord High Steward for the occasion, on the 9th January, 1538, and was convicted and sentenced to die. On the 12th January, the Marquis of Exeter, Lord Montagu, and Sir Edward Nevill, were beheaded on Tower Hill, and the others were drawn to Tyburn, and hanged and quartered. Among the Lansdowne MSS. there is a paper headed "Traiterous Speeches of

Edward Nevill and others, against Bishop Jewell." "Edward Nevell said, that he who brought over Doctor Spreye was a traiterous villain, and that whosoever durst say the contrary was a villain, and lied in his throat. (Signed by five witnesses)." After these executions, Sir Edward Nevill was attainted in Parliament of High Treason on the 28th April, in the 31st year of Henry VIII. (Anno 1540.)

In the latter part of the reign of this sanguinary Monarch the scaffold was deluged with the blood of his subjects. Among other victims of his ferocity was the venerable Countess of Salisbury. This great lady was no less conspicuous for her illustrious birth, than her unbounded munificence, and her innocence of the charges brought against her. She was the daughter of the ill-fated Isabel Nevill, Duchess of Clarence.

"This venerable lady, about seventy years of age, being come to a scaffold, erected in the Tower, was bid to lay her head upon the block, but she would not, saying, 'So should traitors do, but I am none,' nor did it avail, until the executioner told her that it was always customary; but turning her grey head every way, she cried out, 'If you will have my head, get it as you can!' and so he was forced to cut it off barbarously."—*Vide Lord Herbert's Life of Henry VIII.*

PART II.—CHAPTER XI.

THE HOUSE OF ABERGAVENNY.—Continued.

"F rom sinfulnesse preserve me Lord !
R enew thy spirit in my hart,
A nd let my tongue therewith accord,
U ttering all goodness for his part.
N o thought let there arise in me
C ontrarie to thy statutes ten ;
E ver let me most mindful be
S till for to praise thy name, Amen.

A s for my soule, so of my bodie,
B e thou my guider, O my God !
U nto Thee onlie I do crie,
R emove from me thy furious rod.
G raunt that my head may still devise
A ll things that pleasing be to thee ;
U nto mine ears, and to mine eies,
E ver let their a watch set be,
N one ill that they may heare and see ;
N o wicked dede let my hands do,
Y n thy good paths let my feet go."

PLEASE do not say that this acrostical hymn is not all that it ought to be, for the authoress, Lady Frances Abergavenny, the writer of *Precious Pearls of Perfect Godliness*, is ranked by Horace Walpole among the Royal authors. She was the daughter of Thomas Manners, Earl of Rutland, and the first wife of Lord Henry Nevill, 33rd Baron Bergavenny.

This baron was summoned to Parliament in the 3rd and 4th year of Edward VI. In the next year, he accompanied the Marquis of Northampton on an embassy to France, to present the Order of the Garter to the French King.

It appears that Lord Abergavenny was committed to prison for striking the Earl of Oxford in the Chamber of Presence ; but, after a month's confinement, he had a special pardon for the offence.

In the reign of Queen Mary, Sir Thomas Wyatt, of Allington, in Kent, a zealous catholic, but who had, from his travels in Spain, imbibed a detestation of that nation, raised a rebellion in Kent, to prevent the marriage of Queen Mary with Philip of Spain.

Sir Robert Southwell, the sheriff of the county, and Lord Abergavenny, who then resided at his seat, Comforte, in Birling, collected their retainers, and the gentlemen and yeomen in their country to oppose Wyatt.

An encounter afterwards took place between Lord Abergavenny and Wyatt, at Wrotham, "where the rebels were handled so hot and so fiercely," that they fled.

In the year 1586, Lord Abergavenny was appointed one of the judges for the trial of Mary, Queen of Scotland.

This baron died at Comforte, Birling, February 10th, 1586, and was buried with great pomp and solemnity at Birling. Lady Frances died in 1576, and was also buried at Birling.

They had one daughter, Mary, who at her father's death was thirty-two years of age. She married in 1575, Sir Thomas Fane, of Bodsill, Kent. Upon the death of this baron a dispute arose between Lady Mary Fane, as heir of the whole blood, and Edward Nevill, the eldest son of Sir Edward Nevill of Aldington, who was beheaded in 1538. The table in the last chapter shows the Abergavenny pedigree as far as the 32nd Baron. We may now continue it to Lady Mary Fane, to whom the ancient barony of Le Despencer was confirmed, and from whom the present Baroness Le Despencer claims the enjoyment of the premier barony of England :—

ISSUE OF GEORGE NEVILL, 32ND BARON.

1. *Henry Nevill*, 33rd BARON, married Frances, daughter of Thomas Manners. Died 1586. *Mary*, sole daughter and heir, married Sir Thomas Fane. Contested barony as heir-general, with Edward Nevill, heir male and nephew of her grandfather, the 32nd Baron. Barony of Le Despencer allowed to her. Died 1626. Buried at Mereworth. BARONS LE DESPENCER.	2. *Catherine*, married Sir J. St. Leger. 3. *Margaret*, married John, son of Sir Thomas Cheyney. 4. *Dorothy*, married William Brooke, Baron Cobham. 5. *Mary*, married Thos. Fines, Lord Dacre. 6. *Ursula*, married Sir Warham St. Leger.

Sir Thomas Fane, on behalf of his wife, Lady Mary, claimed the barony as heir general to William, Lord Beauchamp, of Abergavenny (summoned as Baron de Bergevenny, 16th Richard II.), treating it as a personal dignity. Sir Edward Nevill claimed the barony as tenant in tail of the castle and honour of Abergavenny, under the entail created by the before-mentioned will of George,

Lord Abergavenny, in the 27th Henry VIII.; and he founded his claim upon the seizin of the castle. Of course they were, as we have shown, both descended from Sir Edward Nevill, who married Elizabeth, the daughter of Richard Beauchamp, Lord Bergavenny.

It appears that the House of Lords could not come to a determination; and they, therefore, moved that information should be given to the King of all the proceedings, and that suit should be made to his Majesty for ennobling both parties, the one to the Barony of Bergavenny, and the other to the Barony of Le Despencer, which baronies both their ancestors enjoyed.

This request was acceded to by King James; but still he required the Lords to determine the right. He directed that the House should proceed to determine upon which of the competitors the Barony of Bergavenny should be settled; and that upon the other, whichsoever it might be, should be conferred that of Le Despencer. Upon this intimation, the Lords proceeded to a final hearing of counsel; and the question having been propounded by the Lord Chancellor, whether the heir male (*i.e.*, Nevill, the tenant in tail of the castle) should have the dignity of Abergavenny, or the heir general; and that they who would give their voice for the heir male should say "Nevill," the others for the heir general by saying "Fane;" it was agreed and resolved by the greater number of voices, that the heir male, Nevill, should be restored to the Barony of Bergavenny; and it is now enjoyed accordingly by the present Marquis. A writ was accordingly issued to call Sir Edward to Parliament, directed "Edwardo Nevill de Bergavenny, Chr.," and tested 25th May, 2nd James, anno. 1604; and he was assigned the ancient place and precedency belonging to that dignity.—*Rowland*.

Edward Nevill of Newton St. Loo, who contended for the barony, died in 1589. His issue is shewn in the following table. His son, Edward, became 34th Baron, and died in 1622, and was succeeded by his son, Henry, 35th Baron. In 1625, this Baron had livery of all his estates by the Crown.

As he held *in capite* of the Crown, certain fines, before the abolition of feudal tenures, were due to the King on the heir having livery of his lands; and on this occasion he paid for his livery a sum equivalent to ten thousand pounds in money of present value.

The manor of Sculton Burdeleys, which came to George Nevill, 32nd Baron Bergavenny, who died in 1546, is held of the King *in chief,* by the service of Grand Serjeanty, to be the Chief Larderer when the Kings and Queens of England are crowned; and the Larderer is entitled 'to take for the performance of the said service, the fees, profits, and advantages due and accustomed, viz., "the remainder of all the beef, mutton, veal, venison, kid, bacon, with all other kinds of flesh meat, and likewise of fish, salt, and all other things, which may remain after dinner in the said office of the Larderer."

In *Testa de Neville,* title "Com. Norff." the right of Hug. de Burdeleys, in respect to the Manor of Sculton, is thus described:—
"Hug. de Burdeleys tenet qu'dam s'jantiam in Sculthow p' s' vicie Lardar' d' ni Reg." *

Mr. Rowland, as deputy of Henry, 2nd Earl of Abergavenny, served the office of Chief Larderer at the coronation of King George IV. in the year 1821, and took a compensation of 200 guineas in lieu of the remnants of the feast, to which he was entitled as perquisites.

ISSUE OF EDWARD NEVILL, OF ALDINGTON, SECOND SON OF 31ST BARON.

Edward Nevill, of Aldington, married Eleanor, daughter of Lord Windsor, and relict of Ralph, Lord Scrope. Beheaded and attainted, 1538. Attainder afterwards reversed.

1. *Edward Nevill,* of Newton St. Loo, Co. Somerset. Heir male and nephew of 32nd Baron. Contended for barony after the death of his cousin Henry, the 33rd Baron, in 1586, but died in 1589. Married Catherine, Maid of Honour to Queen Mary, and daughter of Sir John Brome of Halton, Oxon.	2. *Henry Nevill,* of Billingbeer, Co. Berks. Constable of Windsor. Died, 1592. Buried at Waltham, S. Lawrence. Married Elizabeth, daughter and heir of Sir Thomas Gresham. (She died 1573, and was buried at Waltham.) Ancestor of the Right Hon. Charles Cornwallis Neville, 5th and present BARON BRAYBROOKE. (*See Table.*)	3. *Francis,* married, 1st, Sir Edward Waldegrave; 2nd, Lord Powlett; 3rd, sòn of 1st Marquis of Winchester.

NEVILLS OF BILLINGBEER.

1. *Edward Nevill,* declared BARON BERGAVENNY (34th) by resolution of Parliament, 1604. Died, 1622. Buried at Birling. Married Rachel, daughter of John Lennard, of Knowle, Kent.	2. *Francis,* married Mary, daughter and heir of T. Lewkner, of Selsey, Sussex.	3. *Henry,* married Eleanor, daughter of Edward Poole, Esq., of Poole.

NEVILLS OF CHICHESTER. NEVILLS OF BEDMINSTER.

1. *Henry Nevill,* 35th BARON. Buried at Birling, 1649. Married, 1st, Mary, daughter of Thomas Sackville, Earl of Dorset, Lord High Treasurer.	2. *Sir Christopher Nevill,* of Newton St. Loo, K.B., 1625. Buried at Birling, 1649. Married Mary, daughter of Thomas Darcy, of Tolston Darcy, Co. Essex. *See Table.*	3. *Elizabeth,* married, 1st, Sir John Grey; 2nd, Sir John Bingley.

1. *Sir Thomas Nevill,* died, v.p., 1628. Buried at Birling. Married Frances, daughter of Baron Mordaunt.	2. *Cecily,* married Fitzwilliam Coningsby, of Hampton Court, Co. Hereford.

1. *Henry,* died infant.	2. *Charles,* collum fregit *ex* lapsu equi apud Brackley, 1637.	3. *Margaret,* married Thomas Brooke, son of Sir Basil Brooke, of Madeley

* Testa de Neville was written by a member of the Nevill family, and it contains an account of Serjeanties holden of the King, taken by Inquis. in temp. Hen. III. and Edw. I. Dugdale thinks they were composed by Jollan de Nevill, a Justice Itinerant at the latter end of the reign of Edward II.—*Vide next Chapter.*

ISSUE OF HENRY NEVILL, 35TH BARON, BY HIS SECOND WIFE, CATHERINE, DAUGHTER OF GEORGE, BARON VAUX, OF HARRODEN.

1. *John Nevill*, 36th BARON, married Elizabeth, daughter of Wm. Chamberlain, of Sherborne, Oxon. Died, 1662, s.p. Buried at Birling.	2. *George Nevill*, 37th BARON, married Margaret, daughter of Thomas Gifford, of Birstall, Leicester.	3. *Catherine*, married, 1st, Sir Robert Howard, 5th son of Earl of Suffolk ; 2nd, Robert Berry, of Ludlow.	4. *Elizabeth*, married Thomas Stonor, of Stonor.

1. *George Nevill*, 38th BARON. Died 1695, s.p. Buried at St. Giles in the Fields. Married Honora, daughter of John, Baron Bellasyse, of Worlaby, County Lincoln.	2. *Margaret*, married Sir John Shelly.

ISSUE OF SIR CHRISTOPHER NEVILL, OF NEWTON ST. LOO.
Sir Christopher Nevill.

1. *Richard Nevill*, died at Oxford, 1643. Married Sophia, daughter of George, and sister and heir of Sir Henry Carew.	2. *Anne*, married John, Lord Lucas, of Shenfield, Essex.

George Nevill, died 1665. Married Mary, daughter of Sir Bulstrode Whitelock.

1. *George Nevill*, 39th BARON, died 1720. Married Anne, daughter of Nehemiah Walker, Esq.	2. *Edward*, Captain in Navy, died at sea. Married Hannah, daughter of Jervis Thorpe.

1. *George Nevill*, 40th BARON, died s.p., 1723.	2. *Edward Nevill*, 41st BARON, died 1724, s.p. Married Catherine, daughter of Lieut.-Gen. Tatton.	*William Nevill*, 42nd BARON, succeeded his cousin and married his widow, Catherine, daughter of Lieut.-General Tatton. Died 1744. Buried at East Grinstead.

1. *George Nevill*, 43rd BARON, created EARL OF ABERGAVENNY and Viscount Nevill of Birling, 1784. Buried at East Grinstead, 1785. Married Henrietta, daughter of Thomas Pelham, of Stanmer, County Sussex.	2. *Catherine*, Maid of Honour to Queen Charlotte.

1. *Henry Nevill*, 2nd EARL OF ABERGAVENNY, born 1755. Married Mary, daughter and heir of John Robinson, of Sion Hill, Isleworth.	2. *George Nevill*, of Godstone, Surrey, born 1760. Married Caroline, daughter of Richard Walpole.	3. *Henrietta*, born 1756. Married Sir John Berney.

In the foregoing table, I have not noticed the second marriage of the 42nd Baron to Rebecca, daughter of Thomas Herbert, Earl of Pembroke, in 1732. By this marriage, after a lapse of four hundred years, the Earldom of Pembroke became once more connected with the Barony of Abergavenny. It will be noticed that in the space of eighty years four Barons died without issue, viz., John, 36th Baron; George, 38th Baron; George, 40th Baron, and Edward, 41st Baron.

Of the later barons I need say nothing, "for in the busy scenes of a refined, well governed, and thickly populated kingdom, the tranquil virtues of private life are seldom known far beyond the favoured circle in which they are displayed." By such virtues the noble House of Abergavenny has long been sanctified. We have, therefore, only to add our fervent prayer that by such virtues also it may be long preserved, and thus fulfil its own motto, NE VILE VELIS.

BARONY OF BRAYBROOKE.

Field Marshal Sir John Griffin-Whitwell (heir general of 3rd and last Baron Griffin of Braybrooke), was summoned to Parliament in 1784 as 4th Baron Howard de Walden, and in 1788, was created Baron Braybrooke (peerage of Great Britain) with remainder to Richard Neville Aldworth, Esq., of Billingbere. He died in 1797, when the Barony of Howard de Walden fell into abeyance, and the Barony of Braybrooke devolved upon *Richard Aldworth Neville*, who became 2nd Baron. He was Lord Lieutenant and Vice-admiral of Essex, Provost-marshal of Jamaica, &c. By royal license, 1798, he assumed the additional surname of Griffin. He died 1825, and was succeeded by his son, *Richard Neville*, *LL.D.*, 3rd Baron, editor of the "Diary of Samuel Pepys," born 1783, married 1819, Lady Jane (who died 1856), daughter of 2nd Marquess Cornwallis. The 3rd Baron died in 1858, and was succeeded by his son, Richard Cornwallis, 4th Baron, who died in 1861; when his brother Charles Cornwallis Neville, the present peer, became 5th Baron Braybrooke.—*Vide Debrett.*

ISSUE OF RICHARD ALDWORTH NEVILLE, 2ND BARON BRAY-BROOKE, MARRIED 1780, CATHERINE, SISTER OF 1ST MARQUIS OF BUCKINGHAM.

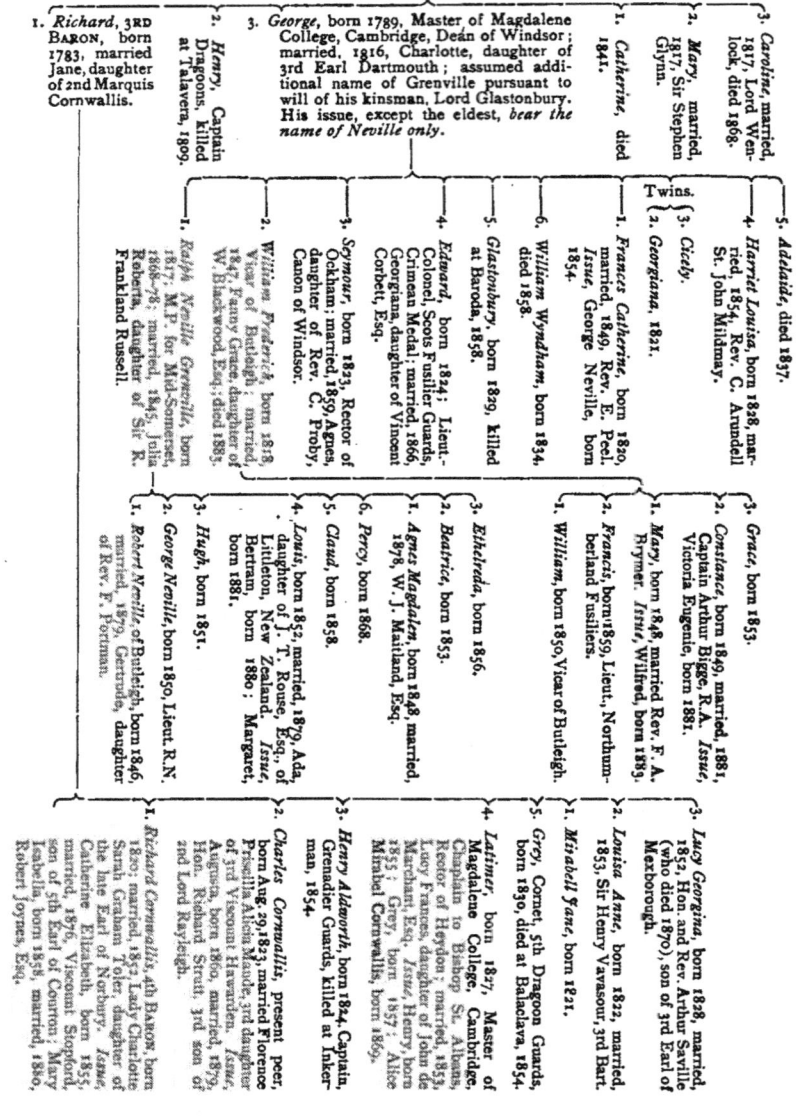

1. *Richard*, 3RD BARON, born 1783, married Jane, daughter of 2nd Marquis Cornwallis.

2. *Henry*, Captain Dragoons, killed at Talavera, 1809.

3. *George*, born 1789, Master of Magdalene College, Cambridge, Dean of Windsor; married, 1816, Charlotte, daughter of 3rd Earl Dartmouth; assumed additional name of Grenville pursuant to will of his kinsman, Lord Glastonbury. His issue, except the eldest, bear the name of Neville only.

1. *Catherine*, died 1841.

2. *Mary*, married, 1817, Sir Stephen Glynn.

3. *Caroline*, married, 1817, Lord Wenlock, died 1868.

4. *Harriet Louisa*, born 1828, married, 1854, Rev. C. Arundell St. John Mildmay.

5. *Adelaide*, died 1837.

---

1. *Francis Catherine*, born 1820, married, 1849, Rev. E. Peel. Issue, George Neville, born 1854.

{ 2. *Georgiana*, born 1821. } Twins.

{ 3. *Cicely*. }

4. *Edward*, born 1824; Lieut.-Colonel, Scots Fusilier Guards, Crimean Medal; married, 1866, Georgiana, daughter of Vincent Corbett, Esq.

5. *Glastonbury*, born 1829, killed at Baroda, 1858.

6. *William Wyndham*, born 1834, died 1858.

7. *Seymour*, born 1833, Rector of Ockham; married, 1859, Agnes, daughter of Rev. C. Proby, Canon of Windsor.

8. *William Frederick*, born 1838, Vicar of Butleigh; married, 1847, Fanny Grace, daughter of W. Blackwood, Esq.; died 1885.

9. *Ralph Neville Grenville*, born 1817, M.P. for Mid-Somerset, 1868-78; married, 1845, Julia Roberta, daughter of Sir R. Frankland Russell.

---

1. *Mary*, born 1848, married Rev. F. A. Rhymer. Issue, Wilfred, born 1883.

2. *Constance*, born 1849, married, 1881, Captain Arthur Bigge, R.A. Issue, Victoria Eugenie, born 1881.

3. *Grace*, born 1853.

---

1. *William*, born 1850, Vicar of Butleigh.

---

1. *Francis*, born 1859, Lieut., Northumberland Fusiliers.

2. *Francis*, born 1859, Lieut., Northumberland Fusiliers.

---

1. *Agnes Magdalen*, born 1848, married, 1878, W. J. Maitland, Esq.

2. *Beatrice*, born 1853.

3. *Elfrieda*, born 1856.

4. *Louis*, born 1852; married, 1879, Ada, daughter of J. T. Rouse, Esq., of Littleton, New Zealand. Issue, Bertram, born 1880; Margaret, born 1881.

5. *Claud*, born 1858.

6. *Percy*, born 1868.

---

1. *William*, born 1850, Vicar of Butleigh.

1. *Mirabell Jane*, born 1821.

2. *Grey*, Cornet, 5th Dragoon Guards, born 1820, died at Balaclava, 1854.

---

1. *Robert Neville*, born 1846, Lieut. R.N.

2. *George Neville*, born 1850, Lieut. R.N.

3. *Hugh*, born 1851.

---

1. *Latimer*, born 1827, Master of Magdalene College, Cambridge, Chaplain to Bishop St. Albans, Rector of Heydon; married, 1853, Lucy Frances, daughter of John de Marchant, Esq. Issue, Henry, born 1855; Grey, born 1857; Alice Mirabel Cornwallis, born 1859.

2. *Henry Aldworth*, born 1824, Captain, Grenadier Guards, killed at Inkerman, 1854.

3. *Charles Cornwallis*, present peer, born Aug. 29, 1823, married Florence Priscilla Alicia Maude, 3rd daughter of 3rd Viscount Hawarden. Issue, Augusta, born 1860, married, 1879, Hon. Richard Strutt, 3rd son of 2nd Lord Rayleigh.

1. *Louisa Anne*, born 1824, married, 1853, Sir Henry Vavasour, 3rd Bart.

2. *Lucy Georgina*, born 1828, married, 1852, Hon. and Rev. Arthur Saville (who died 1870), son of 3rd Earl of Mexborough.

3. *Richard Cornwallis*, 4th Baron, born 1820; married, 1851, Lady Charlotte Sarah Graham Toler, daughter of the late Earl of Norbury. Issue, Catherine Elizabeth, born 1855; married, 1876, Viscount Stopford, son of 5th Earl of Courton; Mary Isabella, born 1858, married, 1880, Robert Joynes, Esq.

The following ECCLESIASTICAL BENEFICES, forming part of the entailed family estates, are in the gift of the Marquis of Abergavenny :—

	Value in King's Books.			Present Value.
	£	s.	d.	£
Sussex.—Rotherfield Rectory	27	12	6 ...	1,150 net
Frant Vicarage	8	5	5 ...	800 gross
West Chiltington Rectory ...	12	16	10½ ...	620 net
East Hothley Rectory ...	7	6	3 ...	250 gross
Rottingdean Vicarage ...	9	10	0 ...	315 net
Kent.—Birling Vicarage	6	9	4½ ...	400 gross
Suffolk.—Otley Rectory	16	6	5½ ...	660 net
Norfolk.—Bergh Apton Rectory ...	13	6	8 ...	——
Sutton Rectory	6	16	8 ...	340 net
Brunstead Rectory	6	5	7½ ...	286 gross
Worcestershire.—Inkberrow Vicarage ...	16	2	1 ...	950 gross
Monmouthshire.—Llanwenarh Rectory ...	26	6	6 ...	333 gross
Llanfoist Rectory	7	4	4½ ...	280 gross
Llanhilleth Rectory	7	15	7½ ...	110 gross
Goytree Rectory	4	7	6 ...	297 gross
Llangattock Rectory	11	7	3½ ...	400 gross
Llanvapley Rectory	10	5	2½ ...	250 gross
Llanvethrine Rectory... ...	14	17	8½ ...	365 gross

The livings of Heydon, Littlebury, Saffron Walden, Waltham St. Lawrence, and Wargrave are in the patronage of Lord Braybrooke.

PART II.—CHAPTER XII.

NEVILL KNIGHTS COLLATERAL WITH THE LORDS OF RABY.

Illustrissimum Nevillorum genus hospes est in Historia Anglicana qui non novit?
et si longa proavorum series tam a regio sanguine Saxonum quam a primoribus
Normanorum deducta, summisque cum honoribus tum et opibus per multa retro
secula clarescens quenquam nobilitare possit palmam omnibus fere regni proceribus
familia hæc merito præripere audeat. Nulla equidem plures aut vegetiores stirps
ramos unquam protrusit.—*Append. ad Honores de Richmund Tit. Observ. in Regis-
trum.*

"So many fighting men were they of the name of Nevill that an honest man
could scarce tell where they all came from."—*Lancastrian Chronicle.*

OUR task is now to notice some of the less prominent names
among those knights who claimed to be directly descended from
Richard de Nova Villa.

The first in the order of time was Robert de Nevill, nephew of
the "Admiral." He held the town of Shrewsbury for that famous
rebel Robert de Belesme, Earl of Shrewsbury, who took arms
against Henry I. After making peace with the Welsh, and having
obtained the aid of two of their princes, he marched with a great
power to encounter the King's army. Dugdale notices that in the
16th year of the same reign the name of a Ralph de Nevill appears
as witness to a charter granted to the monks of Bardney. He
would probably be another nephew, since Gilbert had no son called
Ralph, and his brother Ralph would not be alive in 1116. Alan
de Nevill, the celebrated crusader, was probably a grandson of the
"Admiral," and uncle of Geoffrey Nevill, who married Emma
Bulmer. In the 12th Henry II., he was on his journey to celebrate
the feast of the Ascension when he was excommunicated, with

Richard de Lucy and others, by Thomas à Becket, because he had patriotically maintained the rights of the Crown and people against the usurpations of the Pope. Gilbert Foliot, Bishop of London, being then in the neighbourhood, absolved him upon his promise to go to the Pope and make his submission. Alan was Chief Justice of the Forests in England, and a Justice Itinerant.—*Dansey. Eng. Crusaders.* He died 2nd Richard I., leaving two sons, Alan and Geoffrey.

The latter was Governor of Corffe Castle. In 16th John, being then King's Chamberlain, he was made Governor of Scarborough Castle, and in the following year had a grant of the lands of Simon de Kime and Philip de Kime, who were declared rebels. He was Sheriff of Yorkshire, and joined in a commission on the part of King John to treat with Robert de Ros and other of the rebel barons. In 2nd Henry III., he was Seneschal of Poictou and Gascoigne, and was continued Sheriff of Yorkshire for several years. He had two sons, John and Alan. John, in 48th Henry III., was in the battle of Chesterfield with Robert de Ferrers, Earl of Derby, who was then in rebellion. In the following year he was in the battle of Evesham, siding with the barons against the King. —*Rowland.*

One of the most notable among the companions of Cœur de Lion was Hugh de Nevill, "who, being a servant in Court to the King, went with his Royal master to Palestine, and was one of his ten companions when he charged the infidel host after relieving Joppa." His seal is given on Plate II., No. 2.

With his sword he destroyed a huge lion, after having driven an arrow into the creature's breast. The old bards loved to sing how

> "The strength of Hugh
> A lion slew."

"Eodemque anno obiit Hugo de Nevilla, qui in tota juventute sua tempore Regis Richardi de familia speciali ejusdem Regis extiterat. Inter cetera suæ probitatis et audaciæ insignia in Terra Sancta leonem interfecit: qui prius sagittatus in pectore et postea gladio transverberatus eliquato sanguine expiravit; unde versus:—
> "Viribus Hugonis vires periere Leonis."—*Matt. Paris.*

In 31st Henry II., Hugh held the honour of Werck. In 2nd Richard I., he gave a fine of no less than £200 for livery of his lands. To the monastery of Waltham, he gave the manor of Thorndon, in Essex. He was high justice, guardian, or protho-forester of all England. In 6th Richard I., he attended the King in his expedition to Normandy, and in the following year paid a fine of 100 marks for leave to marry the heiress of Henry de Cornhill, a wealthy citizen of London.—*Dansey. Eng. Crusaders.*

Hugh had two sons, Henry and John. Henry died 2nd Hen. III., and his son Hugh became the ward of William de Albiny. The crusader's other son, John, married Isabel, daughter of Robert de Meynill. He was succeeded by Jollan de Nevill, Justice Itinerant, 24th Henry III. The well known MS. which contains the knight's fees throughout the greatest part of England was composed under his direction, and is therefore called *Testa de Nevill.* In the survey of Clarendon Palace, 1272, mention is made of Nevill's Chamber, so called from Jollan de Nevill.

Another Hugh de Nevill, in 8th Henry III., was warden and justice of all the King's forests. He had livery of the moiety of the manor of Stoke Curcy with the castle and knight's fees, and livery of lands in Fakenham, Suffolk, and in Newnham, Oxfordshire, by right of his wife, Joan. This lady paid a fine, which exhibits the marvellous oppression exercised by the feudal system over domestic rights and liberties. "*6th John.*—Uxor Hogonis de Nevill dat Domino Regi ducentas Gallinas, *eo quod possit jacere una nocte cum Domino suo,* Hugh de Nevill."—*Madox Hist. Exchequer.* Hugh was governor of Sauvey Castle, Leicestershire, and Luggershall, Wilts. He had the King's license for life to hunt, and take the hare, fox, and *cat,* throughout the forests of England. He founded the priory of Stoke Curcy, in Somersetshire; and dying full of years in 1223, was buried in the chancel of Waltham Church, under a noble sepulchre of engraved marble.—*Beattie's Waltham Abbey.*

His son and heir, John de Nevill, succeeded him as justice of all the forests. In 24th Henry III., he covenanted with Roger de Quincey, Earl of Winchester, for the marriage of his son, Hugh, with Isabel, the daughter of De Quincey. She was endowed with lands in Radway and Sideham.

"John de Novavilla, at one time high in rank among the nobles of England, treading in the footsteps of his father, and attaining the very summit of honour, having entered on the common path of all flesh, left a signal example to mankind that they should shun regal favours, and the troubles of a Court; for he, in the flower of his age, being warden of the forests of all England, had great charges brought against him by Robert Passeleve, on account of illegal encroachments on the forests, and other trespasses; and failing in his defence, was found guilty by the verdict of a jury of his countrymen, which sunk him into such a state of despondency as from that day he might date his death. By a judicial sentence he was condemned to pay 2,000 marks (equal to £24,000 in present money, *vide Rowland*), besides the immense debts of his father, which pressed also upon his shoulders. He was expelled with disgrace from his office, without any prospect of being restored to it. Declining then in health, and wasting away with grief, he breathed his last about Midsummer, at Welpercfeld, his manor house, and was worshipfully buried in the Conventual Church of Waltham, near the grave of his father."—*Matt. Paris. Translation.*

His heir, Hugh de Nevill, was summoned to attend the King at Chester, 1265, to oppose the Welsh. He also united with the barons against the King in the battle of Lewes. Whilst engaged in rebellion with Robert de Vipount, he was taken prisoner at Kenilworth by Prince Edward, and carried to Worcester.*

Another Hugh (called *Grossus* and *Hugh the Forester*), is mentioned by Dugdale as Sheriff of Oxford, Hertford, and Essex, 9th Richard I. He was warden of the forests, 3rd John; and held the manors of Halyngbury, Blaaston, Ermhale, and Thoydon, of the same King. He had livery of the lands of Stephen de Camera with *Desiderata*, daughter of Stephen, and obtained grant of a weekly market and fair at Glamford Brigg, in Lincolnshire. In 1207, he was Governor of Richmond Castle, and Sheriff of Cumberland and Hampshire. King John gave him the manor, now called Combe Nevill, in Surrey, and he showed his gratitude by posing as a loyal knight on the plain of Runnimede. His name occurs in *Magna Charta*, as treating with twenty-five dissatisfied barons on the King's behalf. Nevertheless, he afterwards deserted John, and did homage to Louis, son of the French King, to whom he resigned the Castle of Marleburgh. He had previously, 1213, joined William Longespe, Earl of Salisbury, in a naval expedition against the French, and, in one of the ports of Flanders, seized most

* Dugdale considers that from this Hugh, John de Nevill of Essex descended. This John, in 12th Edward III., was in the Flanders expedition, and was in the retinue of William de Bohun, Earl of Northampton, during the French war. The manor of Great Totham, in Essex, called Totham Nevill, was held by his family. He was summoned to Parliament as a Baron, 9th to 22nd Edward III.; and died July 25th, 1359, seized of the manors of Little Welersfeld, Halyngbury, Chigenhale, Qoin, Chigenhale Tang, Pettingdon, with half of the manors of Great and Little Wakeryng.—*Rowland.*

of the French ships, and brought them to England. He was
Governor of the Castle of Pec, in Derbyshire, and Strattondal, in
Cumberland. He died 6th Henry III., 1222, and was buried in
Waltham Abbey.—*Vide Dugdale and Rowland.*

I may fitly conclude this chapter of varieties by appending a
copy of a curious manuscript, bearing date 1652.—*Harl. Coll.*

"Of the most noble, and illustrious, and princely Family of the Nevills, and of
their progenitors and ancestors, there have been of the male line one Duke, which
was of Bedford, one Marquis, which was of Montacute; fifteen Earls, whereof six
were Earls of Northumberland before the Norman Conquest, and six were Earls of
Westmoreland, another was Earl of Salisbury and Lord Monthermer, another was
Earl of Kent and Lord Falconberg, and the other was that most famous Earl of
Warwick and Salisbury, who was commonly called the Kingmaker. There have
also been two Nevills Archbishops of York, whereof one was a favourite to King
Richard the Second; and the other was Lord High Chancellor of England, and
Chancellor of the University of Oxford, in the time of King Edward the Fourth,
who was his cousin-german. And there have been two Nevills Bishops, one of
which was Lord Bishop of Chichester, and was also Lord High Chancellor of
England, and elected Archbishop of Canterbury in the reign of King Henry the
Third; and the other was Lord Bishop and Count Palatine of Durham. There
have been also a numberless company of Nevills (with their progenitors and
ancestors) that have been Lords and Barons, as namely, first of Raby, from Uchtred
the second Earl of Northumberland (and who was also made Earl of York by King
Ethelred) to him that first took the surname of Nevill; and six more of Raby,
before the Lord Ralph Nevill was created Earl of Westmoreland, which was in the
year of grace 1398, 21 Richard II; and there hath been one Nevill Lord Furnival,
two Nevills Lords Ferrars of Oversley, whereof one was also Lord Newmarch; one
Nevill Lord St. Maure (Seymour); seven Nevills Lords Latimer; eight Nevills
Lords Abergaveny; and three Lord Nevills that died married persons, eldest sons
by some of the Earls of Westmoreland, and there have been the Lord John Nevill,
who was a baron in the time of King Henry the Second and of King Richard the
First, and dyed in the 10th of King John, having had issue the Lord John, who
dyed without issue in the 4th of King Henry the Third, leaving his inheritance to
his brother the Lord John Nevill the second, that was one of the judges of the land,
and dyed the 30th of Henry the Third, leaving issue the Lord John Nevill, the
progenitors of the Nevills of Holt, in Leicestershire, whose heir-general was married
in the time of Queen Elizabeth to Smith of Cressing Temple in Essex, upon condition that her heirs should assume the surname of Nevill, which they did accordingly, and nowe retain it, and in right of her do quarter the coat of Ralph Nevill of
Thornton Bridge in Yorkshire, that was a younger son of Ralph, Lord Nevill of
Raby, the grandfather of Ralph Nevill, the first Earl of Westmoreland, and that is
gules a saltier argent, charged with a mullett sable for a difference. The Nevills
of Grove in Nottinghamshire, and of Hoddington, in Lincolnshire, are branches of
Holt, who was first of Rolleston, in Nottinghamshire, and their paternal coat is the
saltire ermine, and their crest is the bull's head ermyne. That of Smith of Cressing
Temple, is argent, a cross gules betwixt four peacocks azure, and they are originally

of the same House as the Lord Carrington. There was also the Lord William
Nevill, in the reigns of Henry the Second and Richard the First, and the Lord
Hugh Nevill, and his son the Lord John Nevill, that were chief foresters of all
England in the times of King John and King Henry the Third. The first of them
had been servant to King Richard the First, and in the wars with him in the Holy
Land. And there was another Lord Hugh Nevill among the rebellious barons, and
had his pardon for it, 48 Henry III. There were also three Nevills: Walter
Alexander, and Alexander (father, son, and grandson), Barons of Bradburne in
Lincolnshire, from one of the sisters and co-heirs of the last of which, (Margaret
Nevill) are lineally descended the Nevills of Haldingworth in Lincolnshire, whose
coat now is (1652) a bend guele and a chiefe indented vert. Not to speak of the
Lord Gilbert Nevill that was High Admiral of the Seas to King William the Con-
queror, and had issue the Lord Geoffrey Nevill, who was father of the Lord Geoffrey
Nevill that was Lord Chamberlain to King Henry the Second, and had issue the
Lord Robert Nevill of Branspeth, Sherry Hutton, and of * * * in the north,
from whose sister and heir, Isabella Nevill, descended the Nevills, Barons of Raby,
and now of Abergavenny. There were many others of the like dignity that were
Nevills, of whom we read in the records in the Tower, and in the books in the
Exchequer; but it is impossible for any man to set down truly all their relations
and branches. There have been one hundred Nevills that were Knights Bachellors;
and divers Nevills Knights of the Noble Order of the Bath; and some Nevills,
Knights Banneretts; and one Nevill (of the house of * * Abergavenny), was
one of the Knights of Rhodes in the time of Henry the Eighth, and he lies buried
in Mereworth Church, in Kent, where he hath a goodly monument. Of the House
of Nevill in the female line (to omit almost an innumerable company, whereof some
were wives, married to Knights Bachellors, and others were married to Knights of
the Bath, to Baronetts, and Privy Councillors, to Knights Banneretts, to Knights
of the Garter, and some to the younger sons of some of the greater nobility, and to
the eldest sons of some Barons, who died before their fathers, and also divers that
were ladies by birth, and were never married), there hath been one Nevill Queen of
England. She was the first wife of Edward Plantagenet, Prince of Wales, the only
son of King Henry the Sixth; and then secondly (being a widow), she was re-
married to King Richard the Third, by whom she had a son that was created Prince
of Wales when he was about ten years of age, but died soon after, before his father.
Moreover, that renowned Princess, the Lady Margaret Beaufort, who was Countess
of Richmond, and an heir of the blood royal, and the mother of King Henry the
Seventh, did carry and bear up the train of this Queen, Ann Nevill, on the day of
her coronation. There have been six Nevills Duchesses, as namely, one the wife of
John Mowbray, the second Duke of Norfolk of that family, and Earl Marshall of
England; one the wife of Humphrey, Lord Stafford, the first Duke of Buckingham
of that family, and Constable of England; one the wife of Henry, Lord Beauchamp,
Duke of Warwick, and King of the Isle of Wight; one the wife of the most excellent Prince Thomas Beaufort, Duke of Exeter, who was brother to King Henry the
Fourth, and who was Lord High Chancellor of England, and some time Lord Protector of the Realm, in the minority of his grand-nephew, King Henry the Sixth;
one the wife of the most illustrious Prince George Plantagenet, Duke of Clarence,
who was Great Chamberlain of England, and Lord-Lieutenant of Ireland, and
brother to King Edward the Fourth; and one the wife of the most high and mighty

Prince Richard Plantagenet, Duke of York, and some time Lord-Lieutenant to King Henry the Sixth, in his Kingdom of France and Dukedom of Normandy, and at length made by Parliament (1455) heir apparent to the Crown, and Lord Protector of the Realm of England; and that Duchess (which was Lady Cecilia Nevill, the youngest sister of Sir Edward Nevill, the first Lord of Abergavenny of that house), lived to see three princes of her body crowned, and four murdered, and she died in the year of grace 1495. Also of the same family of the Nevills (and their ancestors) there have been fourteen countesses; as namely, four of Northumberland; one the wife of Earl Siward; another the wife of Henry Lord Percy, the first Earl of that family; another the wife of Henry Lord Percy, the second Earl of that family; and the other was wife of Henry Lord Percy, the eighth Earl of that house; and her son Earl Henry was father of Algernon Percy (then) Earl of Northumberland, (1652). There hath been also one Nevill, the wife of Sir Gilbert Umfreville, Earl of Kyme and Marshall of France, wherein he was slain in the wars of Henry the Fifth; one Nevill the wife of John Lord Talbot, Steward of England and Marshall of France, and the first and famous Earl of Shrewsbury of that house; one the wife of the Lord John de Vere, Great Chamberlayn and Admiral of England, and the thirteenth Earl of Oxford; one the wife of the Lord John de Vere, Great Chamberlayn of England, and the sixteenth Earl of Oxford; one the wife of the Lord William Fitzalan, Lord Maltravers, and the eighth Earl of Arundel of that family; one the wife of Thomas Lord Stanly, that was the first Earl of Derby of that family, and some time Lord Steward of the Household to King Edward the Fourth, and afterwards High Constable of England; one that was the first wife of Henry Lord D'Aubigny, Earl of Bridgewater; one the wife of Henry Manners, Lord Roos of Hamlake, and the second Earl of Rutland of that family; one the wife of Thomas Lord Cecil, Baron of Burleigh, and the first Earl of Exeter of that family; and one that was wife of George Lord Goring, Earl of Norwich. There hath been also one Nevill, an Abbess, which was of Barking, in Essex, and many of the said house Baronesses; as namely, one the wife of Lord Lumly that was the progenitor of the Lord Lumley of Lumly Castle; one the wife of the Lord Maldred, the son of Crinan; one the wife of the Lord Orme; one Nevill, the wife of Richard Lord Scroope of Bolton Castle; one the wife of Geoffrey Lord Scroope; one the wife of William Lord Scroope of Upsall; one the wife of Thomas Lord Scroope of Upsall; one the wife of Peter Lord Manly of Mulgrave Castle; three wives of several Lord Dacres of Gillesland in the north; one to Thomas Fiennes, Lord Dacres, of the south; one to Walter, the third Lord Falconbridge of Skelton Castle; one to William, Lord Conyers of Hornby Castle; one to Sir John Cobham, Lord Cobham of Cobham; one to Sir John Brooke, Lord Cobham of Cobham; one to Sir Henry Pole, Lord Montacute; one to Sir William Bonvill, Lord Harrington, and she was afterwards married to William, Lord Hastings, that was Lord Chamberlayn and favourite to Edward the Fourth; one to Henry, Lord Fitzhugh; one to a Lord Le Strange of Knocking; one to Thomas, Lord Clifford; one to Walter, Lord Deincourt; one to Ralph, Lord Lumly of Lumly Castle; one to William, Lord Roos of Hamlake; one to Charles Longuevill, Lord Grey of Ruthin; one to Lord Lucas; and one Nevill, in right of her birth, was Baroness le Despencer, and mother of Sir Francis Vane, who was created Earl of Westmoreland and Lord Burgwash, by King James (1624). There have been nine Nevills Knights and Companions of the most noble Order of the Garter; three Nevills Lord High

Chancellors of England, one of which was also Lord President of the Councel. There have been one Nevill Earl Marshall of England; three Nevills Lords High Admirals of the Sea, whereof one of them was also Lord Great Chamberlayn of England, and Constable of Dover Castle, and Lord Warden of the Cinque Ports, High Steward of the Duchy of Lancaster and Lord-Lieutenant of Calis, and the territories thereof. There have been four Nevills Lord Chamberlayns of the King's Household, and one Lord Steward of the Household to King Edward the Third. There have been six Nevills, Chief Foresters of all England, which was then the same office as was of late that of Chief Justice in Eyre. And there have been divers Nevills, Guardians or Lord Wardens of the Marches towards Scotland. And in the absence of Edward the Third (being sailed into Normandy), Ralph Lord Nevill of Rabey (with Henry Lord Percy) was Protector of the Realm. And from Lady Cecilia Nevill the Duchess of York, who was the mother of King Edward the Fourth, and to King Richard the Third, there have lineally descended seven Kings of England, three Queens of England, four Princes of Wales, four Kings of Scotland, two Queens of Scotland, two Queens of France, one Queen of Spain, and one Queen of Bohemia; and this aforementioned Princess Lady Cecilia, was a great-aunt to Sir Henry Nevill, late Lord of Abergavenny, the father of John Nevill, now Lord Bergavenny (1652), and to Sir Henry Nevill, late of Billingbeare in Berkshire, the father of Colonel Richard Nevill of Billingbeare, Esq., and of Henry Nevill of Heathly, in Warfield, in Berkshire, now one of the most honorable Councillors of State (anno. 1652), and to Charles Nevill, Esq., now the senior fellow of King's College, in Cambridge, and one of the Justices of the Peace for the Universitye, and town and county of Cambridge; and she was a great-grandmother to King James (the First), the father of King Charles. And the like honor can not be said of any other English family."

PART II.—CHAPTER XIII.

SHERIFF HUTTON.

—————— "An aged swain, whose hoary head
Was bent with years; the village chronicle,
Who much had seen, and, from the former times,
Much had received. He, hanging o'er the hearth,
In winter evenings, to th' admiring swains,
And children circling round the fire, would tell
Stories of old, of *Hutton's* stately towers,
And tales of other times."

STATELY and sad, very grey and very grand, altogether venerable, and altogether forsaken and neglected—so stand the towers of Sheriff Hutton. Sixty years ago George Todd wrote as follows:—"Many persons who visit Sheriff Hutton Castle will lament to see its ancient walls and towers encumbered with haystacks, pigeon-cots, &c., particularly at the entrance near the eastern portal, even the ruins themselves seem to 'frown resentment' for every insult or injury they sustain."

The same author remarks, in a note, that a local builder had been employed, at a cost of £80, to fasten loose stones with cement, as the state of the building had become dangerous to the cattle in the immediate vicinity.

When a monument of antiquity has been handed over to a local builder, "haystacks, pigeons, &c.," its future cannot be regarded as hopeful, but I certainly was a little astonished at the state in which I saw Sheriff Hutton in the autumn of 1883.

I saw it in the bright and early morning—a morning still, and sad, and beautiful, as autumn mornings sometimes are. The clear sunshine was kissing the hoary stones, and I heard a slow and measured drip, as if the old fabric had been watching and weeping through the night; and I heard, too,—must it indeed be told?—I heard the grunt of a savage sow, for the hall that once echoed to the footsteps of some of the fairest and mightiest of England's nobility is now turned into a veritable pigstye! We often read the ten commandments, and break them too—especially the last—and on this occasion I certainly coveted my neighbour's castle, and longed for it, that I might set the sows at liberty, for I really think they were unhappy, and perhaps slightly conscious of being out of their social plane. But enough of this. The age is liberal, economical, utilitarian. And I do not think that the towers *did* "frown resentment." They looked too sad for that. Deserted even by the ivy, their utter loneliness might have struck the tender heart of the poet, and made him say—

> "Wind, gentle evergreen, thy spreading arms
> Round *Hutton's* ancient towers, and from the blast
> Of winter shield them with thy mantling charms."

Neglected though it be, Sheriff Hutton is a place of surpassing interest. Its early lords followed the wild boar through the trackless forest of Galtres, in which Hutton lay hid, and which stretched far away in a north-westerly direction, covering the hills of Craike, and the plain of Easingwold. The lanthorn of All Saints then shone across the vale of York to guide the traveller through the darkness of the "Great Galtres."

Near to Sheriff Hutton was a holy well. Shaded by the giant oaks of Galtres, and shaded still more by superstition, the waters of the well of St. John were long held in veneration as a sovereign cure for all the ills of man.

Hard by Hutton, was, and still is, Stitenham, the home of Gower, the Homer of England, the author of " *Confessio Amantis*," and the friend of Chaucer. He it was, who,

> "In times
> Dark and untaught, began with charming verse
> To tame the rudeness of his native land."

"And, whereas, if any man wante redy words, approved of good effecte and strength, let him resort to this worthy old wryter, John Gower, that shal as a lanterne gyve him lyght to wryte coynningly, and to garnishe his sentences in our vulgar tongue."

> "Large he was, his height was long,
> Broad of breast, his limbs were strong;
> But couller pale, and wan his looke;
> Such have they that ply'n their booke.
> His visage grave, and stern, and grim;
> Cato was most like to him."

"Being very old and blinde he died *carefully*."

"In the Monastery of Saynt Marye Overes he lyeth ryght
sumptously buryed, with an effigie of him over his tomb, habited in
purple damask down to his feet, a collar of S.S. round his neck,
and a garland on his head, in token that he, in hys lyfe days,
flouryshed freshely in literature."

Sheriff Hutton was distinguished also in science—the noble
science of training "the sprightlie horse." "Goodlie sporte had
they of Hotune in the earlie tyme." "Equorum decursus solem-
nis." The "sporte" was marked by the sound sense of our forefathers. Homes were not wrecked, fortunes were not squandered,
hearts were not broken by it, but the cleverest horse in all the
"sporte" wore a little golden bell; and the noble quadruped was
honoured, and loved in the stall, and in the field. The influence
that this "goodlie sporte" had upon the minds of men is seen in
the survival of an ancient proverb, for, even now among us, the
man who is most honoured is he who "bears away the bell."

The castle of Hotune was built by Bertram de Bulmer in 1140.

Bulmer, Stitenham, and Hotune are mentioned in Domesday
Book.

"In Bolemere and Stidnum, Ligulf had two manors of 15 carucates to be taxed,
and there be eight ploughs. There is a priest and a church, and one mill of two
shillings, and twenty acres of meadow. Wood pasture seven quarentens long, and
two broad. The whole one mile and a half long, and four quarentens broad. Value
in King Edward's time one hundred shillings, now forty shillings.

"They say that William Malet bought seven carucates of land of Sprot in
Hotune for ten marks of silver. Nigel Fossard held three manors of four carucates
in Hotune unjustly, but he has given them up, and they are in the hands of the
King. In Hotune, Sprot had seven carucates."—*(Translation.— Clamores de
Euruicscire. Nort Treding.)*

In 1154, Bertram de Bulmer was appointed Sheriff of Yorkshire
pro novem Annis by Henry II., and Hotune became Sheriff Hutton.
The castle and manor (according to Magna Britannia, Vol. 6) were
formerly part of the demesnes of the Bishop of Durham; and in the
civil wars of Stephen's reign the castle was seized for the King, by
Alan, Earl of Richmond. Probably the fabric suffered by the
struggle, for Ralph Nevill, 1st Earl of Westmorland, rebuilt it.[*]
In a sunk tablet on the Warden's Tower are four shields. Three
exhibit the Nevill saltire, or cross of St. Andrew. On the fourth

[*] "Hutton summæ elegantiæ Castrum a Bertramo de Bulmer extructum, et a
Radulpho Nevil primo Westmorelandiæ Comite restauratum inter nemuscula
amænissimè sedet." (Camden. Ed. 1607, p. 588).

are the arms of the first Earl, and his second Countess, Joan
Beaufort, *i.e.*, on the dexter side a saltire, and on the sinister side
three lions passant gardant, and three fleur de lys (Royal arms—
Joan being daughter of John of Gaunt).

"I marked," says Leland, "in the fore front of the first area of
the castle three great and high towres, of the which the gatehouse
was the middle. In the second area be five or six towres, and the
statlie stair up to the haul is very magnificent, and so is the haul
itself, and all the residue of the house, insomuch that *I saw no
house in the north so like a princely lodging.*"

This princely lodging was held by the Nevills for three hundred
years. Richard Nevill, Earl of Warwick, was constable of the
castle; and after his death on Barnet Field, Edward IV. seized
Sheriff Hutton, and gave it to his brother, the Duke of Gloucester,
who subsequently married the Lady Anne Nevill.*

Letters dated from Sheriff Hutton Castle in the handwriting of
Richard III. remain to this day. Two persons celebrated in the
annals of England were confined by him in this castle. Edward
Plantagenet, Earl of Warwick, only son of George, Duke of
Clarence, was a close prisoner during the whole of Richard's reign.
No visitor to Sheriff Hutton can fail to notice the magnificent oaks
in the park. During the last century a venerable tree, said to have
been standing in the days of Richard, was blown down. It was
known as the "*Warwick Oak.*" Beyond it the unfortunate young
earl was not allowed to pass in his daily walks. His detention,
however, was not marked by any exceptional harshness until after
the death of his uncle on Bosworth Field. The day following, Sir

---

* Shakespeare makes Gloucester commence his wonderful wooing of the Lady
Anne by an announcement that he had murdered her late consort.

    "'Twas I that stabbed young Edward,
    But 'twas thy heavenly face that set me on."

The tradition which Shakespeare follows is a comparatively *late* one. There is
no sufficient warrant for throwing the *onus* of the crime upon Richard, who was only
nineteen at the time. The following are the statements of contemporary writers :—

"After the Kinge hadde questyoned with the sayd Sir Edwarde, and he had
answeryd unto hym contrarye his pleasure, he thenne strake hym with his gauntlet
upon the face ; after whiche stroke so by him receyved, he was by the Kynges
servantes incontynently slayne upon iiij. day of the moneth of May." *Fabyan.*

"There. (at Tewkesbury) was slayn Prince Edwarde crying on the Duke of
Clarence for help." *Leland's Coll. ii.* 506.

"Le dit Roy Edoüard en eut la victoire et fut le Prince des Galles tué sur le
champ." *De Commines.*

"Edwarde, called Prince, was taken, fleinge to the towne wards, and slayne in
the fielde." *Historie of the Arrivall of Edwarde IV.*, published by Camden Society.

Polydore Vergil says that when the Prince was despatched "Georgius Clarentiæ,
Richardus Glosestriæ et Gulielmus Hastyngius circumstabant."

Robert Willoughby was sent by Henry VII. to convey him from Sheriff Hutton to the Tower; and, after an imprisonment of sixteen weary years, this poor prince joined his innocent cousins (the children of Edward IV.) in the land "where the wicked cease from troubling," his head being struck off on Tower Hill, November 26th, 1499. So perished the last male of the line of Plantagenet, and the only son of Isabel Nevill.

But one other white rose had been left in Hutton by Richard Plantagenet. Spared by him, and by the far reaching Wars of the Roses, this fair flower yet bloomed as the hope of a stricken land, and Hutton gave up her treasure in answer to the cry of England.

> "O now let Richard and Elizabeth,
> The true succeeders of each royal house,
> By God's fair ordinance be joined together."
> .   .   .   .   .   .
> "As we have ta'en the sacrament,
> We will unite the white rose and the red;
> Smile, heaven, upon this fair conjunction!"

The solemn vow of Richmond had been heard in Rennes Cathedral, and even after Bosworth Field he could not draw back, cold and jealous though he was.

Conducted by Sir John Halewell, Elizabeth of York left the castle of Sheriff Hutton, and on the 25th of November, 1487, was crowned Queen of all England.

At Westminster's "royall bourde" the few barons, who were left after the wars, held a feast of peace.

"Feisant royall, swan with chawdron, capons of high greece, and pike in latymer sause were servid, and the mynstrells played a song, and the kings of armes, harawlds, and pursuyvants went into the cubborde to the Erle of Arundell, great butler, and dranke. And the Queen was servid with fruit and wafers, and ipocras, and departed with God's blessinge, to the rejoicing of every trew Englishman's hart. But Kinge Henry loved her not, though she was passinge beautiful and gentle."—(*Vide Grose's Antiq.*, *Granger Hist. Eng.*, *Drake's Eboracum, and Taylor's Stories of Regality.*)

Thomas Howard, Earl of Surrey, was sent by Henry VII. to quell the insurrectionary spirit of the North; and he resided at Sheriff Hutton, between the years 1490 and 1500. One of his letters, dated from Hutton, will be found in the Fenn collection, and is printed in *Todd's Sheriff Hutton, Ed.*, 1824.

In the following reign, Thomas, Duke of Norfolk, lived for ten years in the castle; and Skelton, the laureate, laid the scene of his poem, "*A Crown of Laurel*," in this "*Statlie Haul.*"

After Norfolk's death in 1524, Sheriff Hutton became the residence of Henry Fitzroy, an illegitimate son of the King, by the Lady Talbois. Though only six years of age, this boy, being the monarch's pet, was made Lieutenant-General of the North, and was attended by a council. He was successively created Duke of Richmond, Earl of Nottingham, Admiral of England, and Lieutenant of Ireland.—(*Vide Lingard.*)

He was a youth of considerable genius, but died in his eighteenth year, to Henry's great grief. One of his letters to the King is published in Todd's work.

With him the history of Hutton Castle virtually ends. James first came to it in 1617; and caused a survey to be made in 1624, but the "*Statlie Haul*" had by that time disappeared from the earth.

"There is a Stately Castle, the inward materials transported, and the walls ruined. The bowels of this worthy pile, and defensive house are rent and torn." (*Survey. Harl. MSS.* 6288.)

From the present appearance of the ruins it is plain that the castle was purposely, though only partially, taken down by workmen, but there is no evidence to show why, or at what particular date, this was done.

One of the lofty towers which had overhung its base was forcibly destroyed during the latter part of the last century. The castle now presents a quadrangular form, with a large open court in the centre, and flanked with high square towers at each angle. The principal entrance was on the east side. Its pointed arch still remains with the Nevill shields above it.

The materials of which the castle is built are a sort of brown grit stone, said to have been brought from the quarry at Terrington (*v.* Leland). "The south-west tower is 100 ft. in height. Underneath is a deep dungeon, measuring 40 ft. by 20 ft., the roof arched over with stone, semi-circular, and the walls of at least eight feet in thickness, cemented with very hard mortar. There are two entrances; one inwardly, from an uncommonly large winding staircase in the north-west corner, and the other outwardly by a pointed door-way. Directly above this dungeon, one of the ancient chambers still remains in good preservation, and is also arched over semi-circular with stone." (*v. Todd's Hutton, Ed.* 1824.)

Charles I. granted the castle and manor of Hutton, with the appurtenances, liberty, franchise, and privileges of park, to Sir Thomas Ingram, his heirs and assigns, for ever.

In the church of St. Helen some armour of the Knights Gower, ancestors of the present noble family of Leveson Gower, may still be seen ; with an effigy of Sir Thomas Bytham in complete mail. There is also an alabaster monument on which I shall have something to say in my chapter on Nevill Monuments.*

In the reign of Edward III. permission was given to Lord Ralph Nevill, in consideration of his important military services, to maintain two priests for the celebration of daily service in this church, for the good estate of himself during life, and afterwards for the health of the souls of his father, and mother, and all his ancestors.

Three years after the battle of Nevill's Cross, a chantry was founded on the south side of the church, at the altar of St. Mary and St. Peter, by Ralph Nevill and Alice his wife, who left an endowment for " one fit priest" to celebrate mass for ever for the soul of the said Alice.—*Torre's MSS., York Chapter Library, quoted in Todd.*

This chantry, together with the Bytham Chapel, has long since been destroyed.

Hutton Church has suffered much from time and neglect, but it still remains a most interesting structure. There are points of resemblance between it and Brancepeth. The hand of that great builder, Ralph Nevill, first Earl of Westmoreland, may be traced in both.

To Brancepeth let us now go, and witness the marriage of Emma Bulmer.

Away then merrily go we along the great north road! We are in the days of the Crusades, the days of the glorious Hugh de Puisset—vulgarly called Pudsey—Prince Bishop of Durham. The Abbey of Finchale, the Church of St. Cuthbert at Darlington, the Hospitals of Sherburn and Northallerton, the Shrine of St. Bede, the beautiful Chapel of Our Lady (Galilee), and the Elvet Bridge at Durham are just springing into existence.

My magician has raised his wand, altered the landscape, and carried me back some seven hundred years!

---

* During the whole of the present century a thick crust of whitewash covered these splendid monuments, until recently removed by the judicious hand of the present vicar, Rev. J. Lascelles.

Is *this* Brancepeth? I see no more the little railway station with its flower beds, neat and trim; nor the picturesque Elizabethan house upon the hill; nor the happy looking cottages, with warm red tiled roofs, and walls trellised by a very paradise of flowers. The ivy-clad lodge, the old rectory house, the church with all its wealth of carved work, the castle with its nineteenth century Norman work, the Russell tower, the Constable tower, the Essex tower, the Nevill tower—are all gone. Gone also, happily gone, are the days of King Coal. No black, belching contrivance of commerce remains to offend the eye as it rests serenely on the distant landscape.

And what is there left, Leland? Tell me, my quaint guide, what is there left? "On the south-west part there cumnith doune a little bek out o' the rokkes and hills not far off."

Ah, yes! the little brook is left in its ever sweet antiquity. And the deer have it all their own way now. There is no fence to close them in. See how gracefully they come down to drink! And look at the trees! What grand trees they are! That is because all the coal is under the ground.

BARNCEPETH CHURCH.
Co? of Durham

PART II.—CHAPTER XIV.

THE CASTLE OF BRANCEPETH.

——"No honourable note,
No chronicle of all its martial pride,
To testify what once it was, how great,
How glorious, and how fear'd."

"After the accession of Henry II., no one was allowed to fortify his mansion without license. There is no record of any license for fortifying and embattling the castles of Barnard and Brancepeth. These two are the only exceptions in the county; from which fact we draw an inference of their great antiquity."—*Rowland.*

THE word Brancepeth has been variously derived.

1.—"The arms of Richard, Duke of Gloucester, were a boar, or brawn passant, and in contempt of his memory this place had that appellation."

The person who offered this ingenious derivation did not recollect that Brancepeth had a place in English history some four hundred years before Richard of Gloucester was thought about.

2.—In the latter part of the 12th century, Hugh de Puiset issued a grant, restoring the borough of Elvet to the convent of Durham. In this document mention is made of Broun Spittel— the hospital of Broun. *("Terre vel more continetur inter Bearepair et viam regiam qua itur de Crosegate versus Brounspittel quod est juxta Rilleybridge.")* Brancepeth is supposed to be a corruption of Brounspittel.

The third derivation at least enjoys the license of poetry. Brawnspath is the path of the brawn or boar that once roamed here at his own sweet will.

> "He feared not ye loute with his staffe,
> Ne yet for ye knyghte in hys mayle,
> He cared no more for ye monke with hys boke
> Than ye fyendis in deep Croix Dale.
>
> Then out spake Hodge yt wyghte so bolde
> Yt wous on Ferie hye.*
>
> And he hathe sworne by Seynct Cudberte hys rode
> Yt thys horride brawne shall dye.
>
> And he hath dygged a depe depe pitte
> And strewed it with braunches so grene.

This is certainly a very pretty story, but it seems to me that Bertram de Bulmer was here before the knight of Ferie, and he found not one, but many brawns at Brancepeth.†   In the 12th

---

* The seal of Roger de Ferie still remains in the palatinate treasury, bearing a boar passant; and in the churchyard of Merrington there is a flat stone sculptured with his supposed insignia, a rude cross having a sword on the dexter, and a spade on the sinister side.   His posterity occur in the freehold records as late as 1617.   A large stone trough was a few years ago shown at Ferryhill as that from which the brawn was accustomed to drink, but it does not appear who provided accommodation for so unwelcome a visitor.—*Fordyce, Hist. Durham.*

† If the Brancepeth brawn had been represented as a purely mythical creature, and a relic of Saxon superstition, I should feel disposed to regard him with a little more reverence, for the boar was sacred to Freyr.   The vows made upon the head of this creature in the middle ages had their sanction from ancient paganism; and the custom of introducing the same hideous figure at our festive tables, especially at Christmas, is doubtless a heritage from heathendom.   It was the Saxon amulet; indeed the Anglo-Saxon poets consider a boar's form or figure so essential a portion of the helmet that they use the word *eofor* for that part of the armour.

> "He commanded them to bring in
> the boar, the ornament of the head,
> the helmet lofty in battle.
>
> The forms of boars they seemed
> above their cheeks to bear,
> adorned with gold;
> various and hardened in the fire,
> it held the guard of life.
>
> But the white helmet
> guarded the head;
> adorned with treasure,
> set about with lordly signs,
> as it, in days of yore,
> the armourer made;
> wondrously produced;
> set it about the shapes of boars,
> that afterwards neither
> brand nor war-knife
> might penetrate it."

Brandon has been derived from *Bury-Dane*, and the tumulus on the summit of Brandon Hill pointed out as the last resting place of some old hero who fell in battle. This also is ingenious.

çentury the forest district north of London was full of wild boars and wild oxen. ("Latebræ, . . . aprorum et taurorum sylvestrium." *v. Fitz Stephen's Life of Becket).*

Prior Lawrence, in his Latin poem, written about 1140, describes a great boar hunt in the ancient forest of the bishoprick; and he incidentally mentions the fact that five hundred foals were killed by wolves in one winter in Durham.

Had the Ferie hero lived in those days perhaps he would not have considered it necessary to make such elaborate preparations for the slaughter of a solitary brawn.

I fear that this tale of "ye horride brawne" is only "another injustice to Ireland," for the Abbot of Clonfert is really the central point of Brancepeth story; and around him both the Bulmer and the Nevill gather. We may as well accept this fact—the Irish are at the bottom of everything.

To S. Brandon the church of Brancepeth is dedicated. The most ancient portion of the present building dates from 1260, but Reginald speaks of an earlier structure dedicated like the present one to S. Brandon. "*Quia autem in eâdem villulâ Sanctus Brand-damus ecclesiam suo nomini dicatam habuit.*"—*(Reginaldi Monachi Dunelm. Libellus, cap. xlvi.)*

Hœming is the first recorded rector (1085); but it is not unreasonable to suppose that the primary church was a Saxon edifice. The Bulmers of Brancepeth, were descended from Ligulf the Saxon. S. Brandon was a sixth century saint, a saint to suit any Saxon soul—stern in sanctity, fearless to a fault, and a mariner who had sailed over seas whereon the most dauntless had never sailed before—his shrine was sure to be held in peculiar veneration wherever set up; a path would be made to it even through the loneliest waste; and Brandon's path might easily grow into Brancepeth. But a truce to derivations. Let us to the castle.

Reginald, after describing events which happened in 1104, speaks of Brancepeth Castle as a fortified place. "*Pontifex sanctus illi prævius effectus est, ac saxis ingentibus ante illum de ambitu murorum oppidi divulsis, extra mæniorum septa, pene usque ad consita nemorum perductus est.*" *Cap.* 46.

The story that Reginald relates of the miraculous deliverance of a prisoner from the lowest dungeon of the castle, through the aid of S. Brandon, shows the veneration in which Brancepeth held her patron saint in the early part of the twelfth century. S. Brandon is numbered among the Twelve Apostles of Ireland, who attended the expositions of Finian the Wise, in the Abbey of Clonard on the river Boyne.* It is somewhat singular that after the lapse of so many hundred years the words Brancepeth and Boyne should once more become closely allied.

Leland saw Brancepeth "strongly set and builded." "It hath 2 courtes of high building. There is a little moat that hemmith a peeice of the first court. In this court be 3 towers of loggings, and 3 smaule adornaments. The pleasure of the castell is in the 2 court, and entering into it by a great toure I saw in 'scochin in the fronte,

---

* S. Brandon, or Brendon, as he is generally called, was born (A.D. 483) in Kerry, and his tender age was cared for by that remarkable virgin saint of Ireland, St. Ida, who devoted herself specially to him.

He founded the celebrated Abbey of Clonfert, which is said to have had at one time within its walls no less than 3,000 monks; and its schools were frequented by students from all parts of Britain. He was a man of wonderful sanctity, and was frequently visited by the most eminent saints and bishops of his day. Whatever opinion we may hold as to the traditional discovery of America by him, there can be no doubt that considerable credence has been given to it, Eleven Latin MSS. in the *Bibliotheque Imperiale* at Paris, dating from the 11th to the 14th centuries, and other records in French, Dutch, German, Italian, and Portugese, have been brought forward in support of it.

Rafn, the Danish historian, in his edition of the Norse Sagas, drew attention to the traditional visit of the Norsemen to Huitra-Mannaland, (Carolina?), where they found a white people different from the Esquimaux of the 'North, *having long robes or cloaks, and frequently bearing crosses in a sort of religious procession, and their speech was Irish.*

"The Shalholt Saga, bearing date 1117, carefully delineated several bays and shores, and mentioned the death of an Icelandic woman named Suasa, who had accompanied the Norsemen; and so minutely described the topography of the place where she was buried that Sir Thomas Murray conjectured that the spot should be in the immediate vicinity of the Great Falls, on the Potomac river, above Washington."

Mr. Thomas C. Raffinson, the celebrated English antiquary, M. Louis Lequereux, the distinguished geologist, and two American gentlemen, after a long search discovered a Runic inscription cut deeply in a rock, called "The Arrow Head."

> " Here lies Syasy, or Suasa,
> The fair-haired,
> A person from the East of Iceland,
> The widow of Kjorder,
> And sister of Thorgor,
> Children of the same father,
> Twenty-five years of age.
> May God make glad her soul.
> 1051."

Human teeth and bones, three bronze trinkets, and some other relics, were subsequently found. It is said that the legend of St. Brendon suggested to Christopher Columbus the idea of a Western Continent. In his own expedition, however, Columbus was forestalled by an Irishman, for Baptisti Fornitori tells how one Patricius Maguirus was the first to reach the shore. It does not require much knowledge of Latin to translate Patricius Maguirus into Paddy Maguire.

St. Brendon died at the venerable age of 94, and was buried in his Monastery of Clonfert. His festival was long observed with the greatest ceremony.—*Vide Conyngham's Lives of the Irish Saints published by Sadlier & Co., Montreal.*

a lion rampaunt. On the southe west part of the castelle cummith doune a little bek out o' the rokkes and hills not far off. Sum say that Rafe Nevill, the first Erle of Westmereland, builded much of this house A.D. 1398. The Erle that now is hath set a new peeice of work to it." During the excavations made in the castle quadrangle, in the spring of 1883, I was able distinctly to trace the course of the "little mote" above mentioned.

" Within the works is a spacious area, which you enter from the north by a gate with a portcullis, and defended by two *square* towers. The parts now inhabited lie to the south-west of the area, and appear to have been connected by works of various ages. The original plan in that part seems to have consisted of four distinct towers, whose angles project as buttresses, with a small turret at the top of each angle, hanging on corbels, open at the sides, and not in front. From the gate on the east side is a long stretch of wall with a parapet which communicates with a large square tower, having projecting angles turretted like those described; from this tower the wall communicates at no great distance with another large tower similar to the last, and thence the wall stretches to the inhabited part of the castle, broken only by a small turret, square in front but octagonal towards the court. From the gate on the west is a high wall, the parapet in many parts hangs on corbels; where the wall forms angles, it is garnished with small square turrets, on the area side supported by an arch; and in the floor of each is a square aperture to receive materials from persons below, whereby the guard should annoy those who assailed the wall. Towards the north and east the castle has been defended by a moat; to the south and west the walls rise from a rock nearly 40 feet in height, watered by a small brook. It is probable that the whole fortress consisted originally of a race or series of towers of similar form, for the west wall and angular turrets are much more modern than the fortifications on the east. If this conjecture is allowed, then the fortress would contain a cantonment of eight large towers, exclusive of those defending the gateway." *Hutchinson's Hist. Dur.*, published 1794.

The restoration of the castle was undertaken, at enormous expense, by Matthew Russell, Esq., and completed in 1818, under the direction of John Patterson, Esq., of Edinburgh. The Russell tower is new from the foundation. Billings, although taking exception to certain modern details which might readily be removed, says that "*Brancepeth Castle stands superior to any other battlemented edifice in the north of England.* The bold and irregular masses of its towers, with their angular projecting buttresses and turrets, are upon a high scale of grandeur."

"This is, indeed," says Howitt, "one of the noblest houses in the country. The rooms are splendid, and furnished with corresponding taste and richness."

"In repairing the ceiling of the present drawing room, a groined roof was exposed to view of singular beauty. The groining was covered with the inscription, '*Mais droite,*' and the interstices were abundantly charged with the armorial ensigns of the order of the garter, with faint traces of the motto, and also the Nevill Cross, encircled with a garter without any inscription."[*]

Pennant describes Brancepeth as "a habitable house impending over a steep and woody dell. The part of the wall that is quite entire has small square towers on the summit, with *corbal trusses*, for pouring down hot water and boiling pitch on the assailants."

Surtees considered the western part of the castle to have been "an addition of later date than the original building. From the Stafford knot, which appears everywhere repeated on the labels of the windows, it may be conjectured that the towers in question were the work of the fourth Earl, who married a Stafford. The dell and rivulet, above which the south and west fronts of the castle are erected, are extremely romantic."

Brancepeth being nearer to the Palatinate city, and nearer to the northern marches, of which the Nevills were wardens, it seems to have been used more frequently as a residence than Raby. I have examined a mass of correspondence written by various mem-

---

[*] A large stone, exhibiting the saltire surrounded by a garter, and the inscription, MOYS DROYT, was discovered during the restoration. It is now a conspicuous object on the exterior wall of the Nevill Tower, in which tower the drawing room is situated. This room contains the remarkable picture, called "Charity in the Cellar," painted by Hogarth for the first Viscount Boyne. It represents certain members of the "Hell-fire Club" assembled in a cellar, and resolved not to separate until they have consumed its contents. Sir Philip Hoby is seated on a cask of claret. Behind him with his hand held up is Mr. De Grey; and below him Lord J. Cavendish, who has drawn a spigot from the cask to let the wine flow into a bowl. Lord Sandwich is kneeling down, holding a bottle to his mouth. Lord Galway, unable to stand or kneel, is extended on a form in such a manner that the liquor from the cask above him is flowing into his mouth. The grouping of the four centre figures is an ingenious imitation of a statue of Charity, which is seen in the cellar. The position of the bottles brings the comparison still nearer ; and is one of those little incidents for which Hogarth was so particularly distinguished from all other painters, in omitting nothing that might carry out his intention.—*Vide Hogarth's Complete Works, by Ireland and Nichols.*

bers of the Nevill family, and a very large number of these letters
are dated from Brancepeth. The fourth, fifth, and sixth Earls
especially spent much of their time at Brancepeth; and the last
Countess of Westmoreland lingered fondly there, hoping to welcome
back her lord to the old ancestral home. But her presence was
viewed with suspicion. It was feared that she would in some way
incite the rebels to make another stir, and so she was sent to
London in the spring of 1570. Then Brancepeth ceased to be the
home of the Nevills.

"The vast confiscations which followed the suppression of the
rebellion produced a more extensive change in the landed property
within the bishopric than any preceding revolution since the
Norman era. The immense forfeitures of Brancepeth and Raby,
with their dependent manors, should have been vested in the See
of Durham, which still retained, under Henry's Act of Resumption,
the full right to forfeitures of high treason within the Palatinate."
—(Surtees.) But Pilkington, who was specially obnoxious to the
insurgents, both as a Protestant and a married prelate, fled in the
greatest consternation to the south, at the first rumour of rebellion;
and Elizabeth soon had the estates vested in the Crown, under the
ridiculous pretence of defraying the cost of suppressing the rebellion, though, perhaps, no expedition had ever been conducted with
such a spirit of penuriousness. Pilkington eventually made a suit
against the Queen, which, of course, was unsuccessful.

It is painful to think of the vast treasures of antiquity which
had been slowly accumulating through the ages at Brancepeth and
Raby; and which, during this terrible season of social and religious
upheaval, were ruthlessly dispersed and destroyed.

The Survey of the Nevill Manors, taken for James I. in 1614,
shows us a shocking scene of desolateness in the once proud home
of Westmoreland.

" Brancepeth Castle is in the keeping Mr Henry Sanderson and his son Samuel,
or one of them, as constables thereof by patent, with a fee of £10 per annum.
There is a garden belonging to the said castle, for the keeping whereof there was,
and is, a yearly fee of £5, with the herbage of three kyne winter and summer in the
Frythe, and great wood of the East Park, for a gardener to look unto the same.
And when the said Henry Sanderson came first to be constable of the castle the
same was trimmed and kept by the gardener there, as well as with sweet walks and
pleasant arbours, till of late the said Henry Sanderson, having gotten the said
gardener's fee and beast gate by patent, and taken upon him the custody thereof,
the said arbours and walks are grown ruinous, and clean out of all good order.

There are deer toward the number of three hundred, which the said Henry Sanderson being constable hath from time to time both killed for his own use, given away to his followers and friends, and disposed of at his own pleasure. Also there are wild beasts of all sorts, elder and younger, in the East Parke to the number of twenty-eight or thereabouts." *

Then we hear of the deer dying fifty or sixty in a winter, "*being overstinted and famished.*" In 1630, the old forest trees fell before the ruthless axe. Phineas Pett, Esq., a Naval Commissioner, "superintended timber cutting" at Brancepeth, for the service of the navy, and the trees were sent to Sunderland to be shipped. James I. made his favourite, Robert Carr,† Baron Brancepath, and Earl of Somerset, and the castle was in the occupation of that baron from the year 1613 to the date of his condemnation. In the survey made by his steward, Thomas Emerson, the windows of the castle are described as filled with marvellous glass of Normandy, wrought with arms and imagery, the gallery being adorned with the whole history of our Saviour Jesus Christ, from his birth to his ascension, "the like not to be got for almost any money."

* "Memorandum within her ma'ties East Parke of Brancepethe in the Bishopricke of Durham, there haithe been of ancient tyme certain wilde beastes and kyen whiche in the tyme of the late Earles of Westmerland were cherished and kept, and yearlie there was one or two of the said wilde chattail killed and bestowed on thee poore and most needie people at the pleasure and appointment of the said Earles." (*P'ticular conc'ninge the wild chattail of Brancepethe Jan. 13. 39. Eliz. 1596. Chaytor MSS. at Clervaux Castle.*) "The profits of the herbage are stated to have been received by the under tenants and assigns of the Lady Anne one of the daughters of the late Earl of Westmoreland by virtue of a lease granted by Queen Elizabeth of the herbage."

† Carr was of the family of Fernihirst, where Westmoreland found a brief home in exile. The boy had a face full of charm ; his features being delicate, almost effeminate ; his eyes large and eloquent ; his complexion brilliant, with "a frequent trick of blushing." James, who piqued himself on his indifference to the fair sex, was strangely susceptible to handsome looks, a graceful figure, and winning ways in young men. Carr completely captivated him. Nothing was too good for Carr, and nothing was denied him.

He conceived a passion for the Countess of Essex ; a favor which that lady's husband had never accorded her. Though married at the age of thirteen, and very beautiful, she had never been happy with Essex. James decided to terminate her misery. "I mun have her for Carr!" he exclaimed, in his awful Scotch brogue. The Countess sued for a divorce on the plea of nullity of marriage. She offered to satisfy a jury of her own sex that she was a virgin wife ; but, "during her platonic alliance with her husband, she had so amply avenged herself for any marital shortcomings, that, to prevent unpleasant disclosures, another gentlewoman, closely veiled," kindly took her place at the investigation ; and she shortly afterwards appeared in the Chapel Royal, as the bride of the favorite, with her hair hanging in curls to her waist, the appropriate distinction of a virgin bride. Sir Thomas Overbury, who opposed the marriage, was poisoned ; and Somerset was eventually declared accessory to the crime. Such was the man who for a short time flourished as Baron Brancepeth. All the lands in Dorsetshire, which had belonged to Raleigh, also fell into his hands. In vain the sailor's widow pleaded for her children. James replied briefly, "I mun have it for Carr!"—*Vide Ewald's Stories from State Papers.*

"An enquiry into the power and authority of the Earls of Westmoreland, signed by George Brabant, and Wm. Conyers, and others, states that the lord of the manor had all waifs, estrays, goods of outlawed felons, fugitives, and other forfeitures; the tenants were free from toll at Durham and Auckland; and the Earl's bailiff served the writs of the sheriff in the manor.

"In this enquiry, one Thomas Lonsdale, aged 73, deposed that he heard his father and other ancient men say that a sheriff's bailiff coming into the lordship to serve process, was taken by the Earl's officers and tenants, and *made to eat the process*, and was set upon his horse, with his face backwards towards the horse's tail."—*Sir Cuthbert Sharp.*

After the occupancy of the Earl of Somerset, Brancepeth Castle was for some time assigned by the Crown for purposes connected with the household of the Prince of Wales.

In the year 1629, the estates were, by letters patent, granted to certain citizens of London, upon trust to sell the same; and on the 25th of April, 1633, they conveyed the castle and manor of Brancepeth, with their appendages, to Lady Middleton, Abraham Crosselis, and John Jones; who, on the 24th of May, 1636, conveyed the same to Ralph Cole of Newcastle, Esquire, in trust for his son Nicholas Cole of the same place, merchant (afterwards Sir Nicholas). His son, Sir Ralph Cole,* on the 19th of April, 1701 (in consideration of £16,800 paid, together with an annuity of £500 secured to himself for life, and £200 to his wife for life, if she survived him), conveyed the castle and estates to Sir Henry Bellasyse, who died 1719. He left an only son, William, who died 10th Feb., 1769, leaving an only daughter, who departed this life April 6th, 1774, and by her will devised the castle, manor, and estates to her kinsman, the Earl of Fauconberg, who, in 1776, sold the same to John Tempest, Jun., of Winyard, Esq. (the estate then comprising 4,600 acres, all of freehold tenure, and the rental £2,134 8s. 4d.). Sir Henry Vane Tempest, Bart., sold the estate in 1796 for £75,000 to

* There is something very sad about the memory of the family of Cole, who, for a brief period, found a home in the old feudal fortress of Brancepeth. "They rose almost *per saltum* from the smithy to the baronetage. Sir Ralph was a pupil of Vandyke, and retained Italian painters in his house, to the injury of his fortune. He died in 1704, and was buried in the family vault at Brancepeth. The family fell as suddenly as it rose, like a bright exhalation in the evening, and the grandchildren of Sir Ralph died in landless poverty. Sir Ralph represented Durham in the first and second Parliaments after the Restoration, and commanded the Durham Militia in 1685."—(*Sir Cuthbert Sharpe.*)

William Russell, Esq., whose son, Matthew, was considered the richest commoner in England. But not on that account will he be remembered in Brancepeth, for he

——"Who props the sinking pile, renews its sway,
Lives o'er the past, and joins the future day,'
He from oblivion wrests the hoary name,
And on a falling ruin builds his fame."

"Thy landmarks he cast not down. Thy stakes he strengthened." So let the grand old Hebrew benediction overshadow his last resting place—"Let his posterity be blessed for evermore!" A simple mural tablet on the south side of the chancel of Brancepeth Church records his worth.

To the memory of
MATTHEW RUSSELL, Esquire,
The only son of William Russell, Esquire,
By Mary his wife.
He married Elizabeth, daughter of George Tennyson, Esq.,
Of Bayon's Manor, in the county of Lincoln;
By whom he had issue, William, and Emma Maria.
He was representative in Parliament for Saltash,
And Vice-Lieutenant for the county of Durham.
While engaged in restoring his castle to its ancient extent
and magnificence,
He died on the 8th day of May, 1822, aged 57.
His extensive but judicious beneficence scarcely left
Within its range a rational want which he could not relieve,
Or a virtuous wish which he had not the means to gratify.
As a son he was dutiful and pious;
As a husband and a parent devoted and affectionate;
In his friendships immutable; just and indulgent to all.
Thus, when he departed this life, in the full enjoyment of all its
blessings,
He was honoured, beloved, and mourned.

The marriage (Sept., 9th, 1828) of Emma Maria Russell with Gustavus Frederic Hamilton, eldest son of the sixth Viscount Boyne, secured for Brancepeth Castle a continuation of loving care.

PART II.—CHAPTER XV.

RABY CASTLE.*

"Even in these remote provinces we see indications of the superior wealth and civilization of the English nation, with that attention to defence which was the natural consequence of their having something of value to defend."—*Sir W. Scott, Border History.*

"AFTER that Aldwinus and his wanderinge mates had reposed the reliques of their great patron Cuthbert, and buylded somewhat of Durham, then begged they hard not for cantels of cheese, as other poore men doe, but for large corners of good countries, as al their profession used, and obteyned of King Canute, (whome they persuaded to go fyve myles of his way barefooted to see Saint Cuthbert), the manor of Staindrop, with all the appendencies† thereto, which were greate."—*(Lambarde's Dict.,* p. 324).

* *Raby* is purely Danish, and derived from *Ra*, meaning a secluded nook, and *by*, a village. Flambard, Bishop of Durham, wrested Raby from the monks for a brief season, but restored it to them on his death-bed.

† "Standropa cum suis appenditiis, Cnapatun, Scottun, Raby, Wacarfeld, Efenwuda, Alclit, Luteringtun, Elledun, Ingeltun, Thiccelea, et Middletun," which rendered into the parlance of these later days, may be taken to mean Snotterton, (for Cnapatun, according to Hutchinson, Keverston according to others); Shotton, Raby, Wackerfield, Evenwood, Auckland, Lutterington, Eldon, Ingleton, Thickley, and Middleton.

The particulars of this grant are given by Simeon of Durham. Staindrop, even at that early period, was the capital of a wide and fertile district. In 1131, Prior Algar of Durham gave Staindrop to Dolphinus, a nobleman of the royal blood of Northumberland, to be held of the church in chief under a rent of four pounds sterling. In addition to this rental, a stag was offered by the lords of Raby on St. Cuthbert's Day, but there is no mention of such an offering in the instrument of Algar, and the right of the priory to the stag was altogether denied by Ralph Lord Nevill in the fourteenth century. All tenants of the priory were sworn to defend the rights and relics of St. Cuthbert, and to serve the saint right loyally against every foe.

"About a mile to the north of Staindrop is Raby Castle, a noble pile of stately towers, giving the most perfect idea of a great baron's palace in the feudal ages. It is probable that on this plot of ground stood Canute's mansion, which he gave to the Church with Staindrop. One of the towers (Bulmer) is of so singular a figure that it prompts a conjecture of its being of great antiquity. We have no examples that we recollect of Danish architecture in the north to afford a comparison; we can only make a supposition that this bulwark was of that era, and from its description leave the reader to determine the probability of the idea."*—*(Hutchinson.)*

* Rev. J. F. Hodgson, who is an authority on Raby, declares that Canute had no more to do with the building of this tower than had Nebuchadnezzar. "In plan a pentagon, formed by the application of an equilateral triangle to a square, it is admirably adapted to its peculiar position and purpose, viz., that of flanking the south and north-eastern fronts, and at the same time presenting a broad and powerful face towards the acute angle of their junction. Owing to the singularity of its form, this tower has given rise to the wildest and most preposterous conjectures. The whole tower, from turret to foundation-stone, has nothing Danish, or Anglo-Saxon, or Norman about it; but is John Nevill's work throughout (very probably of his own design), and belongs to an advanced period in the fourteenth century. Clifford's tower, by far the largest in the castle, is of enormous strength. This tower is planted with consummate skill. In shape an oblong square, standing, like Bulmer's tower at the opposite extremity, almost detached; and set diagonally to the north and west fronts, it not only completely flanks them both, but also from its close proximity to the moat-house, could either lend it efficient help in case of assault, or render its position, if captured, at once untenable. As originally constructed by Dolfin, the house would probably, following the usual custom of the time, be built principally of wood, and surrounded with a ditch and wooden palisade. This, as time went on, and especially after Robert Fitz Maldred's marriage, would be naturally both enlarged in extent and improved in character; but of such details, of course, we know nothing. The earliest portions of the existing building carry us no further back than the second quarter of the 14th century; and even these have now been so obscured and mutilated by modern alterations as to be practically undecipherable. The present entrance hall—or rather the walls of it; the chapel—or rather its remains; the great heraldic bull, with the Nevill banner displayed; and the external archway of the now destroyed barbican are among those features of the place which may possibly be ascribed either to the days of Ralph Nevill, or to those of his son and successor. The evidence,

"Raby is the largest castel of logginges in all the north countery, and is of a strong building; but not set either on hill or very strong ground. As I entered by a causey into it there was a little stayre on the right honde; and in the first area were but two towers on a ech ende as entres, and no other buildid. In the 2 area, as in entring was a great gate of iren with a tour, and 2 or 3 mo on the right hond. These were all the three toures of the 3 court, as in the hart of the castel. The haul at the houses of offices be large and stately, and in the haul I saw an incredible great leame of an hart. The great chambre was exceeding large, but now it is fals rofid, and divided into 2 or 3 partes. I saw ther a litle chambre, wherein was in windowes of colorid glasse al the petigre of the Nevill's; but it is now taken down and glasid with clere glasse. Ther is a tour in the castel having the mark of 2 capitale B's for Bertram Bulmer.† Ther is another tour bering the name of Jane, bastard sister to Henry IV., and wife to Rafe Nevill, the first Erl of Westmerland. There 'long 3 parkes to Raby, whereof 2 be plenish-ed with dere. The midle park hath a lodge in it; and thereby is a chace bearing the name of Langley, and hath fallowe dere. It is 3 miles in length."—(*Leland.*)

Great part of this noble structure was built by John de Nevill, to whom Bishop Hatfield, in the year 1379, granted license to castellate and fortify the same. (Given under Hatfield's privy seal by the hand of Will. de Elmeden, chancellor, 10th May, 33rd year Pontif; 2nd, Richard II.)

"Raby is a noble, massy building of its kind. Being simply however, it must be confessed, for attributing any of these parts, with the exception of the entrance hall, the windows of which contained distinctly geometrical tracery, to Ralph Lord Nevill, is not by any means as distinct and conclusive as could be wished; but they certainly possess characteristics which belong rather to his period 1331—1367, than to that of John Lord Nevill. * * * * While it would seem probable that though certain portions of the older fabric were so incorporated with the new as in some respects, perhaps, to influence the general design, Raby, never-theless, presents us essentially with the work and ideas of one period—the latter half of the 14th century. The castle plan was as follows:—First, the central nucleus or dwelling house proper, consisting of a closely-compacted mass of towers, connected by short curtains, and of which the block plan forms a figure something between a right-angled triangle and a square. Next, a spacious platform surrounding the central mass; after that, originally, a lofty embattled wall, about thirty feet high (of which a slight fragment only now remains intact), strengthened by a gate-house and barbican, as well as numerous small square bastions rising from its splayed or sloping base; and then the moat, the latter always probably, as at present, owing to the natural conformation of the ground, spreading itself out southwards into the dimensions of a small lake."

† "Probably these letters are denominative of the year in which repairs were made, and that B was then dominical, of which application we have an instance in an inscription in Coniscliff Church."—*Hutchinson.*

magnificent, it strikes by its magnitude, and that idea of strength and command naturally annexed to the view of vast walls, lofty towers, battlements, and the surrounding outworks of an old baron's residence. The castle, with its nearly circular terrace, enclosed within a military wall, is said to measure two acres, and the demesnes annexed to it exceed thirty miles in length.

"By the road leading from Staindrop Bridge the approach is remarkable; the visitor ascends gradually through the park towards the south front of the castle, which presents itself in the noblest point of view as the traveller advances.

"Within the castle the rooms are very numerous, and more modern in their proportion and distribution than one would easily conceive to be possible within the walls of so antient a building; but by means of numerous passages and closets, many of which have been scooped out of the walls and back stairs, the apartments are extremely convenient, well connected, and at the same time perfectly distinct."—(Grose.)

"In the breakfast room the recesses are in the form of semicircles, and scooped out, I may say, of the walls, which are nine feet one inch thick; a window is in each of these. I saw also a recess for a bed gained out of the wall, and several other communications and conveniences quarried out of it; and in some places pillars are left to support the roof. The oven was of dimensions suited to the hospitality of those times, higher than a tall person, for the tallest may stand upright in it, and I think its diameter must be 15ft.; at present it is converted into a cellar, the sides are divided into ten parts, and each holds a hogshead of wine in bottles."—(Pennant.)

"Carriages pass right into the large Gothic saloon, the roof of which is arched and supported by six pillars, the capitals diverging and running in ribs along the roof. A flight of steps leads to the presence chamber—a semi-circular room—where the company set down in the saloon are introduced; from thence passages lead to the chief apartments. A long train of carriages may set down their company without the least interference. Above the saloon is a hall of the first magnitude, which forms one side of the square of the inner area; it is 90 feet in length, 36 in breadth, and 34 in height; the roof is flat and made of wood, the joints ornamented with shields of arms of the family of Nevill.* Here once assembled *seven*

* The length of the Barons' Hall is now 132 feet, its width 36, and its height 34. The original floor was about ten feet lower.

hundred knights who held of that illustrious race. A gallery of stone crosses the west end of this room, used in ancient times for music and that mimicry wherein our ancestors delighted themselves."
—*(Pennant.)*

"From the Bulmer Tower, ascended by eighty-nine steps, a splendid prospect south-eastward lies before you. Coniscliff, Darlington, Sadberg, Long Newton, Stockton with the Cleveland Hills, and Black Hamilton. From other points you catch equally noble and far off views—the mountains of Hope and Arkendale, and westward the vale filled with the woods of Streatlam and Lady Close.

"Raby stands, in its antiquity and vastness, the fitting abode of the mighty Nevills. We can almost imagine that we shall find them still inhabiting it.

"The Royal Joan, walking with her maidens on the green terrace that surrounds it; or the first great Earl of Westmoreland setting out with all his train to scour its wide chases and dales for deer, or to proceed along the Marches to chastise the Scots. The exterior of the whole place has been well preserved[*] in its true ancient character; it is the great, grey, and stately feudal castle,

With all its lands and towers.

But when we step in to find ourselves at once in modern drawing rooms, with silken couches and gilt cornices, the Nevills and their times vanish. We revert to the quaint description of Leland, and wish we could see it as he did.

"The park has many fine woods, but the trees are comparatively young. We are surprised to see so little timber bearing a relative antiquity to the castle, which looks like a grey patriarch left amid a more juvenile race."—*Howitt.*

[*] Most antiquarians will differ from Mr. Howitt as to the preservation of the "true ancient character" of Raby. Mr. Hodgson thus concludes a recent paper upon the architecture of the castle:—"Turning to generalities, one most noticeable characteristic of the work is the entire absence of buttresses; every tower and curtain standing forth in its own unaided and majestic strength. A perfect simplicity and directness of purpose moreover, with constantly occurring change and play of line, will be found to distinguish every part. The great diversity of design, too, as seen in the towers more especially, should also be noticed. Without the least approach to affectation or eccentricity in any, yet, of all the nine included in the central mass, no two can be found which bear the least resemblance to each other. This infinite variety and beauty of proportion in its parts, and the admirable way in which they are combined—producing, as they did once, a sky-line perhaps unmatched in England—must ever have constituted the great glory of the place, and stamped it, while yet untouched and undisfigured, as the veritable work of a master. Alas! that looking back upon its pristine glory by the melancholy light of what is left, we should to-day, and in so large a sense, be forced to say of Raby, as once was said of Troy, '*fuit.*' "

The above was written more than forty years ago, but the same thought will occur to a more modern visitor. Possibly Raby never had many old trees, for the sixteenth century survey describes it as "very barron of tymber." At Brancepeth, too, the old trees are few and far between; and he who wishes to see grand groups of gnarled oaks that were fresh and gay when the sun of the house of Nevill shone in meridian splendour must go to Sheriff Hutton.

"In Langley Dale is a tower on a fine mount, an ancient out-post, and guard to the castle of Raby. It stands upon the banks of a brook, the vale is romantic, and the bower well situated for retirement."—*Surtees' Hist. Durham.*

Tradition tells how a much-loved mistress of Charles, the last Earl of Westmoreland, dwelt in this lonely and beautiful bower, but the "Rising of the North" came like a blast upon Langley Dale. The maiden's lament forms the theme of a beautiful ballad from the pen of the historian and poet of Durham.

> As I down Raby Park did pass,
>   I heard a fair maid weep and wail;
> The chiefest of her song it was,
>   Farewell the sweets of Langley Dale.
>
> The bonny mavis cheers his love,
>   The throstlecock sings in the glen;
> But I must never hope to rove
>   Within sweet Langley Dale again.
>
> The wild rose blushes in the brae,
>   The primrose shows its blossom pale;
> But I must bid adieu for aye
>   To all the joys of Langley Dale.
>
> The days of mirth and peace are fled,
>   Youth's golden locks to silver turn,
> Each northern flow'ret droops its head
>   By Marwood Chase and Langley Burn.
>
> False Southrons crop each lovely flower,
>   And throw their blossoms to the gale;
> Our foes have spoilt the sweetest bower.
>   Alas! for bonny Langley Dale.

Immediately after the Northern Rebellion, a survey was made, June 14th, 1570, and Raby is therein described as follows:—

"The most anncyent house of the Erle of Westmerland and scytuat in the south part of the busshopryk, tenne myles from Darneton, and fyve myles from Barnard Castle. And the Castell of Raby is a marvelouse huge house of buyldyng, wherein

I I

are three wards, and buylded all of stone, and covered with leade; and yet ys there no order or proporcyon in the buylding thereof, and standyth in a playne countrie. The ground and soyle about yt very good and bountefull for corn and grasse, but very barron of wood and tymber. Neyther the scytuacon of the place, or the Castell ytself, of any strengthe, but lyke a monstrouse old abbey, and will soon decay yf it be not continually repayred, yt standeth so open and playne, and subject to all wynd and wether. And albeyt the same is tenne myles further south than Branspeth, yet ys yt more subject to all extremyte of wether than Branspeth, bycause yt standyth naked and bare without covert, and more open upon the great waste called Fends Fell and Weredale, which begyne within two myles of Raby, and so continue to Hexam, a great wast countrey and nothyng so well inhabyted as the est part of the busshopryk, and few gentlemen of any lands or lyving inhabyting there; for the most parte of all the possessions in those partes are eyther belonging to the busshopryk or to the erle. And the gentlemen that were of any possessions were planted in the este parts of the countrey, and that dyd wel appere at this horryble and monstrouse enterpryse, for ther were not many gentlemen of possessions inhabyting between the houses of Raby and Bransepeth on the west parte of the countrey and the est sea, but were infected with this rebellion, and took part with the erle to the utter subversion of themselfs and their posteryte, as shall right wel appere by reason whereof the country is left voyde and barron of governors and gydes, and very much empoveryshed, not without their greate deserte."

In 1613, Raby was granted by James I. to his favourite, the Earl of Somerset; and after a brief possession, it reverted to the Crown. In 1629, the castle, parks, &c., were purchased of the lessees of Charles I. by Sir Henry Vane, the elder, Knight, together with Barnard Castle, on the payment of a yearly rent—a fine of £1,500; the woods to be taken at a valuation; and Sir H. Vane engaged to discharge all the officers' fees, amounting to £51 6s. per annum.— *Privy Seal Records.* On the 29th June, 1645, Sir Francis Liddle, with 120 horse from Bolton Castle, seized Raby Castle by a daring *coup-de-main*, and retained possession for a month. In 1648, it stood a seige, the only record of which appears in the Parish Register of Staindrop, which names a soldier slain at the "*seidge*" August 27th; and states that many soldiers were slain before Raby Castle, and buried in the park. Since that period it has remained in the peaceful possession of the lineal descendants of Sir Henry Vane, and is now the residence of the Duke of Cleveland.—*Sir Cuthbert Sharpe.*

PART II.—CHAPTER XVI.

MIDDLEHAM CASTLE, THE HOME OF THE KINGMAKER.

"The mightiest peers, the most renowned knights, gathered to this hall. Middleham, not Windsor, nor Shene, nor Westminster, nor the Tower, seemed the Court of England. As the last of the barons paced his terrace, far as his eye could reach broad domains extended, studded with villages, and towns, and castles, swarming with his retainers. The name of Warwick was in all men's mouths, and not a group gathered in market-place or hostel, but what the minstrel who had some ballad in praise of the stout earl found a rapt and thrilling audience."—*Last of the Barons, Book V., Chap. I.*

> "Where are they now? The eternal hills survive:
> The vales bloom on with flowers and fruits: the river
> In undimm'd beauty sparkles on for ever—
> God's handywork: while all that men contrive
> Sinks to decay; and yet Death's angel smile
> Still lingers o'er this cold and silent aisle."

MIDDLEHAM, or, as it is called in Domesday, Medelai, formed a portion of those extensive possessions which the Conqueror bestowed on his nephew, Alan Rufus, Earl of Bretagne, first Earl of Richmond, and Lord of Middleham, after the conquest of England. Alan, who died without issue A.D. 1089, gave the manor and honor of Middleham, with its appurtenances, and various other lands which, in the time of the Confessor, belonged to Ghilpatric, a Dane, to his youngest brother Ribald, whose grandson Robert built the castle of Middleham.*

* "Middleham Castel joyneth hard to the town side, and is the fairest castel of Richmondshire next Bolton. Middleham is a praty market town, and standeth on a rokky hill, on the top whereof is the castel meatly well dyked. All the upper part of the castel was of the very new setting of the Lord Nevill called Darabi; the inner part of Middleham Castel was of the antient building of the Fitz Randolph."

The massive and gloomy keep, which formed the original pile, and still survives the lapse of centuries, was the work of this Robert Fitz Randolph, third Lord of Middleham.

We have already shown how this property came into the hands of the Nevills by the marriage of Mary of Middleham with Robert de Nevill, who was buried at Coverham Abbey in 1271. Mary of Middleham survived her husband forty-nine years, and settled her property upon her eldest grandson, Robert Nevill, " The Peacock of the North;" but as he died without issue in his grandmother's lifetime, his brother Ralph had free warren granted him of Middleham and other possessions in Yorkshire. The estate then descended to Ralph's son, the celebrated John de Nevill, who built Raby and was buried in Durham Cathedral. His son became Earl of Westmoreland, and had a special grant for life of the Earldom of Richmond, from Henry, Duke of Lancaster (Henry IV.), as a reward for his services to that prince. He did not, however, use the title of Earl of Richmond. His widow, Joane, most undoubtedly possessed, with the castle, the advowson of the church. This is evident from the following record :—

> " Johanna nuper comitissa
> Westmoreland.
>
> Middelham advoc' Ecclesial. ⎫
> Middelham Castr' maner' et domin' ⎬ Ebor. '

The Countess Joan bequeathed the estate to her eldest son, Richard, Earl of Salisbury.

The first Earl of Westmoreland was the last of the Nevills in the elder line who died seized of Middleham and its dependencies. Henceforth we hear no more of the Nevills of the first line at Middleham, except that Sir John Nevill had a grant for life from Henry VI. (an. reg. 38) of Middleham Castle, with an annuity of 100 marks, accruing from certain lands in Wensleydale, by forfeiture of Richard Nevill, Earl of Salisbury. On the accession of Edward IV., the estates reverted to Salisbury's heir, Richard Nevill, Earl of Warwick; and after his death on Barnet Field, and the subsequent marriage of his daughter, the Lady Anne Nevill, with the Duke of Gloucester, it became the property of that duke. In the same way and at the same time, another old Nevill stronghold, Sheriff Hutton, fell into the hands of Richard Crookback.

Middleham is rich in English history. From hence, Salisbury marched at the head of 4,000 men of Richmondshire to the battle of Bloreheath. In these halls many of the dark scenes in the Wars of the Roses, and in the life of Richard III. were premeditated. Here Edward IV. was guest or prisoner; and here, according to Stow, the bastard Falconbridge, after being foolish enough to trust the Duke of Gloucester, was beheaded in 1471. With Richard III. the sun of Middleham set. Though transferred to the Crown, it was neglected by the House of Lancaster.

"The small remains of this once magnificent castle stand on the south side of the town, and consists of an outwork fortified with four towers, enclosing a body or keep. This envelope is in figure a right angled parallelogram of 210 feet by 175; its greatest length running north and south, and each of its sides forming one of the cardinal points of the compass. As a specimen of architecture Middleham is a unique but not a happy work. The Norman keep, the fortress of the first lords, not being sufficient for the vast trains and princely habits of the Nevills, was enclosed by a complete quadrangle, which almost entirely darkened what was dark enough before, and the first structure now stands completely insulated in the centre of a later work. The entrance into the castle was by a very strong arched gateway on the north side. Within the original building are the remains of a magnificent hall and chapel, but it might be difficult to pronounce whether the first or second work consists of the more massive and indissoluble grout work. The castle has been surrounded by a moat, which can be partially traced."—*Whittaker's Richmondshire.*

Grose, in his *Antiquities*, notices the wonderful echo that may be heard on the south side. He also draws attention to the ancient tumuli, or military earthworks, near to that side of the castle. Tons of stone have been ruthlessly removed from these grand old ruins, to be employed as building materials, &c. This sort of thing has, however, been put a stop to, and the castle is properly cared for; thus forming a happy contrast to the abominable condition in which Sheriff Hutton is allowed to remain. The person in charge is an intelligent man, well acquainted with the history of Middleham. He can return both a civil and a direct answer to most of the questions that may be addressed to him, and if you are disposed to examine the place carefully, and meditate quietly thereon, he will respect your mood. If there is anything I especially hate, it is being hurried through an ancient building in charge of a garrulous keeper, resolute to repeat his lesson verbatim for the nine hundred and ninety-ninth time.

From the year 1609, to the reign of Charles I., the castle was in the possession of Sir H. Linley, and his representatives: and one of his daughters married a Lord Loftus, who succeeded to the estate. Before the death of this lord, the manor was disposed of by the Crown to the citizens of London, who, in 1661, sold it to — Wood of Littleton, in Middlesex, ancestor to the present lord of the manor. —*Rowland.*

Middleham has recently been in the market, but no person could be found sufficiently enthusiastic to bid earnestly for the old ruin. The "lot" therefore remains unsold.

Majestic even in decay, Middleham Castle is the noblest work of man in the old county of Richmond; and it stands amid scenery of surpassing interest. To the west lies Bolton Castle, where Mary of Scotland was kept in durance by the lord of Scrope; and the summer house at the Queen's Gap marks the spot where, having attempted to escape, she was recaptured. Opposite Bolton Castle, towers Penhill, the mountain of Wensleydale, and on its slope are the ruins of a preceptory of Knights Templars. At Cappel Bank is the summer house built for Lavinia Fenton, the original Polly of the Beggar's Opera, who, from the position of an actress at fifteen shillings a week, rose to become Duchess of Bolton. Hard by is the village of Thoresby, where was born John de Thoresby, who became Archbishop, and built the choir of York Minster. Beside the banks of the silver winding Yore, is the pretty village of Wensley, whilst in a charming situation above the falls of Aysgarth Force stands Aysgarth Church.* To the north, is the magnificent natural terrace known by the name of Leyburn Shawl, "a delightful spot on a summer's day to fleet the time carelessly as they did in the golden world in Arden's shade, according to William Shakspere, when the thrush and the linnet sing sweetly, and when the air is laden with the smell of tedded grass and summer flowers."— *Pickford's Yorkshire Dales.*

Northwards also, within a pleasant drive, is Richmond Castle, with its lofty and massive keep, as fresh and sharply chiselled as when, 700 years ago, Earl Conan, laying its foundation upon the rocky bank of the Swale, reared that huge square tower, the walls

---

* The advowson of this valuable living was obtained from Ralph, Lord Nevill, in the 20th Richard II., by the Abbot and Convent of Jervaulx, in exchange for their barony and manor of Warton (*i.e.* Cravenholme, two closes called Buroughsclos and Copwyk, and other lands). The incumbent was Alexander Nevill, who voided it by promotion, and having for some years enjoyed the dignity of Archbishop of York, was driven from that high station, and fled to Flanders.— *Vide Part I., Chap. V.*

of which, with their pinnacled turrets, have braved the dilapidating hand of time, and retain at this day their original dimensions and stability.

To the south-west lie the remnants of Coverham Abbey, where some of Middleham's earliest lords are entombed; and in a sequestered spot, close by the romantic bed of the Cover, are the little known but curious fragments of St. Simon's Chapel and holy well. —*Atthill's Middleham.*

In the brook that babbles over the limestone, Charles Kingsley, who was a canon of Middleham, used to wet the line; and in this retired dale Myles Coverdale was born. To the east are the extensive and well-kept ruins of the once splendid Abbey of Jervaulx; and further still the castle and church of Tanfield, where lie enshrined the renowned lords Marmion, each under his marble sepulchre. Close beside us is the hamlet of Spennithorne, the birth-place of John Hutchinson, the author of *Moses's Principia,* a book written in opposition to Sir Isaac Newton. Hutchinson was the son of a Wensleydale yeoman, and a collection of fossils made by him is still in the Cambridge Museum. Here, too, was born Hatfield, the lunatic, whose extraordinary features are figured in Grainger's Biographical History, wherein his attempt on the life of George III. is also described. "There is a wealth of beauty in Wensleydale. There are lofty dells and heath-clad mountains; there are hanging woods and precipitous rocks; there are rivers winding like the beauteous Yore through rich and verdant meadows, or, like the Cover, foaming and tearing its way over rocks and stones, far, far beneath the feet of him who stands on the summit of its wood-bound banks."

> "Ever charming, ever new,
> When will the landscape tire the view?
> The fountains fall, the rivers flow,
> The woody valleys warm and low;
> The windy summit, wild and high,
> Roughly rushing on the sky!
> The pleasant seat, the ruined tower,
> The naked rock, the shady bower."

In the year 1305, Mary de Middleham gave to the abbot and convent of Coverham, in perpetual alms, certain lands in Crakehall, with two cottages in Thoraldeby, valued at £13 15s. 3d. a year, to found a chantry to be served by two chaplains in the great chapel of All Hallows in Thoraldeby, valued at the dissolution at £4 14s. 8d.

a year; Adam Middleham being then chantry priest. Maria had another sister, Johanna, married to Robert Tateshal, Lord of the Barony of Tateshal, in Lincolnshire, who, dying without issue, the whole inheritance came to the Nevills. Ralph, first Earl of Westmoreland, endowed Middleham Church with glebe and the tithes of the town, 21st November, 1405—7th Henry IV. He also left a legacy of £20 for the finishing of Houseway or Ulshaw Bridge over the Eure, and 100 marks to make a bridge at Winston over the Tees.

I append a translation of the charter granted by Richard II. to the first Earl of Westmoreland, for a fair and market at Middleham:—

"The King to all, &c., greeting,—Know ye that we of our special favour have granted, and by this our charter confirmed, to our beloved and right faithful Ralph de Nevill that he and his heirs for ever may have a market every week on Monday, at his village of Middleham, in the county of York, and a fair there every year on the Feast of St. Alkelda the Virgin, except that market and fair be to the hurt of neighbouring markets and fairs.

"Wherefore we will and firmly command for ourselves and for our heirs that the foresaid Ralph and his heirs for ever have the foresaid market and fair at the foresaid village, with all the liberties and free customs belonging to a market and fair of this sort, except that market and that fair be to the hurt of neighbouring markets and fairs as aforesaid. Besides, of our own special favour, we have granted and given licence for ourselves and our heirs, as much as we can, to the foresaid Ralph, to inclose his wood of Raskelf—called Raskelf Wood—near our Forest of Galtres, in the county foresaid, and thereof to make a park and three places to keep deer in, adjacent to the same park, the length of each of those places to keep deer in to be an hundred feet; and he may hold for himself and for his heirs for ever that wood so inclosed and the park thereof, and the three foresaid places made to keep deer in without any occasion or impediment of us or of our heirs, justices, sheriffs, escheaters, or other bailiffs or ministers of ours whatsoever, provided, however, that wood be not within the limits of our forest. These being witnesses, the venerable fathers, William, Archbishop of Canterbury, Primate of all England; Thomas, Archbishop of York, Primate of England, our Chancellor; William, Bishop of Winchester; John, Bishop of Hereford, our Treasurer; John, Bishop of Sarum, Keeper of our Privy Seal; our very dear uncles, Edmund, Duke of York, and Thomas, Duke of Gloucester; our very dear kinsmen, Richard, Earl of Arundel, and Thomas, Earl of Warwick; Richard Le Scrope; and John Devereux, Steward of our Household; and others.—Given by our hand, at Westminster, the 16th day of February. By the King himself."

PART II.—CHAPTER XVII.

NEVILL HAUNTS AND HOMES.

" Combien de souvenirs ici sont retracés !
J'aime à voir ces glacis, ces angles, ces fossés,
Ces vestiges épars des siéges, des batailles,
Ces boulets qu'arrêta l'épaisseur des murailles."

SHERIFF HUTTON, Brancepeth, Raby, and Middleham have each their glories, but in point of antiquity, perhaps, the Castle of Abergavenny may bear the palm. It is the *Caput Baroniæ* of Abergavenny. The town is situated on the confluence of Usk and Gavenni, and therefore called Abergavenny, since *aber* in Welsh signifies *mouth.* George Owen, in 1602, describes it as a fine town, wealthy and thriving, and the very best in the shire. On account of its disaffection to the new government, and attachment to the old religion, it lost its charter in the reign of William III., and from that time declined.

The position of Abergavenny is celebrated. It stands at the extremity of a pass where the mountains abruptly terminate, and the vale of the Usk begins to take a greater expansion. The town lies at the feet of hills and mountains, which, gradually swelling from the vale, unite the extremes of wildness and fertility.

To the west rises the Blorenge, forming the northern extremity of the chain, which reaches from Pont y Pool and terminates near the confines of the county. To the north are the Pen y Vale hills, which rise in four undulating eminences, called the Derry Hill, the Rolben, the Graig Lanwenarth, and the Lanwenarth. These four hills support on their broad and extensive base the Sugar Loaf, which assumes the form of a pyramid, and is the highest object in the vicinity.

"The western gate of the castle still exists; it is called Tudor's Gate, and is a strong Gothic portal defended by a portcullis, of which the groove is visible. In passing through the arch, the eye catches a perspective view, which is much admired; in the foreground, the river is seen under the arches of the bridge, gliding along the meads. A more pleasing assemblage of picturesque objects never entered into the composition of a landscape; the whole harmonises together, and produces an effect which neither the pen nor the pencil can adequately delineate."—*Rowland.*

The principal remains are situated on an eminence overlooking the Usk; they consist of a pointed arch doorway, a high round tower, and part of a pentagon tower. To the south-east is a tumulus environed by a trench, with the foundation of a building on the top; this was probably the keep or citadel. The doorways and windows of which the shapes are visible are Gothic. The great beauty of these remains is derived from their situation.

> "Far and wide,
> Blackening the plain beneath, proud Blorench lowers,
> Behind whose level length the Western sun,
> Duns his slope beam."—*Cox's Monmouthshire.*

Local tradition tells how the castle was built in the time of the early Britons by a giant named Agros.

It doubtless owes its origin to very remote times, but no real evidence is now to be obtained as to its date. According to Carodock's "History of Wales," it was surprised in 1172, by Sissilth ap Dyfnwal, and Jefan ap Sissilth, who took the garrison prisoners, and burnt the castle. In 1175, as we have already seen, it was taken possession of by William de Braose on behalf of Henry II.—*Vide Part II., Chapter X.* In the reign of King John, 1215, it was again taken by Llewellyn, notwithstanding the anathema of the Pope, to whom John had reconciled himself by submission. In 1257, Peter de Montfort, son of the Earl of Leicester, was put in command of the castle by Prince Edward, and his letter reports the barony as being in a state of violent insurrection. In 1404, Owen Glendwr caused a general rising in Wales, and burnt the Castle of Abergavenny.

In the Act of Resumption of Offices, in 3rd Henry VII., 1487, there is an exception in favour of John Morton, our Serjeant Porter, Steward of the Lordship of Burgavenny, and Constable of the Castle there. The castle was then in Henry's hands, and he afterwards granted it to Jasper, Duke of Bedford.

A manuscript in the British Museum, entitled *Notes of the State of Castles and Garrisons in Wales* (by one Richard Symonds, who served in the royal army), contains the following clause :—"Sunday, July 3rd, 1645. His Majesty lay at Rupperie, a fare seat of Mr. Morgan's, Com. Monmouth. The castle of Abergavenny is burnt, viz., the habitable part, and the garrison drawn out."

In the 13th Elizabeth, Henry Nevill, Knight, Lord Burgavenny, was summoned to show by what title or warrant he used and claimed within the Manor and Lordship of Burgavenny, courts baron, leet, view of Frankpledge, with suit of all inhabitants and resciants within the lordship, &c. Whereupon the said Henry Nevill appeared. The Attorney-General gave judgment for him, and the bounds of the barony were fully described and ordained.

Camden says that "the Castle of Abergavenny has been oftener stained with the infamy of treachery than any other castle in Wales ; first by William, son of Earl Miles, and afterwards by William Braos, both having, upon public assurance, and under pretence of friendship, invited thither many of the Welsh nobility, and basely murdered them. But they escaped not the just vengeance of God, for Braos being deprived of all his effects (his wife and son also starved with hunger), died in exile. The other having his brains dashed out with a stone, while Breulas Castle was on fire, received at length the due reward of his villainy."

Abergavenny has been less used as a residence than any other Nevill stronghold, probably on account of its remote position, and its long association with Welsh treachery and Border fued. Since the rebellion in the reign of Charles I. it has never been used as the home of a Nevill.

It is now rented by a Board of Improvement Commissioners, and is "tastefully laid out with walks, terraces, flower beds, and lawns for tennis, dancing, and other amusements. Parties are allowed to bring their own refreshment, and can arrange at the refreshment rooms at the castle for hot water and other necessary articles. There are cloak rooms and a ladies' lavatory. Certain rooms are also set apart for visitors, free of charge. Admission to the castle grounds twopence."

A guide book may also be obtained, price twopence. I am now quoting from it. This little book states that "the castle stands near the southern entrance of the town ; and before the present tall erections, which partly surround it, were built, it commanded an extensive view of the vale on every hand. At present only two crumbling towers and a few shattered walls remain to mark the positions of the different apartments of the stronghold. On the site of the Keep was erected, about the year 1800, the villa residence which has been converted by the town authorities into refreshment rooms. This modern travesty was almost entirely built of stones from the ruins of the Keep."

For many years the ruins were altogether closed to the public, but now thousands of over-worked people come here to enjoy one of the pleasantest prospects to be found in South Wales. It would be difficult to estimate the amount of sunshine thus thrown into the lives of a busy population.

" In all things charity."

But antiquarians are not remarkable for charity. Rather are they remarkable, like farmers, for grumbling. The aspect of things at Abergavenny Castle will not suit the antiquarian. He will most certainly grumble. The bright-eyed children with their jaunty nurse-maids, the town apprentices with their penny cigars, the lawn tennis courts, the flower beds, the cloak rooms, lavatories, and tea cups will all glare upon him like so many sacrilegious atoms. He will look sadly upon Abergavenny, and go away with Leatham's words upon his lips :—

> " Oh for a bard of olden time
> To yield thee back thy life in rhyme !
> To sing afresh thy glorious prime,
> When wassail rout convulsed thy tower,
> When banquet shook thy festive halls.
> All, all are gone ! Thy crumbling walls
> No more shall echo back the tread
> Of prancing steeds ; no more shall War
> Roll at thy feet his iron car ;
> Nor trumpet's clang, nor clashing swords,
> Nor prisoner's sigh, nor love's last words
> Whisper among thy voiceless dead."

ERIDGE CASTLE, near Tonbridge Wells, is now the magnificent residence of the Marquis of Abergavenny. The Manor of Eridge, or Ewridge, as it was anciently spelt, is one among several small manors, viz., Frant, Walshes, Bullock's Town, and Relf Hedges,

which are subinfeudations of the great paramount manor or lordship of Rotherfield, within the ambit of which they are comprised.

Rotherfield was of the fee of Odo, brother to the Conqueror.
The Saxon Earl Godwin held it, and it was taxed for three hides.
There can be no doubt that there was a large mansion at Eridge
from very early times. But after the reign of Charles I., the
family of Abergavenny deserted it for more than a hundred years.
During the latter part of the last century, Henry Nevill, the second
Earl, left Kidbrooke, the house near East Grinstead, and turned his
attention to the old mansion of Eridge, then occupied as a farm-
house. There were considerable remains of the old buildings; and
the ancient gallery occupies the entire front of the present castle,
which stands in the midst of picturesque grounds, laid out in drives
measuring more than fifty miles.

The old house at Eridge seems to have been large enough to
entertain Queen Elizabeth. In 1573 she made a progress through
Kent, and into parts of Sussex. It is thus recorded:—

"She was at her own house, Knowle, for five days. From thence
she went to Byrlingham (Birling), the Lord Bergavenny's, where
she remained three days, and thence made a visit to Sir Thomas
Gresham, at Mayfield. Thence to Eridge, another house of Lord
Bergavenny's for six days."

Henry Nevill, Lord Bergavenny, who died in 1586, was a
favourite of the Queen. Sir Thomas Gresham, who was connected
with the Nevills by marriage, and who then owned Mayfield Palace,
must have been a splendid merchant, for the furniture and chattels
in his house at Mayfield were then valued, as appears by his own
journal, at £7,553 10s. 8d., a sum probably equivalent to £70,000
in present money. Sir Thomas Gresham bequeathed Mayfield to
Sir Henry Nevill.

In Eridge Park are the remains of a military station of the
Saxons, which still retains the name of Saxonbury Hill.

———

"The MANOR OF BIRLING, in Kent, was part of the vast possessions of Odo, the great Bishop of Bayeux, half brother to the
Conqueror; and is mentioned in Domesday. Birling place was an
ancient residence of the Abergavenny Nevills. There are some
remains yet left, particularly a gateway of stone. The park has

long been disparked, and the family appear to have totally given it up as a residence about the year 1730, when they built Kidbrook,[*] in Sussex, and the old seat is now occupied as a farm house."— *Vide Rowland*, 1830. Birling is now the residence of the Hon. Ralph Pelham Neville, brother of the Marquis of Abergavenny.

BARNARD CASTLE.—"From whatever front observed, Barnard Castle, standing cheerfully on her southern slope; and, grouping her varied buildings around and under the church and ruined castle, presents an interesting object; and not ill fulfils the idea of the capital of a wild but lovely district; half river-valley, half hill, and heath, and moorland. The borough itself, in the midst of much modern improvement, is sprinkled over with vestiges of antiquity; here and there a house retains its ancient mullioned windows and stone gateway; or exhibits, built up in its masonry, fragments from the castle or its chapel; and, not least, the cognizance of Richard, still existing, throws a gleam of interest over the ancient moorland borough, which is wanting in many a place of greater wealth and pretension."—*Surtees.*

Barnard Baliol, son of Guy, who came into England with the Conqueror, built the castle, and called it Castle Barnard. It remained in his family until the attainder of John Baliol, King of Scotland, when it was granted by Edward I. to Guy Beauchamp, Earl of Warwick; and remained in the hands of his descendants for nearly two centuries. Richard, Duke of Gloucester, was Lord of Barnard by right of his wife, the Lady Anne, daughter of Richard Nevill, the Kingmaker, by Anne, sister and heir to Henry Beauchamp, Duke of Warwick. Gloucester was popular in the north, where he was best known, and Barnard Castle appears to have been favoured by him as a place of residence.

The latest portion of the building is acknowledged to have been his work. After his death it remained in the possession of the Crown. It was granted, with Brancepeth, by James I., to his favourite, Somerset, and resumed after his condemnation; being afterwards sold to Sir Henry Vane (2nd, Charles I.), from whom

---

[*] The Kidbrooke estate was purchased and the house built by William Nevill, forty-second Baron Bergavenny, in 1730. It was sold about 1805 to Charles Abbot, first Lord Colchester, and re-sold by the present Lord Colchester to Henry Ray Freshfield, Esq., who is this year (1885) High Sheriff of Sussex. The house has been greatly altered.

it descended to its present possessor, the Duke of Cleveland. Hutchinson, on the authority of the Egleston MS., declares that Barnard Castle was certainly the property of Charles Nevill, 6th Earl of Westmoreland at the time of his attainder, but the evidence for this assertion appears to be very insufficient.*—*Vide Sir Cuthbert Sharpe's Memorials of the Rebellion.*

The story of the surrender of the castle to the Earl of Westmoreland is told by Sir George Bowes himself in his letter to Secretary Cecil.

"I had gathered thether bothe horsmen, and allso fotmen, kepyng them there to repayer to the Lord Lieutenant upon his Lordship's call, as he had dyrected me. I was in the mene tyme beseged by the rebells and contenewyng there in strayte seage, wythe very hard dyett and great want of bread, drynck, and water; which was our onely drynck, save I myxed yt with some wyne.

"I fownde the people in the castle in continuall mutenyes, seakyng not only by greatt nombers to leape the walles and run to the rebells, but also by all menes to betraye the pece (fortification), and with open force to deliver yt and all in yt to the rebells—so far, as in one daye and nyght two hundred and twenty-six men leapyd over the walles and opened the gaytes, and went to the enemy, off which nomber thirty-fyve broke their necks, legges, or armes in the leaping; upon which especyall extremytyes, and that day our water being strayt (the leaden water pipes were cut by deserters), and by other great occasyons, I was forced by composytyon offered to leave the pece, takyng with me all the men, armor, weapons, and horses; levyng my household stuffe, which I mayd no accompt off, in this tyme of servyce, tho' the valewe wer greatt. At my comyng abrode, my storers and kepers off my houses repayred to me with the sayme speache that Jobe's servants repayred to him, for I am utterly spoylled off all my goodes, my corn and cattle karried away, and my housses fully defaced by pulling away off the dores, wyndowes, and chymnees; so that I now have nothing but my horse, armor, and weapon, which I more esteem than twenty times so much off other things, for that by yt I am enabled to serve

---

* "Barnard Castle, on the death of Richard, came to Henry the Seventh, and so hath continued in the Crown ever since, as appeareth by several records and accounts made by the constables of the castle and the bailiff of that liberty, till it came to the Earl of Westmoreland by marriage, and by him was forfeited, 12th Elizabeth."— *Egleston MS.*

my good Quene, whom God preserve, and I wey not all my losses; and thus I praye God preserve you."—From Sysaye, Dec. 14th, 1569.

Ten years after the rebellion, Sir George Bowes earnestly sought permission from the Lord Treasurer to cut down sixty trees in Gainford Wood to repair the bridges, the south tower, the west gatehouse, and the Brackenbury Tower, but the request was denied. The survey of 1592 shows Barnard Castle tenantless, mouldering, and weather-worn. Her "doors are without locks," her "windows without glass."

Three hundred years have passed. Some six and a half acres of ruin remain of Barnard Baliol's stately home. Upon the brink of the steep rock, eighty perpendicular feet above the river, the Bowes tower still rears its huge circular body of perfect ashlar work. No architectural education is necessary to convince the beholder of the august nature of this grey giant who bids defiance to the strong hand of Time, and still guards the north-western angle of the shattered fortress, where noble knights and high-born dames met together in the olden time.

From the narrow terrace upon the castle crag the view is indeed magnificent, and the words of Leland are still true—

"Barnard Castle stondith stately apon Tese."

WARWICK CASTLE, the home of Richard Nevill, the Kingmaker, has been so often described that I need say but little of it here. It remains among us as a proud monument of baronial grandeur—a connecting chain between ourselves and those that have passed "adown the gulf of time." It is ever approached with anticipations of pleasure, and its princely halls and time-worn battlements left with "lingering fond regret." Warwick Castle was a place of importance long before the time of the Norman Conquest. Earl Turchil received the Conqueror's commands to refortify it.

The present approach to the Castle was formed, at considerable expense, by the father of the late Earl. It commences with a recently embattled gateway on the eastern side of the town of Warwick. Passing through this the visitor enters a fine, broad, winding road, deeply cut through the solid rock; the ample branches of the variegated and thickly planted coppices create a canopy above, while the moss and ivy creep in fertile wildness beneath. Proceeding about a hundred yards, a sudden turn in the road brings you to the outer court (formerly the vineyard, renowned for its rich clusters as far back as the time of Henry IV.), where the stupendous line of fortifications breaks upon the sight in all its bold magnificence, bidding defiance to the all subduing power of time. On a nearer approach the whole front of the outer works becomes clearly defined; on the right appears the fine polygon tower, dedicated to Earl Guy, having twelve sides, walls ten feet in thickness, a base of thirty feet in diameter, and rising to the height of 128 feet. It is machicolated, and, from its exactness of design and beauty of execution, is considered a remarkably fine specimen of 14th century work. On the left the venerable Cæsar's Tower—said to be coeval with the Norman Conquest—arrests the attention. It is of irregular construction, and although it has braved the ravages of time, and depredations of man for 800 years, it still continues firm as the rock on which it was founded. This tower rises 147 feet, and is also machicolated. It is connected with Guy's Tower by means of a strong embattled wall, in the centre of which is the ponderous arched gateway, flanked by towers, and succeeded by a second arched gateway, with towers and battlements rising far above the first; they were formerly defended by two portcullises, one of which still remains; before the whole is a now disused moat, with an arch thrown over it at the gateway, where formerly was the drawbridge.

Passing the double gateway the visitor enters the inner court—the area of which is clothed by a carpet of rich sward—and he now sees before him the grand house of Warwick, still retaining that bold irregular outline so peculiar to the ancient Gothic castellated style.

There are two unfinished towers to the right, one called the Bear Tower, begun by Richard III., and having a flight of steps descending to a subterranean passage. Below Cæsar's Tower lie those dark, damp dungeons, wherein many a poor wretch has been confined until driven mad by the depth of his own misery. A follower of Charles I. scratched this inscription upon the wall:—

" Master John Smyth Gunner to his
Majestye Highness was a prisoner in this
Place and lay here from 1642 tell th
William Sidiate rot this same.
And if my pin had bin better for
His sake I would have mended
Everri letter ——"

K K

On Advent Sunday, 1871, a fire broke out in one of the upper
private rooms to the left of the great hall, and in a few hours the
great hall, library, breakfast room, and private rooms on the east
side, together with the many priceless treasures therein contained,
were destroyed.   Happily, the books were saved.   Many curious
features of the older building were disclosed by the action of the
fire, and under the care of Mr. Salvin, these have been preserved.

From the great hall a view is obtained at a single glance of the
grand suite of state rooms on one side, and domestic apartments on
the other, extending in a right line 333 feet, terminated at the
western extremity by a window.—*Vide Cook's Warwickshire.*

It now only remains to speak of the old town houses of the
Nevills.   The house of the Earls of Westmoreland was in Aldersgate.   It was a magnificent pile, but Pennant speaks of it as frittered
into various tenements, though still keeping up the old name in its
appellation of Westmoreland Court.   Of the Erber, Warwick's
house, we have already spoken.

" In Silver Street (this leads out of Aldersgate Street), at the
south end of Monkswell Street, there stood Lord Windsor's house,
in 1603 ; it was built of stone and timber, and was in ancient days
called Nevel's Inn, belonging to the Nevels."   In the 19th of
Richard II., it was found by inquisition of a jury, that Elizabeth
Nevel died seised of a great messuage in the parish of St. Olave, in
Monkswell Street, in London, holden by the King in free burgage,
which she held of the gift of John Nevel of Raby, her husband ; and
that John Latimer was next son and heir to the said Elizabeth.

" This house was called Nevel's Inn, and was possessed by that
noble family until the time of Henry the Sixth, in the 4th of whose
reign, Ralfe Nevel, Earl of Westmoreland, died seised of that
messuage, in the parish of St. Olave, in Farringdon Ward, London,
and the heirs male of his body begotten on Jane, his wife; and of
another messuage called Le Erbor, in Dowgate Ward ; both held
in burgage, as the city of London was held."—*Maitland.*

Abergavenny House (known in the sixteenth century by that
name), was a large mansion at the corner of Paternoster Row.   On
the site of it, Stationer's Hall now stands.

The old Nevill mansion in Green Street, East Ham, E. (known
as Anne Boleyn's Tower), is now a Roman Catholic Reformatory.

DURHAM CATHEDRAL.

PART II.—CHAPTER XVIII.

NEVILL MONUMENTS.

"Out of monuments, names, words, proverbs, traditions, private records, and evidences, fragments of stories, passages of books, and the like, we do save and recover somewhat from the deluge of time."—*Lord Bacon.*

"Old moniments which of so famous sprights
The honour yet in ashes do maintain."
—*Spenser. Ruins of Rome.*

CANTERBURY CATHEDRAL.—In the north transept are the arms of Anne Nevill, daughter of the first Earl of Westmoreland, and also the arms of the Kingmaker, and those arms of Cicely Nevill, Duchess of York, and George Nevill (the son of Montague), who was created Duke of Bedford. On the monument of Henry IV. the arms of Nevill and Despencer are visible, and in various parts of the Cathedral are the arms of Beauchamp and Bergavenny.

CHICHESTER CATHEDRAL.—Ralph Nevill, elected bishop in 1222, is said to have designed and commenced the spire of this cathedral, which was far from being completed at the time of his death in 1244. The plan of the presbytery was also prepared by him about the year 1230, and was adopted in his time, and continued with the addition of the Lady Chapel by Bishop St. Leofard. The chapter house, a small square room, the arched roof and windows of which plainly indicate that it was built about the beginning or towards the middle of the thirteenth century, is probably the work of Bishop Nevill, by whom the dean and chapter were first established. He greatly improved the revenues of the see, and built the episcopal residence in London, the site of which is now occupied by Lincoln's Inn.—*Vide Winkle's Cathedral Churches.*

"Ralph Nevill, Bishop of Chichester, received the great seal in 1226, by the advice and consent of the great council of the nation; and he refused to surrender it to the king, except at the express command of the assembly by which he had been appointed. Henry III., however, succeeded in wresting the seal from him in 1238; but he retained the income and title of chancellor until his death."—*Vide The Early Plantagenets. Stubbs.*

DURHAM CATHEDRAL.—The Nevill chantry, where formerly mass was said daily for the souls of the founders, occupied two bays of the south aisle. Ralph Nevill, the hero of Nevill's Cross, who died in 1367, was buried here. No layman had ever before been allowed place of sepulture in the Cathedral. Alice de Audley, his wife, who died seven years later, was buried beside him. His son, Lord John Nevill, the builder of the Nevill screen, was interred in this chantry; also, Lord John's first wife, Maud Percy.

Their monuments are now to be found in a most grievous state of dilapidation between the piers of the nave arcade. The shapeless mass, which lies easternmost, formerly exhibited the effigies of Lord Ralph, and Alice, his wife.

Lord John's monument is less disfigured. The effigies still remain, though greatly mutilated. The shields of arms are also visible, and the canopied niches, containing small figures representative of Lord John's children.

Before the *Protector* came into the world this must have been a magnificent monument. I may relate briefly why it ceased to be so. Before the battle of Dunbar (1650), Cromwell "called upon the Lord, and his spirit was enlarged within him. A supernatural voice was heard conveying an assurance of victory." The morning sun broke upon the Scots as they struggled in the pass. Cromwell, turning to his own favourite regiment, exclaimed, "Let God arise, and let his enemies be scattered." The bodies of three thousand Scots covered the ground. Cromwell had received another "crowning mercy." He sang the 117th Psalm. Nine thousand prisoners had been taken. Five thousand of these were so maimed that their days for soldiering were over. These Cromwell released. The rest were marched towards Durham, and many died on the road. The remnant arrived at Durham in mid-winter, and three thousand were shut up in the cathedral. Ill clad and cold as these poor wretches were, we need scarcely wonder that they pulled down the woodwork of the choir, and made fires of it. Their exertions were then directed to the demolition of the Nevill monuments; but Cromwell himself was the real author of this sacrilege.

The matrix of the brass to the memory of Robert Nevill, Bishop of Durham, will be noticed on the marble slab close by Lord John's monument. I have before observed that the Bishop's will directs his interment in the Galilee, and Leland says, "Robert Nevill, Bishope of Durham, lyithe in a highe playne marble tumbe in the Galile;" but other accounts place his monument among those of his relatives in the Nevill chantry.

In a paper, read September 24th, 1879, Canon Greenwell states that "the remains of the painted glass which once occupied the windows lighting the chantry, containing amongst others the Nevill shield of arms, have entirely disappeared within my recollection."—*Vide Transactions Durham Archæolog. Society*, Vol. II., p. 220.

If such disappearances are noticeable in cathedrals possessing an affluent and erudite Chapter, perhaps it ought not to surprise us that very remarkable disappearances indeed may be noticed in some smaller churches, whose interests are watched over by incumbents not quite so affluent or erudite.

Let us now pass through the choir, and examine the Nevill screen.

" This screen was finished in 1380, and cost 800 marks (£533 6s. 8d.), of which Lord Nevill contributed 600. The whole is of Caen stone,* previously executed in London, and conveyed by sea to Newcastle. Its erection occupied seven expert masons for a year, during which time they were allowed diet and wages

* Or *French peere*, as it is called in the *Rites of Durham*, though the stone is really Dorsetshire clunch. The other contributors to the screen were Prior Fossor and Prior Berrington.

from the Convent. As a detached altar screen with its accompanying sedilia, it is, perhaps, the most remarkable in the kingdom, either as regards magnitude or richness of detail. Besides the profusion of architectural ornaments, there were formerly no less than 107 statues in the now empty niches, nine of which in the lower range of canopies were of life size. These statues were all painted and gilt, and no doubt were as beautiful as the other portions. The Reformation swept the whole away, deteriorating much from the effect of the screen. The central niche, wider than the others, had a statue of the Virgin, and on each side were statues called the picture of St. Cuthbert and the picture of St. Oswald, all richly gilt. The interiors of the canopies of the niches are beautifully groined with numerous small rib mouldings and bosses at their intersections, and all the subordinate details are worked out with elaborate richness and singular beauty. There are four sedilia on each side of the altar, of the same period and character as the screen. The altar to which the screen forms so magnificent a background was formerly garnished with extreme splendour. It was dedicated to the Virgin, St. Oswald, and St. Cuthbert, and was the goodliest in all the church, if not in all the land. Its decorations were rich and numerous. Curtains of white silk were suspended at each of its ends, and the daily ornaments above and in front were of red velvet, embroidered with large flowers in gold and other embellishments. The ornaments for the day of Assumption were of white damask, set with pearls and precious stones. Above the altar was suspended by gilt rods of iron fixed in the screen a splendid canopy, containing a pix of pure gold, over which was spread a covering of lawn, embroidered with gold and red silk, with tassels of gold at its corners. Upon the canopy stood an emblematical pelican of silver, vulning her breast for the sake of her young ones, and upon the altar itself was laid a book richly covered with gold and silver, called the Liber Vitæ, containing the names of the benefactors to the church from the earliest period of its history, all of which were once a year gratefully recited during the solemnity of mass. Three lamps suspended by chains of silver, and standing in silver basins, threw a dim but perpetual light in sunshine and at midnight, in token that the house was always watching to God."— *Fordyce Hist. Durham.*

I understand that the empty niches are about to be refilled with statues according to the original design.

"In the South Alley of the Lanthorn of Durham was a most lively and beautiful Image of Our Lady, which was made to open with Gimmers, from her breast downwards, and within was painted the Image of our Saviour, finely gilt, holding up his Hands, and betwixt his Hands a fair and large Crucifix of Christ, all of gold, which Crucifix was to be taken out every Good Friday, and every man crept into it that was then in the Church; after which it was hung up again within the said Image. And every principal Day the said Image was opened, that every Man might see pictured within her the Father, the Son, and the Holy Ghost, most curiously and finely gilt; and both the Sides within her very finely varnished with Green Varnish, and Flowers of Gold, an elegant Sight for all Beholders; and underneath the Stone she stood on was a beautiful Cross upon a 'Scutcheon, called the Nevil's Cross, signifying that the Nevils had born the charges thereof."

LINCOLN CATHEDRAL.—Monument of Joan, Countess of West-moreland.—*Vide Part II., Chap. I.*

This tomb has been curtailed, squeezed, removed, and otherwise maltreated. The original inscription has been already given.

"The Countess lay with her mother, wyfe to John of Guant." A beautiful canopy at one time surmounted the tomb, but was re-placed by a Corinthian cornice. The brasses long ago disappeared.

Lincoln suffered much from the *Protector*.

"These men went in with axes and hammers, and shut them-selves in till they had rent and torn off some barge loads of metal, not sparing even the monuments of the dead, so hellish an avarice possessed them."—*Evelyn.*

"They have torn to pieces monuments and tombs, shot down escutcheons and arms of benefactors, and filled each corner of that holy place with their own and horses' dung, in so horrid a manner, as the Lord Kimbolton would turn away his groom that should suffer his worst stable to lie half as nasty as he and Cromwell have made the house of God."—*Mercurius Anlicus.*

"Such were the doings of those who would justify any crime by a text, or pick their neighbour's pocket whilst singing off the same psalm book."—*Sir Charles Anderson.*

OLD ST. PAUL'S CATHEDRAL.—"Here in a monument broken all a-pieces, lieth entombed the body of John Nevill, Lord Latimer, whose widow, Katherine Parr, daughter of Sir Thomas Parre, of Kendal, and sister to William, Lord Parre, Marquesse of Northampton, was the sixth and last wife to King Henry the Eight. He died in the year 1542."—*Weever's Monuments. Ed.* 1631.

YORK CATHEDRAL.—George Nevill, Archbishop, lies beside his successor, Rotherham, on the north side of our Lady's Chapel, in the Choir.—*Vide Leland.*

Stone in the Minster Floor.—Here lieth the body of Dorothea Nevil, widow of George Langford Nevil, Gent., of Nottingham, who departed this life December 20th, 1785, aged 90.—*Vide Hist. Ch. of S. Peter, York,* 1786.

ABERGAVENNY PRIORY CHURCH.—A recumbent effigy in this church was long considered to be the monument of Edward Nevill, first Baron Bergavenny of that name, who married Elizabeth Beauchamp, and died in 1476; but Mr. Octavius Morgan, F.R.S., F.S.A., discovered that it was really the monument of Lawrence de Hastings, Baron Bergavenny, who died in 1344. There is no subsequent record of the interment of any Baron Bergavenny in this church.

BRANCEPETH CHURCH.*—The colossal effigy of Robert Nevill, "the Peacock of the North," forms a conspicuous object in the chancel. This monument has been moved from the position it formerly occupied in the north transept. It has been slightly chipped in several places, but after the lapse of more than five hundred and fifty years, it remains the best preserved Nevill monument in existence.

The effigy is seven feet nine inches long, clothed in chain mail, with surcoat reaching to the knees. The head rests on two cushions, supported on six lions, with two small kneeling figures

* The portion of this chapter relating to Brancepeth was read before the members of the Royal Archæological Institute, on the occasion of their visit to Brancepeth, August 13th, 1884.

between them. The hands are elevated, the legs crossed. The feet rest on a lion. Beside one leg is a dragon, beside the other a muzzled dog, and the space between is covered with foliage. The sword is small, and dependent from a belt under the shield. The shield bears the Nevill saltire, and the label of cadency, by which the effigy can be identified without any manner of doubt. Robert Nevill died in 1319, during the life of his grandmother, Mary of Middleham, being her heir. There is no other Nevill to which this label could apply, and the whole character of the monument is agreeable to the age in which Robert Nevill lived. Stone effigies of crossed-legged knights were sculptured down to the time of Edward II. The hauberk was worn by knights having estates, called in the Norman parlance *fiefs d'haubert*. The crossing of the legs is probably due to the whim of the sculptor, who adopted this disposition in order that he might the better exhibit the detail of the monument. Knights with their legs crossed are not necessarily crusaders, and Robert Nevill was certainly not a crusader, although he has often been described as such. The whole design of the monument was boldly conceived and carried out. It is a magnificent relic, and well deserves the reverent guardianship which it has so long received from successive generations of Brancepeth people, who have been content to pass away into the silence of the church-yard without carving their names upon, or otherwise disfiguring, this splendid monument of antiquity. Let us hope that a like spirit of intelligence may guide the hands of future generations.

The oak monument on the south side of the chancel has been less fortunate. It met with the fate of the prophet Isaiah. The name of the individual by whom it was sawn asunder has not come down to us, his memorial having perished for ever.

Leland says that "in the paroch chirch of Saint Brandon, at Branspath, be dyvors tumbes of the Nevills. In the quire is a high tumbe of one of them, porturied with his wife."

The "high tumbe," having been sawn asunder, is now a low one. The upper part of the monument, on which the effigies rest, and the plinth, with the bases of eighteen canopied niches, alone remain. The main body of the tomb, with all its richly-carved figures, will never be seen again.

A view of the monument as it originally appeared has been preserved in the Herald's College, and a copy is given in *Surtees' History of Durham*. By many writers it is held to be the

L L

monument of the great Ralph Nevill, first Earl of Westmoreland,
and Margaret, his first wife. Stothard, however, describes it as
that of the *second* Earl, and Margaret, his *second* wife.[*] Mr. John
Hewitt, in his learned and exhaustive supplement to Stothard's
work, is evidently perplexed over this monument. I cannot do
better than append his remarks *in extenso.*

"The remarkable points in these effigies are the collars which
decorate the necks of the figures. The Lancaster badge of S.S. is
now discarded, and we find that of York, the white rose in the
sun, adopted.

In his body armour the knight is a good hundred years behind
the fashion of his day. His suit is almost identical with that of the
Black Prince. It is not easy to assign the cause of this resemblance.
It may be attributed to the remoteness of his province from the
metropolis, to the custom of wearing inherited armour, to the artists
having copied some older monument, or to his having affixed a new
head to a more ancient body. All these are probable causes, and
all these may be very far distant from the truth.

In the head piece of our knight, however, we have a novelty, the
visored salade or sallett with its mentonnière. This kind of head
defence approached so nearly to that of the ancient Greeks that the
Italians contrived the ocularium after the classic model, and that
head piece now known to collectors as the Venetian salade is a
facsimile of the Greek casque, so familiar to us from the numerous
representations of the armed head of Minerva. In fight the salade
was brought down over the face so as to join the gorget. Subsequently a visor was added to it, the mentonnière retaining its form
and duties. The Nevill effigy gives but a very imperfect idea of
the visored sallet. It is evident that no artifice could bring that
ocularium in useful proximity to the knight's eyes, and the mentonnière seems equally shorn of its fair proportions. Let us, however, respect the sculptor's motive, which was, no doubt, to bring
into view as much as possible of the knight's countenance.

This head defence appears but very rarely in monumental
sculptures. At Meriden, Warwickshire, is a good example, figured
in Bloxam's *Monumental Architecture.* In brasses it is by no
means of frequent occurrence. One of the best is that of Edmund
Clare, Esq., in Stokesley Church, Norfolk, which is engraved in
Cobman, Vol. I.

[*] Margaret, daughter of Reginald, Lord Cobham.

Lady Nevill wears the kirtle with tight mitten sleeves, made very low in front. The girdle worn loosely is attached by an ornament of suns similar to those of the collar; its chain probably suspends an aulmoniere. The sideless surcoat is curious from its deep facing, most likely of fur. The mantle offers nothing unusual. The head-dress, which we must carefully disentangle from the tassels and corners of pillows, is a mitigated form of the steeple-head, and may be regarded as transitional between that and the pedimental coiffure."—*Stothard's Monumental Effigies, Hewitt's Edition*, 1876.

The York badge of the white rose in the sun parhelion exhibited on the collars of these effigies was assumed by Edward IV. after the battle of Mortimer's Cross, in consequence of which victory he added the device of the sun to the white rose.

If, as Stothard asserts, this monument was erected to the second Earl after his death in 1484, it seems strange that the Yorkist badge, so fatal to the Nevills at the battle of Barnet, should appear such a prominent object on the necks of both effigies. If it be a late erection to the memory of the first Earl, and placed in the church at a time when the Nevills were in close fellowship with Edward IV., I can understand the introduction of the Yorkist badge. The body armour of the male figure is certainly more in keeping with the time of the first Earl than the second. Margaret, the second wife of the second Earl, was not buried at Brancepeth, but at Doncaster. Margaret, the first wife of the first Earl, *was* buried at Brancepeth.

The first Earl lies at Staindrop; but I have not been able to discover the burial place of the second Earl. He was not a very remarkable character, and but for the fact that he was the founder of the Jesus chantry, I see no sufficient reason for the association of his name with the Brancepeth monument.

I have seen it stated that the canopied niches of this monument were filled with figures of the second Earl's children, but the author of this statement failed to remember that this Earl had only two children, and there are the remains of eighteen niches.

Leland says "there lyith in the chapelle on the south of the quier a Countess of Westmoreland, sister to Bouth, Archbishop of York. There lyith in that chapelle also the Lord Nevill, father of the Erle that now is (4th). This Lord Nevill dyed, his father the Erle yet lyving: whereupon the Erle tok much thought and dyed at Horneby Castle in Richmondshire, and ther is buried in the paroche church. The Erle of Westmerland that is now had an elder brother, and he lyith in a little tomb of marble by the high alter, on the south side; and at the feete of hym be buried four children of the Erles that now lyvith."

The high marble tomb that now lies under the tower (having been moved from the Jesus Chapel in 1876), is doubtless that of Matilda (daughter of Sir Roger Booth, of Barton), wife of the third Earl, and Ralph, her son. It is ornamented with quartrefoils encircling plain shields. The shields on the south side have evidently been painted, and the Nevill saltire can be indistinctly traced.

Lady Boyne, Rev. J. Lawson, and H. T. Peirson, Esq., were present during the removal of this monument. The skulls and other remains of two persons were discovered, and re-interred.

Hutchinson (edition 1794) speaks of a table monument in the Jesus Chapel without inscription, but exhibiting a shield with the Nevill arms dexter, sinister three boars' heads. Before the restoration of the church in 1863, an altar tomb, without inscription, is described (by Rev. J. T. Fowler, and also by C. Hodgson Fowler, Esq.) as standing in the centre of the chapel. A large marble slab is still recumbent under the organ.

Above the corbels of the nave roof will be noticed on the north side a bull, on the south an angel, each bearing a shield with the Nevill saltire. The bull's head of the Nevills also appears on the coloured panelling placed over the chancel arch, above the geometric tracery.

Bishop Dudley granted licence, September 20th, 1483, to Ralph Lord Nevill and Isabel* his wife, to found a chantry for one chaplain at the altar of our Saviour in the south part *(ex australi parte)* of the church of S. Brandon, Brancepeth, with an endowment in lands of ten pounds yearly. I have in my possession an exact copy of the original instrument.

EAST GRINSTEAD CHURCH, SUSSEX.—This church was ruined by the fall of the tower in 1785, and was rebuilt soon after. Members of the Nevill family were buried here from 1744 to 1840; but only one mural memorial tablet remains, with the following inscription:—

* Probably synonymous with Elizabeth.

Hic juxta depositæ sunt reliquæ
Honoratissimi Domini
GULIELMI Domini ABERGAVENNY,
Baronis Angliæ Primarii;
Qui dignitatem à longa traditam Majorum serie.
Gerendo vere illustrem
Merendo fecit suam
Obiit 21 Septembris, 1744, suæ ætatis 47.

Arms: a saltire charged with a rose of the field. Crest: a bull's head. Supporters: two bulls. Motto: *Ne vile velis.*

This is the monument of William Nevill, forty-second Baron Abergavenny, who purchased the estate of Kidbrooke, near East Grinstead, in 1730, and built the house in which the Abergavenny Nevills resided for about seventy years.

The Vicar of East Grinstead informs me that during certain re-seating alterations undertaken in 1874, he entered the old Nevill vault, where twenty members of the family are buried, and records of name, date, age, etc., are inscribed upon the walls.

EAST HAM CHURCH, ESSEX.—At the extreme east end of this church there exists the fine monument of Edmond Nevill, who claimed to be seventh Earl of Westmoreland.—*Vide Part II.*, *Chap. III.* It is about 14 feet in height. The lower part is formed by a huge block of black marble, in front of which are the kneeling effigies of Edmond Nevill's seven children. The upper portion of the monument exhibits the kneeling figures of Edmond and his wife, dame Jane. He is bareheaded, his helmet lying at his feet; but the lady wears a coronet.

The shield of the old lords of Raby retains its original colouring (a rare occurrence); the silver saltire appearing on a red ground. A crown surmounts the shield, which is supported by two bulls. There is also a shield with the original Nevill arms:—Or fretty gules, on a canton, per pale ermine, and or, a ship with three masts, sable.

The inscriptions, so far as they are legible, have already been given.—*Vide Part. II*, page 158.

HACKNEY CHURCH.—*Monument of Lady Lucy Latimer.*—This monument, with inscriptions, was remaining in the north aisle of the old church of S. Augustin when it was taken down, and fragments of the monument, together with the effigy of Lady Latimer, in a dilapidated state, reposed for many years amid an accumulation of rubbish in the sexton's tool house beneath the old tower.

Lady Latimer, it will be remembered, had four daughters, the effigies of whom were placed kneeling under her, two on one side of the monument and two on the other. This effigy is figured in Dr. Robinson's *History of Hackney*, published in 1842. He describes it as exquisitely sculptured, and fixed on the top of the table monument.

"She appears to be dressed in a scarlet robe, with a coronet on her head, and the other parts of her dress richly gilt. The effigy is probably intended for a portrait."

The poetical inscription, composed by her son-in-law, Cornwallis, appeared on this monument, and will be found hereafter, under the head of "Well Church."

"Upon the tomb of the Lady Lucy Somerset (where she is represented, in alabaster, with her four daughters, according to her last will, in which she gave 500 marks* for ye erecting of it) is Somerset impaled by Nevil, Lord Latimer, viz., gules, a saltire argent, charged with an annulet sable."—*Dingley, pub. by Camden Society.*

The vault where the Lady Lucy lies buried in the old church, at the east end of the north aisle, has probably never been disturbed. The monument was partially hidden by the schoolmaster's pew; and it appears to have been in a bad state of preservation when the old church was pulled down. The fragments were then relegated to the tool-house, whence they found their way to the mausoleum of the Marquis of Downshire, formerly the Rowe Chapel, an independent building on the site of the old church. Miss Goodwin, the sextoness, was one day engaged in trying to discover, for some Leeds gentlemen, the tomb of Thoresby, when the floor of the mausoleum gave way, and the sextoness was killed. The consequent repairs brought to light a great quantity of sculptured stones, among them a very beautiful alabaster shield belonging to the Latimer monument, with the arms of Cecil impaling Nevill. This shield attracted the attention of the Rev. J. W. Kenworthy, then (1879) curate of Hackney; and Mr. Simpson, the churchwarden, to prevent further

* Equal to £2,000 present money.

damage, carried it home under his arm. Every particle of the Latimer monument was then carefully collected, and, at the cost of some £600, a complete restoration of the old tomb was effected by the Baroness Burdett Coutts,* whose praise is in all the churches. The monument now stands in the vestibule of the new church of S. John.

The work was carried out under the supervision of Mr. Tucker, Somerset Herald, Mr. Powell being architect, and Messrs. Farmer and Brindley executing the restoration.—*Vide Simpson's Memorials of S. John's, Hackney.*

Weever gives the following epitaph relative to Lady Latimer, though it is doubtful whether the lines ever appeared on the Hackney tomb:—

> "My soule in Heaven, my body here, tyll day of dreadfull dome,
> They joyn and hope, and hope agayne for ever time to come.
> Lucy Lady Latimer,
> Ob. 23, Feb., 1582; buried at Hackney."

Dr. Robinson says that in one of the pews of the old church there was a loose stone leaning against the wall under the gallery, which had apparently been taken from an ancient tomb. It bore the following inscription :—

"The Right Honourable Baron John Nevil, Knyght, Lorde Latimer, departed this lyfe at his manor of Snape, in the countye of York, ye 22nd of April, 1577, in ye yeare of his age 61; and lyeth buried with his ancestoures at his church in the Towne of Well."

This tablet was also brought to the new church of S. John.

Hackney old church was a very fashionable sanctuary in the seventeenth century.

In the year of grace 1667, Mr. Pepys was informed that "at Hackney Church they have a fine pair of organs, which play

---

* *Descent of the Baroness Burdett-Coutts from John Nevill, last Lord Latimer :*—
Lucy, Third daughter of John Nevill, last Lord Latimer, married Sir William Cornwallis, by whom she had four daughters. Frances, the eldest, married Sir Edmund Withipool, and had issue William, who died in 1645, leaving an only daughter, who married Leicester Devereux, Viscount Hereford. Their daughter, Frances Devereux, married Viscount Tracy, by whom she had issue Elizabeth Tracy, who married Robert, eldest son of Sir Robert Burdett, and had issue Sir Robert Burdett, fourth Baronet of Foremark. He married Elizabeth, only daughter of Sir Charles Sedley, Bart., by whom he had a son, Francis. This son married Mary Eleanor, daughter of William Jones, Esq., of Ramsbury Manor, co. Wilts, and died in 1794, leaving a son—the celebrated Sir Francis Burdett, the father (by Sophia, daughter of Thomas Coutts, Esq.) of the Baroness Burdett-Coutts.—*Vide Pedigree by Stephen Tucker, Esq., Somerset Herald; given in Mr. Simpson's "Memorials of Hackney." Privately printed.*

while the people sing," consequently, on the 21st of April, Mr. Pepys went dressed in his best, and found great difficulty in obtaining a seat.

"My wife and Mercer ventured into one pew and I into another. A knight and his lady were very civil to me—being Sir George Viner and his lady—rich in jewels, but most in beauty—almost the finest woman that I ever saw. That which I went chiefly to see was the young ladies of the schools, whereof there is great store—very pretty *—and also the organ, which is handsome, and tunes the psalms, and plays with the people, which is mighty pretty."

Hackney old church was pulled down in 1798; and the church of S. Augustine is now known as the church of S. John.

＊

— — —

HOLT CHURCH, LEICESTERSHIRE.—Over the porch :—

Thomas Nevill of Holt, Knight, built this porch at his coste.—A.D. 1635.

The church has small transepts; that on the north is separated from the nave by an iron screen, and is entirely occupied by monuments of the Nevill family.

Against the east wall there is an alabaster tomb, supported by three small pilasters of black marble, on which appears the effigy of an armed knight, with short hair and pointed beard, his head reclining on a cushion, his right hand on his girdle, the left, with his sword under it, lies down by his side.

Against the wall, over this tomb, upon pedestals, are two cherubs, one holding a spade, the other kneeling on a death's head, adorned with hour glasses, etc., and between the cherubs, on a square of white marble, are the arms:—Quarterly 1 and 4, Nevill of Raby and Holt. 2 and 3, or fretty of 12 pieces, gules. On a canton, per pale ermine, and of the field, a galley with sails furled,

* The young ladies of the schools must have taken a leaf out of Mr. Pepys' diary, for, in 1711, *The Spectator* asserts that they went on in the most winsome way, glancing out from behind their fans to the utter agitation of all men. At last matters came to such a pass that the following notice appeared in *The Advertiser*, Jan. 9, 1712:—"All ladies who come to church in the new-fashioned hoods are desired to be there before divine service begins, lest they divert the attention of the congregation." The days of the fan and the non-academic hood are now numbered, for girl graduates are raised even in Hackney. The lady principal of a Hackney college assures us, in a recent prospectus, that "her system of education aims at the most complete and intelligent development of the dispositions." This, like the "fine suit of flowered tabby vest and coloured camlotte tunic" of our old friend Pepys, is "*mighty pretty !*"

sable. Crest out of a ducal coronet, vert. A bull's head, ermine, armed or. Below the arms is the following inscription :—

> This monument is erected in memory of
> Sir Thomas Nevill, Knight,
> Who had two wives; Jane the daughter of
> Toby Haughton, Esq.,
> His second wife being Elizabeth Ferne,
> Sir John Ferne's widow.
> By his first wife he had seaven sons and three daughters:
> Thomas (who died an infant), Henry, William,
> Thomas, Nevill, Clement, and George.
> Daughters: Dorothy, Mary, and Jane.
> He lyeth buried in the upper end of the chancill,
> and dyed the 2nd of March, Anno Dom. 1636,
> In the yeare of his age 81.

Against the west wall, there is an alabaster monument having under a canopy, the curtains of which are held up by two angels, the effigy of a lady in black, with sleeves open or sashed, kneeling on a cushion, her hands joined, and raised in devotion; before her on an altar tomb her book opened, and at the top a death's head. Arms :—Argent, a chevron embattled between three lions rampant, sable. Thursby impaling quarterly Nevill and Nevill as before. Inscription :—

> Here lyes shee dead that yet doth live.
> Cause she dying, life did give,
> Her vertuous life prepar'd a way
> For the peace of her last day,
> And her devotion, at her death,
> Opened Heavne with her breath.
> Thither was she making hast
> When she prayed and liv'd her last,
> Leaving behinde the worlde to shame
> The glory of a spotlesse name.
> Surviving thus in heaven and earth,
> Both in herself and in her birth.
>
> In memory of Jane Thursby, wife of
> Christopher Thursby of Bocking, in the
> County of Essex, Esquire.
> She died the 10th day of October, 1631,
> and left behinde her 2 sonnes,
> William and Nevill.
> Deflevit frater ejus Clemens Nevill.

A large marble table monument beside the west wall in the same transept bears the following inscription :—

This monument was erected at the proper cost and chardg of Sir Thomas Nevill, Knight, of this place. Anno. Dom. 1633. In memorie of his grandfather, Sir Thomas Nevill, Knight, who departed this life the 5th of March, 1569, and hee lyeth buried in the upper part of the chanscell.

Arms:—Nevill of Raby and Holt, as in the first mentioned monument.

On the west wall of the transept there is also a marble tablet bearing the following inscription:—

NE VILE VELIS.
To the memory of
Cosmas Henry Joseph Nevill of Holt, Esq.
He was born 1st of February, 1716, O.S.
Lived a pattern of Prudence, and Piety, and every Christian
and social virtue.
Died 20th September, 1763, N.S.
And is here interred.
Also of his wife, Lady Mary Lee, second daughter of George
Henry, Earl of Litchfield, by his Lady, Frances Hales.
She was born in 1722; married 31st July, 1742, O.S., and
Departed this life in London, 25th July, 1758, N.S.
Her body remains there interred in South Audley Street Chapel.
They left issue George, Henry, Mary, Charles, Cosmas,
William, Frances, and Anne.
R.Q.P.
To the best of parents, George Nevill erected this monument.

Arms:—Quarterly 1 and 4 Nevill of Raby and Holt, impaling, argent, a fess between three crescents, sable.

NOTE.—The daughter, Frances, mentioned above, was buried in the north aisle of Bath Abbey, with this epitaph:—

Here lyes the body of Miss Frances Nevill, the daughter of
Cosmas Nevill of Holt, in Leicestershire, Esquire;
By the Hon. Mary Lee, daughter of
George Henry, Earl of Litchfield,
Who departed this life May 4th, 1772,
In the 22nd year of her age.

Marble tablet on the north wall of chancel:—

NE VILE VELIS.
In memory of Cosmas Nevill, Esq.,
Who departed this life on the 1st June, 1829,
Aged 82 years.
Whose virtues and example will long live
In the remembrance of his family and friends;
Also of Maria Annabella Nevill, his wife,
Who departed this life on the 31st January, 1832.

The Raby arms impaling three crescents.

On the same wall, nearer the altar, is another marble tablet:—

NE VILE VELIS.
In memory of
Charles Nevill, Esq.,
Who departed this life on 18th Oct., 1848,
Aged 57 years.
Also of his wife, Lady Georgiana Nevill,
Youngest daughter of Richard, Second Earl of Lucan,
Who departed this life on 13th July, 1849.
Aged 50 years.
Requiescat in pace.

Arms :—Nevill of Raby and Holt impaling Lucan.

On the south wall of the chancel a marble tablet bears the following inscription :—

Sacrum Memoriæ.
Dilecissimæ (heu nuper) conjugis
Annæ Nevill Guilmi Wilkinson Armigeri Londinensis,
Filiæ unicæ ac hæredis
Quæ relictis post se Anna et Melior filiabus.
Filiumq, enixa, nomine Henricum
Grassante heu bello vix gavisa, at paci data
Die Septembris 21, A.D. 1644.
Quiescit in Domino.
Posuit flevitque superstes Guill. Nevill.

Achievment in South Transept.—Migliorucci impaling *Nevill.*
Gules, an eagle displayed argent, crowned and legged, or. This coat is half covered by another in pale ; or, a lion rampant azure ; over all a fess embattled, gules ; a chief azure, three fleur de lis, or.

(NOTE.—The Lady Migliorucci died March 30, 1742, according to the register at Medbourn, a village adjoining Nevill Holt.)

Nevill and Nevill on an escutcheon of pretence, argent a saltire engrailed between four roses, gules. *Napier.*

LITTLEBURY, Essex.—The chancel of this church was restored by the present Lord Braybrooke, regardless of cost, to the memory of his father and mother. The family vault was formerly in Saffron Walden Church, but is now in Littlebury Churchyard.

The following notices occur in the parish registers :—

Jane, Lady Braybrooke, died Sep. 30th, 1856, aged 57.
Richard Griffin Neville, Baron Braybrooke, died March 19th, 1858, aged 74.
Richard Cornwallis Neville, died Feb. 28th, 1861, aged 40.

MEREWORTH, Kent.—In this church a splendid monument was erected to the memory of Lady Mary Fane, daughter of Henry Nevill, 33rd Baron Burgavenny, with the following inscription :—

"Here sleepeth in the Lord with certain hope of Resurrection, the body of that High-borne lady, Mary, Baroness Despenser and Burwash, who departed this transitory life into an æternal, upon the 28th day of June, Anno. Dom. 1626, and the 72nd yeare of her age. She was sole daughter and heire to Henry, Baron of Abergavenny, all which Three Baronies were derived to him from Elizabeth, sole daughter and heire of William Beauchamp, Baron of Abergavenny and Earl of Worcester, his great-grandmother, and from Isabella Despencer, her mother. This noble lady was wife only to one husband, Sir Thomas Fane, Knight of Badsell, in Kent, whoe left her a widowe at the age of 35 years, and he left this life the 28th day of February, Anno. Dom. 1589, in the 52nd yeare of his age. He was first buried at the Church of Tudley in Kent, and now in obedience to the command of her last will, her executors, executrix, her humble daughter-in-law, Mary, Countess Dowager of Westmorland, whoe erected in her memory this monument in the year 1639, hath translated his body to accompany her's heere until the general day of the Resurrection."

For other monuments at Mereworth and Narden, *vide Part II., Chap. X.*

SAFFRON WALDEN CHURCH, Essex.—A white marble monument is placed against the west wall of the south chancel, with representations of the helmets and swords of the deceased. It bears the following inscription :—

Sacred to the memory of two gallant young officers, the third and fifth sons of Lord and Lady Braybrooke, who, having accompanied their regiments to the Crimea, were both cut off in the short space of one week whilst nobly fighting for their Queen and their country.

The Honourable Henry Aldworth Neville, Captain in the Grenadier Guards, after sharing in the glories of Alma, was mortally wounded in the battle of Inkerman, Nov. the 5th, 1854, and expired a few hours after. Aged 30 years.

The Honourable Grey Neville, Cornet in the 5th Dragoon Guards, died in the Hospital at Scutari, Nov. the 11th, 1854, of wounds received in the charge of Balaclava, October the 25th. Aged 24.

"In the sight of the unwise they seemed to die, and their departure is taken for misery, and their going from us to be utter destruction ; but they are in peace."— *Wisdom, III. Chapter, 2nd and 3rd verses.*

STAINDROP CHURCH.—Leland says that the south aisle was the burial place of the line of Raby, and in especial of "three ladys."* A question arises whom of the line of Nevill are these three female effigies (one of which still wears the coronal mentioned by Leland) intended to represent? From the architecture of the canopied arch 1300 is the very highest period which can be assigned for the sepulture of the individuals commemorated. Mary Fitz-Ranulph, grandmother of Ralph Nevill (who founded the chantries in 1343), died in 1320, but is buried at Middleham. Eufemia and Margery, first and second vives of John, Lord Nevill, are the only females of the line whose decease took place between 1300 and 1343, of whose place of burial there is no record, and to them perhaps the two principal effigies may be fairly attributed.—*Raine.*

"Rafe Nevill, the first Erl of Westmerland is buried yn a right stately tumbe of alabaster yn the quire of Stanthorp College, and Margarete his first wife on the lift hond of hym, and on the right hond lyith the ymage of Johon his second wife; but she is buried at Lincoln by her mother."—*Leland.*

"The tomb is of alabaster with rich niches at the sides. The Earl is represented in plated armour, a pointed helmet, with a flowered wreath, and mail gorget. In the frontlet of the helmet the letters I. H. S., and from the sides a strap charged with S. S. closed by a triple ring. He has a large pair of curled whiskers. The seams of his armour are richly ornamented. The saltire is on his breast; a belt crosses him with a sword at his left side, and a rich studded belt girds round the flaps of his armour, under which is a skirt of mail; his knee pieces, and the beltings and seams of his cuises and gabardines, and the instep pieces are also richly ornamented. Under his head is his helmet, supported by an angel, with the bull's head his crest. At his feet a lion, and behind the lion two monks at desk. His second wife Joan, daughter of John of Gaunt, at his left hand is habited in a mantle, kirtle, and surcote, all richly edged and faced; her hair braided and coomed with quatrefoils with a cordon from two lozenge-fashioned studs; her sleeves buttoned to the wrists; on her head, which rests on two

---

* "In the wall of this isle appere the tumbes and images of three ladys whereof one hath a crounet, and a tumbe of a man child, and a flat tumbe *varii marmoris.* There is a flat tumbe also with a plain ymage of brasse, and a scripture wher is buried Richard, sun and heire to Edward, Lord of Bergavenny." The *ymage and scripture* have long since disappeared. Lord Edward Nevill here alluded to lies in the Priory Church of Abergavenny.

cushions, the undermost tasselled, supported by three angels, is a coronet, and round a collar of S. S., fastened with a triangular ring and a medal appendant. His first wife, Margaret Stafford, on his right hand has a similar coronet and collar of S. S., at the feet of each of the ladies are two dogs collared, peeping out from under their robes, and at the feet of all two monks kneeling at their desks. The whole work was (from apparent remains) gilded and painted. It represents the purest style of the best age of sepulchral monuments."—*Gough*.

"The sides of the altar tomb are richly adorned with architectural decorations, corbels, pinnacles, and niches, surmounted by elegant little minarets with pointed roofs. At the feet of each of the figures are two chantry priests, with open missals, celebrating divine offices; these are in a sadly mutilated state, the heads being broken off. All the figures have the collar of S. S. Under the Earl's head is a helmet bearing the crest of the family, a bull's head, and on his surcoat is a saltire; Gules a saltire Argent, being their coat. Two dogs, wearing collars studded with bells, are at the feet of the Countesses; these animals, so frequently found with the figures of females on tombs, are the appendages of high rank. They are, indeed, the ladies' pet. Thus Chaucer:—

> "Of small houndes had she, that she fedde
> With rosted flesh and milk, and wastel brede,
> But sore wept she if one of them were dead."
> —*Vide Stothard's Monumental Effigies.*

"The females are similarly habited in a mantle, kirtle, and surcoat, richly edged and faced; the hair is braided and adorned with quatrefoils, and enclosed within a covering richly wrought; round their necks are collars of S. S., fastened with a triangular ring, and a metal appendant; and on each side of their heads is a coronet studded with precious stones. The arms of both the principal figures are broken off, and the terminations representing the kneeling priests are sadly defaced. The canopy work of the small shrines on each side has also suffered great dilapidation, partly from the removal of the tomb, and partly in consequence of its present unprotected situation. Although not a single canopy is now entire, enough remains to furnish a very precise idea of the pristine beauty and magnificence of this costly monument."—*Blore's Monumental Remains.*

Nothing in ancient or modern art can surpass the grace, refinement, and delicacy of the delineation of the Earl's effigy. Witness the exquisite finish of the camail, every portion of which looks as fresh and fine as if sculptured yesterday.

All archæologists must deplore the condition of this monument, which, as a work of art, may be considered priceless in its matchless beauty. *It is a question surely worthy of consideration whether it could not be protected from future spoliation by being surrounded by some light railing sufficiently far from the tomb to admit of it being seen*, a work very successfully accomplished at Harewood Church, and elsewhere.—*Vide Paper in the Antiquary, June*, 1881.

This monument formerly stood within the altar rails, and was seriously injured by removal to its present position at the west end of the church. It was further abused by being subjected to the influence of a stove placed in proximity to it. How *could* vicars and churchwardens be so stupid?

The Rev. H. C. Lipscomb describes Staindrop Church as "a dreadful place" in 1846, the year of his institution. The church in his time has been judiciously restored, the old stove has long ago disappeared, and no harm has been done of late years to the Nevill monuments, though they occupy a perilous position.

I notice that a marble monument of one of the Dukes of Cleveland, which stands immediately in front of the altar, and would look better elsewhere, is carefully covered over.

The large wood monument in the north-west corner of the church formerly stood in the chancel, and has been mutilated by removal. It represents Henry Nevill, fifth Earl of Westmoreland. By his will, dated 1563, he desired burial in the church of Staindrop. The Earl is recumbent between two of his wives. He is in complete armour, except the head, which is bare; the hair curled, and the beard pointed; the hands bare and elevated; the feet rest on a greyhound. The females are in the dress of the age, stiff and without ornament; their hands clasped and elevated. The effigy of the third wife is deficient. The north and south sides of the tomb are each divided into four compartments, in every one of which is placed the effigy of one of the Earl's eight children, in the dress of the times, and above them their several names—Elinor, Catherine, Rafe, Charls, Edward, Ihon, Mare, Adelin. The Lady Adeline was the last survivor of the wreck of her family. The seventh name is effaced, likewise the eighth figure, that of Madeline.

An inscription in raised letters runs round the margin of the tomb, beginning on the west :—

This tombe, made in the yeare of our Lord God, 1560, and in ye second yeare of Elizabeth, by the grace of God, Queene of England, France, and Ireland, defender of the fayth, by the commandement of the right honourable Henry, Erle of West-merland, for himself and his three wives, that is to say Anne, daughter to the Erle of Rutland, and Jane and Margaret, daughters—(the rest is lost.)

Under the panels :—

> All you that come
> To the Church to praye
> Sa Pater noster and a crede for
> To have mercy
> Of us and all our progenye.
> Made by the Ha
> Ndis of John Tarbotons.

The east and west ends had each three carved shields, charged with different quarterings, the details of which are given in Surtees.

"In the year 1343, Ralph de Nevill obtained license from Prior Fossor and the Convent to found three chantries in Staindrop Church. How the Convent became entitled to exercise this juris-diction is not easy to prove; the records remain silent, save as to the fact. Bishop Bury then held the See, and the rolls of his time show no confirmatory instrument. Probably the south aisle was appropriated for chantry purposes. Bishop Hatfield granted license, Jan. 24, 1378, to Ralph, first Earl of Westmoreland, to erect and found a college or hospital at Staindrop. The church of Latham in Lancashire, which was a cell to Durham, and Brigham Church in Cumberland, were appropriated to this hospital in aug-mentation of its revenue. The original foundation was for one custos, eight chaplains, four secular clerks, six esquires, six gentle-men, and six other poor persons. Probably the Earl intended this house for the reception of any of his retainers who should become reduced by misfortunes, or otherwise disabled."—*Hutchinson.* It was endowed at the Dissolution with £170 4s. 6d. per ann. in the whole, and £126 5s. 10d. clear.—*Tanner's Notitia.*

"In digging the earth away from the chancel of Staindrop Church, under the tomb of the first Earl of Westmoreland, *it having been moved to the other end of the church to make the family vault of the Earl of Darlington,* the workmen came to the skeleton of the Earl, quite entire, which was of uncommon large bones, and appeared to have been a very tall man. One of the leg bones exhibited a number of hard pimples, and was of a red colour, whence it was supposed that he must have had a diseased leg." *Brancepeth MS. Signed, M.T.*

WALTHAM, ST. LAWRENCE, Berkshire.—In the parish church there is a stately monument to Sir Henry Nevill of Billingbeer (son of Sir Edward Nevill of Aldington, ancestor of the present Lord Braybrooke). It exhibits the statue of the knight in kneeling position, and facing the east. Behind him are the statues of his two wives, also his son in armour, and the son's wife. Underneath are six Latin verses, and the following epitaph :—

"Here lyeth Sir Henry Nevill, Knight, descended of the Neviles, Barons of Abergavenny, who were a branch of the House of Westmerland. He was (besides Martial Service) of the Privy Chamber to King Henry the Eight and King Edward the Sixth. He died the 13th of January, 1593. Issue he had by Dame Elizabeth, sole heir to Sir John Gresham, Knight, by Dame Frances, sole heire to Sir Henry Thwaites, Knight, which Dame Elizabeth died 6th November, 1573. Dame Frances Gresham buried the 27th October, 1580, and are both here also buried with Elizabeth Nevell the eldest daughter."

Sir Henry Nevill, the son of this nobleman, was knighted by Queen Elizabeth, and became a very eminent statesman in her reign.

WARWICK.—Beauchamp Chapel.—Nearly in the centre of the chapel stands the costly and magnificent monument of the founder, Richard Beauchamp. It consists of a high tomb of grey Purbeck marble, bearing his recumbent effigy. The sides of the tomb are divided into five compartments, and each end into two compartments. Each compartment contains a large canopied niche, and each of these niches is flanked by divisions of sunk panel work, with a smaller niche above. The principal canopied niches contain seven male and seven female "weepers." Commencing with the figure at the west end of the south side, and going round the tomb from left to right, we find representations of the following persons : –

1st Figure—RICHARD NEVILL, Earl of Salisbury, holding a scroll in his right hand.
2nd—EDMUND BEAUFORT, Duke of Somerset.
3rd—HUMPHREY STAFFORD, Duke of Buckingham, husband to Anne, daughter of Ralph Nevill, Earl of Westmoreland.
4th—JOHN TALBOT, the great Earl of Shrewsbury.
5th—RICHARD NEVILL, the Kingmaker.

N N

At the East End.

6th—GEORGE NEVILL, Lord Latimer, holding a rosary.

7th—ELIZABETH, wife of Lord Latimer, holding a chaplet of beads.

North Side.

8th—ANN, wife of Richard Nevill, Earl of Salisbury and Warwick. She is represented holding her right hand to her chin, a rosary being in her left hand.

9th—MARGARET, Countess of Shrewsbury.

10th—ANN, Duchess of Buckingham, and daughter of Ralph Nevill, first Earl of Westmoreland.

11th—ELEANOR, Duchess of Somerset.

12th—ALICE, daughter of Thomas Montagu, Earl of Salisbury, and wife of Richard Nevill, Earl of Salisbury.

At the Head of the Tomb.

13th—CICELY, daughter of Richard Nevill, Earl of Salisbury.

14th—HENRY BEAUCHAMP, son of Richard, Duke of Warwick.

Elizabeth, Lady Latimer, third daughter of Richard Beauchamp (the founder), was buried in this chapel. Her son, Sir Henry Nevill, and her son-in-law, Oliver Dudley (both slain at Edgcote), were likewise buried here. Her husband, George Nevill, is, by tradition, reported as resting by her side. Joan, widow of Sir Nenry Nevill, left instructions in her will that she would lie in the same company. Leland visited the chapel in 1539, and failed to find any monument to the memory of Sir Henry; so that the will of Lady Latimer was apparently neglected. I append a copy of this instrument :—

"My body to be interred in the Chapel of our Lady, in the Collegiate Church at Warwick, which the right famous, renowned, honourable, and Christian Prince of noble memory, my lord, my father, Sir Richard Beauchamp, late Earl of Warwick, caused and ordained to be made, and that my said body be laid over both the head of my lord and father, between my natural born son, Harrie Latimer, and Oliver Dudley, late my son-in-law; and I will that there be four several stones of fair marble, with images upon them of copper and gilted, convenient for mine estate and their degrees, with the epitaphs of our births and deceases, and other meetly things, to such purpose written upon the same stones, be purveyed and laid upon us, and the like stone upon my lord my husband. Furthermore, I will that there be bought a pair of goodly vestments of white damask, powdered with bears and ragged staves of gold, and in the orfraie my scutcheon to be well and richly embroidered, given and delivered to the said chapel in Warwick; a vestment of black stuff, with a like scutcheon in the orfraie, to be used in the church for my lord my husband's soul."
—*Test. Vetusta*, Vol. I., p. 358.

WELL CHURCH, Yorkshire.—Against the east wall of the south aisle there is a well-cut monument of Sir John Nevill, the last Lord Latimer, in York stone, erected by his son-in-law, the Earl of Exeter, in 1596. The effigy is in armour, and the face seems intended for a portrait. The monument was formerly protected by iron rails, and stood against the south wall of the chancel. The inscription is as follows :—

> Here lyeth buried Sir John Nevill,
> Knight, last Lord Lattimer, who died
> the 23rd of April, 1577, who married the Lady
> Lucy, the eldest daughter of the erle of
> Worseter, and shee lyeth buried in Hacknee
> Church by London, and by her left four
> Daughters, whose matches
> are hereunder expressed.

The shield over the inscription bears the arms of Nevill, with seventeen other quarterings.* Supporters, two Griffins. Crest, a Griffin. Motto—*Sic transit gloria mundi*. Four shields are placed below the effigy, for the matches of the four daughters, but only two of them have been supplied. Percy impaling Nevill, and Cecil impaling Nevill. The other two shields are divided in pale, and have the arms of Nevill on the sinister side, but the dexter on both is plain. The inscription formerly appeared above the effigy; but, at the restoration of the church, the monument was moved from its original position, and the inscription is now placed on the left side of the effigy—an arrangement much to be deprecated, as the beauty of the monument is entirely marred.

The Lady Lucy died at Hackney, February 23rd, 1582, aged 59. The "matches" of her daughters were expressed in verse composed by her son-in-law, Sir William Cornwallis. His poetry was formerly to be seen engraved upon her tomb; and this was how it ran :—

* 1. NEVILL—Gules, saltire argent, an annulet for difference.
2. OLD NEVILL—Or fretty gules, on a canton parted per pale, ermine and or, a ship rigged sable.
3. BEAUCHAMP—Gules, a fess between six cross crosslets or.
4. WARWICK—Checky, or and azure, a chevron ermine.
5. BERKELEY—Gules, a chevron between crosses patée argent six and four.
6. GERARD—Gules, a lion passant guardant argent, crowned or.
7. LISLE—Or, a fess between two chevrons sable.
8. TYAS—Argent, a chevron gules.
9. VERE—Quarterly, gules and or, in the first quarter a mullet argent.
10. BULBECKE—Vert, a lion rampant argent.
11. SAMFORD—Barry wavy of six, argent and azure.
12. BODLESMERE—Argent, a fess between two bars genelles gules.
13. A saltire.
14. HOWARD—Gules, on a bend between six crosslets fitched argent, an ermine spot for difference.
15. SCALES—Gules, six escallopes argent.
16. Parted pale, and a lion passant.
17. STAFFORD—Or, a chevron within a bordure engrailed gules.
18. LITCHFIELD—Parted per chevron argent and sable, in chief three leopards' heads caboshed or.

> " Such as she is, such surely shall ye be,
>   Such as she was, such if ye be, be glad ;
>   Fair in her youth, tho' fat in age she grew,
> Virtuous in both ; whose gloss did never fade.
> Though long alone she led a widow's life,
>   Yet never lady lived a truer life.
> From Wales she sprang, a branch of Worster's race,
>   Graft in a stock of Brownes, her mother's side ;
> In Court she held a Maid of Honor's place,
>   Whilst youth in her, and she in Court did bide.
> To John Lord Latymer, then she became a wife,
> Four daughters had they, breathing yet in life.
> Earl of Northumberland the first to wife,
>   The next the heir of Baron Burleigh chose ;
> *Cornwallis hap the third for term of life,*
>   And Sir John Danvers pluct the youngest rose.
> Their father's heirs ; them mothers all she saw.
> Pray for or praise her, make your list you law."

Sir William Cornwallis must have been a person of considerable *nonchalance*, if one may judge him by the spirit of his muse.

Against the south wall of the south aisle there is a black marble table monument, with the following inscription, inlaid in brass, to the memory of the Lady Dorothea, first wife of John, fourth Lord Latimer, and mother of the last lord :—

𝕳𝔦𝔠 𝔧𝔞𝔠𝔢𝔱 𝔇'𝔫𝔞 𝔇𝔬𝔯𝔬𝔱𝔥𝔢𝔞 𝔑𝔢𝔟𝔢𝔩𝔩, 𝔮'𝔫'𝔡'𝔪, 𝔲𝔵𝔬𝔯 𝔍𝔬𝔥'𝔦𝔰 𝔑𝔢𝔟𝔢𝔩𝔩, 𝔪𝔦𝔩𝔦𝔱' 𝔣𝔦𝔩𝔦𝔦 𝔢𝔱 𝔥𝔞𝔢𝔯𝔢𝔡 𝔇'𝔪 𝔡𝔢 𝔏𝔞𝔱𝔶𝔪𝔢𝔯, 𝔲𝔫𝔞 𝔰𝔬𝔯𝔬𝔯𝔦𝔦 𝔢𝔱 𝔥𝔞𝔢𝔯𝔢𝔡𝔦𝔦 𝔍𝔬𝔥'𝔦𝔰 𝔙𝔢𝔢𝔯 𝔈𝔬𝔪𝔦𝔩' 𝔒𝔯𝔬𝔫𝔦𝔢 𝔮𝔲𝔞𝔢 𝔬𝔟𝔦𝔦𝔱 𝔳𝔦𝔦 𝔡𝔦𝔢 𝔉𝔢𝔟𝔯𝔲𝔞𝔯𝔦𝔦, 𝔄.𝔇. M. Dni. XXVI. 𝔠𝔲𝔧. 𝔞.'𝔦.'𝔢. 𝔭𝔯𝔬𝔭𝔦𝔠𝔦𝔢𝔱𝔢𝔯 𝔇𝔢𝔲𝔰.

Whitaker describes two very ancient slabs of black marble, tapering from the head to the feet.   On one of these the inscription is almost wholly obliterated, and that on the other is so extremely imperfect that it is scarcely safe even to guess at the person to whom it belonged.   The characters, however, are Longobardic, and therefore not later than the time of Edward III.; and they have surrounded the stone in two parallel lines on each side and at the ends.

Whitaker considers it most probable that this formed a portion of the tomb of Margery de Thweng, second wife of Ralph, Lord Nevill, who died in the fifth year of Edward III.   Could it be known how the lines were at first connected, the difficulty would be greatly diminished.   The following attempt to decipher and supply it may perhaps go as far as any antiquary can venture without imputation of rashness :—

> HIC *jacet* MER*ge* R*ia* DO*mina*
> N*evil uxor secum*
> . DA R DN*i* NE*vil cui* DEVS *propicietur.* A*men*
> M*er* CI *ei*T DE LA*lme*

It seems evident that the outer line beginning with CI is old French.—*Vide Whitaker's Richmondshire.*

A manuscript in the College of Arms mentions the following inscription :—

"Circa ferream clausuram, miles, D'n's de Latimer, et Anna uxor ejus filia Humfridi Stafford, D'n'i de Latymer filii Henrici Nevill militis, filii Georgii Nevill, D'ni de Latymer tertii et Elizabethæ uxoris prædicti Georgii tertii, filii Ranulphi de Nevill Comitis Westmerlandiæ et Johannæ uxoris ejus, filiæ et unius hæredum Richardi de Beauchampe Comitis Warwici et Elizabethæ uxoris ejus, filiæ et hæredis Thomæ Domini de Barkley et Margaretæ uxoris ejus, filiæ et hæredis Warini Lisle. Orate pro hiis et omnibus fidelibus."

WORKSOP.—Inscription on the "fair tomb" of Thomas de Nevill, Lord Furnival, in the chapel of St. Peter, on the south side of the chancel of the Priory Church :—

> "This Thomas Nevyll first gan uppere,
> Brother that was to Erle Westmoryland,
> By Dame Johanne Lord Furnival we understand,
> And he marryed dame Johanne, daughter to Sir William,
> And they had a doghter, dame Molde that hight,
> With which doghter marryed the most noble of fame
> Sir John Talbot warryor, that noble Knight, &c.
> Dame Johanne is beryed aboven the hye quere
> Next Thomas Nevyll that was her husband,
> In alabaster an ymage Sir Thomas right nere,
> As he is tumulate on her right hand ;
> And by her doghter Molde, we understand,
> Went out the Furnivals, as by their name,
> As Lovetots by dame Molde afore did the same,
> And Sir Thomas Nevyll, Treasorer of England,
> Aboven the quere is tumulate, his tumbe is to see
> In the middes, for most Royal there it doth stand ;
> And his doghter Molde of right hye degree
> In Saint Marye Chapel tumulate lyeth shee,
> Afore our blessed Lady, next the stall side,
> There may she be seen, she is not to hyde."
> —*Monast. Angl. ii. Stemma Fundatorum Prioratus de Wyrksop.*

ADDENDA.—NEVILL MURAL TABLETS.

BIRLING CHURCH, KENT.

Shields in Chancel, north side.—Sir Christopher Nevill, Knight of the Bath, ob. June, 1649.

Henry Nevill, Lord Abergavenny, married Mary, daughter of Earl of Dorset, Lord Treasurer of England, ob. December 24th, 1641.

Sir Thomas Nevill, Knight of the Bath, married Frances, daughter of Henry, Baron Mordaunt, ob. 1628.

Sir Edward Nevill, Dom. Burgavenny, ob. December 1st, 1622.

Henricus Nevill, Dom. Burgavenny, married Frances, daughter of Earl of Rutland and Baron Roos, ob. February 9th, 1586.

George Nevill, Dom. Bergavenny, Knight of the Garter, Constable of Dover Castle, and Warden of the Cinque Ports; married, 1st, Joan, daughter of Thomas Fitzallan, Earl of Arundel; 2nd, Mary, daughter of Duke of Buckingham, ob. 1536.

South Side.—Edward Nevill, Lord Abergavenny, ob. anno 1723.

George Nevill, Lord Abergavenny, ob. March, 1720, ætat 63.

George Nevill, Lord Abergavenny, ob. June 14th, 1666.

John Nevill, Lord Abergavenny, ob. December 12th, 1662.

Shield in recess, north side of the Altar.—In the vault beneath are interred the bodies of Henry Nevill, aged 3 years, and Augusta Nevill, aged 14 months, the children of the Honourable and Rev. William Nevill, Vicar of Birling, youngest son of Henry, Earl of Abergavenny, by Caroline, his wife, who both departed this life March 28th, 1828.

In recess immediately over the foregoing is another shield bearing the Abergavenny arms and motto, *Ne vile velis.*

Large Shield over Family Pew in Chancel.—Sir George Nevill, Milit. Dom. Bergavenny, ob. anno 1492, born at Raby Castle, in Co. Durham, son of Edward, Lord Burgavenny, who was sixth son of Ralph, 1st Earl of Westmoreland, Lord of Staindrope, Branspeth, Sheriff Hoton, Middleham, Warkworth, and Coverham, Earl Marshall of England, Knight of the Garter, Constable of the Tower of London, Warden of the Forests north of the Trent, by Lady Joan Beaufort, daughter of John of Gaunt, Duke of Lancaster, fourth son of King Edward III., and which Edward Nevill married Elizabeth, daughter and heir of Richard Beauchamp, Lord Burgavenny and Earl of Worcester, by Isabel, daughter of Thomas, Baron Le Despencer and Earl of Gloucester. Sir George, Baron Bergavenny, married Margaret, daughter and co-heir of Sir Hugh Fenne, Under-Treasurer of England, and was the father of George, Lord Burgavenny, buried here 1536.

This Lord directed, by his will made at Birling, his body to be buried in the Monastery of St. Pancras, called the Priory of Lewes, Sussex, on the south side of the altar, where he had made a tomb for his body.

"Diste mori mundo vivere diste Deo."

Shield in recess, south side of the Altar.—Here lyeth Lady Frances Bergavenny, ob. 1576, wife of Henry, Lord Bergavenny, and daughter of Thomas Manners, Earl of Rutland and Baron Roos; also, Margaret Nevill, daughter of Edward, Lord Burgavenny, ob. 1602; also, Lady Rachael, wife of Edward Nevill, Lord

Burgavenny, ob. October 15th, 1616; also, Lady Elizabeth, wife of Sir Henry Nevill, Lord Abergavenny, and afterwards wife of Sir William Sedlye, Knight and Baronet, ob. August 15th, anno 1617; also, Lady Caroline Nevill, second wife of Sir Henry Nevill, Lord Abergavenny, and daughter of George, Baron Waur, of Harroden, ob. July 10th, 1641.

"Expectamus adventum Domini Jesu Christi."

Memorial Window in south Aisle.—To the glory of God, and in memory of William Nevill, 4th Earl and 16th Baron of Abergavenny, who died August 17th, 1868. This window was painted and erected as a humble tribute of affection to the memory of a kind father by his three daughters, Caroline, Augusta, and Isabel.

"The memory of the just is blessed."—*Prov.*, x., 7.

Small Memorial Window on north side of Church, over Vestry door.—To the glory of God, and in grateful memory of William Nevill, 4th Earl of Abergavenny, and Caroline, his wife. Erected by the parishioners, A.D. 1874.

"Lovely and pleasant in their lives; in their death they were not divided."

Large Window westward of the above, and in same wall.—To the glory of God, and in memory of Caroline, wife of William, 4th Earl of Abergavenny, who died May 19th, 1873. This window was erected in grateful and affectionate remembrance of a beloved mother by William, Caroline, Augusta, and Ralph.

"Those also which sleep in Jesus will God bring with him."—1 *Thess.*, iv., 14.

Small Memorial Window (Christ blessing little children) north side of Chancel.—In memory of Henry Nevill, aged 3 years, and Augusta Nevill, aged 14 months, who both died on March 28th, 1828.

This window was erected by their parents, the Earl and Countess of Abergavenny.

"Suffer little children to come unto me, and forbid them not, for of such is the kingdom of God."—*Luke*, xviii., 16.

The arms of Sir George Nevill, Lord Bergavenny, who died September 20th, 1492, were placed in the east window of Birling Church—1st, *Nevill;* 2nd, *Warren;* 3rd, *Clare and Despencer*, quartered; 4th, *Beauchamp.* His son, Sir George, who made large additions to the estate, was buried at Birling. Henry, Lord Bergavenny, died at Comforte, February 8th, 1586, and was buried at Birling with great solemnity. Edward, Lord Bergavenny, died 1622, and was buried at Birling. He was succeeded by his son, Sir Henry Nevill, Lord Bergavenny, or Abergavenny, as it came about that time to be called. He had a son, Sir Thomas Nevill, by Frances, daughter of Lord Mordaunt, who died in his lifetime, and was buried at Birling. Sir Henry, Lord Abergavenny, died December, 1641, and was buried at Birling, also his lady who died 1649. George Nevill, Lord Abergavenny, died June 2nd, 1666, and was buried at Birling. Sir Christopher Nevill, Knight, of Newton St. Loe, co. Somerset, died June, 1649, and was buried here; also Lady Catherine Nevill, widow, July 10th, 1649. The registers also show the interments of Lady Frances Abergavenny, September, 1576; the Lady Margaret Nevill, daughter of Edward, Lord Abergavenny, 1602; the Lady Rachel, wife of Edward, Lord Abergavenny, October 15th, 1616; the Lady Elizabeth, first wife of Henry, Lord Abergavenny, August 15th, 1617; John, Lord Abergavenny, December 23rd, 1662. The church of Birling with certain lands was given by Walkelin de Maminot, lord of this place, in 1168, to the Priory of Bermondsey, in Southwark, after which it was appropriated by Walter, Bishop of Rochester. George Nevill, Lord Abergavenny (13th Henry VIII.) enclosed Birling Park and rectory, and all tithes belonging thereto, with 150 acres of land and the advowson of the vicarage, late belonging to the Prior and Convent of S. Saviour, Bermondsey, and held by them by annual pension of 20s. to the Bishop of Rochester.

EXTRACTS FROM BIRLING REGISTERS.

Baptisms.

John Nevill, the sonne of the Right Worshipfull Mr. Edward Nevill, was baptised the eighth (?) day of June, 1588.

1727. St. Margaret's, Westminster.—The Right Honourable George Nevill, Lord of Abergavenny, was born June the 29th, 1727. His Majesty King George the Second, His Grace Lionel, Duke of Dorset, and her Grace the Duchess of Newcastle being sponsors.

Burials.

1576. Frances, Ladie Aburgavenny, wife to the Right Honourable Lord Aburgavenny, was burried the eighth (?) September, 1576.

The Right Honourable Sir Henry Nevill, Knight, Lord Aburgavenny, was burried February 10, 1586.

Margaret Nevill, daughter of Edward Nevill, Lord Aburgavenny, was buried the 6th (?) day of October, anno 1602.

Edward, the second son of the Right Honourable Edward Nevill, Lord Aburgavenny, was burried the sixth of December, 1610.

Lady Rachell, wife to the Right Honourable Edward Nevill, Lord Aburgavenny, was buried the fifteenth day of October, anno Dom. 1616.

Lady Elizabeth, first wife of the Right Honourable Sir Henry Nevill, Lord Aburgavenny, and now wife to Sir Wm. Selby Smyth, (?) Baronet, was burried the 15th day of August, A.D. 1617.

The Right Honourable Edward Nevill, Lord Aburgavenny, was burried the eighth day of December, ann. Dom. 1622.

The Right Honourable Sir Thomas Nevill, sonne and heir apparent (?) to the Right Honourable Sir Henry Nevill, Knight, and Lord Aburgavenny, was burried the sixteenth day of May, an. Dom. 1628.

The Right Honourable Henry, Lord Abergavenny, was buried the 24th of December, 1641.

Sir Christopher Nevill, burried June 27th, 1649.

The Lady Catherine Nevill, widdow, was burried July 10th, 1649.

The Right Honourable John, Lord Abergavenny, was buryed the 23rd December, 1662.

The Right Honourable George, Lord Abergavenny, ye 14th day of June, 1666, was buryed.

EAST HAM CHURCH, ESSEX.

Through the kind attention of Rev. S. H. Reynolds, I am able to add the remainder of the inscription on the tomb of Edmond Nevill, which was considered illegible. That portion which appears above the effigies will be found on page 158.

Northern Tablet under the Figures—

From Princly and from Honorable Blood
By true succession was my high descent
Mallignat Crosses oft Opos'de my good
And adverse chance my stat did circumvent
Yet howsoe're my will was counterchck't
By faith my Earthly hopes on Heave were laid
Assur'd y^t God ye same would not Reiect
Throgh Christ, my Saviour and Redeemer's ayd,
In ioy, Griefe, weale, woe, I my life did spend
In hoop to gaine ye life y^t ne're shall end.
Let Honor, life, and fortune sink or swimm
Thogh God shold kill me I will hoop in him.

South Tablet below Figures—

Amidst a world of Crosses and of Cares
I past my transitory Pilgrimage
By God's great mercie guarded from ye stars
Of world and flesh, and Sathan's cruell rage
The gratious Vertue (Prudence) was my guide
Throgh all ye wavering waves of tottering stat
Sweet Prudence told me, honor henc wold slid
And earthly glorie, must have ending date
W^{ch} made me lay all hoop, all faith, all trust,
In Christ to live in heaven, amongst the Just
My soule doth magnifie ye Lord, my spirit
Reioyceth in my God and Saviour's Merrit.

On a Slab above the Tomb : Southern part—

An Epitaph

Upon the Death of the Right Vertuous faire and Noble Ladie Katherin Nevill,
first daughter of Edmund Earle of Westmerland and Jane his wife, who died a
Virgine the fift of December, 1613, being of the age of xx 3 yeares.

Northern part—

Surviving Marble Choysly Keepe
This Koble Virgine layde to sleepe
A Branche untymeey faln away
From Nevill's Royallised Tree
Great Westmerland too deere a pray
For Death if she could ransom'd bee
Hir name was Katherin. Not in vaine
Hir nature held true reference
Hir Beutie and hir parts againe
Were all compos'd of excelence
Blud, Beuty, Vertue, Did contend
All thies advanc'd in eminence
Which of them, could her most comend
When Death Enamor'd tooke her hence
Yet Marble tell the tyme to come
What earst she was When I am dumbe.

O O

The Vicar of East Ham commends this very interesting old monument to the attention of all whom it may concern.

"In 1641, Jane Nevill, Countess of Westmoreland, did, on the eighteenth of July enfeof Sir Francis Holcroft of Green Street and two parcels of land in Middlemarsh in West Ham : and out of the Rent, which was to be paid in even payments on Lady Day, and Michaelmas Day, 10s. was to be paid for preaching a Sermon on St. John Baptist's day, &c., &c. Also, 5s. a year for repairing the monument of her husband, Edmund Nevill, Lord Latimer, Earl of Westmorland, in the Chancel of East Ham Church."—*Morant's Hist. Essex.*

HOLY TRINITY CHURCH, ERIDGE GREEN, SUSSEX.
Brass on Black Marble Mural Tablet.

In
affectionate remembrance
of
Violet,
Wife of Lord Henry Nevill,
who died on
Christmas Day, 1880,
Aged 25.
This tablet is erected by William, Marquess of Abergavenny.

FLETCHING CHURCH, SUSSEX.

It is reported that several of the Abergavenny Nevills are buried under the church, but there are no records, monuments, or tombstones to substantiate this report, nor were any relics found at the restoration of the church in 1880. In the north transept there is hung, on each side, a small trophy of arms, consisting of helmet, gauntlets, and short sword; one helmet being surmounted by the Nevill bull entire, and the other by the bull's head surrounded by a coronet.

FRANT CHURCH, SUSSEX.
Mural Tablet over the Eridge pew, with Abergavenny arms and motto—
John Nevill,
Third Earl of Abergavenny and Viscount Nevill,
Forty-fifth Baron of Abergavenny.
Born the Twenty-fifth of December,
Seventeen hundred and eighty-nine,
Died the Twelfth of April,
One thousand eight hundred and forty-five.

Brass in chancel floor near the altar rail—
To the glory of God, and in memory of
William Fourth Earl of Abergavenny by whom
this Chancel was built, 1868.
The east window was erected by his widow, 1869.
" The memory of the just is blessed."
The above-mentioned window is a beautiful representation of the Ascension.

PART II.—CHAPTER XIX.

NEVILL BADGES, SEALS, AND SOUVENIRS.

"Upon his surcoat, valiant Nevill bore
A silver saltire, upon martial red."
—Drayton's Baron's Wars, Book I.

*   *   *   *   *

"Lord Westmoreland his antient raised,
The Dun Bull he raised on hye;
Three dogs with golden brave,
Were there set out most royally."
Now spread thy antient, Westmoreland,
Thy Dun Bull fair would we spye;
And thou, the Earl of Northumberland,
Now raise thy Half-moone on hye:
But the Dun Bull is fled and gone
And the half-moone vanish'd away.
—The Rising in the North Countrie.

*   *   *   *   *

WARWICK:—
"The rampant Bear, chained to a ragged staff,
This day I'll wear aloft my Burgonet."
—Henry VI. Part II. Act 5.

*   *   *   *   *

"The Fishere hathe lost his hangulhooke,
Gete theym agayne when it wolle be
The Bere is bound that was so wild
For he hath lost his ragged staffe.
—Political Song. Cott. MS. II., 23.

(The Fishere signifies William Nevill, Lord Fauconberg.)

"Coates of Armes," says Sir John Ferne, "were invented by our wise auncestors to honour and adorne the family of him that had well deserved towardes his countrye." Morgan, who was a great enthusiast in heraldry, quickly deciding that our forefather Adam "had well deserved towardes his countrye," assigned to him a shield gules, and to Eve a shield argent; which latter Adam bore over his as an inescutcheon, his wife being sole heiress. After the Fall the house of Adam became still further distinguished, for the old gentleman bore a garland of fig-leaves, which his son Abel quartered with argent; an apple vert (probably a crab apple), in right of his mother.

More startling even than this is the announcement contained in the *Boke of St. Alban's* that, "of the offspringe of the gentilman Japeth came Habraham, Moyses, Aron, and the Profettys, and also the Kyng of the right lyne of Mary, of whom that gentilman Jhesus, by his moder, Mary, prynce of cote-armure."

In spite of their obsolete jargon and grotesque monstrosities the old heralds have rendered us a vast amount of actual service.

"Many are the incidents but faintly written in the pages of history, which would have remained for ever dark and illegible, but for the light flashed upon them by the torch of heraldry. A shield of arms, a badge, or a rebus depicted on a glass window, painted on a wall, carved on a corbel or a monument, will frequently indicate with unerring precision the date to which such relics are to be ascribed, and whose memory they are intended to perpetuate, when all verbal descriptions are wanting."—*Cussan's Heraldry*.

Let us take one instance. On entering the chancel of Brancepeth from the little chapel of St. John (now used as a vestry), I notice a huge stone effigy lying before me. The shield bears the saltire. I know it to be a Nevill. It bears also the label of cadency called by the old heralds a file of five flambeaux. I know, therefore, that this particular Nevill must have died during the lifetime of his grand-parent, being heir to that grand-parent. History tells us only of one Nevill who so died, viz., Robert de Nevill, who died in 1319, being heir to his grandmother, Mary de Middleham. The details of the monument agree with the supposition that the effigy represents Robert de Nevill; and I go away without any doubt in my mind about the identity of this figure. But in the absence of any heraldic devices upon the shield this would be impossible.

Yet you meet people, alas! scores and hundreds of them, who

tell you that such devices are the devices of the devil, invented to feed the vanity of the few, and excite the envy of the many.

"I would rather be without such things," says my revolutionary friend, and if he speaks *sincerely*, I think he is quite right. A man *is* better without that which he cannot understand or appreciate.

"If we cannot attain to greatness ourselves, we may have our revenge by railing at it in others," says Montaigne.

Rail as you may, you can't improve on Oliver Cromwell. He hated all vanity and lying quite as much as you are supposed to hate such unholy practices. He was simply Oliver Cromwell, the Protector, (though he forgot to protect many of the things that most needed protection.) But their came a time when men commenced to address him as "Your Highness," just to see how he liked it; and he liked it quite as much as a plain girl likes to hear herself described as pretty.

Then the humble Protector spoke of himself as *We, Oliver Cromwell, by*———. Soon an admiring world was favoured with the sight of Oliver's family escutcheon with all its quarterings, and a representation of Oliver himself, in regal robes. Thus the Protector displayed himself as proud a peacock as any of his predecessors, only *his* plumes were borrowed.

I wonder what Master Rolt thought of vanity and lying? Master Rolt was the undertaker at Oliver's funeral, which cost £28,000, and "the said Master Rolt was payde but a small part, if any, of his bill."—*Harl. MSS.*

The original arms of Nevill were, or fretty gules, on a canton, per pale ermine and or, a ship with three masts sable; but in the reign of Henry III., the heiress of the Nevills having married Robert Fitz Maldred of Raby, he assumed the name of Nevill, in honour of his wife, but retained his own arms, viz., gules, a saltire argent. His posterity followed his example, exhibiting differences on the saltire for the purpose of marking the different branches. The eldest branch, however, as Earls of Westmoreland, always bore the saltire plain.

The earliest appearance of this well known bearing occurs on the seal of Robert Fitz Maldred. Planchè considers it to be really the cross of St. Patrick, assumed in commemoration of an ancestor named after that saint. Cospatrick, son of Uchtred, was the direct progenitor of the Lords of Raby.

To Geoffrey Nevill, of Hornby, a roll of arms of the time of

Edward III. attributes the device of a ship. The same roll assigns the saltire to Robert de Nevill of Raby. Planchè regards the ship on the seal of Henry de Nevill (preserved in the Duchy of Lancaster Office, and dating from about 1200), as a mere allusive badge; and he does not think that there is any authority for supposing that the arms given by Surtees at the head of his Nevill pedigree were the original arms of the family.

In a roll of arms of the reign of Henry III. mention is made of "John de Nevill, Cowerde, Mascule d'or et de goules ung quartier de Hermyne; and John de Nevill le Forestier, d'or ung bend de goules croiselles noire."

Alexander Nevill of Raskell, third son of Ralph, Lord Nevill of Raby, bore gules, a saltire ermine. Thomas Nevill, Lord Furnival, gules, on a saltire argent, a martlet sable. Richard Nevill, Earl of Salisbury, gules, a saltire argent, a label of three points checquy, argent and azure. This earl sometimes bore *Nevill* in the second quarter and *Montague* in the first. Wm. Nevill, Lord Fauconberg, bore gules, on a saltire argent, an annulet sable. George Nevill, Lord Latimer, gules, on a saltire argent, a pellet. Edward Nevill, Baron Burgavenny, gules, a saltire argent, a rose of the first.

In a manuscript in the British Museum, dated 1640, forty-five families are mentioned as quartering arms with the Nevills.

The first is Nevill.—Paternal coat (saltire) from the Lords of Raby..

The second is Nevill.—Fretty of + pricy, or and gules, on a canton partie per pale ermyn and or, a shippe of three tops sable, from the Norman Admiral.

The third is Bulmer.—Gules, billete, a lion rampant, or.

The fourth is Fitz Randolph.—Or, a chief endented, azure.

The fifth is Britayne.—Ermine, borne by the name of Eudo, Duke of Britayne, and Earl of Richmonde, progenitor of Fitz Ralph, Lord Middleham, and a near kinsman to the Conqueror. Henry VII. of the House of Lancaster had for his cognizance the rose, parti gules, argent, crowned proper; portcullis crowned. From him the Nevills take the portcullis still shown in the arms of Abergavenny.

The crest of the Nevills of Raby appears in the fourteenth century as a bull's head, and was borne subsequently by Ralph, Lord of Raby, 1437, issuant out of a ducal coronet, and by others of the same family at that period, on a chapeau. Planchè considers it an adaptation of an old badge of the family, a pied or dun bull, assumed in honour of their Bulmer descent. It appears on the seal of Robert de Nevill, husband of Mary Fitz Ranulph, and was affixed to a charter in the possession of the Duke of Norfolk. This seal exhibits a bull grazing, and is circumscribed Robert de Nevill. It is figured in the rare and costly work of the late Henry Drummond, M.P. The earliest seal of the ancient family of Arsic displays a border charged with the heads of twelve bulls. The name of Manasser de Arsic occurs several times in the 12th century in connection with that of Nevill, and Planchè suggests the probability that a lady of the family of Arsic married Gilbert de Nova Villa.— *Vide Norman Ancestry of the Nevills.*

Among the manuscripts of the industrious Vincent in the Heralds' College, there is a Nevill pedigree, wherein the bull's head is given as a crest to the Saxon line. The Norman line has the ship with three pointed shields beneath.

The lion, assigned to the Bulmers as their crest, was, of course, never worn by Bertram de Bulmer, because he died before the introduction of coat armour; but it was invented to quarter with the coat of Fitz Maldred in order that the Bulmer descent might duly appear in the Nevill insignia.

The seal of Ralph Nevill, Lord of Raby, appears on the letter from the Barons of England to Pope Boniface the 8th, anno 1301. —*Vide Plate No.* 1.

"Seals are, of all records, those on which the greatest reliance can be placed ; for being contemporary witnesses, no doubt can exist of their historical value."—*Cussan's Heraldry.*

Of all the Nevill seals that of Richard Nevill, Earl of Warwick, is the most curious and interesting. It was taken from his person after he was slain on the field of Barnet, by Sir Roger Kynaston, Knight of Hardwick, Salop, who was knighted on the occasion by Edward IV. The seal, which is of iron, was preserved in the Kynaston family, and deposited in the latter end of the last century in the British Museum. Dallaway says that between 1430 and 1440 seals were wrought in the highest degree of perfection, and he alludes to this seal as a very fine specimen. The Earl wears on his head the tournament helmet on which are his crest and coronet. His breast plate is globular, with taces, to the lowest of which are tuiles. The scalloped edged sleeves are attached to a silken vest, which, as the fancy of the wearer induced, was worn under or over the armour. The steel burrs and cantle of the saddle are very visible, as well as the saddle cloth. On the horse's head is the chanfron, having the projecting spike and attached to a mainfaire, which extended but a little way down the neck. The caparison is emblazoned on the front portion quarterly, the arms of Monthermer and Montacute quartered, for his maternal descent. On the rear four grand quarters; the first and fourth quarterly, of Beauchamp and Guy, Earls of Warwick; the second and third quarterly, of Clare and Despencer, Earls of Gloucester. On his arm the paternal coat of Nevill, distinguished from that of the Earls of Westmoreland by a label of three points gobonie, argent and azure. Inscription:—"The seal of Richard Nevill, Earl of Warwick, and Lord of Glamorgan and Brecknock." (Sigillum Richardi Comitis Warwici dni: Glormorgancie et Morgancie.)—*Vide Plate No.* 1.

The device of the bear and ragged staff, used as the ensign of the Earls of Warwick from the earliest times, was, according to Rous, "taken from the name of one of the British Earls of Warwick, Arthgal, which signified in the British language a bear; and when another British Earl, named Morvi, had vanquished a giant in a duel, with a young tree plucked up by the roots, and stripped of its branches, in token of that event, there was added to the device of the bear that of the ragged staff."

A manuscript in the Harleian Collection, No. 5,854, folio 23, gives the following badges :—

The Dun Bull for *Nevill:* collar, horns, and chains proper.

The Griffin, or and silver, for *Spencer*.

The Pied Bull for *Raby*.

The Squirrel for *Dabigny*.

The Black Bull, golden collar, for *Clare*.

The Buck for *Nevill*.

A manuscript in the Herald's College bears a representation of the standard of George Nevill, Baron Bergavenny, and Constable of Dover, 1497, whose first wife was the daughter of the Earl of Arundel, and his third of the Duke of Buckingham. The standard bears on a ground per fesse vert and argent, semée of double staples, interlaced or, a bull passant argent, pied sable, collared, chained, hoofed and horned of third, the horns tipped of the first. The points of the standard bear the significant motto :—

> "A Tenir Promesse
> Vient de Noblesse."

Mottoes frequently have an allusion to the arms or crest of the bearer, but by far the greatest number of allusive mottoes may be traced to the family name. Thus the Nevills have *Ne vile velis.* The Vernons have *Ver non semper viret.* The Dixies have *Quod dixi, dixi.* Perhaps the best pun is the *Festina lente* of the Onslow family. The punning motto now used by the Nevills has superseded the more ancient one, *Ou Je Tiens Firme.*

Mottoes are rarely altered, being apparently as hereditary as the arms themselves. The motto, however, of Henry Nevill, 5th Earl of Westmoreland, was, *Esperance me Comforte,* rather an apt motto for him, by the way.

Richard Nevill, Earl of Salisbury, bore for arms on the back of his stall at Windsor, as Knight of the Garter, first and fourth quarter counter quartered, viz:—

1st, Argent, three fusills in fess gules for *Montacute;* 2nd, or, an eagle displayed sable for *Monthermer;* 3rd as 2nd; the 4th as 1st, being the quartered arms of his father-in-law, with which he quartered in the second and third quarters his own paternal coat for *Nevill,* viz., gules a saltire argent, and in chief a label of three points compony of the last and azure.

The arms of George Nevill, Baron Bergavenny, and Maria, his wife, daughter of the Duke of Buckingham, appear in the window of the chapel of Lincoln's Inn.

The following notes are given in *Burke's Armoury:*—

NEVILL, Scotton, Lincoln.—Gules, three fusils in fesse argent, a bordure engrailed or.

NEVILL, Faldingworth, Lincoln.—Or, a chief indented vert, over all a bend gules.

NEVILL, Chenston, co. Stafford.—Gules, a saltire argent, charged with a crescent sable; crest, a griffin passant or, charged on the breast with a crescent.

NEVILL, Chevet, co. York (Granted 1513).—Argent, a saltire gules, a mullet and label of three points vert; crest, a greyhound's head erased or, charged on neck with a label of three points vert.

NEVILL, Thornton Brigg, co. York.—Gules on a saltire argent, a mullet pierced sable.

NEVILE, Grove, co. Nottingham.—Gules, a saltire argent; crest, out of a ducal coronet a bull's head pied. This was a branch of the Raby Nevills, derived from the marriage of George Nevill, Esq., with Barbara, sister of Sir John Hercy, of Grove. The last male heir in the direct line, Edward Nevill, of Grove, Esq., was created a baronet in 1674, but died S.P. in 1686, when the title expired.

NEVILL, Thorney, co. Nottingham.—Derived from George Nevill, of Thorney, Esq., second son of George Nevile, of Grove, by Barbara Hercy, his wife. Quarterly, 1 and 4 gules, a saltire argent, for Raby; 2 and 4, or, fretty gules on a canton, per pale ermine and or, a ship with sails furled sable.

P P

NEVILL, Badsworth, York.—Derived from Dyonisius, 5th son of George Nevile, of Grove, by Barbara Hercy. Arms the same as Nevile, of Grove.

NEVILL, Reresby, co. Leicester.—Ermine a chief indented azure.

NEVILL or NEVILLE, Furness, co. Kildare.—Derived from Richard Nevill, son of Edward Nevill, Esq., by Margaret, his wife, daughter of Sir Francis Palmer, and grandson of the Hon. Francis Nevill, of Kyner, Sussex, younger son of Edward, 5th Lord Abergavenny. Gules, a saltire argent ; crest, out of a ducal coronet or, a bull's head pied attired of the first.

NEVILL, of Marymount, co. Kilkenny.—A branch of the Nevills, of Furness, bearing same arms.

NEVILL, Billingbeare, Berks.—Gules, a saltire argent; crest, a bull passant pied, collared, lined, and armed or.

The following seals are figured on Plate II. :—

No. 1.—Cecily Nevill, Duchess of York, A.D. 1450.
No. 2.—Hugh de Nevill, 1190.
No. 3.—Henry de Nevill, 1200.
No. 4.—Richard Nevill, Earl of Salisbury, 1442.
No. 5.—William Nevill, Lord Fauconberg.
No. 6.—Ralph de Nevill, Lord of Raby, circum. 1350.
No. 7.—John Nevill, Lord of Raby.
No. A.—Eufemia, daughter of Ralph Lord Nevill, wife of Reginald Lucy.
No. B.—John Nevill.

My task is now nearly done. The following lists, although incomplete, will not be without interest to the reader :—

NEVILLS WHO HAVE BEEN LORD HIGH CHANCELLORS.

1213. Ralph de Nevill, Keeper of the Seal, and Lord High Chancellor of England.
1226. Ralph de Nevill, Bishop Chichester, made by the Parliament Lord Chancellor for life.
1232. The same, made Chancellor of Ireland for life.
1323. Ralph de Nevill, Lord High Chancellor of England.
1454. Richard Nevill, Earl of Salisbury, made Lord High Chancellor of England by Parliament.
1460. George Nevill, Bishop of Exeter, and afterwards Archbishop of York, Lord High Chancellor of England.

ARCHBISHOPS OF YORK.

1373. Alexander Nevill.
1465. George Nevill.

BISHOP OF DURHAM.

1438. Robert Nevill, translated from Salisbury.

BISHOP OF CHICHESTER.

1222. Ralph Nevill.

NEVILLS AND ANCESTORS OF THE MARQUIS OF ABERGAVENNY, IN THE MALE AND FEMALE LINE, WHO HAVE BEEN KNIGHTS OF THE GARTER. (ORDER CREATED BY EDWARD III., 1349.)

1. John of Gaunt, ob. 1362.
2. Thomas Beauchamp, Earl of Warwick, ob. 1369.
3. Edward, Baron Despencer, ob. 1375.
4. William, Baron Latimer, ob. 1380.
5. John Nevill, Baron, ob. 1388.
6. Thomas Beauchamp, Earl of Warwick, ob. 1401.
7. William Beauchamp, Baron Burgavenny, ob. 1410.
8. Ralph Nevill, Earl of Westmoreland, ob. 1425.
9. Richard Beauchamp, Earl of Warwick, ob. 1439.
10. Richard Nevill, Earl of Salisbury, ob. 1460.
11. William Nevill, Earl of Kent, ob. 1462.
12. Richard Nevill, Earl of Salisbury and Warwick, ob. 1471.
13. John Nevill, Marquis Montacute, ob. 1471.
14. George Nevill, Baron of Abergavenny, ob. 1535.
15. Ralph Nevill, Earl of Westmoreland, ob. 1549.
16. Henry Nevill, Earl of Westmoreland, ob. 1563.

NEVILLS WHO HAVE BEEN NAVAL COMMANDERS.

Gilbert Nevill, Admiral (?) to the Conqueror.

Hugh de Nevill, A.D. 1213. *Vide* p. 247.

Sir John Nevill, Baron of Raby, Admiral of the King's Fleet from mouth of Thames northwards, 44th Edward III.

Richard Nevill, Earl of Warwick, Lord High Admiral of England, 1470.

Edward Nevill, Captain R.N. *Vide* p. 240.

Richard Aldworth Nevill, second Baron Braybrooke, Vice-Admiral of Essex, 1797.

Ralph Viscount Nevill (born 1786, married 1813 Mary Ann, daughter of Bruce Elcock, Esq., died S.P. May, 1826), Lieutenant, 22nd January, 1806; "Courageux," 22nd May, 1806; "Spencer," 29th May, 1806; "Victory," 31st March, 1808. Commander, 30th May, 1808; "Falcon," 30th May, 1808; "Actæon," 7th August, 1809. Captain, 16th February, 1811; "Boadicea," 16th February, 1811.

LIST OF NEVILLS PRESENT ON VARIOUS BATTLEFIELDS.

1066. Hastings—William de Nova Villa (?)

1264. Chesterfield—Geoffrey Nevill. *Vide* p. 245.

1265. Evesham—Geoffrey Nevill. *Vide* p. 245.

1333. Halidon Hill—John de Nevill.

1346. Nevill's Cross—Ralph, Lord Nevill, and John, his son.

1346. Creci—Robert Nevill.

1378. French Campaign—Sir William Nevill.

1415. Agincourt—Ralph Nevill, first Earl of Westmoreland.

1455. St. Albans (1st)—Richard Nevill, Earl of Warwick.

1459. Blore Heath—Richard Nevill, Earl of Salisbury; Sir John Nevill, afterwards Lord Montague; and Sir Thomas Nevill, afterwards slain at Wakefield.

1460. Northampton—Edward Nevill, Lord Burgavenny; Richard Nevill, Earl of Warwick; William Nevill, Lord Fauconberg.

1460. Wakefield Green—Richard Nevill, Earl of Salisbury, beheaded ; Sir Thomas Nevill, slain.

1461. St. Albans (2nd)—Richard Nevill, Earl of Warwick.

1461. Towton—Richard Nevill, Earl of Warwick ; Lord John Nevill, slain.

1464. Hedgeley Moor—John Nevill, Earl of Northumberland.

1464. Hexham—John Nevill, Earl of Northumberland.

1469. York, Robin of Redesdale's Insurrection—Defeated by John Nevill, Earl of Northumberland ; Sir Henry Nevill, afterwards a leader in this insurrection.

1469 Edgcote—Sir Henry Nevill, son of Lord Latimer, slain.

1469. Lancastrian Insurrection in the North, under Sir Humphrey Nevill—Defeated by Richard Nevill, Earl of Warwick.

1471. Barnet—Richard Nevill, Earl of Warwick ; and John Nevill, Marquis Montague, slain.

1471. Tewkesbury—Sir George Nevill, Baron Bergavenny, Knighted after this battle, May 9th.

1497. Blackheath—George Nevill, thirty-second Baron Bergavenny.

1513. Battle of the Spurs—George Nevill, thirty-second Baron Bergavenny.

1513. Flodden—Richard Nevill, Lord Latimer ; Sir John Nevill, "a Knight of the North Countrie."

1554. Insurrection of Sir Thomas Wyatt—Defeated by Henry Nevill, thirty-third Baron Bergavenny.

1569. Siege of Barnard Castle—Charles Nevill, sixth Earl of Westmoreland.

1809. Talavera, Spain—Henry Nevill, Captain Dragoons, son of second Baron Braybrooke, died after the battle. Monument in Waltham St. Lawrence Church.

1854. Alma, Sept. 20th—Henry Aldworth Neville. *Vide* p. 242.

1854. Balaclava, Oct. 25th—Grey Neville, Cornet 5th Dragoon Guards, fifth son of the third Lord Braybrooke, and brother of the present peer, died Nov. 11th, of wounds received at Balaclava.

1854. Inkerman, Nov. 5th—Henry Aldworth Neville, Captain Grenadier Guards, third son of the third Lord Braybrooke, killed in action.

1854-5. Crimean Campaign—Edward Neville, Lieut.-Col. Scot's Fusilier Guards.

1858. Barodia, near Ratghur—Glastonbury Neville, Captain Royal Engineers, killed in action. *Vide Braybrooke Pedigree*, p. 242.

1879. Zulu War—Horace John Nevill *(see conclusion to Introductory Chapter, Part I.)*

Very imperfectly have I traced the pathway of Nevill in sunshine and shade, from the days of Uchtred the Saxon to the reign of Queen Victoria. If in some places I have lingered too long, or in others not long enough, my patient readers will perhaps forgive me before I take my leave of them, wishing

> " To each and all a fair good night,
> With rosy dreams and slumbers light."

NEWCASTLE-ON-TYNE: PRINTED BY ANDREW REID, PRINTING COURT BUILDINGS, AKENSIDE HILL.

CPSIA information can be obtained at www.ICGtesting.com
Printed in the USA
BVOW06s0119050915

416575BV00024B/688/P